THE IRISH ADMINISTRATION
1801–1914

by

R. B. McDOWELL
Fellow of Trinity College, Dublin

GREENWOOD PRESS, PUBLISHERS
WESTPORT, CONNECTICUT

Library of Congress Cataloging in Publication Data

McDowell, Robert Brendan.
  The Irish administration, 1801-1914.

  Reprint of the 1964 ed. published by Routledge &
K. Paul, London, which was issued as v. 2, 2d ser. of
Studies in Irish history.
    Bibliography: p.
    Includes index.
    1. Ireland—Politics and government—19th century.
2. Ireland—Politics and government—20th century.
I. Title. II. Series: Studies in Irish history ;
2d ser., v. 2.
JN1425.M3 1976   354'.415   75-35336
ISBN 0-8371-8561-0

Originally published in 1964 by Routledge & Kegan Paul,
London

Reprinted with the permission of Routledge & Kegan Paul, Ltd.

Reprinted from an original copy in the collections of the
Brooklyn Public Library.

Reprinted in 1976 by Greenwood Press
A division of Congressional Information Service, Inc.
88 Post Road West, Westport, Connecticut 06881

Library of Congress catalog card number 75-35336
ISBN 0-8371-8561-0

Printed in the United States of America

10 9 8 7 6 5 4 3 2

TO N.P. AND C.N.

PREFACE

THE PRIMARY AIM of this work is to describe in general terms
the duties and organization of the government departments
functioning in Ireland between the union and the outbreak of
war in 1914. However, while it aims at providing a guide, it may
also fill a gap. The functioning and development of the central
administration in Ireland, overshadowed by the more spectacu-
lar aspects of Irish history, have received relatively little attention.
But it would be a serious mistake to ignore the administration
when considering the elements which together constituted
Ireland during the nineteenth century. The century was an era
of constructive energy and amongst its achievements was the
creation of the modern civil service. In the British Isles the civil
administration had its roots deep in the pre-industrial age and
it has changed and developed greatly since 1914. But its animat-
ing ideals, its principles and organization, and many of its
working techniques were evolved during the nineteenth century.
Though the century rendered allegiance to *laissez-faire*, paradoxically it was a period when the state was steadily, if unob-
trusively and even apologetically, extending its sphere of action.
It was, too, by the application of practical rules deduced from
laissez-faire principles that a rationally planned administrative
system, which provided the state with an instrument for intervention in political and economic life, was created. And it may
be added that in many of the outstanding administrators of the
period there can be discerned something of the determination,
resourcefulness, planning capacity and concentration of purpose associated with the great entrepreneurs.

The administrative history of Ireland during the union era
is of course to a great extent included in British administrative

vii

history. But it has nevertheless an interest of its own. To begin with, the principles of the union were not after 1801 applied systematically in the administrative sphere. Some Irish departments were merged in their British equivalents and occasionally a British department was charged with responsibilities in Ireland. But a few pre-union Irish departments survived and other distinctively Irish departments were established as time went on. The system was not severely logical, as is strikingly illustrated by the survival of the historic office of lord lieutenant, an anomaly, it could be argued, in a United Kingdom. Moreover Irish conditions encouraged or compelled the state to exert itself vigorously on a more extensive front than in contemporary England. For instance in Ireland the police were government controlled, education was closely supervised by the state, and important schemes for agricultural development and agrarian reform were administered by three great Irish departments, the board of works, the land commission, and the congested districts board. The able and energetic civil servant, who in nineteenth century Ireland might have been trained as a soldier, lawyer or engineer, had plenty of scope.[1] And in a country where there was little industrial development the civil servant was more conspicuous than in England. Indeed an observer of Irish life at the beginning of the twentieth century with a bent for cheerful exaggeration, George A. Birmingham, once wrote that it was impossible to walk the length of an Irish railway-station platform without meeting two or three government inspectors.

In the first chapter of the present work an outline is given of the Irish administrative system at the beginning of the nineteenth century and an attempt is made to indicate the main changes in the departmental pattern and in the recruitment and remuneration of the civil servants employed in Ireland which occurred between the union and 1914. In each of the succeeding chapters the development of a group of departments is discussed. The departments are grouped on the basis of sharing a common sphere of activity. In some instances it may seem that a department has been placed in the wrong chapter.

[1] Mr K. M. Drake has drawn my attention to the fact that William Thomas Mulvany was successively a senior civil servant in Ireland and a very successful industrialist in Germany (see p. 208, footnote 1).

This may be so, but at least it has been dealt with. The courts of law have been included partly because of their close links with the administration and partly because of the offices attached to them. These were very similar to the civil departments and their staffs may reasonably be regarded as forming part of the civil service.

Something must be said in conclusion about three terms which are frequently used in this work, government department, Irish government department, and civil servant. While a government department is usually a recognizable entity the construction of a definite list of departments can produce some nice problems. Sometimes it is arguable whether an office constitutes a separate department or is merely a section of a department. Again there are departments so constituted that they are not government departments but independent statutory authorities functioning under a degree of state supervision. Fortunately in nineteenth century Ireland little attention was paid to this distinction, and contemporary opinion, which regarded several organizations controlled by unpaid boards simply as government departments, has been followed. The appendices show which offices the present writer considers to have been separate departments. An 'Irish' government department means a department concerned solely with Irish business. The term civil servant is employed to indicate a member of the staff of a government department.

ACKNOWLEDGEMENTS

I AM most grateful to my colleague Professor T. W. Moody for advice, help and encouragement at every stage of this work. I am also very grateful to Professor J. C. Beckett of Queen's University, Belfast, for many helpful suggestions.

My thanks are due to the Plunkett Foundation for Co-operative studies and to Dr J. G. C. Spencer Bernard for permission to use manuscript material in their possession; to the Board of Trinity College, Dublin for a generous grant in aid of publication; and to the staffs of the libraries and record offices in which I have worked.

CONTENTS

I

THE ADMINISTRATIVE
FRAMEWORK AND
THE CIVIL SERVICE

ANGLO-IRISH administrative history may be said to have
begun in April 1172 when Henry II appointed Hugh de Lacy
justiciar of Ireland. From then onwards departments were
founded and offices created so that at the close of the eighteenth
century Ireland possessed by contemporary standards a complete administrative machine closely modelled on the English
pattern. During this span of six hundred years there was never
much interest in administrative theory but there was always a
profound respect for established routine and prescriptive rights.
Since posts survived whose functions had atrophied and large
scale reorganization was never contemplated, there was a considerable amount of administrative untidiness. It might be
thought that the size and complexity of the Irish administrative
machine would have been severely limited by the eighteenth
century conception of the duties of the state, summed up by
Locke as being simply the regulation and protection of property
and the defence of the community. But the performance of
even these duties, together with raising the necessary revenue,
required a surprising number of departments. Moreover, the
eighteenth century Irish parliament was remarkably ready to
use the resources of the state in a wide variety of fields. Its
members dispensed public money in the spirit of a benevolent

landlord spending his own income, assisting education and industrial development. Usually this aid was granted to local authorities such as grand juries or to institutions or corporate bodies. But even so, two departments, the inland navigation board and the linen board, were set up to promote economic development. And a third department, the commissioners of accounts, was largely concerned with auditing the accounts of independent bodies which received grants of public money.

The civil administration of Ireland at the time of the union was conducted by twenty-two departments.[1] In addition there were some officials who did not pertain to any of these departments, such as the officers of the viceregal court, the printer of the Dublin *Gazette*,[2] the compiler of the *Gazette*, the inspector general of prisons, the inspector general of His Majesty's royal mines and the directors of the public coal-yards. The inspector general of mines, who was unpaid, had few if any duties, but the creation of his office towards the close of the eighteenth century faintly foreshadows some later interventions of the state in the economic sphere. The first inspector was Richard Kirwan, the celebrated Irish chemist, who was very active in the social as well as the scientific life of Dublin.[3] The public coal-yards, one in Dublin and one in Cork, were stores maintained by the government, from which the poor were supplied with cheap coal when prices were high.[4]

At the head of the Irish administrative system was the representative of the crown in Ireland, the lord lieutenant, who had wide powers by patent and custom. The lord lieutenant had an assistant, the chief secretary, who by the close of the eighteenthe century had become his partner. During the century the

---

[1] In arriving at this figure the offices attached to the law courts have been excluded with the exception of that attached to the revenue side of the exchequer which is counted as a civil government department because it was involved in collecting and accounting for by complex and archaic methods a small proportion of the revenue. For a list of the departments in 1801 see appendix 1.

[2] See J. W. Hammond, 'The king's printers in Ireland' in *Dublin Hist. Rec.*, xi. 29–31, 58–64, 88–96.

[3] For Kirwan see *Proc. RIA*, iv. xciv. On Kirwan's death the office of inspector of mines was conferred on Griffith, the celebrated civil engineer, and seems to have been absorbed in his other posts.

[4] 1 Geo. III, c. 10, 3 Geo. III, c. 17, 1 & 2, Geo. IV, c. 68.

chief secretary's office had grown up, a small but important department with three sections, civil, military and yeomanry. It was the department through which the lord lieutenant's will was expressed and it also performed in Ireland many of the functions of the home office. Besides the chief secretary's office there were at the time of the union twenty-one other Irish government departments. The total number of departments could be raised to twenty-eight by including the forfeiture office, the quit rent office, the surveyor general's office and the offices of the auditor general, the clerk of the pells and the teller of the exchequer. But since the first three of these offices were controlled by the excise commissioners and the other three by the treasury, it seemed unrealistic to treat them as being separate departments.[1]

Of the twenty-one departments which along with the chief secretary's office constituted the civil administration in Ireland, two (the privy council office and the privy seal office) were concerned largely with the formal authentication of acts of state, eight (including the post office) with fiscal matters, one with ecclesiastical finance and five with the paying, equipping and provisioning of the units on the Irish military establishment. There were two departments (including the office of arms) responsible for the preservation of records and the functions of the remaining three—the inland navigation board, the trustees of the linen manufacture and the wide streets commissioners for Dublin—are indicated by their titles.

Of the twenty-two departments twelve were managed by boards. Of these boards, eight were composed of paid and four of unpaid members. Theoretically the fashion of appointing a board or commission to manage a department could be justified on the ground that its members would both share responsibility and pool their knowledge and experience. There was also a practical political advantage in instituting a paid board. It meant a multiplication of places which could be used to reward government supporters.

The departments varied considerably in size. The revenue board controlled a staff of nearly 3,000,[2] the commissariat had

[1] *Commissioners of inquiry into fees . . . in public offices in Ireland, fourth report*, p. 47, H.C. 1806–7 (2), vi, and *Fourteenth report*, p. 3, H.C. 1813–14, (102), vii.
[2] This figure does not include the crews of the revenue cruisers.

a staff of over 1,000. At the other extreme were six departments each with a staff of less than half-a-dozen. Indeed, of the twenty-two departments, only six (the two already mentioned, the chief secretary's office, the linen board, the post office and the board of stamps) had staffs of over fifty. The twenty-two departments employed in all just over 4,700 persons. This figure includes the commissariat wagon train (800 strong), the revenue commissioners' boatmen (over 500) and tide waiters (about 400), the post office letter carriers (76). The Inland navigation board's lock-keepers (18) and finally what may be termed the domestic staffs of the offices—housekeepers, porters, messengers and cleaners—amounting to at least 170.[1]

The heads of departments, for instance the members of a board, were appointed by the lord lieutenant and were usually active politicians or at least owed their appointments to political influence. During the eighteenth century the line between the highest civil servants and politicians holding office was not clear. Indeed at the close of the century the Fitzwilliam crisis was partially caused by the difficulty of distinguishing between them. Beresford, the chief revenue commissioner, and Cooke, the under-secretary, who were removed from office by Fitzwilliam, would probably in any event have resented being the victims of a coalition. But their sense of grievance was increased by their belief that they had been for years devoted and industrious servants of the crown. However, in the three decades following the union the Irish boards on which politicians had seats were all abolished and by 1830 there were only three Irish posts which were 'political', those of lord lieutenant, chief secretary and vice-treasurer, and the whigs on coming into office took steps to render the last named a permanent civil service appointment.[2]

At the beginning of the nineteenth century vacancies in Irish government departments were filled by the lord lieutenant or by the heads of the office, or by a subordinate

[1] For the departments' establishments see appendix I.
[2] The officer of vice-treasurer had existed in the eighteenth century but was abolished in 1794. The office was again in existence 1816–37. For the under-secretary, whose position until the middle of the nineteenth century verged on the political, see pp. 63–5.

official possessing some patronage in his own section of the department. Recruitment by patronage has obvious dangers. A dramatic account of how badly a department could suffer was given by Mulock, the comptroller of the stamp office, when he appeared before a committee of inquiry in 1823.

'One young man', he said, 'was sent to me who had been on board a man of war. I asked him what he could write, he said he had written a log book a good deal, and a very bad clerk he was; but he ran away to the East Indies and so I got rid of him; the next man I got in was a man in a state of derangement; I got rid of him; now they have put in another man, a poor gentleman of broken fortune formerly of near £2,000 a year, and he is glad to get £80 a year in my office; he is an elderly man without knowing the business but extremely diligent and attentive; I have another, the son of Mr Glascock [a commissioner], who is only fifteen or sixteen years of age, and whom I may make something of in time. I went in June last to Mr Gregory [the under-secretary] and entreated him to give me the appointment on a vacancy which had then occurred; he said "I have heard of this before, but I assure you it is not in my power to give the appointment, the lord lieutenant has lost all patronage in the customs and excise and has nothing left but that in the stamp office" and he sent me a man blind of an eye and in the last stage of a consumption. Providence has stood my friend, and taken him away, since he has gone I have now a boy, a nephew of Mr Milliken's, a cool, steady lad; I think he will do in time; there is another who has been training up to be a clergyman, he intends to stay there until he is three or four and twenty, and then he will go into orders and settle; it cannot be expected that people of that description will pay any attention to the business. I think three or four of the lads are rather clever young men, Mr Stanley particularly so; I have a son of Colonel Belford's, an extremely proper, steady young man, as also is Mr Lewis, and a young man who came in later, as to all the rest they are not worth one farthing . . . when I came to the office first in 1798, of the two people who were clerks there at that time, one was a man that hawked rabbits about the streets with a pole over his shoulder, a most ignorant brute; the other was a man who attended the tea kettle of the countess of Westmor-

land; I was very glad to get him out of the office; on the recommendation of the board they were dismissed; and they have
been upon the incidents of the house ever since, actually upon
their full salary'.[1]

Promotion within a department often depended on seniority.
By what was termed by a successful civil servant rising 'by
graduation'[2] a man entering at the bottom of a list of clerks
might climb to the top or go to some better-remunerated post
or office. Indeed as early as 1784 the Irish house of commons
in an effort to check political influence in the revenue departments had resolved that all appointments in the higher grades
should be 'filled by persons only who have gone through certain
inferior departments' and who would owe their promotion to
merit. Almost immediately, eighteenth century officialdom had
discovered a method for evading this resolution. A person
destined for a higher appointment would be placed in a lower
office *pro forma* so that it would appear that he had been
promoted from within the service. The result was that the
higher officials were often inexperienced and the lower discouraged. Moreover, it was pointed out in 1822 that since the
holders of senior posts owed their appointments to political
influence, there was a 'tendency to render those offices more
suitable in point of emolument to persons of superior education
and habits of life, habits often ill-adapted to the laborious
attention required to the performance of the duties annexed
to their situations'.[3]

Promotion by seniority combined with the absence of a
superannuation system (though pensions were occasionally
granted to elderly or disabled civil servants) could have pathetic
consequences. At the beginning of the nineteenth century there
were in the post office several posts, the clerkships of the roads,
which were exceedingly well remunerated. And the prospects
of succeeding to these offices had, it was said, 'induced officers
to continue on the establishment at low salaries, though in

---

[1] *Commissioners of inquiry into . . . the revenue . . .*, pp. 254–5, H.C. (7) 1828,
xiv.

[2] *Commissioners of inquiry into fees . . . fourteenth report*, p. 14, H.C. 1813–4
(104), vii.

[3] *Commissioners of inquiry into . . . the revenue . . .*, p. 14, H.C. 1822 (563),
xii.

some instances scarcely able from age and infirmity to do any duty'.[1]

Influence of course could thrust a man into a department well up the official ladder. For instance Lees, the secretary to the post office at the time of the union, before receiving that appointment had been private secretary to a lord lieutenant and then under-secretary in the war department. Cooke, the under-secretary in the civil department, had come to Ireland about 1780 as private secretary to an under-secretary. Having served several under-secretaries he was in 1785 appointed a clerk to the house of commons and in 1789 under-secretary. Cooke, a Cambridge man, had the unusual distinction amongst his colleagues of being a university graduate, the day being still far distant when an academic training was to be regarded as a desirable preliminary to a civil service career. Indeed one of Cooke's contemporaries, Corry, secretary to the linen board, when he found himself involved in an administrative embroglio suggested as an extenuating circumstance that he was a university man unversed in the details of official life.[2] It may be added that, perhaps on account of his background, Cooke early in his career, when writing to a friend who held a similar post, emphasized that their occupations were a profession 'as much as if we had fixed on law or physic'.[3]

It is not easy to give within a reasonable compass a satisfactory account of the financial position and prospects of the eighteenth century civil servant. A high degree of departmental autonomy, along with sinecures, pluralities and fees, complicates the picture. In many offices some members of the staff were paid or partially paid by fees, which meant that their incomes could sharply fluctuate, bear little relation to the importance of their duties and be improperly increased. Payment by fees nevertheless was defended. When it was suggested that customs officials should no longer be paid by fees it was argued that the practice attracted to the revenue service a superior description of man, and provided the government with valuable patronage. The chief revenue commissioner prophesied that if the officer's remuneration was to consist solely of a salary there would be lacking 'the incitement of those

[1] *Commissioners of inquiry into fees . . . ninth report*, p. 29, H.C. 1810 (5), x.
[2] See p. 196.   [3] Cooke to Bernard; 1 Aug. 1783 (Bernard papers).

7

emoluments which are now dependent upon the performance of a duty'. And he pointed out merchants would be the first to suffer from 'the delays attendant upon the mere cold performance of a duty'. This last argument was also advanced by the barons of the exchequer when the abolition of fees in their court was being considered. 'It is clear', they wrote, 'when an officer has a salary and nothing more, the less business the court has in which he acts the better for him; he is therefore interested in the place of courtesy and kindness to substitute repulsive and disobliging manners, and to discourage business instead of attracting it'.[1]

Sinecures were either posts to which no duties were attached such as the attractively named 'taster of wines', 'one of the ancient customs offices at common law', or posts the duties of which were discharged by a deputy who divided the income with the holder. They were regarded as the rewards of public service or as political trophies and usually went to the members or connections of the great political families, though occasionally a zealous civil servant might in addition to his post hold a sinecure. It would not be easy to say how many sinecures there were at any one moment. But in the customs alone there were in 1804 thirty-six patent offices 'the duties of which appear to be useless' with incomes ranging from £8 to £2,000. And a few years later over eighty Irish sinecures were listed in a parliamentary return.[2] It may be added that as a result of the fee system fantastic incomes were enjoyed by the holders of some great offices attached to the law courts and the revenue at the beginning of the nineteenth century, an era of great and growing activity. The holders of these offices, who frequently were not resident in Ireland, treated them as sinecures, nominating deputies to perform the duties, the principals of course receiving the lion's share of the income.

As well as sinecurists there were pluralists, many of whom were relatively humble officials. For instance at the beginning

[1] *Correspondence relating to the suppression of fees in the customs in Ireland*, pp. 99–100, H.C. 1810 (97), xii, *Commission of inquiry into fees, first report*, pp. 99–100, H.C. 1806 (6), viii, and *Communication of the barons of the exchequer*, p. 2, H.C. 1821 (401), xi.

[2] *Commissioners of inquiry into fees . . . first report*, pp. 380–1 H.C. 1806 (6), viii and *Committee on public expenditure, third report, appendix*, pp. 284–5.

of the nineteenth century a clerk in the excise was also pay-master at the Royal Hospital, a clerk in the customs was a fisheries inspector and three other customs clerks were respectively a sorter in the post office, a barrack-master and a page to the lord lieutenant.[1] One post office sorter was working in the excise, another was in a bank, and a clerk in the secretary's department of the post office was also an inspector of franks in the inland department of the same office. Owing to the bad ventilation of the inland room he began, he explained to the revenue inquiry commission, to suffer from 'imperceptible' fainting fits. He ceased to work as an inspector but continued to draw two-thirds of the salary attached to the post. The president of the inland department, who prided himself on his health, was also accountant general of the Bank of Ireland. He had entered the post office at the age of twelve and about thirty years later had entered the service of the bank. He sat in the chair in the inland department daily from six in the morning until nine. He then, as he said, 'cleaned myself, breakfasted and went to the bank' where he stayed until after three, returning to the post office at five in the evening. He drew a salary of about £800 a year from each of his posts and never sought 'more than domestic pleasures'.[2]

One pluralist, William Shaw Mason, whose official career had an unhappy termination, is still remembered for his contributions to Irish history and sociology. Mason was simultaneously joint-remembrancer of first fruits, secretary to the record commission at a salary of £400 per annum and comptroller of legacy duty in the stamp office at a salary of £600. When his fees as remembrancer are taken into account he must have been at one time enjoying an official income of about £1,200 a year. In two of his offices he was to an exasperating degree punctilious on particular issues. In the stamp office, shortly after he was appointed, he caused some trouble by, 'from a mistaken scruple of conscience', refusing to make affidavits concerning the payment of duties before he took office. Some years later in 1822 as remembrancer of first fruits he pressed for a new valuation of benefices (the last having been made in

---

[1] *Commissioners of inquiry into fees, first report*, pp. 249, 257, 267, 283.
[2] *Commissioners of inquiry into the . . . the revenue, nineteenth report*, pp. 182, 813, 859–93.

the reign of Charles I), overwhelming the government with arguments drawn from antiquarian research and refusing to accept the traditional payments from recently promoted clergymen. Understandably the government shied away from a project which would have been construed by conservatives as an attack on the church and Mason was peremptorily informed by the under-secretary that his patent would be revoked if he did not accept the customary payments.

Mason was a most industrious secretary of the record commission, organizing pioneer work on a large scale in the archives, and a few years after he became comptroller of legacy duty he produced his three volume parochial survey of Ireland (a work which involved a considerable amount of correspondence and editorial effort). But he seems to have been trying to do too much at once. In 1823 a commission of inquiry when investigating the stamp office asked 'was it not notorious that he [Mason] did not attend to his work?'. The chief commissioner of stamps, Glascock (who incidentally was joint-remembrancer of first fruits with Mason), did his best for his colleague, explaining that Mason attended the office daily, but he had to grant that though the office kept returns of the daily attendance of its staff it did not record the period spent in the office. In conclusion Glascock was constrained to admit that while the public had not suffered from Mason's non-attendance, 'his duties might be performed fully as well by his assistant'. Some years later, in 1827, just after the British and Irish stamp offices were amalgamated, Mason was charged with negligence and inattention to duty and after what seems to have been a thorough and fair investigation, dismissed from his comptrollership. Other disasters followed. In 1830 the record commission was wound up and in 1833 it was discovered that Mason was badly behindhand in his work as remembrancer. Consequently, when in the same year that office was suppressed he did not receive compensation. And a few years later when the treasury relented and assigned him a pension he considered it was calculated on a faulty basis. Mason was certainly unlucky. Having built up his position under the old regime, he found himself exposed to the winds of change and reform. Bitterly aggrieved by loss of office and in his own eyes scandalously ill recompensed for his services, he bombarded government departments and people of influence with memorials setting out in pertinacious detail his grievances and claims.[1]

Given then the highly erratic distribution of incomes which could occur, what can be said about the financial prospects of an Irish civil servant at the beginning of the nineteenth century? The bulk of the lowest paid clerks and minor revenue officials had incomes of about £50 per annum. Then there were over 230 officials with incomes of £200 or more, and another hundred-and-thirty with incomes of £500 or more. Finally about 50 posts yielded an income of at least £1,000. It must be said at once that most of the posts in this last category were secured by political influence and were often sinecures to their holders, the duties, if any, being performed by deputies usually for a small proportion of the total income of the post. Thus it might be safely said that the working occupants of government offices in Dublin at the time of the union had rarely less than £50 per annum and shared amongst them over three-hundred posts with incomes ranging from £200 to £1,000. Porters and messengers usually received about £25 to £30 per annum. But there were porters at a guinea a week or door-keepers at £60 per annum receiving more than clerks at the bottom of the ladder or provincial tide waiters (of course the revenue officer in a small port might be merely a part time official).

It is a help towards appreciating the significance of these figures to take into account some other contemporary incomes. The Irish agricultural labourer at the beginning of the nineteenth century usually earned not more than ten pence a day. Assuming his wife earned something, a labourer would probably be fortunate if the income of his household amounted to a trifle over £20 per annum. A skilled artisan might earn from 7/7 a week to twelve shillings a week. A weaver might earn as much as half a crown a day. But it was most unlikely that the higher rates could be earned throughout the year, so probably the skilled artisan earned from about £20 to £30 per annum. Moving to a different social level a captain in the army was

[1] *Accounts and papers relating to first fruits in Ireland*, H.C. 1830–31 (12), vii, *Commissioners of inquiry into . . . the revenue, sixteenth report*, p. 109, H.C. 1828 (7), xiv, Mason to Peel, 13 Sept. 1842 (Add. MSS 40515) and T. 1/3980.

paid £172 a year and a curate in the diocese of Dublin was usually paid about £75 a year.[1]

Undoubtedly, then, civil servant clerks and officials of equivalent rank belonged to the upper or middle classes. And all the evidence indicates they were generally speaking recruited from those classes. On one occasion Gregory, the well known undersecretary, went so far as to say that 'none but young men of good connections and considered as gentlemen' should be admitted to the chief secretary's office. And he successfully resisted the appointment of a candidate whose social status was settled in Gregory's eyes, by his dining with the lord lieutenant's servants.[2]

A considerable number of applications for places in the Irish civil service written about the beginning of the nineteenth century have been preserved. They seem to have been largely unsuccessful but they often reveal the social background of the applicant. For instance Sir Hercules Langrishe recommended his son-in-law, a younger son of a well known landed family, for a 'small employment' which 'would place two virtuous people in reach of the comforts of life'. His conception of a 'small employment' was a post yielding £200 to £300 per annum.[3] But most of the requests were more modest. When George Cavendish, the secretary to the treasury and a son of a peeress in her own right, wanted posts for his two cousins, he remarked that 'situations of £100 to £150 a year would be great things for them'.[4] The master of the rolls recommended an old college contemporary with an estate worth £200 to £300 a year (but also with eleven children) for a post with a salary of £50 to £60.[5] A father with a son a cornet of dragoons was delighted to get a £50 per annum government clerkship for another son (though he was anxious to know what were the boy's prospects of promotion).[6] Another

---

[1] *Papers relating to the establishment in Ireland*, H.C. 1807 (78), *Commons Journ., Ire.*, xix. dxxvii, 1204, xv. cccxli.

[2] Gregory to Goulburn, 21 July 1822 (Goulburn papers).

[3] H. Langrishe to ———, 9 Apr. 1805 (Official papers, 2 series, 521/226).

[4] G. Cavendish to Marsden, 18 Jan. 1802 (Official papers, 2 series, 521/137).

[5] E. Smith to Sir M. Smith, 9 Sept. 1802 (Official papers, 2 series, 521/137).

[6] Richard Jones to Marsden, 3 May 1803 (Official papers, 2 series, 527/183).

father, Newenham (son of Edward Newenham who had been M.P. for County Dublin) who had a son an ensign in the 9th foot and another son who was a lieutenant in the navy, was concerned about a third son who was a civil servant. This son had a post worth £70 per annum in the post office. His health had been badly affected by long hours of work and cramped quarters and his father was anxious to secure him 'a situation in any respectable office' with a salary of about £80.[1] Finally a major with twenty years service in the line applied for a post in the customs, which his father had once held, worth about £300 per annum.[2] These examples, and they could be multiplied, all indicate that appointments in the Irish civil service were sought after by men with respectable middle or upper class backgrounds.

The twenty-two departments which have been dealt with may be taken as forming the civil administration of Ireland. There were also, however, three other great institutions closely connected with the civil government, the courts of law, the army and the established church. The law courts and the congeries of offices attached to them, which were in many ways similar to the departments which have just been mentioned, will be discussed in chapter IV. But at this point something must be said about the relations of the civil administration of Ireland to the church and the army.

To contemporaries one of the most important features of the eighteenth century British and Irish constitutions was the existence of an established church. The more profound implications of the connection between church and state need not be discussed here. All that will be attempted will be to indicate through what departments the Irish administration handled ecclesiastical affairs. The crown appointed bishops, deans (with three exceptions), and a few other dignitaries and possessed the patronage of fifty-three livings.[3] Episcopal appointments were a matter on which the lord lieutenant consulted

---

[1] E. W. Newenham to C. Saxton, 30 Oct. 1812 (Official papers, 2 series, 551/376).
[2] William Moore to ———, 1823 (Official papers, 2 series, 588B/569).
[3] For crown patronage see *His Majesty's commissioners on ecclesiastical revenues and patronage in Ireland, second report*, p. 15, H.C. 1834 (589), xxiii. 23 and *third report*, p. 15, H.C. 1836 (246), xxv.

the prime minister. Family connections and political sympathies certainly influenced promotions, but the names of those appointed to the bench between the union and disestablishment show that successive governments were genuinely concerned about the welfare of the church. The lord lieutenant in council sanctioned the union and division of parishes and the board of first fruits, composed of archbishops, bishops and the holders of high legal offices managed a portion of the church's revenues.[1]

The board of first fruits had been created in 1712 when Queen Anne handed over to the church the first fruits, vested in the crown since the sixteenth century, to be used for the augmentation of poor livings. Later both the Irish and United Kingdom parliament granted large sums to the board to be used for erecting churches and glebe houses. In 1833 the board was abolished on the creation by the church temporalities act of the ecclesiastical commission. The commission was composed of the archbishops of Armagh and Dublin, the lord chancellor, four bishops appointed by the crown and three paid members, two appointed by the crown and one by the archbishops. The commission was empowered to levy a tax on all benefices worth more than £300 per annum and the temporalities of ten bishoprics which were united to other dioceses were vested in it. With the revenues at its disposal the commission was expected to provide requisites for churches, pay clerks and sextons, build and repair churches and augment poorer benefices.[2] The commissioners had a fairly large staff by the eighteen sixties, comprising a secretary, a treasurer, a travelling agent, two architects and twenty-five clerks) and an excellent system of account keeping instituted by Sir Benjamin Lee Guinness. According to its secretary the commission did not consider itself to be a government department. Though, he added, the government nominated paid commissioners, and the commission had to submit to the government an annual report and accounts and secure the lord lieutenant's approval of the salaries paid to its staff.[3] And in 1869 when the commission was abolished, the bulk of its staff were transferred to

[1] 2 Geo. I, c. 15 and 10 Geo. I, c.7.   [2] 3 & 4 Will. IV, c.37.
[3] *Report on the revenue and constitution of the established church (Ireland)*, pp. xvii, *appendix*, p. 26, H.C. 1867–8, [4082, 4082–1, xxiv. 19], 678.

the newly established church temporalities commission which was indubitably a government department.[1]

There was not an Irish army in the eighteenth century; there was, however, 'the army on the establishment of Ireland' composed of regiments paid and equipped by Ireland. These regiments were changed from time to time and part of the force was stationed outside Ireland. At its head was the commander-in-chief in Ireland, assisted by an adjutant-general, a quarter-master, a judge-advocate general and an army medical board. As has been pointed out, five of the departments which formed the civil administration of Ireland, the ordnance, the commissariat, the barrack board and board of works, the muster-master general's office and the comptroller of army accounts office performed services for the forces stationed in Ireland. Moreover, a section of the chief secretary's office, the military branch, sometimes referred to as the war office, expressed the lord lieutenant's wishes on military matters, conducting correspondence with the departments which have just been mentioned and with the commander-in-chief whose head-quarters were at Kilmainham.[2]

The ordnance comprised the Royal Irish regiment of artillery, the engineers, a laboratory and a civil branch composed of clerks and storekeepers, totalling about twenty-five. At the head of the ordnance was the master-general and six patentee officers of whom five were in the civil department. At the time of the union the master general was Admiral Thomas Pakenham, an M.P. who while serving in the navy had proved himself to be a cool and resourceful commander. Of the patentee officers five were M.P.s and one had been in parliament when appointed.[3]

The commissariat, which was responsible for providing food and forage for the army, had a large establishment of about seventy including clerks, assistant commissaries and store-keepers. In addition in 1789 it had organized a wagon depart-

---

[1] 32 & 33 Vict., c. 42.

[2] For the duties of the military department of the Chief Secretary's office at the beginning of the nineteenth century see a memorandum dated 12 June 1801. (Official papers, 2 series, 517/105/4).

[3] *Lib. Mun. Hib.*, iii. 136–8, *Account of compensations . . . for losses sustained by the union*, H.C. 1803–4 (158) and H.O. 50/390.

ment which was nearly a thousand strong, with 'conductors', drivers, smiths and farriers. This wagon department made a dramatic appearance in military history in the summer of 1808 when some of its horses and drivers were taken over for the artillery which accompanied Wellington's first expedition to the Peninsula.[1]

The barrack board and board of works was responsible both for barracks throughout Ireland and for a group of government buildings in Dublin. The board was composed of seven commissioners, one of whom was in sole charge of the barrack department, which had a staff of about one hundred, including a secretary, an architect, two inspectors general of barracks, two storekeepers, fourteen clerks and seventy-six barrack masters. Just after the union the king suggested that the British barrack master general should be entrusted with the superintendence of the Irish barrack department, and Freeman who was appointed first commissioner in 1803 was designated deputy barrack master general, but nevertheless the Irish department remained autonomous for another twenty years.[2] Freeman proved incapable of supervising efficiently a large and, during the war, growing organization. In 1811 and 1814 regulations for the barrack department 'framed in the spirit of the barrack instructions in Great Britain' were issued by the lord lieutenant. But in the early twenties a committee of inquiry appointed by the master-general of the ordnance discovered 'general disorder and abuse'. The superintendent general and the inspectors general who were employed 'for the express purpose of acting as a check upon the conduct of others' were drawing their travel allowances for every day in the year, thus converting 'an intended occasional allowance into a regular salary'. Barrack masters' accounts were carelessly checked, the store accounts were in confusion. Some barrack masters neglected their duties, others shared the contractors' profits on stores and repairs. Indeed it was said that barrack masters themselves 'even caused damage to be done to the buildings in order that something more than the usual amount

[1] *Comm. journ. Ire.*, xix, xli, and *Return of persons employed . . . in all public offices . . .*, p. 112, H.C. 1830 (92), vii, Wellington, *Supplementary despatches, correspondence and memoranda . . . of the duke of Wellington*, vi. 83–8, 192.
[2] Hardwicke to Addington, 22 July 1803 (Add. MSS 35768).

of fraudulant profit might find its way into their own pockets'. It was also said that barrack masters in general, while doing all they could for officers so as to forestall complaints, deprived the rank and file of the comforts intended for them. Finally, the committee granted that there were some honest barrack masters, and that they did not 'entertain even a suspicion' of Freeman's integrity but considered him merely incompetent.[1] In 1822 the first step towards reforming the Irish barrack department was taken when it was transferred to the control of the ordnance department, and almost immediately its establishment was reorganized.[2]

The office of muster-master general or clerk of the cheque was responsible for recording the strength of the units stationed in Ireland. The office was of considerable antiquity (it was in existence by the middle of the sixteenth century) and very lucrative, the muster-master general being entitled until 1807 to charge fees for entering on his books the commissions of officers attached to regiments transferred from the British establishment to Ireland. The muster-master general had a very small staff and in 1822 the office was abolished.[3]

The office of examinator and comptroller of army accounts was a new office, having been created in 1799. The first comptroller was Colonel George Napier, the father of a famous group of brothers and himself an able soldier who as the superintendent of the Woolwich laboratory had markedly improved the quality of the gunpowder manufactured there. Cornwallis, declaring 'I want an honest man', appointed him to the Irish army accounts office and Napier began by renouncing all fees and thus considerably reducing his income. The powers of the comptroller of army accounts were in 1812 transferred to the

---

[1] W.O. 44/111.   [2] 5 Geo. IV, c. 108.

[3] *A statement of the average annual salaries . . . of the several individuals comprising . . . the office of muster master general*, H.C. 1824 (28), xxi and *Liber mun. Hib.*, vol. I, pt. iii, p. 138. Mathew Handcock, the last deputy muster master general seems to have been a contented civil servant. His monument in Tallaght church states he was deputy muster master general for fifty years 'and his talents and services were justly estimated and remunerated on the reduction of the office'. Married to a daughter of a clerk in the chief secretary's office he had 14 children. By 'a judicious and honourable economy' he was able to provide for them and show benevolence towards his numerous relatives.

three commissioners of army accounts. The comptroller started with a small staff. By 1822 the commissioners were employing a secretary, a solicitor and thirty-seven clerks.[1]

Even before the union it was being emphasized that though there were 'accidental differences' between the British and the Irish military establishments, it had 'long been understood as an important political principle to assimilate them as much as possible'.[2] And towards the close of the century steps were taken to secure that the British army clothing regulations and schemes for drill and manoeuvres should be adopted in Ireland. Once the union was through, the king himself made it clear that he was determined that 'the British army should be considered as one and the same army however distributed in Great Britain or Ireland and managed and governed by some uniform system commencing from the time of the union.'[3] Symbolically the title commander-in-chief in Ireland was changed to commander of the forces. The vexed question of promotion was brusquely settled. The lord lieutenant lost all military patronage so far as the regular army was concerned. All commissions were to be transmitted to the king through His Royal Highness the commander-in-chief, the duke of York. Hardwick the first post-union viceroy pathetically hoped that the duke would see 'the propriety' of leaving to the lord lieutenant the power of recommending the ensigncies and cornetcies in regiments stationed in Ireland. The duke promised that 'every recommendation of the lord lieutenant would of course be attended to', but he implied that it might not necessarily be accepted. When Hardwicke's successor, Bedford, pointed out that the instructions issued to the commander of the forces in Ireland ignored the viceroy's patent, York amicably agreed to amend the instructions so as to emphasize the lord lieutenant's responsibility for the defence of Ireland. This was, however, a purely verbal concession and when Bedford a month later raised the question of appointments and

---

[1] 38 Geo. III, c. 56, H.A. Bruce, *Life of General Sir William Napier*, vol. i. 4 and *A return of the . . . office of commissioners of accounts in Ireland*, H.C. 1821 (453), xix, *Liber mun. pub. Hib.* i, pt. II, p. 137.

[2] Kilmainham papers, MS 1011, 13 Feb. 1792, MS 1003, p. 93 and MS 1002, p. 9.

[3] Yorke to Hardwicke, 16 June 1801. (Add. MSS 35701.)

promotions the duke would only say that he would try to meet the lord lieutenant's wishes.[1]

Immediately after the union the Irish ordnance was fused with the British, Dublin being given the status of a 'superior outstation.'[2] At the same time the judge advocate general of Great Britain was given a new commission authorizing him to take cognizance of court martial proceedings in Ireland, and when in 1820 Paterson, who for thirty years had been judge advocate general for Ireland retired, the judge advocate general for the United Kingdom appointed a deputy in Ireland.[3] At the end of 1821 the Irish commissariat was united with the British. In 1822 the Irish barrack department was put under the control of the ordnance department.[4] In the same year it was enacted that Irish military accounts should be audited by the secretary at war.[5] Thus by the early twenties Irish administrative autonomy in the military sphere had completely vanished.

The union marks the beginning of a new epoch in Irish administrative history. It perhaps should be said at once that administrative reorganization was not one of the topics raised in the long discussions, public and private, which preceded the passing of the act of union. The parliamentary debates ranged widely, over constitutional, religious and economic issues. But the parliamentary opposition both in England and Ireland was far more concerned with denouncing the principles of the measure than with discussing what sort of administrative framework the United Kingdom should have. It might have been expected that the ministers and civil servants responsible for the union would have devoted some attention to its effect on the civil administrations of the two islands. But the conception that

[1] Yorke to Hardwicke, 16, 19 June 1801. Hardwicke to Yorke, 20 Aug. 1801, 11 Apr. 1803 (Add. MS. 35701) and Bedford to Spencer, 11 July 1806 (H.O. 100/133).

[2] W.O. 44/111, *Accounts and papers . . . relating to the increase and diminuition of salaries* . . . p. 28, H.C. 1821 (287), xiii, Treasury minute, 6 Nov. 1821 (W.O. 59/11).

[3] *Accounts & papers . . . relating to . . . salaries in the public offices of Ireland*, p. 168, H.C. 1821 (287), xiii.

[4] 3 Geo. IV, c. 108.   [5] 3 Geo. IV, c. 56.

sections of the administrative structure might have to be thoroughly replanned from time to time was only just beginning to emerge. And in any event the last thing leading supporters of the union, only too conscious of the formidable interests arrayed against them, wanted to do was to disturb any vested interest unnecessarily.

But at the time the union was enacted a great movement for the reform and reorganization of the British civil service was getting under way. From the close of the American war of independence the archaic and expensive British administrative machine was being severely scrutinized and criticized by the enemies of corruption and the advocates of economy. The revolutionary and Napoleonic wars created a burden of taxation and debt which strengthened the demand for economy. 'No government', a select committee of the house of commons declared, 'is justified in taking the smallest sum of money from the people unless a case can be clearly established to show it will be of some essential advantage to them'. The real wants of the people, it added, should not be made to give way to imaginary wants of the state.[1] And the negative creed of economy was reinforced by a growing belief in a new concept, efficiency. A positive pleasure, it was discovered, could be gained by adjusting means and ends when planning civil and military expenditure.

The first chief secretary appointed after the union, Abbot, had played an important part in directing parliamentary inquiries into administrative abuses in Great Britain. Having prudently secured a valuable Irish sinecure for life, as soon as he arrived in Ireland he set to work, in co-operation with the viceroy, Hardwicke, to introduce improvements in accounting and to tighten up discipline in the Irish offices. A circular letter was issued directing all Irish government departments 'to make returns of their establishments, duties and salaries' to the chief secretary. The results were unsatisfactory. Some departments 'very reluctantly and sometimes evasively' furnished returns, others deferred doing so until Abbot had left Ireland.[2] It may be added that two departments, the board of works and the

---

[1] *Second report from select committee on public income and expenditure*, p. 2, H.C. 1828 (420), v.

[2] *Diary and correspondence of Charles Abbot*, i. 237, 275–330.

stamp office, which Abbot and Hardwicke tried to regulate, were found twenty years later to rival one another as examples of maladministration. Indeed Tyrawly, the first commissioner of works, tried to obstruct Hardwicke's inquiry into the workings of his department. His attitude is understandable. It was not until between 1811 and 1813 that Tyrawly was able to present his accounts for 1796–1803 to the commissioners for military accounts. And he presented them only after extreme pressure had been applied. His defence was pathetic. The barrack department had been overwhelmed with work during the '98 rebellion; two assistant treasurers who could have been of the greatest help to him had died and the widow of one of them, having a dispute with the retired treasurer, was withholding a number of vouchers; lastly Tyrawly was in bad health. Peel, who had just begun his official career by arriving in Ireland as chief secretary, was unsympathetic, pointing out that if the accounts had been kept 'under a progressive state of arrangement' the difficulty of getting them into shape would not have arisen.[1]

In 1804, two years after Abbot left Ireland, John Foster, three times Irish chancellor of the exchequer, shortly before he accepted office for the second time introduced and carried a measure appointing a commission to inquire into fees and emoluments in the Irish revenue departments.[2] Ten years later, in March 1814, Sir John Newport, a keen whig, moved for a return of the fees in the English and Irish law courts indicating those which had been increased during the previous twenty years. And in spite of conservatives complaining that he was implicitly criticizing the whole legal system his motion was carried.[3] In June he advanced further, moving that a commission should be appointed under the great seal to inquire into the emoluments of officials in the law courts of the United Kingdom. And he stressed the fact that abuses were more likely to occur in the Irish courts, 'remote from the seat of sovereignty'. His motion was carried by one vote, but some time elapsed

[1] Hardwicke to Yorke, 6 Nov. 1801 (Add. MSS 35701) and *Proceedings of the commissioners of military accounts relative to the barrack department*, H.C. 1812–13 (187), vi.

[2] *Hansard*, 1 series, ii. 841 and 44 Geo. III, c. 106.

[3] *Hansard*, 1 series, xxvii. 399.

before the commission was issued; the government, when New-port and Romilly complained of the delay, pointing out the difficulty of finding suitable members.[1] However, in 1815 a commission was appointed for Ireland and was soon vigorously at work. In 1821 a second statutory commission was appointed to investigate the working of the Irish revenue departments and report upon the advisability of their being amalgamated with their British equivalents.[2]

The personnel of the three commissions was intelligently selected and their work was impressive in bulk and content. The first members of the commission on the revenue departments constituted in 1804 were John Rochfort, a barrister who had sat in the Irish parliament, Jackson, an English excise commissioner, Traill, under-secretary in the civil department, John Geale, a Dublin banker and Alexander a Bank of Ireland director. Amongst those appointed to fill vacancies were Saxton, Traill's successor, and John Hamilton, a barrister whose brother was M.P. for Dublin. Hamilton, who had been looking for a government appointment for some time, after sitting as a commissioner for five years, emphasized that his experience as an investigator specially qualified him for a permanent post.[3] Hamilton and Saxton were also original members of the courts of justice commission, their colleagues being Daniel Webb Webster, K.C., John Leslie Foster, later a baron of the exchequer, and Bertram Mitford, a barrister and nephew of Redesdale, the Irish lord chancellor. Later John Doherty, who was to become chief justice of the common pleas, served as a member of the commission. The second statutory commission on the Irish revenue departments was composed of Thomas Wallace, an expert on commercial policy, Herries, who beginning as a junior clerk in the treasury rose to be chancellor of the exchequer, two barristers, and Lewis, who as the *D.N.B.* puts it was frequently employed 'in political and administrative posts of the second rank'.

The commissions all worked on similar lines. They had the power to take evidence on oath and they issued written interrogatories and then examined each official concerned on his answers (sometimes compared with other people's). In addition

---

[1] *Hansard*, 1 series, xxviii. 375, xxix. 475.   [2] 1 & 2 Geo. IV, c. 90.
[3] Hamilton to Peel, 4 Aug. 1813 (Add. MS 44229).

to examining officials, the commissioners also heard members of the general public and collected much documentary material. Witnesses were sometimes shifty and disingenuous, but the commissioners were alert and pertinacious.[1] And their reports on the working of the departments they inquired into are masterly expositions spiced with effectively restrained comment on many of the facts disclosed.

These three commissions surveyed large sections of the Irish administration. Other aspects of it were dealt with by select committees of the house of commons, such as the committee on the public expenditure of the United Kingdom and the committee on the Irish miscellaneous estimates. The material these commissions and committees published suggested the immediate reforms required and by the 'thirties an immense amount had been achieved. Payment by fees had been abolished, sinecures were rapidly disappearing, a superannuation fund had been established, administrative processes had been simplified and efforts had been made to settle departmental establishments and salaries in accordance with the work which had to be done. In Ireland these reforms were facilitated by structural changes in the administration which will be discussed in more detail later. For the moment it suffices to say that, by the middle 'thirties, of the twenty-two Irish departments existing at the time of the union, eighteen had disappeared either by abolition or absorption into a British or new Irish department. Thus the way was cleared for the introduction of new administrative methods into Ireland.

With obvious abuses eliminated, two important and closely related problems could be discerned: how was the civil service to be recruited and how was it to be graded. As early as 1833 the treasury directed departments to take steps to ensure that persons appointed to vacancies in them should be qualified to perform their duties.[2] Appointments were still made by patron-

---

[1] On one occasion at least there seems to have been an attempt to victimize an official who assisted an inquiry. In 1822 it was alleged that Fitzgerald, an inspector in the excise department, was being disciplined, theoretically for irregularities, in fact, because he had given information to the commission inquiring into the revenue. G. Hill to T. Wallace, 14 Feb. 1822; Hill papers.)

[2] *Copy of treasury minute . . . on the . . . regulations for ascertaining the fitness of persons appointed to situations in the public service*, H.C. 1833 (680), xxiii.

age, however, those to junior posts in Irish departments being made by the patronage secretary to the treasury 'usually on the nomination of the Irish supporters of the administration for the time being'.[1] But in 1855 the administrative reformers won a major victory. Though nomination was retained for a time, the civil service commission was appointed to conduct qualifying tests and sixteen years later, in 1871, competitive examination was made the normal mode of recruitment.

The introduction of tests at admission immediately raised the question on what level of the service recruits should enter. The schemes of reorganization formulated before the middle of the century usually provided that there should be more than one grade of clerks in a department, each grade having a fixed salary scale. Vacancies in the higher grades would be filled by promotion from the lower and new entrants naturally started in the bottom grade. But, from the fifties, it was being forcibly argued that such a system ignored the fact that very different types of intellect were required in a service where the work ranged from the purely mechanical to the highly intellectual. If it was a pity to waste good minds for years in dreary copying it was also unwise to trust to long experience in official grooves alone to fit a man for high administrative responsibility. In the event it was accepted that there should be sections in the service whose functions differed in kind and that these sections should be recruited on distinctly different lines. As a result there emerged between 1870 and 1890 the great tripartite division of the service into the administrative, executive and clerical classes which by 1914 was one of its most striking characteristics. In 1871 two schemes of recruitment for clerks came into operation. Those entering under Regulation I were 'expected to be drawn from the best class of university men and were intended to join the superior class in those offices which need high social and educational acquirements'. Those coming in under Regulation II were to be 'persons of less mature age and less extended acquirements'.[2] These two important groups were at first termed the higher and lower divisions. Later, in 1890, for 'sentimental'

[1] *Commissioners to inquire into the condition of the civil service in Ireland report with minutes of evidence*, pp. 3, 66, H.C. 1873 [C. 789], xxii.

[2] *Civil service inquiry commission, first report*, p. 6, H.C. 1875 [C. 1113], xxiii.

reasons they were renamed, being designated First and Second Divisions. For a time there was some uncertainty and confusion over the allocation of work between the different groups. But towards the end of the century the principles determining this were generally recognized. Higher administration, routine administration and mechanical or semi-mechanical work were respectively the province of the first division, the second division and of the categories below the latter—assistant clerks, boy clerks and temporary clerks.

The developments discussed in the last few pages were reflected in the structure and staffing of the Irish administration. During the first three decades of the nineteenth century efficiency and economy were responsible for the high mortality among the pre-union departments which has already been mentioned. As has been said, the government, even before the union, was anxious to unify the military administrations of the two islands, and this meant the disappearance by the 'twenties of three Irish civil departments concerned with military matters together with the barrack 'wing' of the barrack board and board of works and the military department of the chief secretary's office. Again at the time of the union the fusion of the fiscal administrations of Great Britain and Ireland was clearly contemplated. This process began in 1816 and may be said to have finished in the early 'thirties. The unification of British and Irish offices or the absorption of the latter by their British counterparts led to the disappearance of nine pre-union Irish departments. Four others were victims to the spirit of the age. The muster-master general's office was abolished as unnecessary, the revenue side of the exchequer as archaic, the lottery board as undermining public morality and the Linen board as offending *laissez-faire* principles. Four offices were absorbed by other Irish departments, the repository in the Bermingham Tower by the record commission, the privy seal office by the chief secretary's office, the board of first fruits by the ecclesiastical commission and the board of works and the board of inland navigation by the new board of works created in 1831. By 1835 only four of the pre-union offices were still surviving and of these two were very small departments.

But as departments disappeared new ones were established. On the day the union came into force the board of charitable donations and bequests began to function.[1] It was composed of unpaid commissioners and employed a small staff. Of the nine other departments created between the beginning of the century and 1830 eight were on this model. The only department set up in the first three decades of the century under the control of a paid civil servant was the boundary survey. The eight commissions or boards had very limited spheres of activity but their creation suggested the lines state action was to develop along in the future. Four of them were concerned with economic development, two with public health, and one with education. The eighth was concerned with the preservation of public records.

The 'thirties was a great era of administrative reform. Admittedly *laissez-faire* was in the ascendant and current political theory demanded that the activities of the state should be severely limited. But even in England pragmatism and humanitarianism kept breaking through. And it was generally acknowledged that Ireland was a special area where extraordinary measures might have to be tried. In 1831 shortly after coming into office the whigs reorganized the board of works, making it an agency for the promotion of economic development and set up the national board to supervise a nation-wide system of primary education. Before the close of the decade they had set up the ecclesiastical commission, established a national police force and introduced into Ireland the new English poor law. This last step led to a branch of the English poor law commission being established in Dublin. Later, in 1847, an Irish poor law board was constituted and this department, having been entrusted with important duties in the field of public health, was in 1872 transformed into the local government board. After the foundation of the registrar general's office in 1844, nearly a quarter of a century elapsed before another department of any size was established. And the foundation of the public record office in 1867, the creation of the church temporalities commission in 1869 and the foundation of the prisons board in 1877 can scarcely be regarded as major events in administrative history.

But the creation of the land commission in 1881 marks the

[1] 40 Geo. III, c. 75. The board was reconstituted to make it representative of religious interests in the country in 1844 by 7 & 8 Vict., c. 97.

undoubted beginning of a new era. From then onwards the state was intervening in Irish social and economic life on, by contemporary British standards, a large front, and this led before the end of the century to the formation of two other large departments devoted to improving economic conditions—the congested districts board and the department of agriculture and technical instruction. Finally, as a result of the liberals' welfare legislation in the years immediately preceding the outbreak of the Great war, an insurance commission for Ireland was set up. And it is perhaps worth noting that the four departments set up from 1881 onwards to deal with economic problems which have just been mentioned were amongst the six largest government departments in 1914 and between them employed just over fifty per cent of the total staff in specifically Irish offices.

It is apparent from a cursory glance at Irish administrative history in the nineteenth century that there was a strong tendency to tackle newly-appreciated problems on simple *ad hoc* lines, which often meant the creation of a new department with little regard for the general structure. Though functions were from time to time transferred between departments, no attempt was made to plan systematically the distribution of duties between all the departments, British and Irish, functioning in Ireland, nor were the arrangements for controlling and co-operating their activities adequate. And the general situation about the turn of the century was not propitious to administrative reform. For nationalists and liberals home rule completely transcended problems of administrative re-organization, and unionists were obviously reluctant to criticize the existing regime in any respect.

Two under-secretaries, Ridgeway and MacDonnell, both trained in India, were in turn very critical of the Irish administrative system. Ridgeway, who had served as a soldier and political agent on the north-west frontier, arrived in Ireland in 1887. A man of drive and ideas, he was easily irritated by inefficiency and inertia. He believed that there had been a regrettable decline in the status of the chief secretaryship, which he declared had been stripped by recent legislation of some of its most important and interesting duties.[1] In fact

[1] Ridgeway to Balfour, 29 Aug. 1889 (Add. MSS 49810).

27

Ridgeway's own letters show that the tendency was not so much to cut down the duties of the chief secretary's office as to increase the responsibilities of other bodies which were not closely controlled by that office. For instance he was afraid that the land commission would become 'a monster of Frankenstein to the Irish government'.[1] And in 1889 he pointed out that recently the lord lieutenant in council had been empowered to decide numerous important issues. Now, Ridgeway emphasized, the lord lieutenant in council was usually in fact the lord chancellor and the attorney general. 'The danger of putting so much power in the hands of political lawyers is great', he wrote, 'the great blot of English rule here has always been that England rules through lawyers'. And he suggested that some 'lay' officials should be appointed to the privy council.[2]

After two years experience of Ireland, Ridgeway produced a powerful memorandum in which he asserted that 'nothing could be more chaotic and effete than the present system of government by boards. For at present Ireland is ruled by a congeries [sic] of boards who are by statute semi-independent and by the treasury in London. These boards have the power and licence to commit blunders but on the chief secretary rests the responsibility. When the chief secretary happens to be a man of commanding influence and when a common danger threatens the existence of the Castle this complicated machine works smoothly, but in a cumbersome and unproductive fashion. But if this centripetal force were withdrawn all branches of Irish administration would fly off in their old aimless worn out grooves'. Ridgeway's remedy was an extensive reorganization of the whole Irish administrative system. Elected local authorities were to be established in the counties and provinces, extensive powers were to be devolved on these bodies, the boards were to be replaced by one or two under-secretaries and all the threads of the Irish administration were to be gathered into the hands of a single cabinet minister.[3]

MacDonnell before he became under-secretary in 1902 had been 'impressed by the want of efficiency resulting from the

[1] Ridgeway to Balfour, 20 May 1891 (Add. MSS 49812).
[2] Ridgeway to Balfour, 29 Aug. 1889 (Add. MSS 49810). See also Ridgeway to Balfour, 16 Feb. & 27 Apr. 1891 (Add. MSS 49811, 49812).
[3] Ridgeway, memorandum, 6 Oct. 1889 (Add. MSS 49810).

uncontrolled and divergent action of the numerous Irish public boards'. And being an administrator of fire and drive, he seems for the moment to have contemplated drastically simplifying the administrative structure.[1] But at first he was absorbed in land reform, then he became enthusiastically interested in devolution, and his one attempt to modify existing administrative procedure was unsuccessful. He tried to arrange that bodies such as the local government board and the congested districts board should submit papers to the chief secretary through the chief secretary's office (i.e. through the under-secretary). Experienced Irish officials suspected him of trying to magnify the importance of his own post and he failed to establish the administrative principle he was contending for.[2]

In 1914 there were forty government departments functioning in Ireland.[3] Of these eleven were United Kingdom departments which had Irish branches, twenty-nine were Irish departments concerned solely with Irish affairs, and, with the exception of the chief secretary's office which had a small London outpost, functioning only in Ireland. It may be added at once that the distribution of functions between United Kingdom and Irish departments did not follow a line logically dividing imperial from local affairs. Admittedly fiscal matters and defence were in the hands of United Kingdom departments, but so also were factory inspection and company registration. Of the Irish departments four or five were concerned with public health, five with education and four with agricultural development. Again, of the Irish departments, seven were controlled by United Kingdom departments, six of them by the treasury, and one (the quit rent office) by the commissioners of woods and forests. Of the remaining twenty-one Irish departments ten were considered to be under the immediate control of the executive government, that is to say, they continuously received directions and advice from the chief secretary's office. These departments were concerned with law and order, police, pris-

---

[1] Memorandum by MacDonnell (Bd. MSS c. 351).

[2] H. Robinson, *Memories wise and otherwise*, 1923, pp. 141–6 and W. L. Micks. *An account . . . of the congested districts board*, 1925, pp. 112–5, Plunkett, diary, 4, 5 July 1904.

[3] See appendix II and *Public departments (Scotland and Ireland)*. . . H.C. 1912–3 (104), lvi.

ons, crown prosecutions, petty sessions clerks, lunatics, statistics, benefit societies and heraldry. The Chief Secretary was also technically at the head of three other departments, being chairman of the local government board and the congested districts board and president of the department of agriculture and technical institution.[1] In practice he took no part in the administration of the department, since the vice-president who was a junior minister was responsible for its working, though on two occasions when the vice-president could not find a seat the over-burdened chief secretary had to answer parliamentary questions on behalf of the department. The chief secretary frequently presided at the congested districts board, but as the great majority of his fellow commissioners were unpaid they definitely regarded him as simply *primus inter pares*. He only occasionally attended the local government board but kept in close touch with its business by regular meetings in Dublin and London with the vice-chairman who was its permanent head.[2] In twenty of the Irish departments the senior appointments were made by the lord lieutenant or were subject to his approval. The exceptions to this were, besides the seven offices controlled by United Kingdom departments, the department of agriculture and technical instruction and the National Gallery. There was another way in which the Irish government could impose a measure of centralized control on a number of departments. Of the twenty-one departments which have been referred to, seventeen submitted their estimates to the treasury through the chief secretary's office, the remaining four being the chief secretary's office itself, the department of agriculture and technical instruction, which dealt with the treasury directly, and the registry of petty sessions clerks and the loan fund board which were supported by fees—the latter indeed being hard put to it to keep going. When these estimates were passing through the finance division of the chief secretary's office criticisms and suggestions could be made and transmitted to the treasury which had the ultimate decision. Also the treasury might return an estimate with a request for the lord lieutenant's views on

[1] *Royal commission on civil service: memorandum as to the organization and staff of the Chief Secretary's office.*

[2] *Royal commission on civil service, fourth report, evidence,* p. 204, H.C. 1914, [Cd. 7340], xvi.

some item of suggested expenditure. This meant that the chief secretary's office as well as the treasury had a say on the size and shape of establishments in these seventeen offices—though the congested districts board was in the strong position that it was paying (resentfully) most of its staff out of its endowment. And the whole official establishment attached to the supreme court was 'outside the jurisdiction of the Irish government', its estimates being presented directly to the treasury.[1]

Though departmental autonomy was a striking character-istic of Irish administrative life, it was diminished to some extent by the powers exercised by the chief secretary's office. Another centripetal force was personal contact between senior officials. Dublin was a small capital, some of the departments, including of course the chief secretary's office, were housed in the Castle, and all the others, as well as the clubs to which many of the higher officials belonged, were within quarter of an hour's walk of College Green. It is not surprising then that George Wyndham found that the government of Ireland was 'conducted only by continuous conversation'.[2]

The system obviously threw a considerable strain on the chief secretary who had to carry a burden which was not only large but which was composed of a distractingly varied range of subjects. Birrell once described with irreverent gusto the relationship existing between the chief secretary and one department he represented in the house of commons, the board of national education. So far as primary education was concerned, the chief secretary, Birrell remarked, was a mere gramophone, answering questions about a board of which he was not a member and which he could not even attend. The board, he explained, every year

presents through the treasury demands for more money and is per-fectly justified in making the demands. It puts them under eighteen or nineteen ancient heads—very ancient and some of them almost hoary. The only person to whom they are a novelty is the chief

[1] *Ibid.* p. 181, *Royal commission on the civil service: memorandum as to the organization and staff of the Chief secretary's office.* The term 'Irish government' which was used from time to time seems to have implied the lord lieutenant, the chief secretary and their advisers.

[2] J. W. Mackail and G. Wyndham, *Life and letters of George Wyndham,* ii. 407.

secretary who as a rule does not last more than two years and therefore comes fresh to them every time. He selects as best he can those that appeal most to his own idiosyncrasy or appeal to the idiosyncrasy of the guardian of the public purse, his Right Honourable friend the chancellor of the exchequer. . . . That is the way it is done. It is not done by discussion or by pressure brought to bear upon the government. It is done by the work and sense of activity and conscience of the chief secretary operating upon the more or less willing or reluctant treasury.[1]

Mutatis mutandis this description must have at times applied to a chief secretary's relations with other offices.

Admittedly the chief secretary was usually supported in parliament by at least one Irish law officer and he was assisted in the house of commons from the union to 1816 by the Irish chancellor of the exchequer and from 1816 to 1830 by the vice-treasurer. But from 1830 until 1899 (with the exception of the session of 1887) he had to deal with almost the whole range of Irish business, and the relief afforded in 1899 by the creation of the post of vice-president of the department of agriculture and technical instruction was lessened on two occasions when the vice-president could not secure a seat.

In 1878 a treasury committee pointed out that it had been suggested that a responsible minister might represent in parliament the board of works and the local government board and so relieve the treasury and the chief secretary of some of their parliamentary work. Nine years later in 1887, when the chief secretary was extremely hard pressed, Edward King Harman, a courageous, high-spirited Irish landlord was appointed parliamentary under-secretary for Ireland. He dealt with many questions covering a wide range of Irish topics and in 1888 the government introduced a measure—which the Irish nationalists dubbed the King-Harman relief bill—making his post a paid one whose holder could sit in parliament. It also provided that the parliamentary under-secretary could exercise the chief secretary's powers in respect ot granting and revoking tickets of leave and discharging offenders from reformatories and industrial schools. Balfour, speaking in defence of the bill, asked was it desirable that the chief secretary should be the only member of the cabinet who could not attend

_____
[1] *Hansard*, 5 series, xxxviii, 444–5.

to anything except departmental matters. But Morley, one of his predecessors, freed from the trammels of office, argued that the chief secretary learned a lot by being compelled to deal with a mass of minor administrative questions—he himself had found that 'transfers to reformatories shed a most interesting and instructive light upon the details of the conditions of Irish life'. King-Harman died in June 1888 shortly before the Parliamentary Under-Secretary (Ireland) Bill was due for its third reading and the government dropped it.[1]

Thirteen departments were governed by boards—eight of which were unpaid and five paid. And the office of the Inspectors of Lunatics was managed by the two inspectors. An attempt has been made earlier to explain why management by commission was favoured in the pre-union era. In the nineteenth century the creation of an unpaid board meant that different sections of opinion could be associated with the management of a department. The unpaid boards worked of course through permanent staffs and in two instances the heads of the permanent staff were members of the board. It is worth noting that in one respect unpaid boards were inclined occasionally to disregard an important civil service convention. At times they publicly criticized the government, usually for failing to grant them the financial support they wanted.

Members of the paid boards on the other hand behaved as men brought up in an hierarchial tradition might be expected to do. On at least four of these boards the chairman was accorded the status of a departmental head. Robinson, the vice-chairman of the local government board explained that his colleagues could never out-vote him. 'It is not a board', he breezily explained, 'we do not put things to the vote, we never differ. We talk the whole thing out and decide'. Very often on a difficult matter he called in the secretary and the legal adviser and 'they would sit round the table and discuss it but the decision would be given by the president or vice-president'.[2]

---

[1] *Report of the committee appointed to inquire into the Board of works, Ireland,* p. lxx, H.C. 1878, [C 2060], xxiii, *Hansard,* 3 series, cccxiii, 1003–6, cccxix, 1110, cccxxv. 910–49; R. D. King-Harman, *The Kings, earls of Kingston* (1959), pp. 197–203.

[2] *Royal commission on the civil service, fourth report, evidence,* p. 206, H.C. 1914, [Cd. 7340], xvi. ·

Stevenson, the chairman of the board of works told the Mac-Donnell commission on the civil service that he had been a member of the board for over twenty years and that he had never known a difference of opinion 'necessitating a vote'. Theoretically he thought that if any commissioner was in a minority he could appeal to the treasury and the chairman if he was outvoted 'would certainly appeal to the chancellor of the exchequer'. The treasury had in the early 'seventies contemplated replacing the board by a single responsible head but Stevenson produced one argument against this—'in Ireland', he explained, 'people like to get at a responsible head and to be able to do business with him and that power is certainly given by the existence of our board'.[1] The chairman of the national health insurance commission explained that the other commissioners were 'not allowed to decide any point of principle unless it is brought before the commission or sent to me'.[2] The chairman of the prisons board could not conceive a vote having to be taken at his board: 'Everything', he said, 'must be settled by compromise', though he granted that in the past matters in dispute had been decided by a majority.[3]

But one paid board, the estates commissioners, on one occasion proclaimed their dissensions in an unusual manner. Their second report includes bracketed passages in which one of the three commissioners, Wrench, who before entering the civil service had been a land agent, records his disapproval of some of the opinions expressed in the report.[4]

The staffs of the forty offices functioning in Ireland in 1914 totalled over 26,000. Of this total about 2,500 were employed in the twenty-nine Irish departments and nearly 24,000 in branches of United Kingdom departments functioning in Ireland. This latter figure, it should be said, was greatly inflated by the staff of the post office which numbered about 20,000, including over 2,700 sub-post masters and about 7,000 postmen. The total staff of civil servants employed by the Irish departments was, as might be expected, divided very unequally between them. Eight departments, each with a staff of over one hundred (one of them, the land and estates commission, had

---

[1] *Ibid.*, p. 272. [2] *Ibid.*, p. 332. [3] *Ibid.*, p. 280.
[4] *Report of the estates commissioners for the year 1906*, H.C. 1906 [Cd. 3148], xxv.

a staff of 550) employed about 83 per cent of the total force and at another extreme seventeen departments were manned by a mere nine per cent. The total staff of the twenty-nine Irish departments might be divided up in another way. It was composed of three great blocks. The first numbering about 300 comprised what may be termed the domestic staff of the offices —porters, messengers, cleaners. The second numbering about 700 was comprised of officials having professional or technical qualifications—lawyers, medical men, surveyors, professors in the College of Science, museum officials. The third numbering about 1,500 comprised the administrative and clerical staffs of the offices.[1]

By 1914 women had arrived in Irish government offices. During 1902 two 'lady inspectors' of boarded out children were appointed by the local government board. Ten years later 'a female inspector' of reformatory and industrial schools was appointed. And in 1914 the recently constituted Irish national health insurance commission had 17 women officials and 20 women card tellers. Moreover about 1901 the department of agriculture and technical instruction had engaged six 'female typists'. By 1914 about 60 were being employed in Irish offices. But Dougherty, the under-secretary explained that it was impossible to employ them in the chief secretary's office because it was a comparatively small office and 'public opinion in Ireland would insist on the segregation of the sexes'. On being asked what he thought of this, Robinson of the local government board said he hoped public opinion would not penetrate into his old age pensions branch where men and women were working side by side.[2]

Methods of recruitment and schemes of grading in Ireland on the whole conformed to the pattern of British administrative development. Indeed it was claimed that 'the earliest instance of a competitive examination for public office was established in Ireland'.[3] By the grand jury act of 1833 the lord lieutenant was empowered to appoint the county surveyors who were

[1] Appendix II.

[2] *Royal commission on the civil service, fourth report, evidence*, pp. 189, 206, H.C. 1914 [Cd. 7340], xvi.

[3] Larcom in a volume of his papers relating to civil service examinations (N.L.I. MS 7753).

to advise grand juries on the planning and execution of public works. Candidates for surveyorships were to be examined by a board of three military engineers appointed by the lord lieutenant, and in practice the board returned the names of the examinees in order of merit and the lord lieutenant selected names for vacancies in the order listed.[1]

Among the departments which before 1855 applied tests of competency to candidates for clerkships were the chief secretary's office and the Irish poor law board, and the Irish offices under the control of the chief secretary were amongst the first to adopt the system of competitive examination.[2] This is scarcely surprising since the under-secretary from 1853 to 1868 was Larcom, a scientifically trained soldier with wide interests and great organizing powers who was in close touch with Trevelyan, the permanent head of the treasury and a leading administrative reformer. Early in 1853 Trevelyan advised him on the standards to be adopted in examining candidates for clerkships in the chief secretary's office and shortly afterwards sent him an off-print of an article on civil service reform in the hope that it might be inserted into an Irish newspaper. A year later Larcom at Trevelyan's request wrote a letter on civil service reform which could be printed and circulated. Larcom thoroughly disapproved of nomination and promotion by graduation and strongly favoured competitive examination and the *carrièr ouverte*. 'Everything here', Larcom wrote, 'was in former days so soiled with politics and religious differences that people thought it the most natural state of things'. For thirty years the government, in Larcom's opinion, had been striving to put an end to this, and encourage industry and self-reliance. Grand jury reform, the national education system, the Queen's Colleges, the poor law, the Irish constabulary all reflected this policy. And Larcom was convinced that the adoption of open competitive examination for the

[1] 3 & 4 Will. IV, c. 78, and 26 Vic., c. 106. The arrangements for this examination aroused criticism, it being pointed out that pupils of an examiner competed. In 1862 the conduct of the examination was transferred to the Civil service commissioners (N.L.I. MS 7752).

[2] *Report from the select committee on civil service appointments*, p. 13, H.C. 1860 (440), and *Thirtieth report of H.M.'s Civil service commissioners*, p. xvi, H.C. 1886 [C. 4753], xx.

civil service would have the same beneficial effect as these measures.[1]

One point, however, should be kept in mind. Though from 1871 it was accepted that the normal method of entrance to the civil service should be by open competitive examination, this principle was not in practice consistently applied. There were a growing number of posts requiring professional and technical qualifications for which it would have been pointless to hold open competitions. And occasionally there was an appointment to be made for which wide experience or other outstanding personal qualities were required. Obviously it would be difficult to ask the presumed possessors of such qualities to submit to an examination. However, in addition to open competitive examination there were three other methods of entering the civil service, by nomination without examination, by nomination followed by a qualifying examination, and by limited competition. At the beginning of the twentieth century there were in the Irish government departments about fourteen hundred officials appointed by one or other of these three methods. Over six hundred had been appointed simply by nomination. These included the inspectors of the Congested districts board, the local government board and the department of agriculture and technical instruction, temporary clerks and assistant commissioners under the land commission. Another six hundred or so (including nearly five hundred officials in the prison service and a number of assistant commissioners and clerks in the land commision) had been appointed by nomination after a qualifying examination. And about two hundred civil servants (including seventy national school inspectors) had entered by limited competitions.[2]

The old view that the best method of selection was on personal knowledge of the candidates still lingered on. The local government board appointed both its auditors and inspectors by nomination without examination. The auditors had to be barristers, solicitors, chartered accountants or accountants in some branch of the public service, the inspectors were selected from the ranks of the temporary inspectors. Robinson, the vice-

[1] Larcom to Trevelyan, 11 Apr. 1854. The Trevelyan–Larcom correspondence is in N.L.I. MS 7752.

[2] *Government departments (Ireland) return* . . . H.C. 1907 (8), lxviii.

chairman and permanent head of the board, delivered a spirited defence of this system when giving evidence before a royal commission. At one time, he explained, there had been a qualifying examination for auditors. A candidate was told that he was appointed and would have to satisfy the civil service commissioners 'by passing an examination in book-keeping or poor law. The candidate then crammed for a fortnight or so and passed, but it only caused delay'. As for the inspectors, Robinson emphasized, 'you want a class of man who knows the country and understands the minds of the guardians . . . and who has some experience of the daily lives of the people who can go down to the locality and diagnose for the local government board the real state of affairs'. 'A man of imperturbable good temper and of great tact' was needed when it came to dealing with boards of guardians. By bringing a man into the department as a temporary official they could see how he shaped and 'if he has the makings of a valuable official he is nearly always kept on and if he is not too old he nearly always gets on the permanent staff'. Robinson could not conceive an examination which would test the qualities required by a local government board inspector and he mentioned as an illustration that one of the best inspectors the board ever had could not write English nor spell. But this inspector could 'turn boards of guardians round his little finger, partly because he had such kindly, good fellowship for all men, and partly no doubt because he was a great figure in the racing world', being the owner of the far-famed White Knight.[1]

Curiously enough MacDonnell, who clashed with Robinson on administrative issues, agreed with him at least in one instance on the advantages of selection by interview alone. In 1899 the land commission besides laying down the qualifications required by assistant land commissioners decided, apparently after consultation with the chief secretary, that persons appointed should take a qualifying examination conducted by the civil service commission. Early in 1906 MacDonnell came to the conclusion that the land commission needed 'fresh

---

[1] *Royal commission on the civil service, fourth report, evidence*, pp. 203–4, 408–10, H. Robinson, *Further memories of Irish life* (*1925*), pp. 190–1. Robinson gives an example of the inspector's spelling. 'Bord of gardians should brighten up the front of the house with a few flour beds'.

blood'. He did not think an examination would be of any value. Instead he himself interviewed all the temporary assistant commissioners and all applicants for the post of assistant commissioner. As a result he decided that the appointments of five of the existing temporary assistant commissioners should not be renewed, the vacancies being filled by five newcomers. MacDonnell emphasized that he was careful during the interviews to avoid politics and religion. But he admitted that all the new men were nationalists. Conservatives, needless to say, professed to be shocked and were not impressed by the government's explanation that it had simply aimed at securing the best men available.[1]

In 1876 lower division clerks were assigned to nine Irish departments, by 1914 second division men were employed in fifteen, including the four largest, and over five hundred second division men were working in the twenty-nine Irish offices. First division men were far less widely distributed in Ireland, being employed in only four departments. Five of the nine principal and first class clerks in the chief secretary's office, nine of the nineteen officials in the 'upper division' of the staff of the local government board, two of the senior officers and seven clerks in the public record office, and the secretary and assistant secretary of the national health insurance commission were men who had entered by the Class I examination. The public record office contained such an extraordinarily high proportion of the administrative élite, simply because it was closely modelled on the English office which had early become a first division one. As first division men appointed to the Irish public record office started on an initial salary £50 below what they would have enjoyed in most other departments and had comparatively poor prospects of promotion it is understandable that, as the deputy keeper complained, they tended to use the office as a stepping stone. By 1914 first division men entering the office were being informed that they would not be permitted to transfer and the deputy keeper had to admit that some of them were 'fretful'[2].

---

[1] *Hansard*, 4 series, clv. 1319–46, clvi. 750–824, clix. 758–60; Memorandum by MacDonnell, 23 Jan. 1906, MacDonnell to Bryce, 8, 10, 16 Mar. 1906 (Bryce papers, MS. 11012); *Irish land commission: assistant commissioners: rules of the Irish land commission dated 13 Mar. 1899*. H.C. 1899 [C. 9226], lxxix.

[2] *Royal commission on the civil service, fourth report, evidence*, pp. 333–5.

The under-secretary, Dougherty, was convinced that his department needed first division men, since the work to be done demanded 'the grasp, intelligence and knowledge of affairs that a first class clerk possesses in an eminent degree'. He quickly added that all first class clerks were not of the same level and that there were second class clerks equal to first class ones. Indeed, he asserted that in the chief secretary's office 'every Second class clerk carries his baton in his knapsack, although he may not become a field-marshal'. But broadly speaking, Dougherty stated that there was undoubtedly a line of demarcation 'which anyone dealing with administration easily detects' between first and second class clerks.[1] Sir Henry Robinson, the permanent head of the local government board, agreed with Dougherty. Not a university man himself, he was impressed by the wide range of interests and the self-reliance of young graduates who entered the service as first division clerks. Shortly after he became vice-president in 1898, on the eve of a great revolution in Irish local government, he turned his office into 'an upper division one'. The lower division clerks in the office were nearly all Irishmen 'who knew almost too much of the political and religious aspect of affairs' so he was anxious to leaven them with a few Englishmen and Scotsmen 'who might break fresh ground of thought in our brains'. Robinson believed that an office in which the three nationalities, English, Irish and Scotch, were represented, was 'perfectly equipped'. 'The Englishmen', he declared, 'we have had from the upper division examination have been stolid, sensible, highly competent persons. The Scotchman is a rock of common-sense, accurate and cautious. The Irishman is brilliant, resourceful and quick, but he is rather impulsive and wants the steadiness of the English and Scotch'.[2] Finally Starkie, the resident commissioner of the national education board, while paying a high tribute to the hard-working second division men in his office, said that he missed the class of men who were 'able to write satisfactory letters on important subjects'.[3]

On the other hand Gill, the permanent head of the department of agriculture and technical instruction, a very late arrival in civil service life, after a career in politics and journal-

[1] *Ibid.*, pp. 186–7.   [2] *Ibid.*, pp. 201–2.   [3] *Ibid.*, p. 430.

ism, was vehemently opposed to the idea of a 'separate class coming in in the manner which is now provided'. 'These men come in', he said, 'with the notion, from the manner in which they have been brought in, and the privileged position in which they are placed in the service from the first, that they are, so to speak, of superior clay to the men of the other divisions they find in the office'. They were, he granted, often 'charming fellows with those they regard as equals'. But he understood some of them would not even salute second division men when they met in the street. The snobbery thus generated, Gill believed, permeated the whole service, second division men looking down on abstractors, and abstractors on temporary clerks. Gill's remedy was to have two grades, the second of which would include the lower ranks of the existing second division and the abstractors. Men would enter his second grade at about sixteen and a half and his first grade at about nineteen. By taking evening classes, members of grade II could prepare themselves to compete for places in grade I, and members of grade I would be encouraged to prepare for a university degree by attending evening lectures which could easily be arranged in Dublin. Gill would also have permitted graduates to enter grade I straight from the university at the rates of pay they would have attained if they had entered the service earlier. But he seems to have visualized a service in which the higher grade would be largely recruited by promotion from the lower.[1]

On the whole, members of the second division working in Ireland were understandably reasonably content. Their work was satisfying, their remuneration compared, not unfavourably, with that of contemporaries working in comparable occupations. Admittedly representatives of the second division men from five Irish departments appeared before the royal commission on the civil service in 1914. But their main complaint was not a very bitter one. They wanted more opportunities for promotion—broadly speaking either more staff posts should be created or in an increased number of instances second division clerks should be promoted to senior posts. But one witness admitted that his financial prospects as a second division man were 'not to be sneezed at'.[2]

[1] *Ibid.*, pp. 227–8.   [2] *Ibid.*, p. 214.

The assistant clerks seem to have been if anything slightly more discontented, and deputations representing the assistant clerks of five Irish departments appeared before the royal commission. Though one witness said that the maximum was too low and another exclaimed that 'at no time in his career had an assistant clerk got a living wage', the main grievance raised by the deputations was that in many instances assistant clerks were allotted the same work as second division men. The remedy they suggested was more frequent promotion from the assistant clerk grade to the second division. A representative from the valuation office thought that one quarter of the vacancies in the second division might be reserved for the assistant clerks; a representative from the national education office went further, asking for half of these appointments to be reserved. The commissioners from the tone of their questions do not however seem to have been convinced that the assistant clerks were in fact frequently performing duties of the kind to which second division men would be assigned.[1]

The temporary clerks of whom there seem to have been about four hundred in Dublin formed the saddest group of all. They were not well paid and, though they might be employed for years, they had neither permanency nor the prospect of a pension. One temporary clerk explained that temporary appointments were 'usually accepted under dire stress of circumstances; very often and in fact in most cases, when things began to run smoothly for the individual, after a few years he sees no prospect, nothing in front of him and no hope of reaching a proper maximum, or anything of that kind. He has no means to provide for his old age, and in a good many cases he cannot even insure himself decently . . . and he drifts along until things become hopeless'. He added that he himself had been in commercial life for two years before he 'accepted a position as a temporary clerk in the government service'. The reason he changed was that a kinsman advised him that 'if I got into what he described as the outer circle I would very likely do well'. The representatives of the temporary clerks association suggested to the commission that any man who had given long and satisfactory service in a department should be made permanent.[2]

There is another question closely connected with the grading

[1] *Ibid.*, pp. 266, 297, 314.   [2] *Ibid.*, pp. 338–9.

which it is hard to handle within reasonable limits, remuneration. As has been pointed out one of the reformers' objectives during the early part of the century was to try to establish a rational relation between remuneration and duties. By the middle of the century this had to a very great extent been attained. The heads of the Irish departments enjoyed official incomes of about £1,000 per annum. At the bottom of the ladder clerks entered the service at about £80 per annum (the initial salary in the chief secretary's and paymaster of the civil service's office was £100 per annum; at the other extreme clerks entering the Dublin metropolitan police office began at £55 per annum). About one in seven of the clerks in the Irish government offices enjoyed salaries of £400 or over, twice as many had salaries of £200 or over, and the remainder (rather over four-sevenths) had salaries of under £200. Probably it would be safe to say that at the middle of the century a clerk in a government office in Ireland had a reasonable possibility of ending his career with a salary of about £300 per annum.

Between the middle of the century and the late 'sixties there was a considerable rise in the salary levels in Irish government departments. Initial remuneration altered little but the maxima of many groups definitely increased. The proportionate increases varied immensely but it might be said that financial prospects generally must have improved by about fifty per cent.

Nevertheless there was discontent which the treasury ignored, and in 1868 a number of civil servants working in Dublin formed a committee which produced a statement showing that their salaries were inferior to those of men performing similar duties in England and that there had been in recent years a distinct rise in the cost of living in Dublin. In the autumn of the following year, 1869, a deputation put this case before the chief secretary (Fortescue), who 'received them very courteously and undertook that no effort on his part should be wanting to obtain for their case' favourable consideration by the government. But when the secretary of the Irish civil servants committee wrote placing the claims of the staff in several departments before the government, and asking for 'the removal of the brand of inferiority which is placed upon their services', the treasury firmly refused to 'entertain applications for an increase of salary in a collective form'.[1]

In April 1872, Plunket, a leading Irish conservative M.P., raised the matter in the house of commons, asking the House to resolve that civil servants working in Ireland should be put 'on an equality as to remuneration with those performing corresponding duties in England'. Plunket's resolution was seconded by an Irish liberal M.P., and though the debate took a strange turn, drifting into a discussion on the cost of maintaining criminal lunatics in Great Britain and Ireland, the government yielded to what was clearly the wish of the house and promised to appoint a commission of inquiry.[2]

The commission, which was appointed by the chancellor of the exchequer in September, was composed of three members, Lord Monck, an Irishman who had been the first governor-general of Canada, Major Myles O'Reilly, the liberal M.P. for Longford who had fought with distinction in the papal forces, and Arthur Blackwood, an able treasury official and a fervent evangelical, who during his stay in Dublin devoted some of his scanty leisure to addressing religious meetings.[3] The treasury suggested to the commission that it should investigate the cost of living and the earnings of professional men and clerks in Dublin. It should also try and discover whether Irish departments were over-manned. It should bear in mind 'the uninterrupted and progressive character of government pay' and remember that civil servants were entitled to 'a fair price for the work required of them, but not a higher price than that for which the government can get the work efficiently performed'.

The commission closely investigated conditions in two departments, considered to be representative, the local government board and the registrar general's office. And they also considered the claims of the R.I.C. and the Dublin metropolitan

---

[1] R. Peel to secretary to the treasury, 29 Nov. 1865, L. Balfour to Naas 6 Feb. 1867, W. M. Burke to Naas, 10 May 1867 (Naas papers, N.L.I. MS 11147), *Civil service gazette*, 30 Oct. 1869. The deputation which was over 30 strong included several first class clerks. Its case was put by G. W. Finlay, a first class clerk from the poor law commission office (Stansfield to chief secretary, 14 July 1870 (T. 14/71 and T. 1/9626). Larcom papers, N.L.I. MS 7755).

[2] *Hansard*, 3 series, ccx. 2019–41.

[3] *Some records of the life of Sir Stevenson Arthur Blackwood*, pp. 312–7.

police for higher pay. They agreed in recommending higher scales of remuneration both in the two departments and for the police. They also agreed that over the previous twenty years there had been a definite rise in the cost of living in Dublin.

But they differed sharply on other issues. Monck and O'Reilly admitted that 'in the past' when the cost of living in Dublin was lower than in London and when junior appointments in the Irish section of the civil service were usually granted to Irishmen, there were good grounds for making salaries in Dublin lower than in London. But with the rise in the cost of living and the disappearance to a great extent of recruitment on a departmental basis, civil servants working in Dublin ought, they decided, to enjoy the same salaries as those performing analogous duties in London. Blackwood considered that in making this general recommendation the commission was exceeding its terms of reference. Realizing that he would be 'stigmatized in parliament as a "narrow minded official" ' he emphasized that adequately qualified persons were being secured for posts in Ireland and that, taking into account 'the many advantages that gentlemen in the permanent service of the government possess beyond those engaged in commercial employment', civil service salaries were high enough. Granting there had been a rise in the cost of living, it was for the treasury, taking all factors into account, to decide which, if any, salaries ought to be increased.[1]

The treasury's reaction to the commission's findings was to express a willingness to consider the case of the officials in any department if submitted through its head. But a deputation of Irish M.P.s to whom the chief secretary announced this decision expressed great dissatisfaction and, in April 1873, Plunket again raised the question in the house. Plunket and his supporters grounded themselves on the majority report of the commission. The government's case was put with considerable force by Lowe and Gladstone who argued that a civil servant's salary was based on a contract between the official and the public and that it was unfair to the latter to vary the contract when the circumstances told against the former. Lowe, a doctrinaire, asked rhetorically were salaries to be lowered if the

---

[1] *Report of the commissioners appointed . . . to inquire into the condition of the civil service in Ireland. . . .* pp. 3–13, 66, H.C. 1873 [C. 789], xxii.

cost of living fell and pointed out that equality of remuneration between English and Irish civil servants could, of course, be secured by revision downwards. In spite of these arguments the government was defeated, Plunket's motion being carried by 130 to 117. And as a result over the next few years salaries in Irish offices were revised so as to move upwards. The Irish civil servants' victory was consolidated soon afterwards by the formation of the lower (second) division and the category of assistant clerks, these groups being paid on the same scales throughout the United Kingdom.[1]

The higher civil servants, those who dealt with administrative problems as distinct from routine duties (including the immediate subordinates of the heads of departments and the men recruited by the Class I examination), did not in 1914 form a division and their salaries varied somewhat between departments. But a member of this group would have an almost certain prospect of ultimately enjoying about £700 per annum, and he might well have a larger salary. The permanent heads of three departments had salaries of £2,000, the heads of two other departments had been paid, when at their maximum, £1,800, and the heads of another twelve offices had salaries ranging at their maximum between £1,000 and £1,500. Of the civil servants employed in Irish departments in 1914, fifty (including those who have just been mentioned) enjoyed, when at their maximum, salaries of £1,000 or over, and over sixty more had maximum salaries of between £800 and £1,000.

Finally, something must be said about a category of civil servants which does not correspond to any of the classes which have been mentioned and which, though important and perceptible, defies precise definition. It was composed of that relatively small number of higher officials, who, under the government of the day, controlled the running of the Irish administrative machine. Obviously there can be differences of opinion over what names should be included in such a group. However, it seems reasonable to assume that it would comprise the heads of most of the Irish departments, along with, for the major departments, their immediate subordinates and the heads of the Irish branches of a few United Kingdom departments. This group formed the official environment in which the lord

[1] *Hansard*, 3 series, ccxvi. 1805–31.

lieutenant and chief secretary worked, and members of it were bound to have some influence on policy. There is another reason why this category of civil servants repays attention. Allowing for the fact that its members were outstandingly successful, an examination of the group is a help towards getting a general impression of the service as a whole.

In 1914 this category, assuming it was composed on the lines mentioned in the last paragraph, contained forty-eight officials.[1] One fact about the group is noticeable on the most cursory inspection. It was overwhelmingly Irish in its origin. Only ten of its members came from across the channel, including two commissioners of works, each of whom had come to Ireland as private secretary to a chief secretary: Taylor, a principal clerk in the chief secretary's office, who as assistant secretary between 1918 and 1920 was to be the inflexible upholder of law and order, and Headlam the treasury remembrancer. Headlam had come to Ireland from the Treasury because the cost of living in Dublin was low compared to London and because he would have an office of his own to run, be able to live in the country and have plenty of fishing.[2] The two assistant secretaries of the department of agriculture and technical instruction, Campbell, who had been a professor at the Yorkshire College, and Fletcher, who had been an inspector of the science and art department, had both been brought to Ireland when the department was set up. Fletcher indeed was said to have been 'almost an Irishman in the persuasiveness of his tongue, sense of humour, quick repartee and facility as a raconteur'.[3]

Twenty-nine of the group had been to a university (twelve to Trinity College, Dublin, six to the Queen's or the Royal Universities, four to the R.C.S.I., five to Oxford, one to Cambridge, and one to Edinburgh. Of those who had not attended a university, two had been called to the bar, three had qualified as solicitors, three had served in the army, one was a qualified engineer, two were valuers, one, Connolly, a principal clerk in the chief secretary's office, had entered by the first-class examination and another (Robinson, of the local government board) was preparing for it when he was able to enter the service by a less arduous route. Their educational qualifications show that

---

[1] See Appendix IV.   [2] M. Headlam, *Irish reminiscences*, p. 25.
[3] *The Times*, 25 Sept. 1934.

the members of the group generally speaking were bound to have middle-class backgrounds. During the nineteenth century a young man of working-class origin would have found it difficult to prepare himself for civil service examinations or acquire professional qualifications. But it can be quickly added that no member of the group could be considered as belonging by birth to the aristocracy. The most that can be said in that respect is that one was the grandson of a viscount and another the brother-in-law of a baronet. Half-a-dozen were the sons of landowners, but of lesser landowners, if importance is measured by acreage and valuation rather than lineage. The fathers of at least sixteen were professional men, including clergymen, doctors, magistrates, engineers, a teacher, an army officer and a journalist. Three were sons of senior civil servants.

There is one question which would certainly have interested contemporaries, the religious affiliations of the members of this category. On the available evidence it seems that it was composed of twenty catholics and twenty-eight protestants, the officials of Irish origin being denominationally divided almost equally. It may be added that it was customary for one of the two secretaries of the boards of national education, intermediate education, and charitable donations to be a protestant while his colleague was a catholic. And the same rule seems to have applied to inspectors of lunatics. A secretary of the board of charitable donations once explained that though he and his colleague did not divide their work on religious lines, and that indeed all their work could be done by one man, the board had decided that it would not retain the confidence of the country if it had not a protestant and a catholic secretary.[1]

The members of the category that has been discussed in the last few pages attained the positions they held in 1914 by a surprising number of paths. Twelve had entered by general examination. Six of these had taken the class I examination. The others had taken examinations roughly equivalent to that for the second division. Of this latter group three had come in by open competition, one by restricted competition and one by a qualifying examination. Nineteen others, though they had risen from another civil service post to the one they held in 1914, had originally been recruited because they possessed some

---

[1] *Royal commission on the civil service, fourth report, evidence*, p. 191.

professional or technical qualification. For instance, three of the land and estates commissioners and the assistant under-secretary had been employed by the land commission; the commissioner of valuation, having built light railways, had been a board of works inspector; the registrar of deeds had been a parliamentary draughtsman; the registrar of petty session clerks had been an R.M.; the inspector-general of the R.I.C. and the chief commissioner of metropolitan police had served in the army, the inspector general having been Roberts's private secretary in South Africa; and Mrs Dickie, the health insurance commissioner (and the only woman in the category) had been an inspector of boarded-out children. Three members of the local government board and one member of the prisons board had been local government inspectors; the chairman of the prisons board had been an engineer in the prisons service, a local government board inspector and private secretary to the viceroy, and the under-secretary, Dougherty, a pres-byterian minister, had been professor of logic at Magee College, Londonderry (and a prominent Ulster liberal) when Morley made him assistant under-secretary in 1895.

Finally the category contained fifteen civil servants who had been brought into the service to fill the important posts they occupied in 1914. These included the permanent heads of two of the more important Irish departments, Gill, secretary to the department of agriculture and technical instruction, and Starkie, the resident commissioner of national education. Gill, before he became secretary to the department at the age of forty-one, had been a journalist, a nationalist M.P. and an enthusiastic propagandist for agricultural reform. Starkie had been a fellow of Trinity College and president of Queen's College, Galway. Others in this group were Thompson, a dis-tinguished Dublin medical man who was made registrar-general in 1909, Wrench a land commissioner, who had been a land agent, the two assistant commissioners for intermediate education, one of whom had been a professor in Cork and the other an inspector of schools in Cairo, and three of the four national health insurance commissioners. One of these com-missioners, Walter Kinnear, who had been the Dublin manager of an insurance company before receiving his civil service appointment, so impressed Lloyd George that he was ultimately appointed controller of the Health insurance department in the ministry of health.[1]

Their careers show that the leaders of the Irish civil service did not conform to a stereotyped pattern. There are other indications that their interests were wide and varied. Two of them after retiring from the service entered politics, Dougherty, as liberal member for Derry, and Sweetman, a secretary of the charitable donations board, who resigned in 1916, as Sinn Fein member for Wexford. Sweetman's colleague Graves, who had captained Dublin University in football and played cricket for Ireland, before entering the civil service, had been a pioneer in technical education. Ross had one of the best gardens in Ireland, Wrench took a keen interest in horse breeding, his colleague in the land commission, Bailey, whose home in Earlsfort Terrace was a vigorous intellectual centre, travelled extensively and at the beginning of the Great War published an informative work on out-of-the-way parts of Central Europe. There were a number of other authors in the group. Ross wrote on military and Indian history, Butler on Irish and Italian history, Starkie edited Aristophanes, Fletcher edited an Irish geography, Mills and Le Fanu published papers on medieval history and the Huguenots, Norway wrote on English bye-ways and post office history, Headlam published a book on fishing and an episcopal biography, Graves printed poems which he modestly described as doggerel, Micks wrote a lucid and at times pungent history of his own department, the congested districts board, Dawson published medical papers and Dilworth a mathematical text-book. Robinson of the local government board produced two volumes of memories which, as he was a shrewd administrator with a quick eye for the absurdities of official life and the amiable weaknesses of his countrymen, are both entertaining and enlightening. Robinson himself was once closely observed by a critical eye. His colleague on an important royal commission, Mrs Sidney Webb, was fascinated by him. She found he was one of the most agreeable companions she had ever come across and she thought that if he was, as his enemies said, 'slim and a timeserver' he was also upright with good intentions. But she was disturbed to discover that he had no preference for one state of society over another. 'After trying',

[1] *The Times*, 4 Apr. 1953.

she wrote, 'to elicit a positive principle or a positive preference, I asked him outright what kind of society he desired in Ireland assuming that he had complete power to bring it about. A dull look came into his grey eyes—giving the impression of a sort of film—an expression of deafness which he has whenever one gets away from the facts of today and after a moment's silence he said, "Well, Mrs Webb, I have lived all my life at concert pitch and I really never thought of all these questions in which you are interested. What has concerned me is keeping my successive chief secretaries out of trouble"!'[1]

[1] B. Webb, *Our partnership*, p. 408. In a moment of despondency Robinson once admitted 'it is very hard to know what is best to do sometimes as there are so many things cropping up which will lead to trouble whatever course we take' (Robinson to Bryce, 6 Apr. 1906, Bryce papers, N.L.I. MS 110 12).

II

THE IRISH EXECUTIVE

~~~~~~

THE HEAD OF the Irish executive was the lieutenant-general and general-governor of Ireland, appointed by patent and holder of a great and historic office.[1] He represented the sovereign; he was responsible for the peace and security of the kingdom; he possessed wide statutory powers; he exercised the prerogative of mercy and he appointed to numerous offices. Moreover he was the embodiment of the 'dignified' aspects of the state, the official leader of Irish social life.

The holder of this important post was always a peer. Of the thirty-four viceroys to hold office between the union and the treaty, ten had been cabinet ministers before coming to Ireland and half-a-dozen others attained cabinet rank after serving as lord lieutenant. Of the remaining viceroys, one, Cornwallis, had been governor-general of India, another (French) had commanded the British army in France, and two (Whitworth, who confronted Napoleon, and Heytesbury) had been distinguished diplomatists. The others were noblemen whose status and wealth made them fitting representatives of royalty. At the beginning of the century the viceroys included Bedford, the head of a great whig family, famous as a collector and practical agriculturalist; Richmond, noted as a duellist and cricketer, and Hardwicke, described by an admirer as 'a model of an English nobleman—courteous and affable, calm and dignified, hospit-

[1] For definitive lists of the lord lieutenants and chief secretaries see *Handbook of British chronology* (London 1961), pp. 147–71 and J. L. J. Hughes, The chief secretaries in Ireland', in *I.H.S.*, viii. 59–72.

able and munificent, intelligent and a highly accomplished scholar',[1] who proved a very conscientious, at times indeed fussy, viceroy. Later amongst the viceroys was Eglinton, the organizer of the celebrated tournament, whose statue stood for years in St Stephen's Green with its eyes fixed on the card room of the University Club at, tradition asserts, Eglinton's own request; Abercorn, a popular resident Irish landlord, created a duke by Disraeli who also used him as the model for the duke in *Lothair*; Dudley, who came in touch with a wide range of Irish life by both entertaining sumptuously and owning a small house in the west; and Aberdeen, who with his wife formed a happy and energetic partnership, active in promoting public-spirited projects such as Irish industries, town planning and housing.

The viceroys were surrounded with considerable state. There was a viceregal court with its officers and ceremonial. At the beginning of the nineteenth century the household included a state steward, a chamberlain, a comptroller, a gentleman usher, aides-de-camp, a master of the revels, gentlemen in waiting, Ulster king of arms with his heralds and pursuivants, the 'master and composer of the musick', 'the state music' (a Restoration foundation composed of a kettle-drummer, trumpeters, violins, hautboys, french horns and a dulcimer), and a company of footguards armed with battle-axes who attended the viceroy on ceremonial occasions. This state was somewhat shorn during the early nineteenth century. The office of master of the revels, which seems to have become a sinecure, was abolished in 1817, and in the early 'thirties the battle-axe guards and the state music were abolished and the number of A.D.C.s and gentlemen-in-waiting reduced.[2] Three-quarters of a century later, under Aberdeen, the gentlemen-in-waiting were finally dispensed with and Sir Anthony Weldon was appointed both state steward and chamberlain.

At the beginning of his viceroyalty the new lord lieutenant was sworn in at a meeting of the Irish privy council and made a state entry into Dublin. The former ceremony was a simple one. The lord lieutenant designate appeared at a council

---

[1] *Gentleman's Magazine*, new series, iii. 205.

[2] *Report from the select committee on civil government charges*, pp. 14, 63-7, H.C. 1831 (337), iv, and *Estimates for civil services for the year ending 31 Mar. 1908*, p. 20, H.C. 1907 (54), li.

meeting presided over by his predecessor or by the lords justices who represented the crown in the absence of a viceroy. The counsellors present were seated and covered (a spectator at the beginning of the twentieth century was much impressed by the unusual sight of top-hatted figures seated round the table).[1] The new lord lieutenant's patent and a letter directing that the sword of state be handed over to him were read; he took the oath of allegiance; the counsellors uncovered, and he assumed the presidency of the council.

The state entry offered an opportunity for military pageantry. On his arrival at the city (from the beginning of the railway age at Westland Row Station) the lord lieutenant was met by the lord mayor and corporation and rode, wearing the star of St Patrick, with a cavalry escort through streets lined by troops to the Castle. When political excitement was running high the atmosphere could be tense, and an unfriendly observer saw Lord Aberdeen in 1886 passing almost unnoticed through College Green amidst an uproar produced by Trinity College undergraduates singing 'God save the Queen' against Nationalists singing 'God save Ireland.'[2] And in 1885 the Dublin corporation declined to meet the incoming viceroy, a decision it adhered to on all other state entries. In 1889 the unionists did their best to provide substitutes for a civic welcome by arranging for the viceroy to be greeted by the commissioners of Blackrock and Pembroke townships and by a citizens' committee at Westland Row. Lord French in 1918 and Lord Fitzalan in 1921 did not make state entries.

The lord lieutenant held levées and drawing-rooms and gave balls and dinners. He was also expected to appear at a wide range of functions, military parades, philanthropic and academic occasions, the dinners of the great corporate bodies, race meetings, and the opening of important public buildings. Performing these social duties with éclat in a hospitable but critical society proved an expensive business. And in 1810 when it was suggested that the viceroy's salary should be increased from £20,000 to £30,000, it was stated in the house of commons that the dukes of Bedford and Richmond had spent nearly £20,000 annually out of their private incomes in supporting the dignity of their office. Though Tierney, the whig leader

[1] *Irish Times*, 15 Dec. 1905.   [2] *Dublin Evening Express*, 20 Feb. 1886.

who was most of his career in opposition, argued that 'it was not usual that a person serving the public in a high office should be able to live entirely independent of his private fortune', and that in any event, the duke of Richmond could well afford £20,000 per annum, the house agreed to the increase.[1] But twenty years later the viceregal salary was reduced again to £20,000 per annum. This obviously increased the difficulties of filling the post, and on one occasion an exasperated prime minister, trying to find a viceroy, complained: 'the wealthy avoid the office and paupers won't fit'.[2] And Lady Aberdeen, whose husband was one of the less wealthy viceroys, ruefully wrote that though he spent as much as he could afford to, 'the jokes which Aberdonians tell against themselves got inevitably connected with our entertainments'.[3]

Nationalists tended to avoid attending the viceregal court. Unionists found their emotions confused when the crown was represented by a lord lieutenant who was a 'home ruler'. During the bitter struggle over Gladstone's second home rule bill, unionists absented themselves from Lord Houghton's court, leaving his levées to 'soldiers, policemen, knights and nobodies'. Houghton, who, even his opponents granted, behaved with dignity, felt obliged to bring the behaviour of the lord chief justice, Sir Peter O'Brien, to the queen's notice. Sir Peter did not only absent himself from a levée, but tried to induce others to stay away. In Houghton's opinion the refusal of unionists to attend his levées after appearing at Londonderry's and Zetland's simply revealed that they attended the viceregal court 'not out of respect for Her Majesty but as a tribute to a political ally'.[4] Again after the third home rule bill was introduced, unionists ceased to attend Aberdeen's receptions. But to some extent the absentees seem to have been replaced, since an indignant court official noticed with distaste 'blue reefer coats and brown boots' appearing at court receptions.[5] On the whole, however, the lord lieutenants seem to have been popular.

[1] *Hansard*, 1 series, xvii. 527–30.
[2] *Letters of Disraeli to Lady Bradford and Lady Chesterfield* (1929), ii. 59.
[3] Lord and Lady Aberdeen, '*We two*' (1925), ii. 79.
[4] *Vanity Fair*, 12 Feb. 1894, 21 Feb. 1895 and *Letters of Queen Victoria*, 3 series, ii. 222–4.
[5] N. Wilkinson, *To all and singular* (1925), p. 195.

They added a touch of spectacle to Irish life and they performed with considerable success the useful social functions of a constitutional sovereign, promoting worthy causes and diffusing amiability.

But, as has been mentioned at the opening of this chapter, the lord lieutenant also had important political and administrative duties to perform. And in exercising the powers he possessed by patent and statute the lord lieutenant had to consider his relations with the government of the day and with the chief secretary. He was a member of the administration, sometimes in fact a cabinet minister. He corresponded with the prime minister both on major questions and on relatively minor issues (including, for instance, the higher legal appointments). He had a comparatively free hand in dealing with Irish matters but of course his general policy had to coincide with that of his colleagues and party. Aberdeen summed up the position by quoting 'Mr Gladstone's admirable formula "the cabinet for policy, the lord lieutenant for administration"'.[1]

The relationship between the lord lieutenant and the chief secretary tended to vary. As the chief secretary's title implied, his office was at first a subordinate one. When it first emerges in official history its holder was the viceroy's personal assistant or chief of the staff, one of the earliest known secretaries to a lord deputy being described an 'inward man' with his master, who used him as a register of all his proceedings and entrusted him with as much as any man could communicate to a servant.[2] The office grew in importance and, towards the close of the eighteenth century, an experienced Irish official could describe the chief secretaryship as 'the most troublesome office in the British empire, comprising every department in the church, law, state, army and revenue, and both houses of parliament'.[3] In short the chief secretary was, subject to the lord lieutenant's supervision, responsible for managing many domestic matters which in England were the business of a secretary of state. Moreover, he was regarded as the most authoritative exponent in the house of commons of the administration's policy. And

[1] Lord and Lady Aberdeen, '*We two*' (1925), i. 250.
[2] *H.M.C. Cecil MSS*, i. 401.
[3] Hely-Hutchinson to Wyndham, 12 Aug. 1784 (Add. MSS 37873).

56

during the century there grew up around the post a department comprising a couple of under-secretaries and some clerks.

But throughout the eighteenth century the chief secretary was always strictly subordinate to and overshadowed by the lord lieutenant who could deal with important issues and persons himself. And this inferiority of status was reflected right up to 1801 by the form of the secretary's appointment: it was by 'a verbal communication to the office of the chief secretary' from the lord lieutenant.[1] Even in the house of commons, the one sphere where he was not overshadowed by his principal, the chief secretary, handicapped by an inadequate knowledge of Irish affairs and frequently by political immaturity, was dwarfed by the tough, quick-witted Irish office-holders on whose advice, in an emergency, viceroys tended to rely. Just before the union, however, by a curious accident, the prestige of the chief secretaryship was suddenly raised. Castlereagh, who functioned as chief secretary from May 1798, was a member of a highly successful Irish political family and had been an Irish M.P. for eight years. A calm, level-headed young man, a first-rate debater and an able administrator, he remained in office when Camden, who appointed him, was replaced by Cornwallis, and the Cornwallis–Castlereagh administration can fairly be described as a friendly and equal partnership.

The union had a considerable effect on the chief secretary's status. From then onwards the chief secretary spent the recess in Ireland and the parliamentary session at Westminster. He had to see Irish legislation, of which there was always a considerable amount, through the house of commons, answer questions and handle the Irish members. His parliamentary duties and the fact that he could be in close contact with cabinet ministers tended to increase his importance at the expense of his nominal chief, who was occupied in supervising the working of the Irish governmental machine from Dublin Castle.

It is not surprising then that from the union the chief secretary ceased to be the lord lieutenant's personal nominee. And as early as 1812 the duke of Richmond felt called on to remonstrate mildly when a chief secretary was nominated before he

---

[1] *Commons journ. Ire.*, xvii. 684. For the form of appointment after the union see J. L. J. Hughes *op. cit.*

could raise any objection. 'Nobody', Richmond wrote, 'cares less about form than I do, but it might have been awkward, for if I had strong grounds of objection to the person they wished I must have refused my consent'.[1] But when one of Richmond's successors, Anglesey, did in fact in 1828 express some reluctance to have Leveson-Gower as his chief secretary, his doubts were swept aside,[2] and after 1830 even the form of securing the lord lieutenant's acquiescence in the appointment of the chief secretary seems to have been dropped. Moreover, in 1831, when conditions were critical in Ireland, the chief secretary, Stanley, was promoted to the cabinet. The lord lieutenant naturally enough asked to be also admitted. But the prime minister refused, pointing out that, owing to his absence from England, Anglesey could not perform the duties of a cabinet minister and that Stanley, 'tho' a member of the cabinet for the advantage of a government here', would, when in Ireland, be subordinate to the lord lieutenant.[3] Stanley's promotion, however, did not initiate a constitutional custom, for during the following thirty-seven years only three chief secretaries, Labouchere (1846), Cardwell (1859) and Naas (1866) sat in the cabinet;[4] Labouchere and Cardwell had already sat in former cabinets, and Naas, who in 1866 was chief secretary for the third time, was an outstanding member of his party.

Of the viceroys during this period, however, five had the prestige conferred by having previously sat in a cabinet. During Gladstone's great first ministry, his chief secretary was always a cabinet minister. Disraeli in 1874, aiming at a small cabinet, reverted to the old practice of excluding the chief secretary. And though, two years later, the chief secretary, Hicks Beach, was admitted to the cabinet, when in 1878 he was moved to the colonial office, his successor as chief secretary remained outside. Gladstone, returning to office in 1880 when Irish affairs were in a critical state, followed his own precedent by appoint-

---

[1] Richmond to Bathurst, 5 Aug. 1812 (H.M.C., *Bathurst MSS*, p. 193).

[2] Wellington to Anglesey, 15, 18 June 1828 (Wellington, *Despatches*, (1871), iv. 489, 491).

[3] Grey to Anglesey, 13 June 1831 (Anglesey, papers). Clarendon told Kimberley that he would never have consented to be lord lieutenant with his chief secretary in the cabinet (Add. MSS 44224).

[4] Naas was in fact admitted six weeks after the formation of the cabinet (G. E. Buckle, *Life of Disraeli*, iv. 445).

ing Forster, a cabinet minister, chief secretary. Forster resigned over the Kilmainham treaty, and since Cowper, the lord lieutenant, though a supporter of a strong policy, was, in the opinion of the queen, the prime minister and the chief secretary, a weak man,[1] Gladstone reorganized his Irish administration drastically. Spencer, the lord privy seal, able, unambitious, public-spirited, a tower of strength to any administration, who had been viceroy in 1870, was re-appointed lord lieutenant, retaining of course his seat in the cabinet. This led to a pathetic situation. For Trevelyan, the chief secretary, after fifteen months' experience of 'this terrible office', implored Gladstone to admit him to the cabinet. Nobody, he said, could form any conception of what it was to be the representative of the central government in the face of the false and unscrupulous men who were for ever seeking to discredit English rule in Ireland. To enable him to conduct Irish business with any semblance of authority he had to be a cabinet minister.[2] Spencer made it very clear that he did not want his personal preference for continuing as they were to stand in the way of Trevelyan receiving his due. After all, during the early 'seventies, when Hartington was in the cabinet, Spencer never felt that he was being overridden or that his views were not being considered carefully.[3] But Gladstone, who could be punctilious on questions of promotion, told Trevelyan that it was dangerous if not impossible to have a chief secretary in the cabinet with 'a working viceroy'. Trevelyan, he emphasized, should realize 'that those portions of our political lives in which we feel ourselves overborne and overwhelmed constitute the most telling and valuable parts of the political education we are all undergoing'.[4] In less than a year Trevelyan, whose hair had turned white, was asking to be relieved of office. 'The life I lead', he wrote, 'is not a human life at all'.[5] And Spencer felt that if he were not relieved he would have a breakdown.[6] In the autumn

---

[1] Foster to Gladstone, 29 May 1881 (Add. MSS 44158) and *Letters of Queen Victoria*, series 2, iii. 164, 271.

[2] Trevelyan to Gladstone, 20 Aug. 1883 (Add. MSS 44310).

[3] Spencer to Gladstone, 7 Oct. 1883 (Add. MSS 44310).

[4] Gladstone to Trevelyan, 23 Aug. 1883, 26 July 1884.

[5] Trevelyan to Gladstone, 26 July 1884 (Add. MSS 44335).

[6] Spencer to Gladstone, 20 Sept. 1884 (Add. MSS 44311).

Trevelyan was sent to the board of trade and promoted to the cabinet. His successor was Campbell-Bannerman, noted for 'his passive good humour and extreme frugality of speech'.[1] Spencer was anxious that he should be admitted to the cabinet, but Gladstone, being unwilling to create a precedent, refused.

When the conservatives took office in 1885 they adhered to their predecessors' arrangements, placing the lord lieutenant in the cabinet and the chief secretary outside. Admittedly, just as the ministry was about to resign, Smith, the secretary of state for war and already a cabinet minister, was appointed chief secretary, an office which he held for a few days. In Gladstone's third and fourth and Salisbury's second governments, the chief secretaries were in the cabinet and the lord lieutenants were not. But when Salisbury formed his third ministry in 1895 the lord lieutenant, Cadogan, was in the cabinet, and the successive secretaries, Gerald Balfour and George Wyndham, were outside it. Wyndham, who was delighted to be chief secretary—'I like my province', he wrote, 'it can be governed only by conversation and arbitrary decisions'—did not approve of the arrangement.[2] In 1901 he wrote to Arthur Balfour: 'I let my spirits sink in the face of eight sheets received from Cadogan. I would gladly devote days to talking to him if I ever supposed he understood what I am saying. But I have known from his remarks he does not and I have reason to fear that he with the best will in the world misrepresents my views to others.' Consequently, Wyndham decided to confine his 'conversational exercises' with the viceroy to the minimum required by loyalty. And he compared himself —trying from outside the cabinet to influence government policy—to a lunatic in a padded cell or a man speaking through a megaphone with a pudding in its mouth.[3] In 1902, Wyndham was admitted to the cabinet and Cadogan was succeeded by Dudley, who was not included in the cabinet. Wyndham's successor, Long, was at the time of his appointment a cabinet

[1] J. A. Spender, *Life of the Rt. Hon. Henry Campbell-Bannerman* (1923) i. 66–7.
[2] J. W. Mackail and G. Wyndham, *Life and letters of George Wyndham*, ii. 412.
[3] *Ibid.*, pp. 425–6.

minister, and after two years in double harness with Dudley his opinion of the lord lieutenant was 'that however a good fellow he may be in private life he is a very bad colleague in government'.[1] He deplored a speech the lord lieutenant had made on the land question, telling him: 'We have been flogged in the house of commons over your speech "about government in accordance with Irish ideas"—this is applauded by the nationalists and derided and flouted by unionists and . . . as you and I exist as ministers on unionist votes it is of course an impossible policy to use language of the kind'.[2] Shortly afterwards, when the lord lieutenant disagreed with the instructions to the estates commissioners which he had signed at Long's request, Long told him that as the instructions were signed his views could only 'have an academic interest'. 'Your position as a member of the Irish executive', he added, 'makes you jointly responsible both for their terms and for their loyal administration'.[3] Finally they differed sharply over a nomination to the senate of the Royal University, the lord lieutenant wishing to increase the catholic clerical representation. Long plainly stated that when he, the minister responsible for the government of Ireland, decided after full consideration on an appointment, it was the lord lieutenant's duty to act on his advice. Even when the lord lieutenant was in the cabinet, and the chief secretary outside it, the former almost invariably gave way to the latter on the ground that, as he had to defend, he ought to control.[4] Dudley insisted that the dispute should be referred to the prime minister. Balfour, in the course of a philosophic letter on that 'practical paradox', the existing system of Irish government, argued that as a result of constitutional developments the real headship of the Irish government belonged to the minister who happened to be both in the cabinet and the house of commons. Thus, while the legal and social status of the lord lieutenant remained what they had been, his political position was quite altered. The views of the chief secretary must prevail, but it would be absurd to regard the lord lieutenant as merely an under-secretary. Rather he was a constitutional monarch.[5]

Dudley's successor was Aberdeen, and after only a year in

---

[1] C. Petrie, *Walter Long and his times*, p. 97. [2] *Ibid.*, p. 87.
[3] *Ibid.*, p. 90. [4] *Ibid.*, pp. 93–4. [5] *Ibid.*, 95–7.

office he sent the prime minister a memorandum on the relationship of viceroy and chief secretary. In this he laid down that though the lord lieutenant could perform his duties better if he were not a member of the cabinet, he must be recognized 'as a partner in the Irish government in respect to his formal functions', for the viceroy being 'the man on the spot' might be in the best position for forming a correct opinion. This implied (1) that the lord lieutenant should be kept informed on matters of policy and administration, and (2) that he should be responsible for appointments other than those which had been recognized as appertaining to the chief secretary.[1]

Aberdeen's successor, Wimborne, discovered when he came into office that, although nominally the head of the administration, his powers had been completely absorbed by the chief secretary and the under-secretary. Moreover, the under-secretary held 'the doctrine of the lord lieutenant's total irresponsibility'. Wimborne complained that he was being kept in ignorance of matters which were being referred to him by those who 'did not appreciate the change in the lord lieutenant's status'. After repeated representations he managed to secure 'a partial insight' into the working of the Irish administration.[2]

The formation of the war cabinet at the end of 1916 meant that the chief secretary ceased to be a cabinet minister. And when Lloyd George reconstituted his government on normal lines in October 1919, he made a curious arrangement. The viceroy and chief secretary were alternatively members of the cabinet.[3] This scheme ended with Lord French's resignation in 1921.

The chief secretary's principal subordinate was the under-secretary. From 1777 the chief secretary's office was divided into two branches, the civil and the military, each headed by an

[1] Aberdeen to Campbell-Bannerman, 28 Dec. 1906 (Add. MS 41210).

[2] *Royal commission on rebellion in Ireland: minutes of evidence*, p. 34, H.C. 1916 [Cd. 8311], xi. It may be added that immediately after the rising Wimborne resigned and lords justices were appointed to act under the general directions of the government conveyed through the home secretary. Wimborne was reappointed in August 1916 (*Dublin Gazette*, 14 July, 24 Aug. 1916, *Hansard*, 5 series, lxxxiv. 1322).

[3] *Hansard*, 5 series, cxx. 271.

under-secretary. But at the close of 1819 the office of under-secretary for military affairs was allowed to lapse and the under-secretary in the civil department became the under-secretary.[1]

The under-secretary, continuously resident in Dublin, was responsible to the chief secretary for the routine working of the whole Irish administration.[2] The importance of the post naturally fluctuated with the personalities of its holders. But even the most outstanding under-secretaries were clearly subordinated to the chief secretary. The post only slowly became a civil service appointment in the modern sense, with its holder a permanent official completely detached from party politics. This is scarcely surprising, since the distinction between a higher civil servant and a subordinate political office holder was only evolved during the nineteenth century. Cooke, the civil under-secretary at the time of the union when Castlereagh, the chief secretary, retired, felt that he could not remain 'a quiet, torpid, useless clerk, going through mere common drudgery and dis-approving every measure that is taken by the government which permits me'.[3] So he resigned and was transferred to the board of control for India. Later Gregory (under-secretary, 1812–30) was compelled to retire on pension by the whigs when they came into office in 1830.[4] For the following twenty-two years all his successors had obvious political sympathies (three of them had been M.P.s and Thomas Drummond was at the end of his career being considered as a Liberal candidate for Belfast) and they left office on changes of government. At the beginning of the fifties the post seems to have been considered a political one, and when Larcom was appointed under-secretary at the beginning of 1853 the lord lieutenant pointed out that he might well object to leaving the permanent appointment he held (he was deputy-chairman of the board of works) 'for one

[1] *Report from select committee on civil government changes* . . . , *appendix*, pp. 64–7, H.C. 1831 (337) iv.

[2] *Report on the organization of the permanent civil service*, pp. 80–6, H.C. 1850 (1713), xxvii. 112–8, and *Royal commission on rebellion in Ireland*, p. 1, H.C. 1916 [Cd. 8279], xi.

[3] *Memoirs and correspondence of Viscount Castlereagh*, iv. 28.

[4] On the change of government in 1827 Gregory resigned but immediately afterwards withdrew his resignation (Gregory to Goulburn, 19 Apr. 1827; Goulburn papers).

he would lose in a change of government'. However, the viceroy remarked, 'he would have his profession to fall back on and
he is so good an engineer that he would not fail to obtain
employment if he applied for it'.[1] In the event Larcom never
had to rely on his professional talents, for he remained in office
for fifteen years (during which the liberals' long lease of power
was only interrupted by two short-lived conservative governments). From his retirement in 1868 the post was definitely
treated as a civil service appointment, and filled by an interesting selection of occupants, comprising four soldiers (Wether-
all, Buller, Ridgeway and Nathan), four distinguished home
civil servants (Anderson, Byrne, Chalmers and Hamilton) an
Indian civil servant (MacDonnell), a post office official
(McMahon), a high police official (Harrel), an official from
the chief secretary's office (Burke) and a sometime professor
of philosophy (Dougherty). Admittedly three of the under-
secretaries appointed after 1868 were removed from Ireland
because they were identified with controversial policies and
Stoney, the secretary of the Queen's University, believed that
the reason why he was not appointed under-secretary in
succession to Larcom was that his politics did not coincide with
those of the government in power.[2] Sir Anthony MacDonnell
(under-secretary, 1902–8) became involved in an important
political crisis. It became known that he had taken an active
part in devising a scheme of devolution which the government
promptly disavowed. However, Wyndham, the chief secretary,
accepted responsibility and resigned. MacDonnell was able to
remain in office but soon after Wyndham's successor, Long,
arrived, MacDonnell felt that owing to a change of policy
'against which my representations were unavailing', his situation was becoming intolerable. At that point a serious illness
put him out of action and by the time he was able to resume
duty a liberal administration was in power. But generally
speaking Balfour accurately described the position of the under-
secretary when he explained that Irish under-secretaries though
'aiders, advisers and suggesters to their official chief' were
'always bound to follow the rulings of the government which
they serve and always bound by those rulings of the civil

[1] St Germans to Aberdeen, 23 Jan. 1853 (Add. MSS 43207).
[2] T. W. Moody and J. C. Beckett, *Queen's Belfast* (1959), i. 227.

service which are the great strength of the administrative machine'.[1]

From what has been said it is patently clear that the system by which the lord lieutenant and chief secretary shared responsibility for the government of Ireland was clumsy and liable to work in an inharmonious fashion. Why then was it retained? The reasons seem simple. In the exhaustive discussions over the drafting of the act of union little attention was paid to administrative problems. Parliamentary representation, religious issues and the economic and financial relations between the two islands were the topics which had been debated for at least a decade. They were all considered in planning the union. Administrative arrangements were left to the future.

The first post-union home secretary, Pelham, did indeed contemplate a drastic reshaping of the Irish government. He suggested that, since the importance of the viceroy and the chief secretary was greatly reduced by the union, 'the present local administration in Ireland cannot require more than a small portion of the patronage it before found necessary'. The office of chief secretary, he implied, might be abolished, and the viceroy's functions reduced to 'directing . . . the police of the country'. The Irish administration was quick to reply. If the lord lieutenant had not adequate authority and patronage the office would soon be abolished, and 'instead of the wholesome principle of British government, a spirit of faction, cabal and party would prevail throughout the country'. As for the chief secretary, Abbot (the then chief secretary) asked who, if his office was abolished, would manage parliamentary business? The only possibility would be the overburdened home secretary, and if he were a peer, would 'the gentlemen of Ireland attend in the ante-chamber of a peer to transact their house of commons business with his under-secretary?'[2]

These vigorous protests seem to have quashed Pelham's tentative scheme and the matter was not raised again until it was mentioned in parliament in 1810, when Tighe asked was it really necessary to keep up the farce of a viceregal court?[3]

[1] Memorandum by Sir A. MacDonnell, 13 Jan. 1906 (Bryce papers, MS 11012) and *Hansard*, 4 series, cxli. 994.

[2] *Diary and correspondence of Charles Abbot, Lord Colchester*, i. 303–30.

[3] *Hansard*, 1 series, xvii. 527.

Ten years later, Sir John Parnell argued that the lord lieutenancy should be abolished as expensive and useless.[1] In the
'twenties, Joseph Hume, the radical advocate of economy, who
sat for Aberdeen, took up the question and with characteristic
pertinacity initiated parliamentary debates on it on no fewer
than three occasions, in 1823, 1830 and 1844.[2] In 1830 his
motion, which implied the abolition of the lord lieutenancy
and the chief secretaryship, was defeated by 229 to 115.[3] On
the other two occasions he did not press it to a division. Eager
to simplify the whole administrative system, he explained that
all the duties of the lord lieutenant and chief secretary could be
performed by departments in London, mainly by the home
office. In 1830 Hume was supported by Spring-Rice and
Althorp. Spring-Rice argued with neat logic that if the lord
lieutenant and chief secretary agreed with the home secretary
they formed a useless piece of expensive machinery, if they did
not there would be a mischievous collision. As for the civilizing
influence on Irish society attributed to the viceregal court by
its defenders, he valued one steam-boat more than a wilderness
of lord lieutenants. Althorp thought that the viceregal office
should be abolished since it gave Ireland all the trappings and
none of the advantages of monarchical government—a theme
which was reiterated by the dangerously witty Bernal Osborne
when he seconded Hume's motion in 1844.[4]

On each occasion Hume was opposed by the serving chief
secretary who did not underrate the importance of his functions.
But Hume was also opposed by a more majestic and experienced
debater, Sir Robert Peel. In 1823 Peel unhesitatingly declared
himself in favour of the existing system. Ireland required 'the
protecting care of some official organ of government residing
upon the spot'. Also the proposed redistribution of powers
would throw too much work on the home secretary.[5] In 1844,
however, his speech consisted of a careful balancing of the

[1] *Ibid.*, 2 series, i. 465.
[2] For the debate in 1823 see *Hansard*, 2 series, ix. 1212. In 1823 it was discovered that a clerk in the chief secretary's office who had absconded owing
to financial difficulties had been supplying Hume with information about
Irish government expenditure (Gregory to Goulburn, 7 May, 18 June, 4
July 1823, Goulburn papers).
[3] *Hansard*, 2 series, xxiv. 555.
[4] *Ibid.*, pp. 566, 570.   [5] *Hansard*, 2 series, ix. 1032.

factors involved. To abolish the lord lieutenancy would increase absenteeism, but it would tend to the amalgamation of the governments of the two islands which *pro tanto* would be an advantage. He advanced one complex constitutional argument against the proposed change. The lord lieutenant was bound to obey the instructions of the home secretary. Thus one mind presided over the internal affairs of the United Kingdom. But, if Irish affairs were transferred to a new secretary of state, as Hume seemed to suggest they should be, this unity of control would be lost. Moreover, when the secretary of state was in England, who was to administer Ireland, and when he was in Ireland was he to share responsibility for cabinet decisions?[1] Though Hume asserted all his arguments remained 'sound and unshaken', he withdrew his motion.

It was significant that three whig cabinet ministers, Althorp, Spring-Rice and Lord John Russell, at different times expressed their disapproval of the existing system. And there is a note in Lord John's handwriting, presumably written in 1847, stating that the impending death of Lord Bessborough raised the question whether the office of lord lieutenant should be retained. 'A separate government—a separate court—and an administration of a mixed nature, partly English and partly Irish, is not of itself a convenient arrangement. The separate government within fifteen hours of London appears unnecessary —the separate court a mockery—the mixed administration the cause of confusion and delay.' And when Clarendon succeeded Bessborough it was apparently clearly understood that the abolition of his office was contemplated.[2]

It was not, however, until 1850 that Lord John introduced a bill for reorganizing the Irish government. The offices of lord lieutenant, chief secretary and under-secretary were to be abolished. The power of issuing proclamations and appointing officials vested in the lord lieutenant was to be vested in the crown. All the powers vested in the lord lieutenant by about twenty-five acts relating to law and order and public health and the powers which could be exercised by the chief secretary or the under-secretary were to be exercised by a secretary of state. Three secretaries of state and three under-secretaries

---

[1] *Hansard*, 3 series, liv. 856.
[2] Russell papers (P.R.O. 30/22/8).

were to be capable of sitting in the house of commons.[1] The bill was introduced in May and in June secured a second reading by a large majority, though opposed by a number of Irish and protectionist members. But early in July Lord John decided that the bill would have to be dropped as the government's legislative programme was in a state of congested confusion.[2]

Later Roebuck, Hume's successor in some respects, in successive sessions (1857 and 1858) moved that the office of lord lieutenant should be abolished. On the second occasion he was defeated by 226 to 115.[3] Nevertheless, in 1860, Cardwell, who had recently been appointed chief secretary, produced a memorandum in which he argued that, with a chief secretary in the commons with a lord lieutenant who was a secretary of state rather than a viceroy and with an under-secretary who was often in practice 'the Irish government', the Irish administration was 'not so constituted as to meet the requirements of the parliamentary system'. Cardwell suggested that the lord lieutenant should be converted into a secretary of state or that his powers should be vested in the home office. Cardwell's memorandum stirred Larcom, the under-secretary, into writing the last of a group of memoranda on the subject which he composed between 1857 and 1860. Larcom agreed that the system would have to be changed but he was sure the time for change had not arrived. Ireland, 'an old country with new institutions' was still in many respects different from England. Party feeling was strong, disaffection was not dead. The government was responsible for the impartial administration of the law and the promotion of social progress. It was pre-eminently a centralized government which often had to act with great promptitude and vigour, and, Larcom emphasized, the lord lieutenant was the mainspring of every movement of the central government.[4]

When the subject of the lord lieutenancy was raised again in the late 'sixties, it was entangled with a delicate question, that of the relations of the royal family with Ireland and even indeed

[1] *Lord lieutenancy abolition (Ireland) bill*, H.C. 1850, iii.
[2] *Hansard*, 3 series, cxii. 899.
[3] *Ibid.*, 3 series, cxlvi. 1048 ff., cxlix. 712 ff.
[4] Copies of Cardwell's and Larcom's memoranda are bound together in the Larcom papers (N.L.I. MS 7504).

with the relations between the Prince of Wales and the queen. In 1858, Archbishop Whateley had remarked that he hoped the time would come when 'the great absentee . . . the queen will be an Irish resident'. There could be no loyalty, he declared, or 'at least no personal loyalty to a mere idea, to a person who is never seen'. And he thought the queen should come to Ireland for visits of five or six weeks.[1] It was suggested in 1868 by Sir Colman O'Loghlen and in 1870 and 1871 by William Stacpoole that steps should be taken to provide a royal residence in Ireland.[2] About the beginning of 1871, Lord Bessborough, an influential whig peer, submitted a memorandum to Gladstone, arguing that a royal residence in Ireland would remove the idea that Ireland was an inferior country and 'benefit Ireland generally by making it the fashion to reside there'. The residence, which need only be a country house, could be used by the queen or more usefully by the Prince of Wales. Bessborough felt that the prince should reside for only a few weeks at a time so that the novelty of his presence would not wear off, and he did not think that the prince should be placed in the position of a lord lieutenant, 'for the Irish are essentially provincial, every act social or political is canvassed more than in London, and a prince placed in such a position would require an amount of prudence far beyond what has been attributed to any of late years'.[3] Gladstone was impressed by Bessborough's arguments, but declared that his awareness of the gravity of the situation made him reluctant to act on a limited plan. Hartington, who also supported Bessborough's proposals, found the chancellor of the exchequer sympathetic and the viceroy, Spencer, ready to allow his right to hold drawing-rooms and levées to be transferred to the Prince of Wales. And he was confident that Bessborough's scheme would not impede the adoption of another plan.[4] This other plan, which Gladstone seems to have had in mind, was the abolition of the lord lieutenancy and the creation of a secretaryship of state for Ireland. In June 1871, Gladstone, with considerable tact, secured the queen's acquies-

---

[1] N. W. Senior, *Journals . . . relating to Ireland*, ii. 140.

[2] *Hansard*, 3 series, cxcii. 346–62, ccvii. 1341.

[3] Bessborough's memorandum and Bessborough to Gladstone, 26 May 1871 (Add. MSS 44430).

[4] Hartington to Gladstone, 20 Feb., 16 May 1871 (Add. MSS 44143).

cence in a proposal for the abolition of the lord lieutenancy. There may, however, have been a misunderstanding. The queen seems to have thought that a royal prince would act as a non-political viceroy; Gladstone said that the prince would merely reside in Ireland for a portion of the year. Finally, there was some discussion over personalities. The queen was in favour of the duke of Connaught occupying the post, provided that it did not mean long absences from London or interfere with his military career. Gladstone favoured the Prince of Wales, pointing out that it would take him away from the London season.[1]

Spencer, the viceroy, on being informed of this, drafted a strong memorandum. If a royal prince came over as lord lieutenant he would be associated in the public mind with the administrative acts performed in his name, and 'it would require a man of remarkable firmness and more than ordinary common sense to retain the position of neutrality that a member of the royal family ought to hold'. But if the lord lieutenancy was abolished on the understanding that the queen was to be represented in Dublin during the Castle season by a royal prince, and the prince failed to come regularly, a grievance would be built up. Defending the existing system, Spencer argued that Irish business could be satisfactorily divided between the lord lieutenant and the chief secretary (assuming they were on good terms), 'the lord lieutenant dealing principally with Irish executive work, the chief secretary being responsible for all new legislation'.[2] Spencer's attitude and the illness of the Prince of Wales in the autumn prevented anything being done, but curiously enough it was Spencer who raised the whole question again fourteen years later when, in 1885, he suggested to Gladstone that the viceroy should be replaced by a secretary of state. Gladstone did not think the time had come

[1] *Letters of Queen Victoria*, 2 series, ii. 136–8.

[2] Spencer's memorandum on Gladstone's conversation with the queen (Add. MS 44307). There is in the Gladtone papers an unsigned, printed memorandum, marked confidential and dated 16 October 1871. With considerable vigour it urges that the lord lieutenancy be abolished and replaced by 'an Irish Balmoral and a secretary of state for Ireland'. This memorandum was produced by H. Y. Thompson, then Spencer's private secretary, and celebrated as a collector of illuminated MSS (N.L.I. MS 7504).

to submit the matter to the cabinet, and soon afterwards far more sweeping plans for the reorganization of the government of Ireland were being discussed.[1]

In all the home rule schemes, since responsible government was being conceded, it was assumed that the lord lieutenant would act on the advice of his Irish ministers and would not go out of office on a change of government in Great Britain. In fact the later home rule bills provided that he was to be appointed for six years. Nevertheless, he was to act on the instructions of the imperial government in granting assent to legislation, and under the 1914 act he could refer constitutional questions to the judicial committee of the privy council. Upon the appointment of a governor-general of the Irish Free State according to the provisions of the Irish Free State constitution act, the lord lieutenant's powers ceased to be operative in the Irish Free State. But under the Irish Free State consequential provisions act, Lord FitzAlan continued to exercise these powers in Northern Ireland for two days longer. As for the office of chief secretary, it lasted until the resignation of Lloyd George's administration in October 1923, the occupant's duties being defined as the 'liquidation' of various departments.

The chief secretary, besides being one of the two senior members of the Irish executive, was also head of a small department, the chief secretary's office, which was the mainspring of the Irish administration. Since it was 'the central office of the Irish government' its duties were wide and varied. It submitted the estimates for a number of other departments and handled questions as to the relations of the civil and military power and correspondence with the English departments, the treasury, the home office, the foreign office, the board of trade and the war office. Above all it was responsible for law and order. All major questions relating to the control, discipline and distribution of the Royal Irish Constabulary and the Dublin Metropolitan Police were referred to the chief secretary's office. The office also supervised the resident magistrates, corresponded with justices of the peace, received memorials from prisoners and convicts, settled problems relating to re-formatories and industrial schools and transmitted the orders of

[1] Spencer to Gladstone, 26 Jan. 1885 (Add. MSS. 44312).

the attorney general (who was the director of criminal prosecutions) to the police and crown solicitors concerned.[1]

Moreover, during the nineteenth century the office absorbed
two other offices of greater antiquity, the privy seal office and
the privy council office, the latter of which had a growing
volume of business. At the union the keeper of the privy seal
was Lord Castlereagh. As he felt that 'pluralities do not become
a young politician', he resigned the office in 1801.[2] This enabled
the government to give his successor, Abbot, 'some certainty' by
conferring the office on him for life.[3] In 1817, however, it was
enacted that on Abbot's death (which occurred in 1829) the
office of keeper should always be held by the chief secretary.[4]
The Irish privy council, composed of high administrative and
legal officials with a sprinkling of peers and distinguished com-
moners, had by the end of the eighteenth century ceased to be
an advisory body. But it performed judicial and administrative
functions. The latter were largely formal but important since it
was by an order-in-council that on many matters the will of the
executive was expressed. And, of course, there were a number
of enactments which entrusted the Irish executive with the
duty of making a series of orders dealing with points of detail.
The council office was responsible for preparing the business
to be laid before the council, and keeping records. At the union
the clerk of the council, Lord Clifden, was a sinecurist, and his
duties were performed by two deputies and an assistant, the
first deputy being also usher to the council chamber. On the
death of Lord Clifden in 1836, the treasury fixed the council
office establishment at three clerks and in 1852 it decided that
the office should be abolished and its duties transferred to the
chief secretary's office, the chief clerk being sworn as clerk to
the council.[5]

The chief secretary's office also had a small off-shoot, the
Irish Office in London. Before the union there was a lord
lieutenant's secretary resident in London and after the union

---

[1] *Royal commission on the civil service, fourth report, evidence*, p. 184, H.C. 1914
[Cd. 7340] xvi.
[2] *Memoirs and correspondence of Viscount Castlereagh*, iii. 387.
[3] *The Diary and correspondence of Charles Abbot*, i. 262.   [4] 57 Geo. III, c. 62.
[5] *Reports of committees of inquiry into public offices*, pp. 87-9, H.C. 1854 (1715),
xxvii. 119-21.

an office was set up to provide a base for the chief secretary when he was in London and to handle official Irish correspondence. Very soon it had a staff of about ten, including an under secretary, a law adviser and eight clerks. In 1831 Stanley diminished the duties by arranging for papers to be transmitted directly between the chief secretary's office and English departments, and reduced its staff to two clerks and a law adviser.[1] Twenty years later a treasury committee found some difficulty in discovering what work was done in the office. The law adviser was hardly required (communications with Dublin having greatly improved since the beginning of the century) and the two clerks seem to have been mainly employed in 'keeping in order a very extensive and valuable library of books'.[2]

The staff was further reduced to one clerk, but even so the office seems in the mid-Victorian era to have been a placid one. Horsman, who became chief secretary in 1855, described how on the day after his appointment 'full of new official ardour' he arrived in the office at ten in the morning. His reception was what any gentleman might have got if he arrived at an inn early in the morning when only the boots was astir. Fires were unlaid, the rooms unswept and he was told that his clerk was expected about mid-day or one o'clock.[3] However at the beginning of the twentieth century the staff in the London office had to be slightly increased to cope with the tremendous pressure produced by parliamentary questions. Many of these, in the opinion of Dougherty, the under-secretary, were of 'an exceedingly trivial character'.[4] But a keen critic of the Irish administration pointed out with evident delight that the parliamentary question 'is the first thing which takes the starch out of the chief secretary'.[5]

From 1777 the chief secretary's office was divided into two sections, the civil and the military. By the close of the century, a third section, the yeomanry, had been added and the office was staffed by about forty clerks. In 1831 the military and

---

[1] Treasury minute, 8 Nov. 1831 (T. 29/323).
[2] *Reports of committees of inquiry into public offices*, p. 81, H.C. 1854 (1715), xxvii.
[3] *Hansard*, 3 series, cl. 1454.
[4] *Royal commission on the civil service, fourth report, evidence*, p. 185.
[5] R. B. O'Brien, *Dublin Castle and the Irish people*, p. 22.

yeomanry sections of the office whose duties had dwindled away were merged with the civil branch, and Stanley's scheme of reorganization in 1831 fixed the establishment at a chief clerk, three senior clerks, a registrar and fourteen clerks. The chief clerk had a salary of £800 a year, the senior clerks £500, and the rest salaries ranging from £100–£350 a year.[1] It was understood that vacancies in the higher ranks would be filled by promotion within the office. But when the first chief clerk, Thomas Taylor, who had entered the office just before the union, died in 1839, Morpeth, the then chief secretary, replaced him by Alexander McDonnell, an able young Oxford graduate, who had been prevented by nervousness from practising at the English bar. McDonnell's two immediate successors, Tighe Hamilton, a barrister, and Pennefather, a country gentleman, were also brought into the office from outside and when Pennefather retired in 1845, the government, eager to have a 'respectable and well-qualified catholic' in a responsible post, replaced him by McKenna, a catholic barrister, who was given the title of assistant under-secretary.[2]

Politics clearly played a part in these appointments. But there was another reason for bringing in outsiders. It was generally considered that none of the senior men in the office was fit to fill the post of chief clerk. The clerks naturally were disturbed by the tendency to appoint 'a stranger' and in 1845 they drew up a series of memorials stating their case. They considered that the level of salaries in the office (which they thought too low) and the absence of increments should be compensated for by prospects of promotion. Therefore, they argued, if nobody in the office could expect to become chief clerk, or, as they put it, if they were deprived 'of the fair prospect of ultimately reaching our reward', their salaries should be increased. The redoubtable Trevelyan, who was beginning his career at the treasury summarily disposed of their case in a letter to the chief secretary. In his opinion the zeal and activity of any body of men depended 'far more on what they have in prospect than what they have in possession'. He opposed an increase of salaries, which would

[1] Minute, 22 Nov. 1831 (T. 29/323 and T. 1/3881).
[2] C. S. Parker, *Sir Robert Peel from his private correspondence*, iii. 184–6 and *Reports of committees of inquiry into public offices*, p. 70, H.C. 1854 (1715), xxvii.

have 'a drowsy' effect. Instead, he suggested, the clerks should be informed that anyone in the office who was fit to be chief clerk would probably be appointed to the post.[1]

Trevelyan, when he went to the treasury, considered that the reform of the chief secretary's office was 'an admitted desideratum', and in September 1852 a treasury committee was appointed to inquire into the working of the office. This committee concluded that the chief clerk or assistant secretary was 'the key both to the past deterioration of the office and its future improvement'. The under-secretary, it was pointed out, was frequently absent from the office attending the lord lieutenant, and when he was there much of his time was consumed by interviews. Therefore the supervision of the whole department should have devolved on the assistant under-secretary. But McKenna, it was found, confined his attention to a limited section of official business. This was not altogether surprising since, a senior clerk pointed out, 'the feelings of dissatisfaction' of 'the older members of the establishment' made it very difficult for the assistant under-secretary to interfere with the running of the department.[2] As a result work was badly distributed, the attendance of the clerks was very irregular (no attendance book was kept in spite of a treasury minute), and several clerks, it was said, had difficulty in finding work to do in the office. At the end of 1852 a treasury minute was issued reducing the office staff by three clerks, establishing new salary scales with increments, changing the office hours from eleven to five to ten to four, and making the chief clerk (the title replacing that of assistant under-secretary) who, the treasury recommended, was in future to be chosen from the staff of the office, responsible for enforcing 'diligence, discipline and regular attendance throughout the establishment'. The minute also directed the abolition of the fines and penalties office (its work being transferred to the audit commissioners) and the council office, and a drastic reduction of the staff of the Irish Office in London.[3]

[1] For the clerks' petitions and Trevelyan to Fremantle, 4 Sept. 1845 and to Bromley, 9 Dec. 1852 see S.P.O.I., Misc. letters-papers, 1799–1868, No. 17.
[2] Misc. letters-papers, 1799–1868, No. 17.
[3] *Reports of committees of inquiry into public offices*, pp. 120–7, H.C. 1854 (1715), xxvii.

One of the clerks retired under this minute, Robert Ball, fourth assistant clerk, was celebrated far beyond the bounds of his department. Ball, a member of an 'ancient and honourable family' having been given an introduction by the duke of Devonshire to William Lamb, when chief secretary, was in 1827 appointed to a clerkship in the chief secretary's office. Already he had displayed keen interest in natural history and during the next thirty years he was to be one of the most prominent figures in Irish scientific life. He toured the west of Ireland in search of algae and antiquities, published papers on zoology, was for twenty years, honorary secretary of the Royal Dublin Zoological society, and from 1844 the director of the Trinity College museum. With wide scientific interests and many friends he not only produced original work of value but strove to co-ordinate the activities of the various Irish learned societies in which he played a leading part. His career as a civil servant was less happy. During his early years in the office he seems to have worked hard, sometimes spending up to ten hours a day on duty. And he obtained some credit by inventing a copying machine on an entirely new principle. But he failed to secure the promotion and salary he expected and was greatly disheartened when a stranger was made chief clerk. He grumbled about 'the soul-subduing slavery of Castle work' which compelled him to devote his attention 'to sheep-stealing and infanticide' and left him sometimes 'without *vis* for anything good'. He thought of trying to become a stipendary magistrate and played with the idea of emigration to India or New Zealand. But, widely known as an energetic and successful scientist, he remained a disgruntled civil servant. Nevertheless 'according to his own conviction' he performed his duties faithfully and he was hurt when the treasury committee recommended his retirement on the grounds that it was a rule of the public service that 'gentlemen in the permanent employment of the government shall not have any other occupation which may call off their attention from their official duties'. Since he had been appointed secretary to the Queen's University in 1851 and was an assistant examiner to the civil service commissioners he was financially secure, but retirement had a detrimental affect on his health. When he was in the chief secretary's office he always took his six weeks leave and went on a holiday. Released from official routine, he devoted himself unceasingly to scientific work, seriously over-taxing his strength.[1]

One of Ball's superiors was also hurt. Wynne, the under-secretary, had been a member of the committee of inquiry. Nevertheless he was deeply annoyed by the treasury minute, based on its report, which he declared was damaging to the office and improper. Trevelyan, when he heard this, was incensed. 'The minute', he wrote, 'gave a bare summary of the facts recorded in the report . . . In other words it told the truth which is damaging only to what is bad. The minute let daylight in upon as dark a corner of our administrative system as anywhere exists'.[2]

The office hierarchy in the 'fifties and 'sixties was simple. Below the chief clerk were first, second and third class clerks. In 1876 the title of chief clerk was abolished, an assistant under-secretary being again appointed. In the same year, lower (later second division) clerks were introduced, and this grade in time absorbed the third class and supplied staff clerks. After 1822, the first class clerks, of whom there were two, were known as principal clerks. From 1884 men recruited by the Class I method were being appointed to the chief secretary's office and by 1914 four of the five first-class clerks had entered the service by this examination. In 1914 the staff of the office consisted of two principal and five first-class clerks, a registrar, a librarian and a parliamentary draftsman. This last-named office was made a whole-time appointment in 1877 and its holder, always a barrister, both prepared legislation and appeared in cases where petitions were lodged by Irish departments against private bills.[3]

---

[1] *Natural History Review*, v. 1–34.

[2] Misc. letters-papers, 1799–1868, No. 17.

[3] *Royal commission on civil service: second appendix to fourth report*, pp. 181–90, H.C. 1914, [Cd. 7340], xvi, *Royal commission on the civil service: memorandum as to the organization and staff of the chief secretary's office.*

III

THE FINANCIAL
DEPARTMENTS

~~~~~~

THE IRISH FINANCIAL administration at the beginning of the
nineteenth century was complex, possessed some exceedingly
archaic elements, and was doomed to be absorbed by United
Kingdom departments during the early decades of the century.
At least three historic strata can be discerned in its composition.[1]
There was the exchequer of medieval origin; there was the
revenue board controlling a number of departments which had
its beginnings in the seventeenth century; and finally towards
the close of the eighteenth century, when efforts were being
made to tighten parliamentary control over expenditure and
improve accounting methods, three auditing offices were
created—the treasury in 1793, the commission of accounts,
which examined the accounts of government departments and
bodies receiving public grants in 1766, and in 1798 the comptroller and examiner of army accounts.[2]

The treasury was responsible for all matters relating to the
collection and management of the revenue and all warrants for
the issue of public money had to be signed by three com-

---

[1] For the development of the Irish fiscal administration see T. J. Kiernan,
History of the financial administration of Ireland until 1817 (1930).

[2] The commissioners of accounts had pre-eighteenth century origins.
But their reorganization in 1766 and the extension of their powers in
1784 in effect constituted a new department. (See Kierman, *op cit.*, pp. 233,
271.)

missioners. The treasury might have become the mainspring of the Irish financial administration. In fact during its short lifetime it showed no signs of developing into a powerful department. The commissioners, being M.P.s, were, after the union, absent from Ireland for a considerable part of the year, so 'a board' (which required three commissioners) could not always be assembled. Treasury warrants and orders were often simply forwarded to London, where the necessary signatures were collected, and at a subsequent board meeting entered on the minutes as the acts of the commissioners then present. The revenue board often ignored the treasury when making regulations, and the lord lieutenant also exercised 'a power of control and superintendence over the revenue from the superior authority belonging to government with much more effect than the treasury'. Departmental estimates were not submitted to the treasury before being laid before parliament. And though the secretary to the treasury asserted that the treasury 'would observe upon any improper conduct' detected by the commissioners of accounts, he did not refer to any specific instance of the treasury taking action. In short, the Irish treasury restricted itself to performing the routine duties of an accounting department and did not attempt to influence the organization or policy of other departments.[1]

The exchequer, a far more venerable department, had of course three sides, common law, equity and revenue, and it is only the last with which we are concerned here.[2] The officers on the revenue side performed two sets of functions. A group of them, including the comptroller of the pipe, the clerk of the pipe, and the summonister, were concerned with the collection of a very small proportion of the total revenue, the casual revenue (fines, forfeited recognizances, custodies, profits of the hanaper) by processes which even an eighteenth century official soaked in exchequer tradition thought could be 'abundantly abridged'.[3] Another group of officers connected historically with the court of exchequer, the auditor general, the

---

[1] *Commissioners of inquiry into fees . . . fourteenth report*, H.C. 1813–4 (102) vii.

[2] *Commissioners respecting the courts of justice, twelfth report*, H.C. 1824 (407), xii.

[3] G. E. Howard, *A treatise of the exchequer and revenue* (1777), i., xxv.

teller of the exchequer, and the clerk of the pells, assisted the treasury in keeping a check on receipts and expenditure. The teller, who had an account at the Bank of Ireland, received and issued public funds. The clerk of the pells' records were a check on the teller's, and the auditor general both examined the teller's accounts and ascertained whether the treasury was authorized to issue the warrants on which the teller had acted.

The revenue commissioners, of whom in 1801 there were nine, controlled the machinery by which most of the revenue was collected. Their staff was divided between two great departments, customs and excise, the latter including two small offices which collected the crown rents, the quit rent office and the forfeiture office. In 1806 two boards were constituted, the one responsible for customs, the other for inland excise and taxes. By 1814 the work of the latter department had been so much increased by wartime taxation that it was divided into two sections, excise (including crown rents) and assessed taxes. There were three other revenue departments, the post office, established in 1785, the stamp office, founded in 1773, and the lottery office, dating from 1785. Finally there was a small office concerned with lessening the burden of taxation, the commissioners for the reduction of the national debt, constituted in 1797.

These departments varied very much in size. The lords commissioners of the treasury were assisted by a secretary, a chief clerk, a revenue clerk, and fourteen other clerks. On the revenue side of the exchequer, fourteen officers and clerks supervised the collection of the casual revenue and the three great accounting officers connected with the exchequer, the auditor general, the clerk of the pells, and the teller, employed about twenty officers and clerks, including the deputies of the first two officers, since Lord Roden, the auditor, and Lord Shannon, the clerk of the pells, each drawing an official income of about £3,000 per annum, were sinecurists.[1] The commissioners of public accounts managed with a small staff. In 1799 they had only three clerks and the occasional assistance of two solicitors. By 1822 they employed a secretary, an inspector-

[1] *Commissioners of inquiry into fees . . . fourteenth report*, pp. 122–3, 148–9, 150–1, H.C. 1813–4 (102), vii.

general and fourteen clerks.[1] By then they were auditing eighty
accounts, including those of a number of bodies which received
government grants and of some government departments and
of a large number of institutions which received state assistance.
The lottery commissioners had a staff of about the same size.
In 1809 there were nine part-time commissioners who employed
a secretary, ten clerks, an inspector and a stamping officer.[2]
As for the commissioners for the reduction of the national debt
they had only a secretary and a broker[3]. The office of the
comptroller of army accounts has already been dealt with in
chapter 1.

It was the revenue commissioners, the board of stamps and
the postmaster-general, who had by contemporary standards
large establishments.[4] The customs was divided into three sections, the central office, the port of Dublin and the outports.
In the central office, which was in the great Custom House,
there were about 125 officials and clerks, working in a number of
departments—those of the secretary, the accountant general,
and the examinator of customs, and the statistical office (in
contemporary terminology the office 'for keeping accounts
respecting trade'). The port of Dublin had a staff of about 150
officers and clerks, divided almost equally between the quays
and the Custom House, where, in the Long Room, merchants
jostled one another to get their cargoes cleared during the short
official day. Attached to the custom house were about seventy-
five porters, messengers and gate-keepers, and on the quay there
were over 200 boatmen and tide-waiters, the latter being stationed on a vessel as soon as it arrived with the object of
preventing an unauthorized landing of any part of the cargo.
The ship's master was responsible for feeding the tide-waiters,
who sometimes were difficult to please. At the other Irish ports
there were in all 500 officials and clerks and 750 tide-waiters

[1] *Comm. Journ. Ire.*, xix, appendix viii, *Return of the establishment of the office
of commissioners of accounts*, H.C. 1821 (453), xix.
[2] *An estimate of the sums necessary to be provided for paying the salaries of the
lottery officers*, H.C. 1809 (54), xi.
[3] *Accounts and papers . . . relating to the increase and diminution of salaries. . . .*,
p. 20, H.C., 1821 (287), xiii.
[4] For establishments of the customs and excise departments see *Commissioners of inquiry into fees . . . first and eighth reports*, H.C., 1806 (6), viii and
H.C. 1809 (52), vii.

and boatmen. Thus the customs establishment numbered about 1,850. In addition there were nineteen revenue cruisers whose crews totalled nearly 700. The excise establishment was rather smaller, numbering in all about 1,300, the bulk of this force being composed of surveyors (500), gaugers (650), and hearth money collectors (about 100). The statutory commission of 1804[1] when dealing with the customs, listed fifty offices whose holders were either sinecurists or performed their duties by deputy, and reported that the department's collecting and accounting systems could be greatly simplified and that customs officials were taking fees considerably in excess of those to which they were legally entitled. When they came to consider the excise department, especially those sections concerned with the collection of duties on spirits and malt liquors, the commissioners were severely critical. Fees were being exacted which were often indistinguishable from bribes. The commissioners were also shocked by the magnitude of the excise board's law charges. For instance 'the facility' with which such charges had been allowed 'seems to have induced the solicitor (for the king's rents) to permit no occasion to escape of adding to the amount of his miscellaneous costs'. Legislation followed the commissioners' reports. In 1808 customs officers were forbidden to take fees, compensation being granted to existing office holders, and their hours of attendance were defined by statute. All out-door officers were to be on duty from May to November from eight o'clock to four, and from November to May from nine to four; the hours of indoor officers were to be nine to four. In the following year it was made a misdemeanour for any officer of customs or excise to take any fees.[2]

The stamp office was managed by five commissioners. Under these commissioners was a staff of about forty officials and clerks, thirty-six stampers and fifty-six distributors. The officials included a secretary, a receiver, a comptroller (who supervised all the accounts of the department), inspectors of law courts, an inspector of newspapers and an inspector of hats. At the beginning of the nineteenth century a comparatively quick survey of the department by the committee on fees disclosed that stamp distributors were being allowed to retain

[1] See p. 21.
[2] 48 Geo. III, c. 56, 49 Geo. III, c. 116.

large balances in their hands, that there were insufficient checks on the office warehouse keepers, that law charges were surprisingly high and that the number of corrections in the office books suggested that the clerks were incompetent. These, however, were venial faults compared to what a later enquiry was to reveal.[1]

The Irish post office was in 1801 a comparatively new office. During the greater part of the eighteenth century the British post office, acting under the powers bestowed by the post office act of 1711, functioned in Ireland. But in 1784, consequent upon the constitutional changes of 1782, the Irish parliament passed an act setting up an Irish post office under an Irish postmaster general. At the beginning of the nineteenth century the Irish postal establishment comprised about seventy senior officials, clerks and sorters and over fifty porters and letter carriers, all attached to the head office in Dublin. And in addition there were about 260 post towns, each with its deputy postmaster, scattered about the country.[2]

Less than a quarter of a century after its foundation the office was reorganized by Clancarty, the more energetic of the two joint postmasters general appointed in 1807. Clancarty, an adroit politician, who changed his views opportunely during the union debates, spent three years at the Irish post office in the course of a successful administrative and diplomatic career. He proposed that there should be a new general post office to replace the cramped quarters in which the mail had to be sorted and he also reorganized the Inland sorting office making the English mail office into a separate branch and raising salaries of the clerks and sorters so as 'to render it worth while for officers to whom so much is entrusted to be honest'.[3]

Clancarty's successor, the earl of Rosse, and his colleague as joint postmaster general, Lord O'Neill, managed the post office for years by a curious system of remote control. In theory, boards were held, minutes bearing the heading 'Present the earls'. In fact the postmasters general infrequently came to the office

---

[1] *Commissioners of inquiry into fees . . . second report*, H.C. 1806 (270), viii.

[2] *Commissioners of inquiry into . . . the revenue, nineteenth report*, pp. 200–7, 238–52, H.C. 1829 (353), xii.

[3] *Ibid.*, pp. 113–21, 435. The new G.P.O. in Sackville Street was begun in 1815.

and were rarely, if ever, there together. Indeed, the secretary asserted in 1824 that he had only once seen Lords Rosse and O'Neill in the same room, and that was at Parsonstown. In practice the secretary, Edward Lees, ran the office, reporting to the postmasters general and securing the sanction of one of them. For extraordinary financial expenditure he was careful to obtain their joint signatures in advance since otherwise he was afraid he might find himself liable. When there were differences of opinion between the postmasters general, Lees 'experienced considerable difficulty', but, he explained, 'without apprizing the postmasters general in all cases of the variance which has existed between them, I have endeavoured on my own responsibility to do the best I could'.[1] On occasions there could be serious disagreements between the postmasters general. In 1823 they took different sides in a quarrel between the Comptroller of the British mail office and the secretary. The secretary's office refused to help the comptroller, Homan, one evening when overwhelmed with work. As a result the mail went out late and Homan complained officially, and in a conversation with a viceregal *aide de camp*. Lord Rosse acquitted the secretary of having delayed the mail but commended Homan for his zeal. Lord O'Neill having read his colleague's minute, suspended the comptroller for making a charge against the secretary privately to the lord lieutenant. Finally, the commissioners for inquiring into the revenue to which the matter was referred, having heard over thirty witnesses, came to the conclusion that the comptroller had not acted improperly and recommended his reinstatement. It may be added that Lord Rosse thought the government intended that he should be the active postmaster general, responsible for the management of the office, Lord Clancarty having told him that 'you must manage the post office yourself, for it is a kind of thing that cannot well be done by two people'. Lord O'Neill, however, was quite unaware that any distinction existed between him and his colleague in respect to their duties.[2]

The routine administration of the office was, as has been said, carried on by the secretary, Sir Edward Lees, an experienced official. His father had been appointed secretary to the Dublin post office under the English postmaster general in 1774.

[1] *Ibid.*, pp. 146, 463, 586.   [2] *Ibid.*, pp. 152–7, 451–2.

Ten years later he was made secretary to the Irish post office and in 1801 his son Edward, was joined with him in his patent 'with benefit of survivorship'. The younger Lees was for the two years at the beginning of his career given a thorough grounding, being put through all the departments of the post office and even sent for some months to Belfast where the branch office was excellently managed. Well paid (his emoluments were over £1,400) he was a zealous official, ready to carry a large load of responsibility and to make improvements in the service. Indeed his superior, the earl of Rosse, thought at times that he was too fond of novelty, instancing the way in which he experimented with the lighting of the general post office. At first it was, of course, lit with candles, then the secretary at considerable expense brought over Argand lamps from Liverpool; next he tried coal gas, with unfortunate consequences for the earl heard that the young men in the office found the smell insupportable. The earl himself came up to Dublin and discovered that 'each gas-light was in an arm with a tube with many joints, so that it could be brought nearer or further from the person; but an obvious consequence of that was the joints would cease to be staunch, and the gas would escape'. Finally, with the earl's approval, Sir Edward installed oil gas.[1]

Besides the secretary's office there were nearly a dozen departments in the Dublin post office. There were the accountant general's, the receiver general's and the solicitor general's, the letter bill office (which checked the letter bills from the deputy postmasters), the inland office, the British mail office, the alphabet (*poste restante*), the bye, dead and mis-sent letter office, the Penny post office (which distributed mail collected within a radius of four miles of the General Post Office), the mail coach office, the surveyor's office (which supervised the country post offices), and the writing office (which supervised the issue of stationery to the other departments in the office). By 1822 the total post office staff in Dublin amounted to over 100 senior officials, clerks and sorters, over 140 letter carriers and porters, and 85 mail guards. In the country there were over 430 post towns, each with a deputy post-master who might employ a small staff. The deputy postmasters' salaries in the smaller places were low but they often had

[1] *Ibid.*, pp. 438, 459.

another source of income, many of them being pensioners or on half-pay, and it is probable that some deputy postmasters increased their emoluments by failing to make prompt remittances to the General Post Office, or even by fraud.[1]

By contemporary standards the post office was a large and complex department. The number of post towns increased by sixty per cent between 1797 and 1822. In 1790 the process of replacing carts by mail coaches on the main routes began. In the early years of the nineteenth century the average speed of the Irish mail coaches was increased from about five to eight miles an hour. And in 1815, Bianconi, the proprietor of a great fleet of long cars, the 'bians', which travelled regularly and with surprising speed even through the most difficult country in Ireland, began his long association with the post office. At first by contracts with the deputy postmasters and later, after 1830, by contract with the post office, he carried the mails over a large area in the south and west, his cars being only slowly superseded by the railways.[2]

Undoubtedly in some respects the department was enterprising and evinced a desire to maintain satisfactory standards of service, but on the other hand two commissions of inquiry, which examined the post offices in 1809–10 and 1823–9, and Sir Edward Lees himself considered that a number of reforms were required. 'Each postmaster-general legislating at a distance of 180 miles from each other, and never meeting and often disagreeing, while the secretary is in danger of acting in contradiction to *both*' was, Lees wrote, 'an absurd anomaly'.[3] It was too an anomaly which was largely responsible for other defects in the office. The financial checks were said to be insufficient. Post office officials were allowed to take letters which they claimed belonged to them from the bags in the sorting room—a practice which enabled the taxing clerks to get their accounts to tally with those of the country postmasters by assuming that the necessary number of letters had been removed. Franking was practised with lavish and illegal generosity. For instance, on government orders (issued *ultra*

---

[1] *Ibid.*, pp. 63–4, 238–53.
[2] A. Trollope, 'History of the post office in Ireland', appendix J to *Third report of the postmaster general . . .* , H.C. 1857 (2195), iv.
[3] *Commissioners of inquiry into . . . the revenue, nineteenth report*, p. 146.

vires) the publications of religious societies were forwarded post free, and Swan, the receiver general who was also a land agent (for most of the year he seems to have disposed of his official duties by a daily visit of about half an hour to the post office) admitted that he despatched an immense business correspondence under his official frank. Mail coach contracts were said to be too favourable to the contractors, the post office, in the opinion of an experienced English official, failing to encourage competition. In the sorting departments officials were allowed to stay on when they should have been superannuated (the president of the inland office, who had been forty-five years in the post office, was sometimes found asleep on duty), promotion was retarded, and the sorting took too long and was partly done by under-paid probationers. Finally there were six posts to which privileges were attached which amply remunerated their holders. The four clerks of the roads and the two express clerks had considerable advantages in the distribution of newspapers. At the time of the union when there was a fall in newspaper circulation the four clerks of the roads were compensated by annual grants, and in 1810, when considerable improvements were made in the postal facilities available to newspaper proprietors, the clerks received further compensation. In the eighteen twenties the secretary of the post office was clerk of the Leinster road, and his brother, Thomas, was clerk of the Munster.[1]

The defects in the working of the Irish post office which were described by the statutory commission in its report of 1829 soon disappeared. The commission recommended the fusion of the British and Irish post offices and in 1831 it was enacted that there should be a single postmaster general for the United Kingdom. Almost immediately afterwards, Augustus Godby, the secretary of the post office in Scotland, an expert in the detection of administrative irregularities, was sent to Ireland (Lees being transferred as secretary to Edinburgh) and a period of brisk reorganization in the Irish branch of the post office began.[2]

The act of union provided that Great Britain and Ireland

---

[1] *Ibid.*, pp. 37, 63–5, 77–82, 85–8.

[2] *Papers relating to the post office, 1834,* pp. 33–47, H.C. (20) 1834, xlix, *Post offices: a return . . .* pp. 11–16, H.C. 1835 (443), xlviii.

should contribute to the expenses of the United Kingdom in the proportion of fifteen to two, each country keeping its own fiscal system and revenue departments. But the act also provided that when the national debts of the two countries were in the same ratio to one another as their respective contributions their finances could be amalgamated. By 1811 this situation had been reached and in 1816 the British and Irish revenues were consolidated.[1] This meant in the administrative sphere the immediate fusion of the British and Irish treasuries, one board becoming responsible for the supervision of the finances of the United Kingdom. At the same time the duties of the Irish commissioners for the reduction of the national debt were transferred to the British commissioners.

The amalgamation of the treasury boards was the first step towards a complete fusion of the financial administration of the two islands. Soon after the new board was constituted the treasury sent over a group of English revenue officials, composed of the solicitor to the excise board, a customs commissioner, an excise commissioner, a surveyor general of customs and eight British officers from the excise service, to investigate the workings of the Irish customs and excise departments. Reporting in minute detail, the two commissioners and the solicitor demonstrated that the Irish establishments were unduly swollen and all the investigators were severely critical. For instance the surveyor general of customs thought that the revenue business of the port of Dublin should have been managed far faster, and he was scandalized to discover landing officers who should have been on duty by nine in the morning arriving about noon or one o'clock. And the four English excise officers after watching Irish excise-men at work were convinced that not one excise duty was fully and efficiently collected in Ireland.[2]

While the English customs commissioner was preparing his report on the Irish system the Irish customs commissioners, spurred into action, tried to anticipate criticism by producing for the lord lieutenant a memorandum in which they pointed to the useless offices and sinecures they had abolished, listed

[1] 56 Geo. III, c. 98.
[2] *Second report of the commissioners of inquiry into . . . the revenue*, pp. 31, 388–90, 1141–52, H.C. 1822 (563), xii.

some further savings they hoped to make, and (adroitly putting the government on the defensive) declared that 'amongst the measures which would tend to improve and facilitate the collection of the revenue none would be so efficacious as a due regard to the advancement of meritorious officers'. This could be attained by directing that, whenever a vacancy occurred in a senior post, the commissioners should report to the government on the qualifications of the two officers next in rank whom they judged fit for promotion. Thus political influence would be eliminated and officers would look to their official superiors for promotion.[1] The Irish excise board also tried to meet criticism in advance by producing some suggestions for the reduction of its staff by amalgamating surveys and walks.[2]

Within two years a second inquiry into the Irish revenue departments was held. This inquiry was conducted by the statutory commission of 1821 which after extensive investigations concluded that the Irish customs, in spite of recent reforms, was managed with much less efficiency and economy than the English. As for the Irish excise department it was 'in so defective a state of management, organization and discipline' that it could only be improved by a complete change of system. Admittedly just after the statutory commission was appointed, the Irish excise commissioners had suggested reductions in their establishment. The statutory commissioners were unappeased. They pointed out that no satisfactory reason was given why 'expenditure thus admitted to be unnecessary had not been curtailed before', adding that 'the proposal bore indeed more the appearance of a hasty attempt to anticipate the result of the inquiry . . . than of a spontaneous and well digested plan of reformation'.[3]

The statutory commission recommended that the Irish customs and excise departments should be fused with their British equivalents, arguing that such a step would both facilitate commercial intercourse between the two islands and open the way for drastic administrative reforms in the revenue system in Ireland. Their views which were in accordance with the government's general policy were quickly implemented, it being enacted in 1823 that the British and Irish customs and excise should be consolidated.

[1] *Ibid.*, pp. 32–5.   [2] *Ibid.*, pp. 834–7.   [3] *Ibid.*, pp. 6–9.

In the same year, 1823, the statutory commission turned its attention to another Irish revenue department, the stamp office. Though the treasury in 1819 had issued regulations for the stamp office, providing new checks on expenditure and reducing its staff, the commission found it was very badly in need of reform. The chief commissioner for stamps, William Gore, who had claimed 'an exclusive responsibility for the general conduct of the department', had become involved in pecuniary difficulties, had persuaded subordinates to back bills for him, and then had taken refuge on the continent. The secretary had a place in Tipperary and was frequently absent from the office, leaving his routine duties to be performed by the chief clerk on the ground that he himself had to be in constant attendance on the board. The board's solicitor had a fantastically high income (about £3,000 per annum) since he was permitted to charge a fee on every reference made to him. The head of the Dublin warehouse for stamped goods, Richard Jones, who was a barrister with a house in the country, was extremely evasive when examined over his attendance at the office. But after being twice warned to be more careful about his answers, he admitted that taking winter with summer he was on an average in the office probably three days a week and that on the days he was there he might be away from the office 'an hour, an hour and a half, or two hours', adding petulantly 'that really the office was given to me not to be attended at all'. In 1813, considering himself overworked, he secured the appointment of an assistant warehouse keeper. The holder of this post in 1823 was Richard Graydon, who was also irregular in his attendance at the office, the best he could say himself being that during office hours 'more frequently it happened that I was in the office than not', and he added he had become much more regular in attendance as soon as the commission of inquiry was expected. There was an office attendance book but Graydon sometimes arranged to have it signed for him. As for his superior, Jones, he did not think it was necessary to sign the book at all, as he regarded 'my responsibility as of more importance than my attendance'.

The comptroller whose office was meant to be 'a check upon the accuracy of all the pecuniary transactions of the department' had to contend with lethargic superiors and incompetent subordinates, appointed in spite of his earnest remonstrances. The accounts of the country stamp distributors were left unchecked for far too long and Holmes, the Dublin distributor, committed so many irregularities that it was almost impossible to check his accounts. Moreover, in the course of the inquiry it was discovered that he owed the office something approaching £17,000. With difficulty he met his obligations, pathetically pointing out that he had not used public money 'for his own aggrandizement' but that he was financially embarrasssed, since 'to extricate a numerous and unhappy family from utter ruin and under an engagement which I thought I could depend upon' he had gone security for Mr Gore, the first commissioner. Holmes was also involved in a more dubious transaction. It was discovered that Graydon had secured the post of assistant warehouse keeper by paying several hundred pounds to his immediate superior, Jones, and that Holmes had negotiated the arrangement. The revenue inquiry commissioners reported these facts to the treasury immediately they emerged and the treasury acted promptly. At the beginning of 1824 a minute was issued dismissing Jones, Graydon and Holmes, and suggesting to the lord lieutenant that the patent appointing the stamp commissioners should be revoked.[1] A provisional commission of civil servants was appointed to administer the office, and three years later, in 1827, the commissioners of stamps for Great Britain were constituted stamp commissioners for the United Kingdom.[2]

In 1827 as a logical consequence of the amalgamation of the revenue boards, the land revenues of the crown in Ireland were placed under the management of the commissioners of woods and forests.[3] The commissioners took over the control of the quit rent office and promptly abolished the forfeiture office. As for the post of surveyor general of crown lands, it disappeared with the death of its last holder in 1829. Since the commissioners managed to sell a considerable amount of landed property from the middle 'fifties most of the property under their management consisted of quit rents.

One interesting result of the commission's connection with

[1] *Commissioners of inquiry into . . . the revenue, sixteenth report*, pp. 77–8, 95–6, 220, 231, 280–2, 310, H.C. 1828 (7), xiv.
[2] 7 & 8 Geo. IV, c. 55.   [3] 7 & 8 Geo. IV, c. 68.

Ireland was the improvement of Phoenix Park, which was under its control until 1851. The chief commissioner of woods and forests in Grey's government was Duncannon, a leading whig and a member of a great Irish landed family. In 1832, shocked at the way the park had been neglected, he arranged for a survey by Decimus Burton as a prelude to extensive improvements, and in 1847, when viceroy, he persuaded the commissioners of woods and forests to carry out a major drainage scheme.[1] In 1851 the park was placed under the control of the commissioners for works (a United Kingdom department) and in 1860 it was transferred to the (Irish) board of public works.[2]

Thus by the 'thirties, the Irish revenue was being collected by United Kingdom departments. As for the accounting offices in 1816, by the act consolidating the public revenues of Great Britain and Ireland, the treasury was given the power—which it immediately exercised—of appointing a vice-treasurer for Ireland who was to be responsible for all issues out of the Irish exchequer, his accounts being audited by the British commissioners for auditing the civil accounts. The treasury was also given power, on the determination of existing interests, to regulate the offices of auditor general, clerk of the pells and teller of the exchequer, offices 'with respect to which it is expedient that a more economical execution of their duties should be secured'.[3] Five years later, in 1822, as the existing interests had not expired, the treasury was empowered to dispense with the offices, giving reasonable compensation. The treasury, at once used its powers to abolish the offices of auditor general and clerk of the pells. Their records were handed over to the vice-treasurer for Ireland who kept the accounts previously kept by the auditor general and who transmitted weekly abstracts of the receipts and issues of the Irish exchequer to the treasury.[4]

The vice-treasurer was permitted to sit in parliament and

---

[1] *Commissioners of H.M. woods, forests . . . and buildings, twenty-second report*, pp. 5–6, 39–43, H.C. 1845 (617), xxvii; *Twenty-eighth report*, pp. 64–76, H.C. 1851 (631), xxix; *Thirty-first report, appendix*, pp. 600–6, H.C. 1852–3 [865], lvi; *Thirty-third report*, pp. 35–40, H.C. 1854–5 (358), xxix.

[2] 14 & 15 Vict., c. 42, 23 & 24 Vict., c. 42.

[3] 56 Geo. III, c. 98. After the consolidation of the two treasury boards, the treasury directed that Irish accounts were to be shown in British currency (Treasury minute, 23 Jan. 1818, Hill papers).   [4] 3 Geo. IV, c. 56.

the government intended that his salary should be £3,500 per annum. Since there also was to be a deputy vice-treasurer the opposition considered that this salary was far too large and denounced the proposal as one of the most shameless jobs that had ever come before parliament. Castlereagh argued that some situations should be overpaid being, 'ulterior rewards for a long period of able services'. Also, he thought, the chief secretary needed the support of another Irish minister in the house. But the opposition by two votes managed to reduce the salary to £2,000. The first vice-treasurer was Sir George Hill, the member for Londonderry city. Shortly before Wellington's government fell, Sir George was appointed governor of St Vincent and departed for the West Indies, leaving his accounts in such confusion that his friend Dawson was reduced to begging the house of commons to remember what a great difference there was 'between the non-settlement of accounts and defalcation'. Sir George's successor, the Knight of Kerry, resigned with Wellington's ministry and the whigs replaced him by the chief clerk in the Irish department in the treasury, John Smith. It was made clear that the vice-treasureship was no longer to be regarded as a political appointment and the post of deputy was abolished.[1]

In 1832 it was enacted that Irish accounts were to be audited by the commissioners of public accounts in Great Britain and the power of the lord lieutenant to refer accounts for audit was transferred to the treasury. If the commissioners of public accounts were in doubt over a point in an Irish account they could require the deputy remembrancer to investigate the matter.[2]

In 1835 an Irish whig, Spring Rice, became chancellor of the exchequer. He seems to have thought that the financial machinery in Ireland was still needlessly elaborate, and shortly after he took office most of the offices on the revenue side of the exchequer were abolished and the system for collecting the casual revenue drastically simplified.[3] In the following year (1836) the treasury was empowered to abolish the offices of vice-treasurer and teller of the exchequer, making suitable arrangements for the performance of their functions.[4] Some

---

[1] *Hansard*, 2 series, xxxiv. 1109–22, 1129 and 3 series, i. 778, ii. 82, vi. 934.
[2] 2 & 3 Will. IV, c. 99.   [3] 5 & 6 Will. IV, c. 55.   [4] 6 & 7 Will. IV, c. 83.

months later, in 1837, the treasury abolished the two offices, and laid down that the receipt and issue of revenue in Ireland was to be under the supervision of the comptroller general of the exchequer, who would have an account in the Bank of Ireland. Issues were to be made on the authority of a treasury warrant and a paymaster of civil services in Ireland was to be appointed who was to make detailed payments. He also was to keep accounts with county treasurers, pay and issue exchequer bills and carry out any other duties he was directed by the treasury to perform.[1] In 1861 the last remnant of an autonomous financial administration in Ireland was swept away when the office of paymaster of civil services in Ireland was abolished. The commissioners of public works were entrusted with his responsibilities relating to loans for public works, and his other duties were transferred to a branch of the paymaster general's office which was established in Dublin.[2]

As a result of these amalgamations, by the 'thirties the whole of the Irish revenue machinery was managed by United Kingdom departments. Consequently the treasury, which had been steadily acquiring a predominant position amongst public departments in England, was able from 1817 to exercise considerable influence in Ireland. It was customary when a department was constituted to entrust the treasury with the duty of settling its establishment, and all departments, as the treasury was quick to point out, had to submit their annual estimates to the treasury. This meant that the treasury could state and often impose its views, not only on questions relating to the size, salaries and grading of a department's staff, but on innumerable other matters in which financial issues were involved. Moreover many officials working in Ireland belonged to finance departments closely supervised by the treasury, and three Irish departments, the board of works, the valuation office, and the national school teachers' superannuation office (established 1879), were directly under treasury control. Finally, between 1837 and 1861 the treasury was represented in Dublin by the paymaster of civil services, and nine years after this post was abolished the post of treasury remembrancer in Ireland was created in 1870, the intention being that its holder

[1] Treasury minute, 21 Feb. 1837 (S.P.O.I., T. 12, 1837).
[2] 24 & 25 Vict., c. 71.

should be the confidential adviser of the treasury on all Irish administrative and financial problems. Being on the spot he was easily able to have personal contact with Irish officials and when an Irish department sent a proposal over to the treasury he investigated the facts and reported to the treasury.[1]

Though treasury correspondence was carried on by the lords commissioners of the treasury, 'a degree of prestige and authority' as Trevelyan said, being associated with the formula, Irish business was normally handled by the principal clerks. From 1817 until the middle of the century there was an Irish junior lord who was frequently consulted on Irish business and who often interviewed Irish visitors to the treasury, presumably on the assumption that he would know how to cope with his importunate fellow countrymen. But about the middle of the century the custom of assigning Irish business to a specific junior lord lapsed.[2]

From early in the nineteenth century the treasury, with crusading zeal and Puritan precision was engaged in enforcing severe administrative standards. A civil servant, it assumed, should have an austere sense of vocation. Waste was to be sternly discouraged. Economy, so far as it was commensurate with efficiency, was to be strictly enforced, and all departmental expenditure should be justifiable and, if the treasury required it, justified. The treasury's correspondence with the Irish departments shows how comprehensively and consistently these principles were applied. The department of agriculture was warned not to multiply statistics unnecessarily; the board of national education was encouraged 'to keep expenditure within the parliamentary grants' by employing monitors; the prisons board was informed that the treasury was not satisfied with its reasons for increasing lodging allowances for married warders; the chief secretary's office was reminded that measures involving financial considerations should not be introduced into parliament without the consent of the treasury; the board

---

[1] *Report from the select committee on miscellaneous expenditure minutes of evidence*, pp. 121–2, H.C. 1847–8 (543), xviii and M. Headlam, *Irish reminiscences* (1949), pp. 26–8.

[2] *Report from select committee on miscellaneous expenditure, minutes of evidence*, pp. 76–81, 105–6 and A. Todd, *On parliamentary government in England* (London, 1869), ii. 49–50.

of public works was told that a lower division clerk should receive extra pay only if his excess duty was considerable and prolonged; the secretary of the landlord and tenant commission was congratulated for obtaining a reduction in an exorbitant Belfast hotel bill; and the under-secretary was informed that the Treasury would not sanction the expense of engaging St Patrick's cathedral choir to take part in the installation of a knight of St Patrick in St Patrick's Hall in Dublin Castle.[1]

The offices which the treasury found most intractable seem to have been those connected with the courts of law. For instance in 1846 the master of the queen's bench was informed that he would be expected to produce more accurate accounts in future. The implied rebuke is explicable: the treasury were receiving from him accounts for the same quarter differing in amount.[2] During the 'sixties the treasury was engaged with varying success in a series of struggles to reduce the establishments attached to chancery and the common law courts. The sort of opposition the treasury might meet with is illustrated by the fiery letters it received from Whiteside, the lord chief justice, over a clerkship in his court. When in May 1876, Whiteside filled a second-class clerkship in the office of the master of the queen's bench, by the promotion of a third-class clerk, the secretary of the treasury wrote to him pointing out that, as it had been admitted that the office was over-staffed and as the Irish judicature bill was before parliament, the new clerk would not have a claim to compensation in the event of his office being abolished. To this implicit criticism of his action Whiteside replied in a lengthy letter redolent of the sonorous and inflated rhetoric by which he had established his reputation as a parliamentary debater. He had not, he asserted, the power to dispense with an obligation imposed on him by an act of parliament. 'There is', he wrote, 'no safe course to pursue in a country governed by law but to obey the law with unswerving fidelity'. 'You must' he went on 'excuse me for informing you

[1] Treasury to chief secretary, 3 Apr. 1867, 22 Apr. 1886, to under-secretary, 28 Feb. 1877, to National education board, 1 Jan. 1876, to Board of works, 19 July 1880, to department of agriculture, 22 Nov. 1900, to secretary, landlord and tenant commission, 1880 (T. 14/39/61, /48, /47, /53, /80).

[2] Treasury to master of Queen's bench, II, 27 Aug. 1846 (T. 14/30).

that the court of the queen's bench is not a department of the treasury and that the chief justice who happens to be the first magistrate in this kingdom is not accustomed to receive admonitions as to how he is to fulfil his duty'. To the judges had been assigned the task of administering justice in this distracted kingdom, yet from the tenor of the treasury's communication 'it would seem as if the very government whose just authority we strive to uphold, regards the institution to which we belong and its several departments as a vast job'. The treasury contented itself with very briefly reasserting its view, but in the end Whiteside's nominee retained his post and ended his career nearly forty-five years later as an assistant registrar of the king's bench.[1]

Ten years later an attempt by the treasury to reduce the remuneration of the Irish attorney general encountered an obstinate and successful resistance. At the beginning of 1886 Sir Robert Hamilton, the under-secretary, a newcomer to Ireland and an expert in departmental finance, in a memorandum dealing with the remuneration of several legal officials suggested that the attorney general's salary should be £4,000 per annum. The Irish lord chancellor argued forcibly in favour of £5,000, and the treasury after giving the matter very careful consideration, decided in April 1886 that while the then attorney general would receive £5,000, the salary of the office for future holders should be £4,000. And in spite of a strong remonstrance from the lord lieutenant, who pointed out that the attorney general's parliamentary duties in London deprived him of his private practice, the treasury refused to modify its decision. But three months later, when the conservatives took office, the treasury yielded to the argument that the new attorney general, Holmes, having held office under previous conservative administrations, was entitled to the higher salary. But it emphasized that at the next appointment the April decision would be adhered to. Still the Irish government refused to acquiesce, and when Holmes was promoted to the bench in 1887, the treasury again yielded and allowed his successor the £5,000 per annum which the Irish attorney generals continued to enjoy until 1921.[2]

[1] *Queen's bench, Ireland* (*Mr Blackham*), H.C. 1876 (332), lxi.
[2] *Irish law officers' remunerations*, H.C. 1887 (26), (261), (336), lxvii.

The treasury made a strong effort to assert its principles on a far broader front at the most critical stage in Irish history during the nineteenth century. For several years, beginning in the autumn of 1845, successive failures of the potato crop deprived the bulk of the Irish population of its usual subsistence. The government had to intervene, and during 1846 and the early months of 1847 relief was provided by importing grain which was sold at depots in the most severely distressed areas and by encouraging an enormous programme of public works. Since the works devised for the emergency were soon thought to be both extravagantly expensive and to be drawing labour from productive work, they were abandoned and relief given to the destitute in the form of food rations.

Throughout the crisis the treasury held a commanding position, co-ordinating and supervising the government's plans for coping with the catastrophe. Not only was finance inevitably involved in most relief proposals, but of the three principal departments through which the government tried to organize Irish relief, two, the board of works and the commissariat, were subordinate to the treasury. The result was that the treasury, suddenly faced with a mass of novel and complex responsibilities, had to assume an unaccustomed role. Besides checking and controlling it had to initiate and direct. Within the treasury, famine relief was largely managed by the assistant secretary and permanent head of the office, Charles Trevelyan, who, though he had to consult the chancellor of the exchequer on major issues, was empowered to despatch directions to the various officials concerned without informing in advance the treasury board. Trevelyan, decisive in thought and action and forcibly lucid, threw himself energetically into tackling Irish problems. His colleagues assisted him by taking over some of his other duties and Trevelyan himself tried to expedite matters by doing as much business as possible in demi-official letters. Nevertheless at the height of the Irish crisis Trevelyan and some other treasury officials never left the office before seven-thirty in the evening, often stayed much later and sometimes saw dawn breaking as they finished the day's work. Once Trevelyan tried to snatch a week's holiday in the country, but, as he said himself, 'I found such a quantity of work following me and having no assistance with me was harder worked in the country than I was at the treasury, so I came back again'.[1]

Trevelyan had decided views which coincided with those of his official superiors. He was a strong believer in free trade, and quick to see the dangers inherent in state intervention in economic matters. In its anxiety to avert starvation in Ireland, the state, he argued, might easily discourage commercial enterprise, demoralize the Irish poor and deprive the British market of its fair share of the available supplies. He wanted the propertied classes in Ireland, 'to feel the full extent of their responsibilities', and he hoped that the Irish public would realize that 'the machine we have to put in motion and regulate' was 'not only the government officers but the whole body of society in Ireland from the nobleman and gentleman down to the poorest peasant, who must all make one united effort to get through the approaching calamity'.[2] But within the limits fixed by government policy Trevelyan, it should be emphasized, worked with might and main to avert the tragic consequences of famine.

His principal agents in Ireland were two Peninsula and Waterloo veterans, Sir Randolph Routh, who was head of the Irish branch of the commissariat, and Colonel Harry Jones, chairman of the board of works. They were both intelligent and indefatigable and they were both also on the two committees which successively co-ordinated and supervised relief measures in Ireland, the relief commission of eight set up at the end of 1845 and the central relief board of six set up early in 1847. Trevelyan in his instructions to Routh emphasized that the chief responsible authority on Ireland was the lord lieutenant, that the commissary general in Ireland was to act in strict subordination to the relief commission, and that even his private letters to Sir Randolph were to be shown to the chief secretary.[3] But the treasury was so active and self-

---

[1] *Report of the select committee on miscellaneous expenditure, minutes of evidence,* pp. 79, 112, 116–7.

[2] *Correspondence explanatory of the measures adopted for . . . the relief of distress . . . in Ireland,* pp. 16, 25, 27, 81, 91, 101, 143, H.C. 1846 (735), xxxvii. 68, 77, 133, 143, 153, 195, and *Correspondence . . . relating to the measures adopted for the relief of distress (Commissariat series),* 32, 245, 353, 409, H.C. 1847 (761), li.

[3] *Correspondence explanatory of the measures adopted for . . . the relief of distress . . . in Ireland,* pp. 14, 67, H.C. 1846 (735), xxxvii.

assured that official courtesy does not seem to have hampered it when planning Irish relief.

The treasury made arrangements for buying, milling and transporting corn. It corresponded with commercial agents, with the admiralty which provided shipping and ground some of the corn, with the ordnance which provided sacks and with the constabulary which assisted in the distribution of supplies. It advised the poor law commissioners on the repayment of advances for relief, drew up instructions for the central relief board, and took steps to augment the staff of the commissariat in Ireland and of the board of works.

The commissariat opened a number of depots—by the beginning of 1847 it had twenty-nine in action—from which food could be sold at cost price to relief committees, and towards the close of 1846 it appointed about ten inspecting officers each of whom was responsible for a district. These officers were to visit and report on the work of relief committees, encouraging them to keep proper accounts and act on sound economic principles. They were also to examine the way in which lists of persons seeking relief were compiled. The inspectors were instructed to be forebearing and courteous in dealing with all classes of people and to stress that the great social crisis the country was going through could only be met by the united efforts of the whole community. When, early in 1847, the central relief board was set up, the secretary and staff of the commissariat relief office became 'the establishment' of the new board and the inspecting officers who worked under this board were selected from those who were being employed by the commissariat and the board of works.[1]

Some may see in the treasury's efforts to maintain its fiscal and administrative principles in the face of a national disaster an example of conspicuous failure in political proportion. But what should not be forgotten is the devotion to duty shown by the members of the department's staff in Ireland responsible

[1] *Correspondence explanatory of the measures adopted for . . . the relief of distress . . . in Ireland*, pp. 19, 67, 108, 131, H.C. 1846 (735), xxxvii. 71, 119, 183, *Correspondence . . . relating to the distress (Commissariat series)*, pp. 27, 55, 106–7, 142, H.C. 1847 (796), lii. 373, 401, 452–3, 488, *Correspondence . . . relating to the measures adopted for the relief of distress*, pp. 247–9, H.C. 1847 (761), li. 269–71.

for relief. Intensely conscious of the urgency and magnitude of their task and only too well aware of the limitations within which they had to act, they worked unceasingly, blending humanity and resourcefulness with punctilious respect for their department's standards.

At the beginning of the twentieth century, when schemes of national development were in the air, the treasury, in its determination to maintain what it conceived to be sound standards in public finance, clashed heavily with two important Irish departments. Both of these departments were managed by unpaid boards which, lacking the traditional reserve of the civil service, publicly proclaimed their disagreements with the treasury. Until 1887 there was no limit to the amount which the commissioners of national education could annually spend on building and improving schools. If in any year the grants exceeded the estimate, a supplementary estimate was presented. In 1887 the treasury pounced, claiming the right to limit the amount to be paid out in building grants in any year. From then on there was a series of tussles, the commissioners stressing the need to raise the standards of school accommodation, the treasury emphasizing the importance of economy. About 1900 the treasury suggested that the commissioners must 'look forward to the discontinuance of building grants at an early date'. Shortly afterwards, when an interdepartmental committee on which both the treasury and the commissioners, were represented drew up a standard plan for a primary school, the treasury insisted on the plan being revised in the interests of economy. Then, for some years, the treasury disregarded the earnestly pressed demands of the commissioners in the hope that these claims might be met out of the Irish development grant. Finally the commissioners, in their report for 1905–6 set out their case, appealing to the Irish government to try to induce the treasury to be less obdurate. This course was justified, for in the following year the commissioners were able to report a victory, having secured an increased building grant which was to be supplemented by sums from the development fund. But soon the treasury and national education commissioners were fighting on a new front—the amount to be spent on teachers' salaries. The commissioners, who had already accused the treasury of 'cheeseparing' on salaries, wanted to increase the establishment of the higher, better paid, grades of teachers. The treasury refused its consent and maintained its refusal until the outbreak of the great war enabled it to postpone action indefinitely.[1]

The congested districts board shortly after it was constituted disagreed sharply with the treasury on whether a section of its staff should be paid out of its endowment or carried on the estimates. The treasury insisted on the former policy and the board took the unusual step of submitting a case to counsel. Counsel's opinion was that the board was in the right but had no remedy against the treasury. In 1907 a serious dispute began between the board and the treasury. The former emphasized that its future effectiveness depended on an increase of income. The treasury stressed that 'an obligation rests on the congested districts board as upon all other public departments of confining their operations within the limits imposed by the funds supplied by parliament'. The board retorted by resolving that its resources should be increased. The treasury then made the position as it saw it very clear. The board had got into difficulties by trying to do too much at once, it should balance its accounts and accept the fact that the question of increasing its statutory resources would have to be deferred until the royal commission which was investigating the congested areas had reported.[2] In the end, however, the board's views prevailed, since by the land act of 1909 the funds at its disposal were considerably increased. Soon, however, the board was urgently but unsuccessfully pressing the treasury to provide superannuation for the large section of its staff which was unestablished. The treasury refused to approve the board's superannuation schemes until the outbreak of war in 1914, when it was able to defer the question indefinitely. Finally, when the treasury insisted that the board must accept

[1] In 1903 it was enacted that there should be an Irish development grant amounting to £185,000 devoted to land purchase, education and economic development (3 Edw. VII, c. 23, *Hansard*, 4 series, c. 823 ff.) *Commissioners of national education in Ireland, seventy-first report*, p. ii, H.C. 1905 [Cd. 2567], xxviii., 403, *Seventy-second report*, pp. 8-17, H.C. [Cd. 3154], xxix. 646-56, *Seventy-fourth report*, p. 11, H.C. [Cd. 4291], xxvii.

[2] *Royal commission on congestion in Ireland, eleventh report, appendix*, v. pp. 112-29, H.C. 1908 [Cd. 4089], xlii.

certain payments in land stock instead of cash, the board boldly sued the treasury in the high court. The court of appeal decided in favour of the treasury but the board undaunted took the case to the house of lords which decided in its favour.[1]

It may be added that in 1918 another unpaid board, the board of charitable donations and bequests, had a serious clash with the treasury. In 1916 when a new appointment was made the treasury reduced the salary of a secretary to the board by £100. The board 'unanimously and repeatedly' requested that the salary should be restored to its former level, pointing out there had recently been a great increase in the department's work. When the treasury refused to comply with this request seven members of the board resigned. The chief secretary pressed them to reconsider their decision and in the end three withdrew their resignations and four persisted in their protest.[2]

The treasury certainly asserted its principles with consistency and determination, and the application of these principles obviously imposed a salutary discipline on official life. Equally obviously it was bound sometimes to have a cramping effect on beneficient policies. It was natural and inevitable that there should be some tension between other departments and the treasury. But the belief that vigorous and imaginative state intervention was needed in many spheres of Irish life accentuated this tension when Irish departments were dealing with the treasury. 'The permanent officials of the treasury have always hated the name of Ireland', Sir Henry Robinson wrote when he was summing up a lifetime's experience. 'They seem to have considered that the Irish chief secretaries went to too great lengths to propitiate the Irish members and did not hesitate to commit the treasury in favour of unnecessary expenditure to make things easier for themselves in the house of commons. It was because of this that the young watch-puppies of the treasury would start up like the fretful porcupine when schemes from Irish departments came before them.'[3]

[1] *Irish Law Times reports*, lvii. 1–5.
[2] *Seventy-third report of the commissioners of charitable donations and bequests for Ireland*, H.C. 1919 [Cd. 9197], vii; *Hansard*, 5 series, cx. 2526.
[3] H. Robinson, *Memories: wise and otherwise* (1923), pp. 94–5.

IV

THE COURTS OF LAW

AT THE BEGINNING of the nineteenth century there were six superior courts in Ireland—chancery, the three common law courts (king's bench, common pleas and exchequer), the admiralty court and the prerogative court (an ecclesiastical court with jurisdiction over testamentary matters).[1] Four of these courts were of medieval origin. The exchequer was probably in existence before the close of the twelfth century, the Irish chancery was founded early in the thirteenth century, the first Irish chancellor being appointed in 1244, and the antecedents of the courts of king's bench and common pleas are to be found in the thirteenth century.[2] The other two courts were comparatively modern. The court of prerogative and

---

[1] There is of course an immense mass of material relating to Irish legal administration. Two modern works which the present writer has found of value are F. H. Newark, *Notes on Irish legal history* (1947), F. E. Ball, *The judges in Ireland, 1221–1921* (2 vols., London, 1926). A very detailed survey of the working of the Irish courts is given in the twenty-two reports of the *Commission appointed to enquire into the duties, salaries and emoluments of the officers, clerks and ministers of justice in all temporal and ecclesiastical courts in Ireland* (henceforth referred to as *Courts enquiry*), which appeared between 1817 and 1831. The following also contain much useful information: Wood, *Guide to the records deposited in the Public Record Office in Ireland* (Dublin, 1919), M. C. Griffith, 'A short guide to the Public Record Office of Ireland' in *I.H.S.*, viii. 45–58; L. F. Maxwell, *A bibliography of Irish law from the earliest times*; G. F. Howard, *Exchequer and revenue of Ireland* (2 vols., Dublin, 1776); C. J. Smyth, *Chronicle of the law officers of Ireland* (London, 1839).

[2] H. G. Richardson and G. O. Sayles, *The Irish parliament in the middle ages* (Philadelphia and London, 1952), pp. 21–6.

faculties based its rights to exercise jurisdiction on two sixteenth century acts and two seventeenth century patents, one of James I and one of Charles I.[1] And though admiralty jurisdiction had been exercised in Ireland from medieval times, the Irish court of admiralty had been created by statute in 1784.[2] From the court of chancery and the three common law courts there was an appeal to the court of error (known as the court of exchequer chamber) composed of the judges of the three common law courts, and in 1857 it was enacted that the court of exchequer chamber when hearing an appeal should consist of the judges of the two courts from which the appeal did not arise.[3] From the admiralty court and from the prerogative court there was an appeal to delegates in chancery. From all Irish courts there was an appeal to the house of lords. For the greater part of the nineteenth century this in fact meant a court composed of a very few peers who held or had held high legal office, assisted if they desired by the common law judges. From the number of Irish appeals it seems to have given satisfaction, though it was pointed out that the lords when hearing an appeal might in fact be only one peer with a very scanty knowlege of Irish law—on one occasion the lord chancellor while hearing an Irish appeal had to be lent for an evening a textbook on Irish land registration law.[4] Still the Irish judges considered that as uniformity in the administration of the law was desirable, a final court of appeal in England was of the greatest value.[5] And after the enactment of the appellate jurisdiction act in 1876 there was nearly always an Irish lord of appeal in ordinary (or law lord), Fitzgerald holding office from 1882 until his death in 1889 when he was succeeded by Morris who held office for ten years. Then in 1905 Atkinson was appointed, and he

[1] 28 Henry VIII, c. 19; 2 Eliz., c. 1; *Liber mun. pub. Hib.*, pt. II, p. 79–80.

[2] *Stat. Ire., John-Hen. V*, pp. 511–3; 11, 12, 13 James I, c. 2; *Liber. mun. pub. Hib.*, pt. II, pp. 221–2; 23 & 24 Geo. III, c. 14.

[3] 40 Geo. III, c. 39; 20 & 21 Vict., c. 6.

[4] *Report from the select committee appointed to inquire whether it is expedient to make any . . . provision for the more effective exercise of the functions of the house as a court of appellant jurisdiction, . . . minutes of evidence*, pp. 113–5, H.C. 1856 (264), viii. 533–5.

[5] *Supreme court of judicature bill; copy of the resolutions of the Irish judges*, H.C. 1873 (273), liv.

held his seat until 1928, 'his inflexible sense of duty', as his biographer admiringly records, enabling him 'to resist the pressure put on him to resign by the first coalition government in order to satisfy the requirements of the political party leaders'.[1] It perhaps should be added that in 1870 O'Hagan, the first catholic to be chancellor since the reign of James II, was created a peer and between then and his death frequently took part in the judicial work of the house, and that in 1906 Hemphill, who had been Irish solicitor-general, received a peerage. Moreover, between 1868 and 1913 four Irishmen who were distinguished lawyers, though not members of the Irish bar, sat in the house of lords—Cairns, Russell, Collins and Macnaghten.

There was another court of great antiquity and dignity with a peculiar range of business—the Irish privy council. When acting as an administrative body it had been prepared to hear counsel and twice during the nineteenth century judicial committees of the privy council were created by statute. In 1849 by the encumbered estates act a right of appeal to 'the judicial committee' composed of the Irish lord chancellor and such members of the privy council as held high judicial office was granted. This committee must have disappeared when the act expired in 1858. Half a century later the Irish local government act of 1898 gave a right of appeal from certain decisions of a county council to a committee consisting of such members of the privy council as were or had been judges of the supreme court, which was to be styled the judicial committee. From about 1847 the council seem to have occasionally referred matters to committees composed of privy councillors with legal experience. And after 1887 there was only one occasion on which the council as a body heard a contentious issue. From 1867 to 1884 the committees which heard counsel were almost always attended solely by lawyers; between 1884 and 1900 laymen were sometimes summoned to attend them; after 1900 there was a tendency to revert to the pre-1884 practice. Most of the work of these committees arose from the privy council being a court of appeal from the decision of administrative authorities acting under the local government act of 1898, the tramways and public companies act of 1883, the educational

[1] *D.N.B.*, *1931–40*, p. 24.

endowments act of 1885, the Irish education acts of 1892 and 1893, and the labourers act of 1885.[1] By the Irish universities act of 1908 the lord lieutenant was empowered to appoint a committee of the privy council to hear appeals from the commissioners responsible for the establishment of the new universities. The committee, which was styled the Irish universities committee, was constituted and heard a few appeals.

In the six superior courts there were sixteen judges—the lord chancellor, the master of the rolls, the lord chief justices of the king's bench and the common pleas and the chief baron of the exchequer, the puisnes of these courts, the judge of the prerogative court and the judge of the admiralty court. All of these, with the exception of the judge of the prerogative court who was appointed for life by the archbishop of Armagh, were appointed by the crown. All with the exception of this judge and the lord chancellor held office during good behaviour and could only be removed by the crown on an address from both houses of parliament. The lord chancellor had presided over the Irish house of lords and soon after the union it was made clear that he might have to vacate his office on a change of ministry. Moreover from the death of Clare in 1802 to 1846 it seems to have been felt that the Irish chancellor should be a leading English lawyer.[2] But the whigs on taking office in 1846 appointed Maziere Brady as chancellor, and from then onwards the Irish chancellors were always selected from the Irish bar. It may be added that though during the early eighteenth century English lawyers were sometimes placed on the Irish bench, after 1770 Irish judges were always appointed from the Irish bar.[3] There was, too, a clear correlation between political activity and legal promotion. Of those appointed to the bench in the four courts between 1801 and 1877 and after 1877 to the high court and the court of appeal, over one half had sat in the house of commons and nearly three-quarters had been law officers.

---

[1] This account of the judicial work of the privy council is based on papers in S.P.O.I., 6229 A, vi.

[2] Plunket, an Irishman, was lord chancellor, 1830–4, 1835–41.

[3] During the eighteenth century 82 lawyers were placed on the Irish bench. Of these 63 (a few of whom were English born) practised at the Irish bar before being placed on the bench, and 19 were Englishmen who came to Ireland on receiving a judicial appointment.

Judicial salaries were considerably increased near the close of the eighteenth century[1] and in 1821 they were increased again to compensate for the loss of fees.[2] The result was that throughout the nineteenth century a common law puisne judge enjoyed an income of about £3,500. Other judges of approximately the same status (for instance the land judges and the judge of the bankruptcy court) had somewhat smaller salaries, the master of the rolls, the chief justices and the chief baron had substantially larger ones. As for the lord chancellor, he enjoyed an income of £10,000 until 1832, when his salary was fixed at £8,000.[3]

Shortly before the union it was made possible for Irish judges to resign on pension.[4] And between then and 1914 a number of judges took this course, with the result that the average age of the judges of the superior courts remained unexpectedly low. Admittedly there were a few judges who lent an air of antiquity to the bench, and there were two very well known judges on whom considerable pressure had to be exercised before they availed themselves of the right of retirement on pension. Norbery resigned when he was eighty-eight on being given a step in the peerage. Lefroy, who had been promoted from being a puisne in the exchequer to be chief justice of the queen's bench at the age of seventy-six, res'gned in his ninety-first year.[5] If his retention of office was severely criticized he had the satisfaction of being able to delay his resignation until Lord Derby became prime minister for the third time. The departure from the bench of another Irish judge created a constitutional precedent. Jonah Barrington as a reward for his energetic parliamentary services was appointed in 1797 judge of the admiralty court. Genial, good-humoured and careless, he found his salary too small for his needs and the increase he managed to secure insufficient. And if his efforts to evade his creditors showed legal acumen they were undignified and unsuccessful. In the end he withdrew to the continent, delegating his duties

---

[1] 36 Geo. III, c. 26; 50 Geo. III, c. 31.   [2] 1 & 2 Geo. IV, c. 53.
[3] 2 & 3 Wm. IV, c. 116; 40 & 41 Vict., c. 57; *Judges' salaries: a return*, pp. 4–5, H.C. 1850 (525), xxiii. 378–9.
[4] 54 Geo. III, c. 95.
[5] *Hansard*, 3 series, clx. 759–806, clxxxiii. 778–811; T. Lefroy, *Memoir of Chief Justice Lefroy* (Dublin, 1871), pp. 292–330.

to a surrogate (considering that this was financially preferable to retiring on pension). The commission for inquiring into the Irish courts, which began work in 1815, when it reached the court of admiralty discovered two instances in which Barrington appeared to have misapplied moneys paid into his court.[1] Acting on the commission's reports, the houses of parliament having heard Barrington's counsel in 1830 voted addresses to the crown demanding his removal—the first and so far the only occasion on which this procedure has been put into operation. Fifty years later another Irish judge retired for an unusual but very honourable reason. When the crimes prevention bill of 1882, which provided for the trial in certain circumstances of serious criminal offences by judges sitting without a jury, was introduced into the house of commons, the Irish judges met and unanimously agreed to transmit to the lord lieutenant a resolution to the effect that the imposition on them of this duty would impair public confidence in the administration of justice in Ireland. Since the government did not delete the clauses the judges disapproved of, Baron Fitzgerald, an outstanding member of the bench, felt obliged to resign.[2]

Until almost the middle of the century the pattern of the superior courts remained almost unaltered. But in 1821 the court for the relief of insolvent debtors was set up, composed of two commissioners, who had to be barristers of at least ten years' standing, appointed by the lord lieutenant.[3] The act certainly seems to have benefited the first commissioner to be appointed, the popular Peter Burrowes, who was in financial difficulties.[4] In 1836 the system established in the eighteenth century by which commissions in bankruptcy were issued for each individual case was superseded by a permanent commissioner in bankruptcy appointed by the lord lieutenant. In the following year the lord lieutenant was empowered to

---

[1] *Courts inquiry, eighteenth report*, H.C. 1829 (5), xiii.

[2] All the judges of the supreme court were present at the meeting with the exception of the lord chancellor, Baron Dowse, who was ill, and Lawson and Morris, who were away (*Irish Law Times*, 20 May 1882; *Dublin Express*, 1 Aug. 1882; *Freeman's Journal*, 5 Feb. 1897; J. A. Curran, *Reminiscences* (London, 1915), pp. 148–9).

[3] 1 & 2 Geo. IV, c. 59.

[4] W. Burrowes, *Select speeches of the late Peter Burrowes* (Dublin, 1850), pp. 107, 113.

appoint a second commissioner, and it was enacted that the commissioners, who had to be barristers of at least ten years' standing, could only be removed upon an address from both houses of parliament.[1] In 1857 the jurisdiction of the two sets of commissioners was vested in a new court, the court of bankruptcy and insolvency, composed of two judges appointed by the crown with the tenure and approximate status of a judge of one of the superior courts. From this court there was an appeal to chancery.[2] In 1872 the distinction between bankruptcy and insolvency was abolished and the court was called the bankruptcy court.[3]

In 1848 the encumbered estates act threw an enormous mass of complex business into the court of chancery. If the act was to be effective, special machinery was required, and in 1849 the encumbered estates court consisting of three commissioners (of which one was a baron of the exchequer) was set up. It was intended to be a temporary institution, but in 1858 it was made a permanent court, its jurisdiction being extended to embrace in certain circumstances unencumbered estates. It consisted of three and later (after 1860) of two judges whose tenure of office and status were equivalent to those of a common law judge,[4] and from 1858 was called the landed estates court.

Another new court was set up in 1857, the court of probate, to which the testamentary jurisdiction of the ecclesiastical courts was transferred. The judge of this court was to have the tenure of office and status of a puisne judge.[5] Naturally enough the first holder of the office was the last judge of the prerogative court. In 1870, at the time of the disestablishment of the Church of Ireland, the matrimonial jurisdiction of the ecclesiastical courts was vested in the court of matrimonial causes and matters, the probate judge being also the judge of this court.[6]

In 1856 a court of appeal in chancery was constituted consisting of the lord chancellor, a specially appointed lord justice of the court of appeal in chancery and any common law judge whom the lord chancellor might require to act. This court heard appeals from the lord chancellor, the master

---

[1] 6 Wm. IV, c. 14; 1 Vict., c. 8.
[2] 20 & 21 Vict., c. 60.   [3] 35 & 36 Vict., c. 58.
[4] 12 & 13 Vict., c. 77; 21 & 22 Vict., c. 72; 29 & 30 Vict., c. 99.
[5] 20 & 21 Vict., c. 79.   [6] 33 & 34 Vict., c. 110.

of the rolls and later from the landed estates court.[1] In 1867
the court of chancery was strengthened by the appointment of
a vice-chancellor with concurrent jurisdiction with the lord
chancellor.[2]

All the changes which have been mentioned were trifling
compared to the great remodelling of the judicial system which
took place in 1877, the most revolutionary year in Irish legal
history. The supreme court of judicature act, modelled on the
English act of 1873, provided that the courts of chancery,
queen's bench, common pleas, exchequer, probate, matrimonial causes, the landed estates court and admiralty were
to be fused into one supreme court which could administer law
and equity concurrently. It was to have two permanent divisions,
the high court with original jurisdiction and with power to hear
appeals from inferior courts, and the court of appeal exercising
appellate jurisdiction. The appellate division consisted of the
lord chancellor, the master of the rolls, the lord chief justice,
the chief justice of common pleas, the chief baron of the exchequer and two other judges known as lord justices of appeal.
The high court consisted of the members of the supreme court
save the two lord justices of appeal, and eleven other judges.
For the more convenient despatch of business the high court
was to be divided into five divisions—chancery (which included
the land judges), queen's bench, common pleas, exchequer,
and probate and matrimony, and, after 1893, admiralty.[3]
But in 1887 the common pleas division and in 1897 the exchequer and probate divisions were fused with the queen's
bench, which also absorbed the bankruptcy court when the
last judge of that court was appointed to the queen's bench.[4]
Moreover in 1903 the office of vice-chancellor, on the resignation
of Eyre Chatterton, the first and last holder, at the age of
eighty-four, was not filled. Instead a judge was transferred
from the king's bench to sit in chancery, and though after three
years the vacancy so created in the king's bench division was

[1] 19 & 20 Vict., c. 92.   [2] 30 & 31 Vict., c. 44.
[3] 40 & 41 Vict., c. 57; see also 45 & 46 Vict., c. 70. The admiralty court
was to be merged with the supreme court on the first occasion the office of judge
of the court of admiralty was vacated after the passing of the judicature act.
John FitzHenry Townshend, who was appointed judge of the admiralty
court in 1867, held office until his death in 1893.
[4] 50 Vict., c. 6; 60 & 61 Vict., c. 66.

filled, in 1907 it was enacted that the next two vacancies in that division would not be filled.[1] Thus the pattern in 1914 was a court of appeal of six judges and a high court comprising a chancery division of four judges and a king's bench division of eight judges. Since all the members of the court of appeal, with the exception of the two lord justices of appeal, also sat in the high court, there were in all fourteen supreme court judges. To these might be added the judicial commissioners of the land court, who ranked as judges of the high court. Under the land act of 1881 the office of judicial commissioner was created, and under the act of 1903 a second judicial commissioner was appointed.[2]

Turning to courts with a local jurisdiction, in Ireland, as in England the most important of these were originally composed of justices of the peace who performed their duties at quarter sessions or as individuals—the jurisdiction of the justices acting in quarter sessions being of course considerably wider than that of a single justice. The justices of the peace, unpaid amateurs, had to perform a wide variety of duties and even handle questions of some legal complexity, as can be seen from the textbooks prepared for their use, ranging from Bolton's *Justice of the Peace for Ireland* (1633) to O'Connor's *Irish Justice of the Peace* (1911). Traditionally the typical justice of the peace in England was a landed gentleman. But in Ireland, where the landlord was often an absentee and where most of the landlords were protestants and the majority of the tenants were catholics and where agrarian questions were acute, there were obvious difficulties in making appointments to the bench. At the beginning of the nineteenth century it was said that in some parts of the country highly unsuitable persons were placed on the bench. For instance it was said that in one disturbed area (in county Cork) the justices were 'brewsters, maltsters, distillers and rackrent landlords'. And since the first three categories would not offend their customers and the tenants of the last were rioters, it was hard to restore order. In 1822 a general revision of the commission began and within a few months the lord lieutenant noticed 'that the mere knowledge of the existence of a plan of revision had produced salutary consequences by increasing the diligence, accuracy, and careful conduct of the magis-

[1] 7 Edw. VII, c. 44.   [2] 44 & 45 Vict., c. 49; 3 Edw. VII, c. 37.

trates'. About the same time a strong check was imposed on individual failings and eccentricities by the development of the practice of holding petty sessions. This substituted for 'the arbitrary and irregular discharge of his functions by a single magistrate' the joint action of at least two and possibly more justices acting publicly and after the petty sessions act of 1827, sitting at fixed times with a clerk, records, and fixed fees.[1] From about 1830, when justices of the peace were attacked, it was usually not on the grounds of incompetence but for alleged displays of political bias. And the composition of the bench as a whole was criticized, since in 1886 out of 5,000 justices of the peace only 1,200 were catholics, and while there were only 350 justices who were described as farmers, there were 2,700 landed proprietors in the commission. Attempts were made by liberal governments to change the balance and by 1912 out of 6,000 justices of the peace 2,400 were catholics.[2]

Successive governments evolved another method for improving the administration of justice in the local courts—the strengthening of the unpaid magistracy by the presence of professionals. By an act of 1787 the lord lieutenant was empowered in disturbed areas to appoint a barrister who would act as 'a constant assistant to the justices' at quarter sessions. He was to be of at least six years' standing, to receive a salary not exceeding £300 a year and to be ineligible to sit in parliament. The experiment proved so successful that nine years later the lord lieutenant was empowered to appoint an assistant barrister for every county. Moreover the assistant barrister was given power to determine by 'English bill or paper petition', usually called a civil bill, suits involving less than £20.[3] The civil bill offered a relatively quick and cheap procedure, and the assistant barrister's court was more accessible than the assize court, so understandably its jurisdiction was steadily enlarged. In 1851 the status and salary of the assistant barrister were raised, it being laid down that he was to be a barrister of at least ten years' standing and hold office on good behaviour,

---

[1] R. B. McDowell, *Public opinion and government policy in Ireland, 1801–46* (London, 1952), pp. 79–81.

[2] *Commission of the peace (Ireland) return*, p. 132, H.C. 1886 (174), liii. 548, and *Magistrates (Ireland) return*, p. 27, H.C. 1912–3 (396), lxix. 719.

[3] 27 Geo. III, c. 40; 36 Geo. III, c. 25.

being removable only by the crown on an address from both houses. In 1858, however, it was provided that, if an assistant barrister was incapable of discharging his duties, the lord lieutenant could remove him by an order in council, care being taken that all councillors resident in the city and county of Dublin should be summoned to attend the council at which the order was issued. At the same time the title of the office was changed to chairman of quarter sessions, a title which was changed again in 1877 to county court judge. And in 1877 the office of recorder which existed in Dublin, Belfast, Cork, Londonderry and Galway, was merged with that of the county court judge of the adjacent county.[1]

Another category of magistrates also originated from an effort to stiffen the justices of the peace. In 1814, the lord lieutenant was empowered to proclaim an area to be in a state of disturbance and to appoint for it magistrates 'of police' with the powers of a justice of the peace. The magistrates so appointed were to be resident and to receive salaries of £700 per annum. As each of these magistrates was at the head of a force of constabulary, their executive functions also loomed large. In 1822 the lord lieutenant was further empowered to appoint for any district on the application of the justices of the county a magistrate who would be constantly resident with the powers of a justice of the peace. These magistrates, who had a salary of £500 per annum, were not connected with the constabulary. And in 1836, when the police were reorganized, the police magistrate of the type created under the act of 1814 disappeared, but the lord lieutenant was empowered to appoint magistrates to reside in such districts as he thought fit. These magistrates, who were to report regularly to the chief secretary on the state of their districts, were not to hold office in the constabulary, and this separation of the resident magistrate from the police inspector was emphasized in 1853 when it was enacted that the superannuation certificate for the former was to be given by the chief secretary and not by the inspector-general of the constabulary.[2] In a memorandum despatched to stipendiary magistrates about 1846 the government admitted

---

[1] 14 & 15 Vict., c. 57; 21 & 22 Vict., c. 88; 40 & 41 Vict., c. 56.
[2] 54 Geo. III, c. 131; 55 Geo. III, c. 13; 3 Geo. IV, c. 103; 6 Wm. IV, c. 13; 16 & 17 Vict., c. 60.

that 'none but very general instructions for their guidance' could be given. They were simply to make their services as magistrates as useful as possible, especially by attending petty sessions and fairs in their districts. Nevertheless the memorandum was accompanied by copies of about twenty circulars issued between 1835 and 1846 referring to the duties of stipendiary magistrates. They were directed how to take informations and how to make their reports. And as it was important that the government 'should be acquainted with the whole of the duties performed by the stipendiary magistrates even to their minute detail' they were instructed to keep a diary which was to be forwarded to the chief secretary's office monthly. If a stipendiary magistrate was discovered to be absent from his district without having secured leave, he would be immediately dismissed, and leave of absence, it was declared, would only be given on account of private affairs of the utmost urgency or bad health.[1]

By 1860, the resident magistrates (the term is used in the title of the act of 1853) numbered 72; over a dozen had served in the constabulary and about twice that number had previously held the commission of the peace—for in the years following the famine the salary of a resident magistrate seems to have proved attractive to many Irish county gentlemen.[2] But by 1870 the R.Ms. were explaining to a treasury commission of inquiry that owing to the rising cost of living their salaries were insufficient. One witness pointed out that £400 in 1836 represented £700 in 1870 and he added that the resident magistrate 'should hold socially a position of respectability and independence. There is no people in the world more sensitive than the Irish people on this point'. And the R.M. stationed in Belfast, who told the commission that he often had to be out with the police until three o'clock in the morning, said that if he was compelled to live on his pay he would be 'shabby, mean and unbecoming the position'. Fortunately he had private means.[3] As a result of

[1] Professor Moody drew my attention to this memorandum which is to be found in P.R.O.I., S.P.O., Unregistered miscellaneous papers 1846, no. 85 (carton 1417).

[2] *Magistrates (Ireland): a return*, H.C. 1860 (288), lvii. 879.

[3] *Report of the commission appointed by the lords commissioners of her majesty's treasury . . . to enquire into the condition of the civil service in Ireland; . . . on resident magistrates*, H.C. 1874 (923), xvi.

the commission's report in 1874 the salaries and allowances of the resident magistrates were raised. In 1912 the total number of resident magistrates was 64 and their districts included all Ireland except Dublin. Dublin, from the close of the eighteenth century, had had stipendiary magistrates with the powers of a justice of the peace. And after 1808 these magistrates were appointed by the lord lieutenant.[1]

Beside the hierarchy of courts which has been outlined lay a confusing conglomeration of local courts which had been set up under the charters which had created cities, boroughs and manors. They were numerous and varied considerably in respect to jurisdiction, procedure and terminology—and by 1800 in respect to their activity and usefulness. Some played an important part in the life of the area, others scarcely survived and were archaic nuisances. To begin with, eight counties of cities or towns were equipped with an imposing system of local courts corresponding to their special status.

Dublin had four local courts—the court of quarter sessions, the lord mayor's court, the mayor and sheriff's court, and the court of conscience. The court of quarter sessions had cognizance of all crimes (except treason) committed within the city's boundaries; the lord mayor's court exercised a summary jurisdiction in a number of minor offences and settled small disputes (such as those between servants and masters over wages or between masters and apprentices); the mayor and sheriff's court had cognizance of all personal actions, and the court of conscience settled disputes which involved less than forty shillings. The judges in the lord mayor's court were the lord mayor, the recorder and the senior aldermen, in the mayor and sheriff's court the lord mayor, the sheriff and the recorder, in the lord mayor's court the lord mayor himself, and in the court of conscience the lord mayor of the preceding year. But theory and practice did not altogether coincide. Most serious offences, instead of being tried at quarter sessions, were reserved for the commission court (held before two judges of a superior court). At quarter sessions the recorder sat alone, and in the mayor and sheriff's court he heard motions sitting alone. The business of this latter court had greatly decreased during

[1] 35 Geo. III, c. 36; 48 Geo. III, c. 140; 1 Vict., c. 25; 22 & 23 Vict., c. 52.

the early nineteenth century, as cases could be removed to a superior court. The court of conscience was remarkable for the ease with which a rehearing could be secured by the defeated party, with a consequent increase of fees for the officers of the court.

Cork, Limerick, Londonderry, Kilkenny and Waterford all had a quarter sessions court dealing with criminal cases, a mayor and sheriff's court (a court of record) dealing with civil disputes and a court of conscience. In Carrickfergus and Galway there was a quarter sessions court and a Tholsel court which dealt with civil disputes. Waterford had these courts and a mayor's court; and two boroughs, Kinsale and Youghal, which were not counties of boroughs, nevertheless had quarter sessions courts and record courts with wide jurisdiction. In about twenty-three boroughs there were courts of limited jurisdiction presided over by the head of the corporation. The little business they had was usually concerned with the quick collection of small debts. At least thirty other boroughs seem to have at some time possessed similar courts, but during the eighteenth and early nineteenth centuries they ceased to function.[1]

Finally there were the manor courts which possessed a threefold jurisdiction, a common law jurisdiction ranging in amount from five marks to £200, exercised according to the forms of the superior courts; the jurisdiction of a court baron which could be exercised comparatively speedily; and finally a statutory jurisdiction granted during the eighteenth and early nineteenth centuries of a simple, speedy kind for the collection of small debts.[2] The legislature, besides extending the jurisdiction of the manor courts, also tried to regulate them. In 1785 seneschals (as the judges of the courts were termed) were ordered to keep court books, duplicates of which were to be deposited with the clerk of the peace for the county. Two years later seneschals were directed to lodge copies of the charters under which their courts were held with the clerk of the peace. And in 1826 it was enacted that a seneschal, if he were not a

---

[1] City and borough courts are described in great detail in the *Report of the commissioners appointed to inquire into the municipal corporations in Ireland*, H.C. 1835 (23–24, 27–28), xxvii–viii; 1836 (29), xxiv.

[2] For the manor courts see *Report from the select committee on manor courts, Ireland* . . . H.C. 1837 (494), xv.

barrister of three years' standing, was to enter into recognizances at quarter sessions for the proper performance of his duties.[1] There were in 1837 about 200 of these courts, erratically distributed throughout the county, and taken together they had jurisdiction over a wide area and were cheap and easy of access. The seneschal of three courts in West Cork put the case for the manor courts intelligently when he declared, referring to his own courts, 'the people are invariably pleased with being able to tell their story in Irish and to address the jury through me and to tell their story as they like themselves. The jury are conversant with their little manners, customs and bargains much better than gentlemen and all that; I do think that many of them would come to a better and fairer decision than almost any magistrate, at least more satisfactory to the parties'.[2] Critics of the courts pointed out that many of the seneschals were grossly ignorant, that discharged clerks and drunkards often practised as attorneys before them, that the courts were sometimes held in public houses, because publicans believing that a court day was good for business were willing to provide a room, and that the proceedings were often disorderly and dangerously informal.

Most of these city and borough courts were abolished by the Irish municipal reform act of 1840, though Dublin, Galway and Carrickfergus retained their courts of quarter sessions and recorder's courts for the trial of civil actions, and the queen was empowered to grant such courts to any borough which petitioned for them.[3] The manor courts lasted until 1859 when they were abolished by act of parliament.[4]

There were twenty-six ecclesiastical courts:[5] the court of prerogative, which has already been dealt with, twenty-four diocesan courts, and the ecclesiastical court of the exempt jurisdiction of Newry and Mourne, the vicar general who

[1] 25 Geo. III, c. 44; 27 Geo. III, c. 22; 7 Geo. IV, c. 41; 7 & 8 Geo. IV, c. 59.
[2] *Report from the select committee on manor courts, Ireland . . .*, p. 69, H.C. 1837 (494), xv.
[3] 3 & 4 Vict., c. 108.   [4] 22 Vict., c. 14.
[5] For the ecclesiastical courts see *Courts enquiry, fourteenth report*, H.C. (68), 1826, xvii; *Nineteenth report*, H.C. (311),1830, xx; *Twenty-first report*, H.C. 1831 (739), x; *Report from the select committee appointed to inquire into the state of the prerogative and ecclesiastical courts in Ireland*, H.C. 1837 (412), vi.

presided in this court being appointed by the earl of Kilmorey as successor to the abbot of Newry. The four metropolitan courts had both an original jurisdiction for the archbishop's own diocese and an appellate jurisdiction from his suffragans' courts. There was also an appeal from the metropolitan courts to delegates in chancery. The jurisdiction of the ecclesiastical courts embraced testamentary and matrimonial matters, tithe (which, until the enactment of the composition act of 1823, provided the bulk of their business), ecclesiastical administration and discipline, and causes of correction such as defamation. The judge in each of these courts was appointed by the bishop, usually for life, and might be a vicar general (the title by which he was usually known), an official principal, a commissary or a chancellor; and writers on ecclesiastical law carefully distinguished between the respective jurisdictions of each of these officials. But since in Ireland all of these offices were always conferred on the same individual it is unnecessary to pursue the subject. The vicar general could appoint a surrogate or deputy, and each diocese also had a registrar responsible for the custody of its records and for providing copies when required and entering the decisions of the diocesan (or consistory) court.

The consistory court in Dublin was the busiest of the diocesan courts, and during the eighteenth and nineteenth centuries the vicar general of the Dublin diocese was also the judge of the prerogative court, the custom at the beginning of the nineteenth century being for the judge of the prerogative court on court days to sit earlier in the morning as vicar general. The vicar generals of Dublin were therefore highly competent jurists. In the other dioceses they were frequently laymen and lawyers, but in practice it was the surrogate who normally presided in the consistory court, and the surrogates, who were usually clergymen, had according to an active ecclesiastical lawyer 'no knowledge whatever of the principles of law', though he generously added that 'being generally men of education it is to be observed that they seldom stray widely from the landmarks of common sense and the just appreciation of evidence'.[1] In 1864 as a belated result of the Irish church

[1] *Report from the select committee appointed to enquire into the state of the prerogative and ecclesiastical courts in Ireland*, p. 61, H.C. 1837 (412), vi.

temporalities act the number of ecclesiastical courts was drastically reduced. The Irish ecclesiastical courts act of that year provided that there should be twelve united diocesan courts in addition to the two provincial courts and twelve diocesan registries. And the archbishops of Armagh and Dublin were empowered to prepare rules regulating the procedure and fees of the ecclesiastical courts and the preservation of documents. These rules were to come into operation when approved by the lord lieutenant in council. In September 1865 the new rules were approved by the lord lieutenant,[1] but five years later the Irish church act abolished the jurisdiction of the ecclesiastical courts.[2]

The legal official world can be conveniently divided into the law officers and agents of the crown and the administrative staffs attached to the courts. The law officers of the crown in Ireland at the beginning of the nineteenth century consisted of the prime serjeant, the attorney general and the solicitor general, and the king's advocate (who appeared for the crown in admiralty cases). The office of prime serjeant was not filled after the death of Arthur Browne in 1805. In 1886 an under-secretary, trained in the treasury tradition and anxious to prune legal expenses in Ireland, declared the office of queen's advocate to be unnecessary, and consequently the treasury decided to abolish the small salary attached to it and to introduce a clause abolishing the office itself into the first suitable bill.[3] In the event, the office as a dignity with unremunerated honour lasted on until the last holder, Gerald Fitz-Gibbon, was placed on the bench in 1924. Another law office evolved and disappeared during the century, that of law adviser. From 1803 the government was making occasional payments to a member of the bar for assistance given to the attorney and solicitor general. Richard Greene, later a baron of the exchequer, was law adviser when Stanley was chief secretary, and Abraham Brewster, later lord chancellor, held the same post when Peel became prime minister for the second time. The

[1] S.P.O.I., Council order book, 1861–8.

[2] 27 & 28 Vict., c. 54; 32 & 33 Vict., c. 42.

[3] *Correspondence between the treasury and the Irish government as to the remuneration of the attorney general and solicitor general for Ireland*, H.C. 1887 (26) and (336), lxvii. 379–393.

need for such an official can presumably be explained by the number of legal problems the Irish government had to deal with, together with the frequent absence from the country of one or both of the law officers. And though the duties of the law adviser were never defined by minute or otherwise, from 1849 a salary was provided. However, in 1883, a circular signed by the under-secretary informed justices of the peace that the lord lieutenant considered that magistrates at petty sessions should abandon the practice of obtaining advice from the law adviser to the government, and the last holder of the office, John Naish, became solicitor general.[1]

The government's other law agents were the crown and sessional solicitors. In the eighteenth century there seems to have been only one state solicitor for the whole of Ireland, for it was not customary for the crown to prosecute at assizes except 'on very pressing business or in disturbed districts'. However in 1801 crown solicitors responsible for crown prosecutions at the assizes were appointed for each circuit. In 1842 the treasury examined the cost of conducting the government's law business in Ireland, and, being 'well aware from former experience in several departments in England, how difficult it is to check the bills of costs incurred by professional men', insisted that the crown solicitors should be paid fixed annual salaries in lieu of fees. These were to cover all expenses, the treasury refusing to make an exception which was suggested in favour of fees for briefs and the examination of crown witnesses, 'since in these two cases above all there is the greatest temptation to swell, by undue prolixity or irrelevant matter, the cost of the proceedings'. About 1846 the circuits began to be divided, and by 1880 there were twenty crown solicitors as well as the crown and treasury solicitor. In 1842, the treasury had suggested that the crown solicitor for Dublin should act in Ireland as the treasury solicitor in England, managing the civil law business of the government and preparing parliamentary bills.[2] After the death of William Kemmis in 1857, however, the offices of

---

[1] The circular abolishing the office is given in the *Irish Law Times*, 28 Apr. 1883. See also *Hansard*, 3 series, cclxxviii. 378.

[2] *Courts inquiry, sixteenth report, appendix, p.* 67, H.C. 1826–7 (341), xi; *Crown solicitors (Ireland): return . . .,* p. 1, H.C. 1842 (508), xxxviii; *Crown officers (Ireland): return,* pp. 31–43, H.C. 1852–3 (116) xciv.

crown solicitor for Dublin and treasury solicitor for Ireland were separated. The principal function of the crown and treasury solicitor was to act as solicitor for various public departments. He did not conduct prosecutions, 'except state prosecutions as may be directed for instance by the cabinet'. In 1888 the offices of crown and treasury solicitor and crown solicitor for the county and city of Dublin were amalgamated under the title of chief crown solicitor. On the retirement of the holder of this post in 1905 its duties were again divided between two whole-time officers, the chief crown solicitor and the treasury solicitor.[1]

About 1830 the attorney general began to direct a solicitor in each county, who came to be termed the sessional crown solicitor, to conduct government prosecutions at quarter sessions. The sessional crown solicitor, who was paid a small salary, sometimes even prosecuted at petty sessions, but usually government prosecutions at petty sessions were managed by the police. In the middle 'eighties it was decided to amalgamate the offices of crown solicitor and sessional crown solicitor and by 1914 this had been almost completely accomplished.[2]

It is very difficult to summarize the organization and composition of what may be termed the legal administrative service at the beginning of the nineteenth century. Chancery, three common law courts and the court of error each had a staff of officials who were responsible for managing each of the various available legal processes, preparing writs and summonses, taking affidavits, filing documents, noting rulings, enrolling judgments, searching the records, certifying documents, taxing costs, and collecting fines. In the three common law courts the highest and best remunerated officials were sinecurists with large incomes, their duties being performed by deputies. In chancery there were sinecurists, but they held relatively unimportant (but not unremunerative) posts. The

---

[1] *Appropriation accounts, 1887–8*, p. 309, H.C. 1889 (18), liii; *Royal commission on the civil service: memoranda on the organization and staff of the chief secretary's office*, p. 13; *Report of the committee appointed to inquire into the office of public prosecutor with minutes of evidence*, pp. 32–3, H.C. 1884 [C. 4016], xxiii.

[2] *Estimates for the civil service for the year ending 31 Mar. 1888*, p. 281, H.C. 1887 (53), liv. 297.

duties of each court were divided amongst a number of officials who worked in small, semi-independent departments, each labouring by himself or with the help of a small number of clerks which he usually himself paid and appointed. As these officials were largely remunerated by fees, their incomes fluctuated and were not necessarily exactly proportionate to the burden or importance of their work. Also this method of remuneration acted as a positive disincentive to any attempt to simplify procedure.

Of all the courts, chancery had understandably the largest and most ornate staff. There were not only the two judges, the chancellor and the master of the rolls, but there were also the four masters whose office was 'of very ancient institution and high trust'.[1] Their work was semi-judicial and their remuneration compared not unfavourably with that of a common law judge. Each master had a small staff composed of his examiner and clerk and the examiner's clerk. The six clerks who acted as agents for the attorneys practising in chancery could earn very substantial incomes, and of course employed clerks to assist them. And there were a number of other officials, including the lord chancellor's secretary, the examiners, the accountant general, the clerk of the crown and hanaper,[2] the cursitor, the registrars, the usher, and the sergeant-at-arms. Omitting the judges, the masters, and the sinecurists, the total number was 43 officials, and as they employed 42 clerks, the total staff of the court was 85.

The total staff of the king's bench was 33. The civil side had 16 officials ranging from the two deputy prothonotaries to the crier, and they employed 14 clerks. The crown side was managed at the Four Courts by a very small staff—the two deputy clerks of the crown and a clerk they employed. The court of common pleas had 20 officials employing 16 clerks, so that the total staff of the court was 36. In both the king's bench and the common pleas the core of the office was com-

[1] *Courts inquiry, first report*, p. 22, H.C. 1817 (9), x.
[2] The clerk of the crown and hanaper was responsible for the issue of patents and commissions. From 1884 the holder of the office was also secretary to the lord chancellor (*Courts inquiry, first report*, pp. 89–96, H.C. 1817 (9), x; *Chancery office, Ireland, commission report*, pp. 6–7, H.C. 1859 [2473], xii; *Irish Law Times*, 11 Oct. 1884).

posed of a group of experienced clerks who performed services for attorneys in private practice. In the common pleas nine principal clerks were fed by attorneys 'who employed them to do such part of their business as they themselves are precluded from doing by the usage of the office'.[1] And in the king's bench seven clerks occupied a similar place. Needless to say, the incomes of these clerks greatly varied, but they could be large, a partnership of two clerks in the king's bench enjoying a net income of about £4,000 per annum, and a clerk in the common pleas an annual income of about £3,000. And the attorneys seem to have relied on these clerks to an extent which at times aroused the latter's slightly contemptuous surprise.

The court of exchequer was highly complicated, having three sides, common law, equity, and revenue. And though the revenue side had an archaic connection with the government's financial administration, the custodiam process, which was strictly a method by which the debts of the crown could be recovered, was frequently made available to private citizens through a legal fiction. On the pleas side of the exchequer there were 11 officials, including the deputy clerk of the pleas and a group of clerks acting as agents for attorneys, who employed 14 clerks. The equity side had 17 officials, including the deputy chief remembrancer and three examiners, who employed 11 clerks. The revenue side was smaller. There were only eight officers, including the deputy treasurer's remembrancers, the secondaries, the controller of the pipe and the clerk of the pipe, and they employed only eight clerks. Thus the total staff of the court of exchequer was 69.

Omitting judges and sinecurists, there were employed at the Four Courts about 117 officials, who themselves appointed and paid over 100 clerks.[2] Some of these offices were in the gift of the crown, the sinecurists of course appointed their own deputies, and the lord chancellor, chief justices of the king's bench and the court of common pleas, the chief remembrancer, the lord treasurer's remembrancer, each had some patronage in their respective courts. The judges appointed their registrars. The masters in chancery, who were appointed by

---

[1] *Courts inquiry, fifth report,* p. 97, H.C. 1819 (5), xii.

[2] These statistics are based on the evidence in the reports of the commission set up to inquire into the Irish courts in 1815.

the crown and the Six Clerks, who were appointed by the master of the rolls, had to pay a substantial sum to their predecessors. And lastly, the clerks who did not hold any official post were appointed and paid by the officials whom they served —often themselves comparatively humble office-holders. The tenure of office of the various officials attached to the superior courts varied: it might be at pleasure, for good behaviour, or for life. But they all implicitly agreed on one point: generally speaking, no office holder, unless guilty of grave malversation, should be compelled to relinquish his post.

The anachronistic confusion which characterized the whole legal machinery marked it out as an inevitable target for the administrative reformers. And, as has been pointed out earlier, in 1815 a statutory commission was constituted to inquire into official duties and emoluments in the Irish courts.[1]

Its first members were Daniel Webb Webber, K.C., John Leslie Foster, later a baron of the exchequer, Bertram Mitford, a barrister and nephew of an Irish lord chancellor, John Hamilton, and Sir Charles Saxton, who had been for some years under-secretary. The commission lasted for sixteen years and fourteen persons in all served on it. As Webber, who served on it for thirteen years, pointed out, the inquiry turned out to be 'much more complicated and extensive than anyone contemplated' as 'it was not so easy to extract the information (which used frequently to be of a criminating nature) that it was desirous to extract'.[2] The commissioners sent to every official from the lord chancellor downwards a series of question relating to his duties and emoluments and used his answers (sometimes compared with other people's) as the basis for a cross-examination. It is not surprising that so searching an investigation should discover a variety of scandals. While some fees had fallen into disuse, a number had been introduced or raised by the completely unauthorized action of the officers concerned. As the commission put it, in all offices 'which have concurrent duties there will be observed a tendency, even in those persons who may have been originally most scrupulous,

[1] p. 21.

[2] *Report from the select committee appointed to inquire into the state of the prerogative and ecclesiastical courts in Ireland*, p. 1, H.C. 1837 (412), vi.

finally to assimilate their charges to such as have been successfully established by any of their brethren who may have acted
under less restraint'.[1] In the court of error the clerk had been
given a statutory salary which, considering his very limited
duties, appeared ample remuneration. Nevertheless the clerk
was found to have tripled his income by demanding fees, and
furthermore was over-estimating the length of documents on
which fees were being charged, and charging to both parties
fees which in any event should only have been paid by one.
Admittedly after his first examination by the commission, Sir
James Galbraith, the clerk of errors, hastily repaid some of
his recently collected fees and 'took the opportunity to repeatedly declare in the most solemn manner that he was as
ignorant and as innocent as the child unborn that there had
been any erroneous reckoning to the prejudice of the suitor' in
his office.[2]

In the court of common pleas the cost of enrolling records
was considerably increased by it being supposed that three rolls
were made out though in fact only one was prepared. Worse
still, owing to the negligence of the clerks, a large number of
recoveries, 'these great common assurances of landed property'
lay unenrolled for years. 'It is obvious', the commission remarked, 'that any reasoning that could excuse the delay of
executing the service ought in fairness to extend to postpone
equally the payment of fees attached to its performance'. This
however was not the case. All the fees and even the stamp duties
(which the clerk would not have to pay until the end of the process) were promptly collected.[3] In the king's bench, when
making out charges, there was a tendency for the clerks to over-
estimate the length of an enrolment, and as the attorneys were
also paid according to its length the unfortunate lay client was
badly protected.[4]

Finally one major offender was brought to book, John
Pollock, the clerk of the pleas in the court of exchequer. Pollock, an attorney by profession, was a great legal pluralist,
being clerk of the pleas, clerk of the reports in the court of chan-

[1] *Courts inquiry, fifth report*, p. 35.
[2] *Courts inquiry, third report*, appendix, p. 48, H.C. 1817 (487), xi. 220.
[3] *Courts inquiry, fifth report*, pp. 37–8, H.C. 1819 (5), xii. 41–2.
[4] *Courts inquiry, sixth report*, pp. 21–2, H.C. 1819 (6), xii. 307–8.

cery, transcriber and foreign opposer in the court of exchequer, clerk of the crown for Leinster, and registrar to the chief justice of the king's bench. From the office of clerk of the pleas he derived an income of over £5,000 a year, and when the commission came to investigate the sources of this income, in spite of all their experience, they were shocked. When in 1803, as a result of legislation improving the procedure of the courts of the king's bench and common pleas, it seemed as if some of the business of the exchequer might be diverted to those courts, it was very fairly provided that the officers of the exchequer should be compensated for any consequent loss they might incur. What was scarcely intended was that when an officer was claiming compensation any increase in his income should be ignored. This however was Pollock's contention. Though his total income from the office of clerk of the pleas was steadily growing, he annually claimed compensation for the fees he considered he had lost and this compensation amounted on an average to over £1,000 a year. On being asked if it had not occurred to him that any increase of fees should have been set off in favour of the public against his losses, Pollock replied that 'it did occur as a subject for consideration but after the best consideration I could give it, after conferring with other gentlemen of the office, I was satisfied I was entitled to compensation'. This reply stung the commission into asking with perceptible irony: 'did you ever moot that as a case of conscience with the commissioners of imprest accounts'? To which Pollock replied 'never'. As a result of the commission's activities in the summer of 1817, the attorney general filed a series of charges against Pollock, accusing him of charging excessive fees when taxing bills of costs, of allowing the officers of his court to advance their charges, and, 'on the sole pretext of establishing uniformity', of allowing fictitious charges on bills of costs he taxed. The court of exchequer having heard Pollock's defence found him guilty and he was dismissed, to retire into comfortable obscurity.[1]

The commissioners made numerous recommendations relating to the organization and procedure of the legal offices whose workings they inspected. As regards fees—the subject they were appointed to consider—they insisted that they should be paid

---

[1] *Liber mun. pub. Hib.*, pt. VII, p. 283; *Courts inquiry, second report*, pp. 21–6; appendix pp. 70–4, H.C. 1817, 10 xi.

at fixed, published and reasonable rates and they inclined to the view that officials should be salaried. The traditional attitude on this was put forcibly by the barons of the exchequer, in a communication to the chief secretary: 'The service which an official renders to a suitor is not always confined to a mere discharge of his duties', besides working out of office hours, often to a very late hour of the night, his knowledge and experience enables him to give much advice and assistance in the conduct of a suit, which may reasonably be expected to be withheld when it becomes the interest of the office to withhold it; and it is clear when an officer has a salary and nothing more, the less business the court has in which he acts, the better for him. He is therefore interested in the place of courtesy and kindness to substitute repulsive and disobliging manners, and to discourage business instead of attracting it. We are therefore clear that it will be much easier to punish the extortion which might arise in collecting fees than the remissness and inactivity of which a merely salaried officer might be guilty'.[1]

In spite of this defence of the old regime, the taking of fees by the officers of the common law courts was forbidden by an act of 1821, and they were assigned fixed salaries payable from the consolidated fund. Two taxing officers were appointed for the common law courts and new stamp duties were imposed on legal transactions.[2] In 1835 a more drastic step was taken. All the offices on the revenue side of the exchequer were abolished with the exception of that of lord treasurer's or second remembrancer, and the grant of this office to Sir Hugh Stewart was cancelled, it being enacted that it should be held by a barrister of at least ten years' standing whose duty it would be to report to the barons on the equity side of the court. The chief remembrancer was to audit the sheriffs' accounts and those of corporate bodies which the treasury requested him to examine.[3] Eight years later, when the fines and penalties audit office was established, it was placed under the supervision of the chief remembrancer. When in 1850 the equity jurisdiction of the exchequer was transferred to chancery and all the offices on the equity side of the exchequer were abolished, the

---

[1] *Communication of the barons of the exchequer on the fourth report so far as it relates to the court of exchequer*, pp. 25–7, H.C. 1821 (401), xi.
[2] 1 & 2 Geo. IV, c. 53.   [3] 5 & 6 Will. IV, c. 51.

auditing of Sheriffs' accounts and proceedings relating to debts due to the crown were transferred to the pleas side of the exchequer, and the fines and penalties office was placed under the supervision of the chief secretary.[1] Shortly afterwards the head of the office, the clerk of the fines and penalties, asked for an increase of staff, pointing out that his accounts were seriously in arrears. A treasury commission reported that the clerk who was a practicing barrister went on circuit and 'failed to devote his whole time to his public duties'. The commission recommended that his office should be abolished and its duties transferred to the comissioners for auditing the public accounts. The treasury concurred but the clerk of the fines and penalties argued strenuously that his office could be abolished only by an act of parliament. The law officers to whom a case was submitted agreed with him and the treasury had to retreat.[2]

In 1844 after a viceregal commission had heard evidence and reported, an act was passed abolishing all offices attached to the superior courts of common law (with full compensation to any official who had a freehold in his office) and providing a new establishment for each of the three courts. This consisted of a master, with under him a principal assistant, a clerk of the rules, clerk of the writs, and about half a dozen clerks. Their salaries (over which the treasury was given a measure of control) and duties were clearly set out. The masters and clerks of the rules and writs were to be appointed by the lord lieutenant, the master in each court was to appoint the clerks, and promotion amongst the clerks was to be by seniority.[3] The bill which incorporated these changes had an uneventful passage through the commons, but in the upper house three powerful peers of great legal experience and different political standpoints, Lyndhurst, Campbell and Cottenham, contended that the patronage of all the offices in the Irish law courts should belong the chief justice in each court as was the practice in England. Though some of the lay lords were unsympathetic—Lord Wicklow for

[1] 6 & 7 Vict., c. 56, 13 & 14 Vict., c. 51.
[2] *Report of the committee of inquiry into public offices*, pp. 90-1, H.C. 1854 [1713] xxvii; SPO V/733/3324.
[3] *Report of the commission appointed to inquire and report with a view to the revision of the officers of the superior courts of common law*, H.C. 1842 (378), xxiii; 7 & 8 Vict., c. 107.

instance saying he would support a measure depriving the English judges of their right of appointment—an amendment was carried transferring the patronage granted under the bill to the lord lieutenant to the chief justices. The commons however disagreed with this amendment, and though Lyndhurst protested against the implied insult to Ireland, the lords by a small majority decided not to contest the point.[1] Six years later, in 1850, to equalize the business of the three courts, a consolidated writ, appearance, and seal office was set up. The first clerk of the writs, who was to be in charge of the new office, was to be appointed by the chief justices, his successor by the lord lieutenant.[2] Finally in 1867 the offices attached to the common law courts were still further simplified by the fusion within each office of their pleading and record departments. The clerks were divided into three classes and were to be appointed by the chief justices and the chief baron, vacancies in the first and second classes being filled by promotion. Any clerk appointed to the third class was to receive a certificate of fitness from the civil service commissioners.[3]

Simultaneously the official establishment of chancery was being reorganized. In 1823, to ensure 'the more easy, cheap and expeditious administration of justice', an Act for the better administration of justice in the court of chancery laid down the fees which were to be charged by various officials of the court from the lord chancellor to the crier—and it was also laid down that these fees were to be publicly displayed. The master of the rolls and masters in chancery were not to accept fees, the masters being granted substantial salaries with compensation for the existing holders of the office for loss of fees. And the lord chancellor was given power to dismiss officers of the court (masters excepted) for misconduct.[4] Thirteen years later, in 1836, the offices of usher, cursitor and of Six Clerks were abolished and their duties allocated to officials holding newly created posts—the clerk of affidavits, the two clerks in court, and the clerk of appearances and writs. There were to be two registrars, one attending the lord chancellor's court, the other that of the master of the rolls. All these officials were to be paid salaries and were not to receive any of their remunera-

---

[1] *Hansard*, 3 series, lxxvi. 1649–52, 1752–3, 1944–53.
[2] 13 Vict., c. 18. [3] 30 & 31 Vict., c. 129. [4] 4 Geo. IV, c. 61.

tion from fees. The clerk of the affidavits and the registrars were to be appointed by the lord chancellor, the two clerks in court and the clerk of the appearances by the master of the rolls.[1] And in 1850, by the chancery court regulation act, the secretary to the lord chancellor and the clerks and examiners to the masters were also granted fixed salaries in lieu of fees.[2] In 1845 a new department was added to chancery by the appointment of a taxing master—shortly afterwards three taxing masters were found to be necessary. These officials were appointed by the lord chancellor.[3] Finally in 1867 the chancery (Ireland) act accomplished for chancery what the act of 1844 had done for the courts of common law—giving it a rationalized structure. The office of master was abolished, except that one master was retained to supervise estates under receivers. The following officers were also abolished: the clerk and assistant clerk of affidavits, the clerk and assistant clerk of appearances, the deputy keeper of the rolls, the clerk of enrolment, clerk and assistant clerk of pleadings, the clerk of recognizances. Clerks were divided into first and second class, they were to be appointed by the lord chancellor, first-class clerkships were to be filled by promotion, and persons appointed to second-class clerkships were to produce a certificate of fitness from the civil service commissioners.[4]

The supreme court of judicature act made sweeping changes in the legal administrative machinery. All the officials attached to any of the courts whose duties were vested in the supreme court were transferred to that court, which was to have a common taxing office and common writ and seal office serving all its divisions. The lord chancellor, the chief justice, and the chief baron were empowered to define and distribute duties, and with the concurrence of the treasury to determine what officials and clerks would be requisite for 'the permanent organization of the official staff of the supreme court'. All junior clerkships were to be filled by open competition, the lord chancellor, with the concurrence of the chief secretary, making the necessary regulations. All officers attached to a judge were to be appointed by him, officers attached to any division of the high court were to be appointed

[1] 6 & 7 Wm. IV, c. 74.   [2] 13 & 14 Vict., c. 89.
[3] 8 & 9 Vict., c. 115; 11 & 12 Vict., c. 132.   [4] 30 & 31 Vit.,c c. 129.

by its president, officers attached to the high court or the court of appeal were to be appointed by the lord chancellor, and the lord chancellor, the master of the rolls, the vice-chancellor and the lord chief justice were to retain their rights of patronage.[1]

Partly as a result of the supreme court of judicature act there was between 1870 and 1914 a substantial reduction (about thirty per cent) in the size of the administrative staffs attached to the superior courts. But this reduction was balanced by the establishment of a new office under the control of the land judge (and in some matters of the lord chancellor), the central office of the land registry of Ireland. The local registration of title act of 1891, which provided for the compulsory registration of the ownership of freehold land purchased under the land purchase acts and for the voluntary registration of the title to other freehold land, set up local registries attached to the offices of the clerks of the crown and peace and a central registry. The head of the new office was the registrar of title and from 1892 this post was held by the registrar of deeds who thus was enabled to arrange for the co-operation of two departments working in the same sphere.

The administrative staff of the central registry numbered nearly fifty and amounted to just about a quarter of the whole administrative staff attached to the supreme court. In addition there was 'a subordinate establishment' (consisting of housekeepers, court-keepers, messengers, criers and tipstaffs) which totalled about seventy. Of the administrative staff about forty had salaries (at maximum) of £500 or over, of these eleven had salaries of £1,000 and three, the registrar of the lord chancellor, the master of the king's bench and the official assignee in bankruptcy had salaries of £1,200.

Turning to courts of a more limited jurisdiction, the clerk of the crown was responsible for the routine functioning of the assizes court and kept its records. The clerk of the peace performed similar duties at quarter sessions and was also the principal officer in the civil bill court. The clerk of the crown was appointed by letters patent: until 1820 he held his office at pleasure, from then onwards for good behaviour. The clerk of the peace was appointed by the custos rotulorum of the county.

[1] 40 & 41 Vict., c. 57.

The clerk of the crown was designated in his patent clerk of the crown and peace, and at the turn of the century the crown seems to have determined to try and secure the appointment of clerks of the peace. In 1820 an act was passed affirming the right of the custos rotulorum to appoint the clerk of the peace, but it was specifically stated in the act itself that it was not to affect suits already pending in the courts. In 1819 the claim of the crown to appoint the clerk of the peace for King's County was challenged in the court of common pleas, and after prolonged proceedings the house of lords finally in 1829 decided in favour of the custos rotulorum. And at least one unfortunate lawyer, the clerk of the crown for Kerry, who had discharged the duties of clerk of the peace in virtue of a patent from the crown, not only had to relinquish the office, but pay the custos rotulorum's nominee 'the salary and emoluments which I received as a remuneration for doing the duties'.[1]

It was often suggested that the offices of clerk of the crown and clerk of the peace should be amalgamated, and in 1877 the county officers and courts (Ireland) act provided a machinery by which this would be accomplished. The lord lieutenant was empowered as vacancies occurred to appoint a clerk of the crown and peace for each county. The clerk of the crown and peace was to be paid a salary fixed by the act and could be removed by the lord chancellor. Registrars appointed by the chairman, subject to the approval of the lord chancellor, could be attached to each civil bill court and a suitable staff was to be provided for each court with qualifications prescribed by the lord chancellor and appointed by the clerk of the crown and peace.[2]

Finally there were the petty sessions clerks. In 1827 it was enacted that the justices of the peace meeting in petty sessions could appoint a clerk who would receive the fees set out in the act. In 1851 the petty sessions clerk's duties and qualifications were set out. The latter mainly consisted of a list of offices which the clerk must not hold—he could not practise as an attorney in

---

[1] *Report of the commissioners appointed to revise the several laws under and by virtue of which moneys are now raised by grand jury presentment in Ireland*, appendix, p. 49, H.C. 1842 (386), xxiv. 159; Pollock *v.* Harding (*English reports*, iv. 1300); 1 Geo. IV, c. 27.

[2] 40 & 41 Vict., c. 56.

his own court or at the quarter sessions of the district, nor was he to be a pound-keeper or keep a public house. In 1858 the petty sessions clerks were made salaried officials, stamped documents taking the place of fees in their courts, and the clerks drawing their salaries from and accounting for their stamps with the clerk of fines and penalties, who from the later sixties was termed the registrar of petty sessions clerks. The registrar had a small staff, one of whom, Bram Stoker, produced in 1878 a textbook on the duties of petty sessions clerks. In the same year as he published this work, Stoker, who is better known as the author of *Dracula*, resigned from the civil service to become manager to Henry Irving. From the middle of the nineteenth century there were about 600 petty sessions districts in Ireland, and the clerks salaries ranged widely, the best paid at the beginning of the twentieth century getting £300 or £400 a year. Generally, however, the trend of salaries was upward, the lowest salary in 1904, £28 per annum, being the average salary at the middle of the century.[1]

[1] 7 & 8 Geo. IV, c. 68; 14 & 15 Vict., c. 93; 21 & 22 Vict., c. 100. *Petty sessions clerks (Ireland)*, H.C. 1856 (12), liii. 503 and *Petty sessions clerks (Ireland) (salaries)*, H.C. 1905 (115), lxv. 531.

V

POLICE AND PRISONS

~~~~~~

AT THE BEGINNING of the nineteenth century police and prisons
in Ireland were still under the control of the local authorities,
the grand juries. But already the state had been empowered to
take steps to raise the standards of police and prison administration and as the century progressed it was to take over the
control of both services. For centuries the constable was a
vague figure in Irish social history. He emerged during the
middle ages. Constables are mentioned in the great charter of
Ireland in 1216, and in 1308 the Statute of Winchester, which
provided that two constables should be appointed in every
hundred, was extended to Ireland.[1] By the seventeenth century,
theoretically at least, there were high constables for each
barony and petty or parish constables.[2] From 1734 the high
constables were appointed by the grand jury and the justices
of the peace were empowered to appoint petty constables if
sheriffs and seneschals failed to do so.[3] By an act of 1787 the
lord lieutenant was empowered for each barony or half-barony
in any county to appoint a chief constable under whom there
would be sub-constables appointed by the grand jury.[4] Five
years later, in 1792, by an act from the operation of which
thirteen counties were exempted, the grand juries were auth-

---

[1] *Stat. Ire., John-Henry V*, pp. 13, 158.

[2] R. Bolton, *A justice of the peace for Ireland*, pp. 57–9, *Cal. S. P. Ire.*, 1606–1608,
pp. 577–8.

[3] 7 Geo. III, c. 12; 23 Geo. II, c. 14.

[4] 27 Geo. III, c. 40; 30 Geo. III, c. 35; 36 Geo. III, c. 25.

orized to appoint up to eight sub-constables in each barony.[1] Thus by the beginning of the nineteenth century the Irish counties had a police force composed of small groups of sub-constables. Besides being few in number the men were poorly paid and were only part-time policemen.[2]

Such a force was bound to be ineffective and in 1814, when there were serious agrarian disturbances, Peel decided to supplement the baronial police by a more mobile force under the control of the government. The lord lieutenant was empowered to proclaim an area to be in a state of disturbance and to require extra police. In such an area the lord lieutenant could appoint 'a chief magistrate of police' with the powers of a justice of the peace and with, 'for his aid and support', a clerk, a chief constable and a force of sub-constables.[3] The detachments commanded by the police magistrates comprised the peace preservation force and in 1822 Goulburn, the chief secretary, declared that its operations 'had been attended with the most happy results'.[4]

Inspired by the success of the peace preservation force, the government made an attempt to reform the baronial police. In 1822 the lord lieutenant was empowered to appoint a chief constable for each barony and to direct the justices of the peace to nominate constables and in their default to do so himself. The force so raised was to be equipped at the expense of the county from government stores, and chief constables were to report to the lord lieutenant at three-monthly intervals. The lord lieutenant was also empowered to appoint four inspectors-general of baronial police and (in 1824) a superintendent of constables for County Dublin. A few years later, in 1828, he was empowered if necessary to move constables out of their county.[5] In the early 'thirties the constabulary or baronial police was a force of nearly 7,700 officers and men, managed on a system which represented a clumsy compromise between centralization and local autonomy. There

---

[1] 32 Geo. III, c. 16.

[2] *Accounts presented to the house of commons of the presentments passed by the grand juries of Ireland*, H.C. 1808 (205), xiii and *Grand juries: sums levied in the several counties of Ireland during the two years last past*, H.C. 1824 (287), xxii.

[3] 54 Geo. III, c. 131.　　　　　[4] *Hansard*, 2 series, vii. 852.

[5] 3 Geo. IV, c. 103; 5 Geo. IV, c. 28; 9 Geo. IV, c. 63.

were also stationed in ten counties detachments of the peace preservation force, consisting in all of ten magistrates and about 600 men.[1]

There were two other police forces in Ireland, the Dublin police and the revenue police. During most of the eighteenth century the policing of Dublin was managed by the parishes. Then in 1786 the lord lieutenant was empowered to appoint three police commissioners who were placed in control of a force of about 750 men.[2] The measure constituting this force was bitterly attacked by the opposition who declared that it was 'a bill of patronage not of police' and compared the chief commissioner to Attila.[3] In 1795 there was a change of policy, and the commissioners were replaced by three magistrates chosen by the corporation. But in 1808 the government again were given a share in the management of the metropolitan police. The force was put under the control of eighteen magistrates, of whom six were elected by the corporation and twelve appointed by the lord lieutenant, who also was empowered to appoint one of them chief police magistrate of Dublin.[4] In 1824 the elected and appointed magistrates were reduced to four and eight respectively. These magistrates were to appoint patrolling constables and to report regularly to the chief or under-secretary. In the early 'thirties the force at their disposal amounted to about 200 constables and 500 watchmen. The whole establishment was expensive and inadequate, the watchmen being often 'decrepit, worn-out old men' whom an experienced magistrate refused to parade in daylight on the ground 'that they would excite so much ridicule of the people that there is the risk of their very appearance creating a disturbance'.[5]

The revenue police was a force created by private enterprise. Suppressing illicit distillation could be dangerous in some parts

[1] *Report from the select committee on county cess, Ireland, with the minutes of evidence*, pp. 1–3, H.C. 1836 (527), xii.

[2] For the Dublin police see *First report of the commissioners appointed to inquire into the municipal corporations of Ireland, appendix*, pp. 61–73, H.C. 1835 [23], xxvii.

[3] *Parl. Debates (Ireland)*, vi. 330, viii. 305.

[4] 48 Geo. III, c. 140

[5] *Minutes of evidence taken before the select committee . . . appointed to inquire into the state of Ireland . . .* p. 1002, H.C. 1839 (486), xii.

of Ireland, where it was carried on 'by gangs of sixty or eighty men in glens and fastnesses and mountains, gangs of men that were so ferocious that it required armed men to cope with them'. Understandably excisemen when 'still-hunting' at the beginning of the nineteenth century often sought military assistance. But the military authorities, believing this form of service to be bad for discipline, refused to allow their men to be employed on it. Some revenue officers then hired armed parties as escorts, and these parties under the command of lieutenants who were given commissions as excisemen formed the first revenue police force.[1]

Since Ireland in the 'thirties was suffering severely from agrarian disturbances and sectarian animosities, it was obviously desirable that the police should be properly organized. In 1835 Morpeth introduced a bill for making the Irish police 'more serviceable', which ultimately passed in the following session. By this measure the constabulary and the peace preservation force were abolished and replaced by a single force controlled by the government, the Irish constabulary. In the same session (1836) another measure passed reforming the Dublin police. The lord lieutenant was empowered to appoint in Dublin two paid justices of the peace (from 1841 known as the commissioners of the Dublin police), who were to be responsible to the chief secretary. They were to recruit a sufficient number of 'fit and able men' and to make rules and regulations for the force.[2] Finally in the same year (1836) the government offered the command of the revenue police to Colonel Brereton, an artillery man who had served in the Peninsula. Brereton 'hardly knew what the excise meant' but he accepted the appointment. He found the revenue police 'without discipline and without instruction of any kind. . . . Every man almost was married, with a tribe of children, they were miserably lodged and miserably clothed, their arms in the worst possible condition'. He promptly dismissed two-thirds of the force, insisted that all recruits should be literate and of good character, and set up a depot in Dublin where he had his

---

[1] *Report from the select committee . . . appointed to consider the consequences of extending the functions of the constabulary in Ireland*, pp. 5–6, H.C. 1854 (53), x.

[2] 6 & 7 Will. IV, cc. 13, 29; *Hansard*, 3 series, xxx. 657.

men drilled as a light infantry corps, 'the movement of light infantry being peculiarly applicable to still hunting', since, as Brereton explained, the men could advance in extended order and then, when retiring with prisoners, form a square which could beat off attempts at a rescue. And when Brereton discovered that the last strongholds of illicit distillation were the islands off the west coast, he persuaded the treasury to grant him a steamer and landed detachments on the islands.[1] The revenue police after Brereton's reforms was an efficient force of about 1,100 strong and its activities rapidly reduced the amount of illicit distillation. But in the early 'fifties it was unnecessary to maintain a special police to enforce the revenue laws. So in 1857 the revenue police was abolished, its duties being transferred to the constabulary.[2]

The Irish Constabulary—known from 1867 as the Royal Irish Constabulary or the R.I.C.—had from the outset several interesting characteristics. It was a centralized force, responsible for the peace of the whole country (with the exception of the Dublin area). It was swiftly responsive to the will of the Irish executive, the inspector general keeping in close contact with the chief secretary's office, and it was strictly disciplined. Constables were to be of 'good character for honesty, fidelity and activity'[3] and the first inspector general, Shaw Kennedy, a Peninsula and Waterloo veteran, compiled for the use of the force a manual of rules and regulations. It was a comprehensive treatise, succinct in style, bearing the marks of an intelligent mind trained in Wellington's school. Having dealt with the duties of each rank in the force, Kennedy arranged his material under alphabetical heads beginning with Absence and Accounts and concluding with Wedlock and Witnesses. His readers were reminded that they were expected to use their intelligence to supply the deficiencies inevitable in general orders and that members of the new force must act with 'the utmost forebearance, mildness, urbanity and perfect civility'. After serving for two years Kennedy resigned, having had a conflict of opinion with the government over the appointment of officers. He was

---

[1] *Report from the select committee . . . appointed to consider the consequences of extending the functions of the constabulary in Ireland*, pp. 4, 6–12, H.C. 1854 (53), x.

[2] 20 & 21 Vict., c. 40.   [3] 6 & 7 Will. IV, c. 13.

succeeded by Duncan McGregor, another Peninsula veteran, and McGregor's successors, with one exception, were all retired field officers with distinguished records. The exception was Sir Andrew Reed. Reed, a brilliant student of Queen's College, Galway, was preparing for the Indian civil examination when the lord lieutenant offered the college a nomination for the constabulary cadetship examination. Reed seized the opportunity, rose rapidly in the force, acquired a great reputation for tact, and produced a useful manual of police duties.[1]

From the formation of the force most of its officers were directly commissioned, entering and being trained as cadets. Until the middle 'sixties only one in six of the appointments to the rank of sub-inspector were made from the ranks. A treasury commission in 1866 suggested that a larger proportion of these appointments could be filled by promoted N.C.O.s, and shortly afterwards it was decided that one-fourth of the appointments to the rank of sub-inspector (after 1883 to that of district inspector) should be from the ranks.[2] Finally in 1895, 'with a view to encouraging men of energy and enabling them to advance in the service, the government directed that half the vacancies in the grade of district inspector should be filled by promotion from the ranks.[3]

It was at times suggested that a much higher proportion of the officers should be recruited from the ranks. Understandably some representatives of the rank and file favoured this policy, and a treasury commission in 1873 suggested that 'many of the sub-inspectors' duties could be discharged by a superior class of head constable with a somewhat increased pay and a horse and tax cart'. But there was a strong body of opinion in favour of having a high proportion of directly commissioned officers. It was pointed out that inspectors 'were thrown much in contact with the gentry of their counties both socially and in the performance of their duties'. Therefore they had to be able to move easily in county society. It was said that the men tended to be too familiar with officers who had risen from the ranks

[1] *Irish Times*, 9 Nov. 1914.
[2] *Constabulary, Ireland, report of the commission*, pp. 13-4, H.C. 1866 [3658], xxxiv; *Report of the commission to inquire into the condition of the civil service in Ireland (Royal Irish constabulary)*, p. 9, H.C. 1873 [C. 831], xxii.
[3] R.I.C. circular, 17 Jan. 1895.

and preferred to be commanded by gentlemen who were not too closely acquainted with 'the little details of the duties'.[1] And it was emphasized that the force greatly benefited from 'the fresh and high intellectual element . . . supplied to the service by the introduction through severe competition of young men of high education'.[2]

One result of the R.I.C. method of officer selection was that the R.I.C. district inspectors were better paid than police inspectors in England (incidentally the D.I.s when asking for increased pay in 1914 definitely rated themselves well above inspectors in English forces).[3] It is impossible of course to prove that the increased cost of securing the R.I.C. type of officer was justified. But the success with which the force tackled a wide range of various duties must have been at least partly due to the capabilities of its officer corps. And of course there were many occasions when political, agrarian or sectarian strife placed an Irish police officer in a position which made severe demands on his intelligence, self-confidence and tact.

It may be added that the rank and file of the force as well as its officers showed considerable pertinacity and ingenuity in pressing their claims for higher pay. Their representatives appearing before commissions (treasury or vice-regal) on four occasions (in 1873, 1882, 1901 and 1914) based their case on the rising cost of living and the rising standards of the classes from which recruits for the force were drawn. The commissions scrutinized their arguments closely. For instance the vice-regal commission of 1901 reported that the constabulary witnesses had considerably over-estimated the rise in the cost of living. Nevertheless the force secured substantial rises in pay in 1866, 1883 and 1914. The 1883 rise was preceded by a widespread agitation in the force. The land war imposed a heavy strain on the constabulary and during the summer of 1882 meetings

---

[1] *Report of the commission . . . to inquire into the condition of the civil service in Ireland (Royal Irish constabulary)* pp. 51–2, 56, 65–6, 70, 78.

[2] *Royal Irish constabulary and Dublin metropolitan police: appendix to the report of the committee of inquiry*, p. 183, H.C. 1914–16 [Cd. 7637], xxxii.

[3] *Committee on the police service: report . . .*, Pt. I, p. 22, H.C. 1919 [Cd. 253], xxvii; *Royal Irish constabulary and Dublin metropolitan police: appendix to the report of the committee of inquiry*, pp. 198, 364, H.C. 1914–16 [Cd. 7637], xxxii.

of the men were held and demands for better pay and pensions formulated, and at some stations discipline was subject to severe strains. However, when the government granted a commission of inquiry the agitation subsided.

Immediately afterwards there was a police crisis in Dublin. The D.M.P. had also found their work increased by the political excitement of the early 'eighties and their discontent was stimulated by the constabulary's success in securing a commission of inquiry. At the end of August the men held two large meetings to discuss pay claims. The second of these meetings was prohibited by the commissioner, but a number of men met. The following day (Friday, 1 September) over 200 constables who had attended the meeting were dismissed. Promptly a large majority of the remaining constables refused to go on duty. On the following Saturday Dublin was patrolled by hastily enrolled special constables backed by the military. The rougher elements in the city took advantage of the situation, there was stone throwing, hooting and yelling, and the specials were badly baited.[1] But the behaviour of the roughs brought some of the strikers unexpectedly back to duty, during the following week the bulk of the dismissed men were reinstated and the force gained a pay increase shortly afterwards.

The officers of the Irish constabulary under the inspector general and his immediate subordinates were at the outset designated sub-inspectors and chief constables. The rank and file comprised head constables, constables and sub-constables. In 1839 the ranks county inspector and sub-inspector replaced those of sub-inspector and chief constable. And in 1883 sub-inspectors, constables and sub-constables were termed district inspectors, sergeants and constables.[2] Two years earlier, in 1881, when Ireland was seriously disturbed, a new grade of police officers was created. Six 'special resident magistrates' were appointed, each of whom was responsible for co-ordinating and directing the activities of the forces of law and order in a group of counties. In 1883 their number was reduced to four and they were termed 'divisional magistrates'. Though these officers had the powers of a J.P. their duties were executive and in 1889 they were more happily designated 'divisional com-

---

[1] *The Times*, Aug. 1882, *Irish Times*, Aug./Sept. 1882.
[2] 6 & 7 Will. IV, c. 13; 2 & 3 Vict., c. 75; 46 & 47 Vict., c. 14.

missioners'. In 1898 the post of divisional commissioner was abolished.[1]

At the outset the force numbered about 8,400. From then onwards it fluctuated in size, reaching a strength of over 14,000 in the early 'eighties. In 1913 it was composed of just over 12,000 officers and men occupying about 1,300 stations. Between 1836 and 1846 each county met a moiety of the cost of the constabulary force stationed in it. In 1846 the cost of maintaining the constabulary was transferred to the imperial exchequer, each county being assigned what was considered to be an adequate police establishment (later known as its 'free quota'). If however extra police were temporarily needed in a disturbed area the county had to meet half the cost of the additional force. When in 1865, after violent rioting with which the town police was quite unable to cope, Belfast was made a constabulary district, the town was assigned a 'free quota', and a similar arrangement was made for Londonderry in 1885.[2]

The primary function of the R.I.C. was of course the maintenance of law and order. Keeping the peace in a largely agricultural community was normally humdrum work but it could involve coping with armed rebellion (on three occasions), dealing with serious sectarian rioting (as in Belfast in 1886), or handling widespread agrarian disturbances. And as the government was always concerned about the incidence of political and agrarian discontent, one of the duties of constabulary inspectors was to send up reports on conditions in their districts. From the middle of the nineteenth century a steady stream of such reports was flowing into the chief secretary's office, and from the middle 'eighties these reports were being largely used in the compilation of the 'Notes' on the state of the country which were prepared in the office for the chief secretary's use.[3]

But in addition to preserving the peace the constabulary had a number of other duties to perform. The government, as an

[1] *First report from the committee of public accounts*, pp. iv–v, H.C. 1889 (73), ix, *Hansard*, 4 series, lx, 1107.

[2] 6 & 7 Will. IV, c. 13; 9 & 10 Vict., c. 97; 11 & 12 Vict., 72; 28 & 29 Vict., c. 70; 33 & 34 Vict., c. 83.

[3] *Royal commission on the civil service, fourth report, evidence*, p. 183, H.C. 1914 [Cd. 7640], xvi.

inspector general explained, realizing that the R.I.C. was 'a highly disciplined and well educated body of men, spread over the whole face of the country, in a web of which every thread centres in Dublin', had steadily added to the duties of the force.[1] By the beginning of the twentieth century the R.I.C. was making inquiries on behalf of the congested districts board and the board of works, collecting agricultural statistics, acting as enumerators at the census,[2] enforcing the fishery laws and performing a variety of duties under the food and drugs, the weights and measures, the explosives and the petroleum acts. The department of agriculture and technical instruction greatly appreciated the help of the force in the collection of agricultural statistics and in checking foot and mouth disease. Gill, the secretary of the department, explained that the organization and discipline of the force enabled the department to bring measures for stamping out the disease rapidly into operation. And he stressed the amazing knowledge the police possessed of local farming conditions, adding that many members of the force had what he termed 'a sort of latent knowledge of farming output'.[3]

The other Irish police force, the Dublin Metropolitan Police, was responsible for an area which after 1901 covered thirty-six square miles, 'the police district of the Dublin metropolis'. The area was divided into six districts, each denoted by a letter of the alphabet, in each of which a division of the force was stationed. The seventh, or G division of the force, was its detective branch. And detachments of the D.M.P. were stationed at the Castle, the Four Courts, and the official residences in the Park.

The D.M.P., which in 1913 was nearly 1,200 strong, differed from the R.I.C. in several respects. Its officers, with the exception of the commissioners, had all risen from the ranks, and in training and tone the force was less military than the R.I.C. But the D.M.P. had a slightly higher standard of height than the R.I.C., and its men in their large, silver-faced helmets

---

[1] *Report of the proceedings of the Irish convention, appendices*, p. 122, H.C. 1918 [Cd 9019], x.

[2] See p. 283.

[3] *Royal Irish constabulary and Dublin metropolitan police: appendix to the report of the committee of inquiry*, pp. 310–14.

embodied law and order with massive dignity. When in 1917 it was suggested that the two police forces might be amalgamated, the chief commissioner of the D.M.P. strongly opposed the suggestion, pointing out that Dublin had special problems and that the D.M.P. was a city and civil force while the R.I.C. was largely rural and semi-military.[1]

Both police forces, the R.I.C. and the D.M.P. were efficient. Both played a conspicuous part in Irish life. Both on occasions clashed violently with large sections of the Irish public. In 1913 the D.M.P. found itself badly involved in the violent Dublin labour troubles of that year. The R.I.C. during periods of agrarian and political strife had to face widespread popular hostility. *United Ireland* for years cartooned them as the dark, brutal, sinister upholders of tyranny. And in 1886 the Orange rioters in Belfast denounced them as murderers. But the periods when the police forces were violently opposed to large sections of the public were short. For most of the time over most of the country the police were occupied in routine duties, they were part and parcel of local life and probably about as popular as the enforcers of the law are ever likely to be.

As has been pointed out, gaols in Ireland at the beginning of the nineteenth century were controlled by grand juries. Indeed when the government in 1798 and 1803 made numerous arrests, it had to lodge its prisoners in the Provost's Prison (a military prison) and Kilmainham (the Dublin county prison). The former turned out to be insecure and the latter became over-crowded, the debtors especially being greatly inconvenienced by the need to find space for the state prisoners.[2] But before the close of the eighteenth century the state had important permanent responsibilities in the sphere of prison administration. It controlled the Four Courts Marshalsea, it was responsible for a particular group of prisoners—convicts awaiting transportation—and it was empowered to inspect local prisons.

The Four Courts Marshalsea, near Thomas Street, mainly

[1] *Ibid.*, pp. 9, 254–68, *Report of the proceedings of the Irish convention, appendices*, pp. 126, 130.

[2] Official papers, 2 series, 512/52/11 and *Commons journ., Ire.*, xix. p. dcclx.

built about 1775, was the traditional prison for debtors from all over Ireland and its governor, the marshal, was appointed by the crown. In the early nineteenth century the Marshalsea was seriously overcrowded. Those prisoners who could afford to rent chambers from the marshal were not so badly off. But the poor debtors were crowded into the common halls in loathsome conditions. Living standards in the Marshalsea improved as the century progressed, but it was never easy to enforce discipline and the smuggling in of spirits sometimes led to disorder. In 1874, two years after imprisonment for debt was abolished, the Marshalsea prison was closed.[1]

At the beginning of the nineteenth century, 'convicts'—felons liable to transportation[2]—were often left for some time in the county gaols, the county prison authorities being frequently 'exceedingly incommoded by the incarceration of so many desperate offenders'.[3] Those from the north were ultimately collected in Dublin, being assembled at Newgate (the city prison) or Kilmainham, and then shipped by sloop or brig to Cork. Those from the south and west were collected at Cork. At Cork convicts while awaiting transportation to Australia were lodged in the city gaol. This was an unsatisfactory arrangement, and as early as 1792 the lord lieutenant was empowered to set up a penitentiary where convicts might be reformed by being compelled to work at useful trades. But nothing seems to have been done until the Richmond penitentiary in Dublin was opened in 1818. It housed convicts whose sentences of transportation had been commuted to imprisonment 'in the hope that they might be restored to society with morals corrected and purified'.[4]

In 1817 it was discovered that the Cork prison authorities were misapplying the government grants for the maintenance of convicts. The convicts were removed temporarily to the

---

[1] *Prisons of Ireland, report of inspectors general, 1823*, pp. 11, 18, H.C. 1823 (342), x; *Report from the select committee on the state of gaols*, pp. 207–8, H.C. 1819 (579), vii; *Report from the commissioners appointed to inquire into . . . the state prisons and other gaols in Ireland . . .*, p. 4, H.C. 1809 (265), vii.

[2] 2 Anne, c. 12; 17 & 18 Geo. III, c. 9.

[3] F. Archer to Gregory, 9 Sept. 1817 (Official papers, 2 series, 569/488/43).

[4] 32 Geo. III, c. 27. *Report from the select committee on the state of gaols, minutes of evidence*, pp. 217–8, H.C. 1819 (579), vii.

county gaol and an old barrack in Cork was converted into a convict depot.[1] Six years later two hulks, one at the Cove of Cork, the other at Kingstown, were also provided for the reception of convicts awaiting transportation. The convicts were set to work, the expenses of their maintenance strictly regulated and (at Cork at least) their characters marked weekly as a stimulus to good behaviour. These reforms (according to himself) were carried out by Dr Edward Trevor, who had been medical superintendent at Kilmainham (where he had bitter disputes with some of the state prisoners), and who was superintendent and medical inspector of convicts.[2] In 1836 it was discovered from inquiries conducted by the Irish executive that the convicts on the hulks were left without employment, and at night were locked up below deck without any arrangements for separation or supervision. The lord lieutenant decided that 'the hulk system' was 'most pernicious . . . a worse form of prison could scarcely be devised' and at the end of 1836 the hulks were dispensed with, the convicts awaiting transportation being assembled in Dublin, the male convicts at Kilmainham, the female at the Richmond prison, Grangegorman.[3]

On Trevor's death in 1837 the under-secretary, Thomas Drummond, directed Major Palmer, one of the inspectors-general of the prisons appointed in 1823, to supervise the convict department. This arrangement did not work well. Palmer was careless over certifying accounts and checking contracts (it was discovered for instance that he was permitting too much to be paid for bibles supplied to convicts before sailing), and in 1843 he was relieved of the management of the convict service, being replaced by Major Cottingham who was appointed superintendent of convicts.[4] In the next few years the convict department was to be subject to severe strain,

[1] *Report of the commissioners on abuses in the convict department at Cork*, H.C. 1817 (343), viii, *Report from the select committee on the state of gaols, minutes of evidence*, pp. 206–7.

[2] *Convict department, Cork . . .*, H.C. 1835 (535), xlv; *Report from the select committee on the state of gaols, minutes of evidence*, pp. 207–8; *Rules and regulations for the hulks Surprize and Essex*, Cork, 1832 (T. 1/3564–6).

[3] T. 1/3564–6.

[4] *Convict service (Ireland), returns and reports . . .*, pp. 4–8, 71, H.C. 1843 (547), xlii.

and, as will be explained later in this chapter, in the early 'fifties it was to be drastically remodelled.

At the beginning of the nineteenth century there were in Ireland 41 gaols and 112 bridewells. The former were the county prisons, the latter were 'secondary gaols' to which persons were committed for petty offences or under civil bill processes for the recovery of small debts. They also held prisoners '*in transitu*' to the county prisons.[1]

During the eighteenth century benevolent public opinion had been shocked by the conditions found to be prevalent in Irish prisons. These conditions were the product of a badly compounded blend of gross laxity and excessive severity which itself arose from the simple fact that little or no systematic attention had been paid to penal problems. Prisoners of both sexes and different degrees of criminality were herded together in hard and unhealthy surroundings. The insecurity of the Irish gaols, a prison reformer explained, was largely responsible for the harshness with which the prisoners were treated, and he quoted the instance of Naas where the upper parts of the gaol were so defective that criminals had to be packed in 'most loathsome, dark, damp dungeons, filled with stinking vapours'. But the gaoler was not inhumane and during the day he allowed the prisoners (apparently ironed) to beg in the street.[2] The prison population was greatly increased by the custom of confining debtors in prisons primarily intended for criminals. In Dublin at the end of the eighteenth century there were two debtor's prisons, the Marshalsea and the recently established Sheriffs prison.[3] But both in the capital, and of course in the country, debtors were held in the ordinary gaols. It perhaps may be added that the genteel debtors (carefully described in parliamentary reports as ladies and gentlemen), along with some of the political prisoners who were flung into gaol at the turn of the century, provided emphatic evidence for the prison

---

[1] *Prisons of Ireland: report of the inspectors general*, pp. 69–71. H.C. 1823 (342), x; *Report from the select committee on the state of gaols, minutes of evidence*, pp. 191–2, H.C. 1819 (579), vii.

[2] *Commons journ., Ire.*, xi. cxxxi.

[3] The Sheriffs prison was opened in 1794 with the object of preventing the 'the abuses of sponging houses'. (*Report from the commissioners appointed to inquire into . . . the state prisons and other gaols in Ireland . . .*, p. 21, H.C. 1809 (265), vii.)

reformers. As members of the middle class they found the roughness of prison life insufferable.

As early as 1729 the house of commons appointed a committee to inquire into the state of prisons. It reported that the keeper of Newgate had been guilty of gross cruelty.[1] Half a century elapsed, and then, probably stimulated by the movement for prison reform inspired by John Howard,[2] parliament passed an act for preserving the health of prisoners. Attributing disease to 'a want of cleanliness and fresh air', it directed justices of the peace to order the regular whitewashing of gaols, to arrange proper ventilation and provide a bath or tubs. The cost of these improvements was to be met by the county.[3]

Some years later after a committee presided over by Peter Holmes, an enthusiast for penal reform, had reported, three important measures were passed in 1782, 1783 and 1786. These three statutes increased the powers and responsibilities of grand juries in respect of prisons. In each county the grand jury was to inquire into the state of the gaol and if necessary enlarge it, contracts for this purpose being advertised for. If needs be the land required for prison extension was to be obtained by compulsory purchase. In new gaols there were to be dry and airy cells and distinct yards for debtors, accused persons, convicted felons and lesser criminals. In every gaol there were to be common halls in which during the colder months of the year fires should be kept going for some hours every day. In all gaols certain regulations were to be enforced. The gaoler, who with his assistants was to be paid by the grand jury, was to be resident. He was not to sell malt or spirituous liquors to prisoners. He was to provide threepence worth of food per day per prisoner. Rooms were to be kept clean, livestock was not to be kept in gaol yards. In each county the grand jury was to appoint an inspector of prisons. As the Dublin gaols contained a large population, the grand jury of the city was to submit three names to the court of king's bench, which was to select one. The Dublin inspector was to be paid £100 per annum. If a person of 'public spirit and liberal fortune' was willing to

[1] *Ibid.*, iii. ccclxxxvi–ix.
[2] J. Howard, *State of the prisons*, 1777–80. Howard also describes Irish prison conditions in *An account of the principal lazarettos in Europe* (1789), pp. 78–112.
[3] 17 & 18 Geo. III, c. 28.

act as inspector of prisons in Dublin without taking a salary, then the grand jury could pay a deputy appointed by the inspector £60 per annum. Finally and perhaps most significantly of all, the lord lieutenant was empowered in 1786 to appoint an inspector general, who during his first two years in office was to visit all the gaols in Ireland, receive the reports of local inspectors and present a report on prison conditions to both houses of parliament.[1] The first inspector general was Sir Jeremiah Fitzpatrick, known as 'the second Howard'. Though his views on the propagation of infection were scientifically unsound, he grasped the connection between cleanliness and health and until he left Ireland to be inspector of health in the army he was a zealous advocate of prison reform.[2]

After the union the complaints of the Irish state prisoners and the reports of Fitzpatrick's successor as inspector general drew attention again to prison conditions. Sheridan secured the appointment of a commission of inquiry composed of two lawyers, a clergyman, a medical man and a banker, and following the appearance of its reports, which showed conditions to be very unsatisfactory, the government requested Downes, the chief justice of the king's bench, and the law officers to draft a prisons bill which was passed in 1810.[3] It was both an important consolidation act and the first of a group of measures which were consolidated in the prisons act of 1826. These measures were intended to have the same effect as the legislation of the seventeen-eighties—to fix uniform and fairly high standards of prison administration for the whole country. But the standards were higher, the regulations were far more precise and detailed and the government's supervisory powers were greatly strengthened. Though county prisons were to be built by the grand juries their plans had to be approved by the lord lieutenant who might 'on the faith' of county presentments advance money for their construction from the consolidated fund. In each county the grand jury was to appoint a board of superintendance of eight to twelve members, half of whom were to be justices of the peace. Prison officials, who were appointed by the high sheriff or grand jury and paid by

[1] 21 & 22 Geo. III, c. 42; 23 & 24 Geo. III, c. 41; 26 Geo. III, c. 27.
[2] *Gentleman's magazine*, lxxx. 187.
[3] *Hansard*, 1 series, xi. 1131, xv. 468; 50 Geo. III, c. 103.

the county, were absolutely forbidden to receive fees—and a notice to this effect was to be conspicuously displayed in every gaol. And the king's bench was empowered to dismiss summarily any official guilty of misconduct. In all prisons a rigorous division was to be made between male and female prisoners, but in county gaols and houses of correction a much more rigorous system of classification was to be observed. Debtors, felons, those guilty of misdemeanors, persons awaiting trial and vagrants were all to be separated. Cleanliness was insisted on. There was to be a supply of good water, walls were to be whitewashed, cells were to be washed, bed straw was to be regularly changed and prisoners were to be provided with 'an adequate allowance of soap, towels and combs'. No prisoner was to be put in a dungeon nor—unless it was absolutely necessary—in irons.[1]

And to ensure that standards were maintained the lord lieutenant was empowered in 1822 to appoint two inspectors general who would regularly visit and report on all gaols and bridewells. The inspectors general were directed to supply each prison with a 'dietary table', and empowered to report prison officers guilty of misconduct to the king's bench and to compel the counties to supply their prisons with sufficient bedding and other requisites.[2] The first two inspectors general were Major Benjamin Woodward, who had served in the Cavan militia and who remained in office until his death in 1841, and Major James Palmer. Palmer, who had served in the 96th and on the staff in Ireland, acquired some first-hand experience of prison life: in the early 'thirties he was confined for a short period in Kilmainham as a debtor. But in spite of this mishap he remained an inspector general until some years after Woodward's death.'[3]

The energy with which Woodward and Palmer threw themselves into their duties is evinced by their reports, which describe in minute detail illuminated by terse comment conditions in the prisons they visited. 'Prisoners', they emphasized, 'had not

---

[1] 7 Geo. IV, c. 74.   [2] 3 Geo. IV, c. 64.

[3] *Army list*, 1814, Memorandum by James Palmer, 17 Dec. 1813 (Add. MSS 40232), *Returns of reports . . . on complaints forwarded to the Irish government . . . and of evidence taken relative to the mode of conducting the convict service in Ireland*, pp. 41, 53, 74, H.C. 1843 (547), xlii.

forfeited their claims on society. On returning to the world they would be worse or better men according to the use made of their imprisonment'.[1] Therefore the inspectors general set to work to persuade the boards of superintendence to make extensive and expensive improvements to their gaols. At first the inspectors found 'a great proportion of otherwise enlightened magistrates, active promoters of public good, impressed with almost unconquerable prejudices against a system which, though originating in the philanthropy of individuals, [had] received the sanction of the legislature'.[2] But they soon noticed the readiness of grand juries to take up the subject of prison discipline and the inspectors general generously declared in 1842 that it was to the zeal of the county authorities that most of the improvements in the Irish prison system were due. This is certainly notable in one sphere, building. At the close of the eighteenth century Fitzpatrick had observed with pleasure that new gaols had been built or were being built in almost every county.[3] But the beginning of the nineteenth century was a revolutionary era in prison architecture, and in 1823 the inspectors regretted that there were only five Irish gaols built on up-to-date lines, that is to say, constructed functionally so as to permit the separation and close supervision of the prisoners in healthy surroundings. Of these five gaols, four—Ennis, Galway, Roscommon and Sligo—were built on a semi-circular plan, and one, Limerick, on a 'radical' one. In addition, the city of Londonderry was building a magnificent new prison, modern in lay-out and, as a proud citizen boasted, exhibiting 'a good deal of architectural variety' with its fashionable battlements and castellated turrets.[4] And at least nine other counties were making improvements in their prisons. In the following year four new gaols, Londonderry, Louth, Longford and Monaghan were completed, all semi-circular in pattern. Of the new prisons the most striking was Lanyon's gaol at Belfast, 'the model

---

[1] *Prisons of Ireland: seventeenth report of the inspectors general . . . appendix*, p. 33, H.C. 1839 (91), xx.

[2] *Eighth report of the inspectors general on . . . the prisons of Ireland*, p. 6, H.C. 1830 (48), xxiv.

[3] *Commons journ., Ire.*, xv. ccccviii.

[4] Attached to the governor's house was an 'panoptic' from which all the yards could be surveyed (R. Simpson, *The annals of Derry* (1847), pp. 242–3).

prison of Ireland', with an exterior of heavy gloom calculated to strike terror into the heart of the wrongdoer.[1]

But though properly planned buildings were necessary, 'experience', the inspectors general remarked, 'has convinced us that too much comparative importance has been attached to the nature of the buildings . . . in fact faults have arisen from a want of conscientious and efficient officers, attentive committees, effective inspection, and order and cleanliness in the gaol,[2] governors, the inspectors declared, should be gentlemen 'whose education and rank of life are calculated to secure the respect and obedience of their inferiors'. And they pointed out that a governor's remuneration when all allowances were taken into account was sufficient to attract a gentleman. The turnkeys, the inspectors insisted, should be uniformed, assigned to clearly demarcated duties, and if possible lodged in the gaol.[3] The inspectors general were very pleased when in 1830 the military guards which had been maintained at Irish gaols to prevent escapes were removed, for they believed that this would have a stimulating effect on the prison staffs, compelling them to be alert and take an interest in their charges. As for the prisoners, the inspectors were very anxious that they should be treated with a judicious blend of kindness and severity. Not only were they to be properly fed and exercised and kept in warm and healthy quarters (so that from the material point of view the prisoner's lot might compare favourably with that of many Irish cottars), but they were at the same time to be subject to a system of moral discipline and instruction, so that a prison would be 'a living scene of industry and instruction'. When a governor argued that it would be dangerous to place hammers in the hands of prisoners an inspector general replied that this attitude indicated an inability to control his fellow men.[4]

[1] *Twenty-first report of the inspectors general on . . . the prisons of Ireland*, p. 26, H.C. 1843 (462), xxvii.

[2] *Prisons of Ireland: report of the inspectors general . . .*, p. 7 H.C. 1823 (342), x.

[3] *Report of the inspectors general on the . . . prisons of Ireland*, p. 11, H.C. 1825 (493) xxii; *Sixth report of the inspectors general on . . . the prisons of Ireland*, pp. 13–5, H.C. 1828 (68), xii.

[4] *Prisons of Ireland: seventh report of the inspectors general*, p. 7, H.C. 1829 (10), xiii; *Eighth report of the inspectors general*, pp. 7–8, 58, H.C. 1830 (48), xxiv; *Eleventh report of the inspectors general*, p. 7, H.C. 1833 (67), xvii.

One of the worst features of eighteenth century prison administration had been the facilities afforded for 'contamination by association'. Prison reformers by 1830 were vigorously debating which was the better remedy—'entire separation' or silence. The former system was officially approved for Ireland in 1840, when boards of superintendence were allowed (with the approval of the lord lieutenant) to make rules for the individual separation of prisoners.[1] The inspectors general highly approved of the separate system which they thought afforded every aid to moral improvement, offered the prisoner an opportunity to learn a profitable trade, and 'protected the well disposed against *offensive* while it deprives the hardened offender of congenial society'. They had to admit in 1837 that most of the Irish county gaols had been built or extended before the new system was advocated. But they urged that in every gaol which was to be constructed provision should be made for each prisoner to have a separate cell.[2] They were also eager that prisoners should be provided with 'profitable employment' so that a period of imprisonment as well as being a punishment would be of 'permanent benefit' to the prisoner. And the inspectors general were pleased to be able to report at the beginning of 1838 that a female penitentiary had recently been opened at Grangegorman for female prisoners from county Dublin and female convicts, with a matron chosen by Mrs Fry.[3]

The famine threw a severe strain in the Irish prison system. Understandably, in a period of acute distress, there was an increase in committals, and parliament by passing the vagrants' act, which empowered magistrates to sentence beggars to a month's imprisonment, increased the strain on accommodation. The prison population rose steeply. Gaols were crammed. Individual work had to be given up. Classification was disregarded; separation was impossible; disease and death increased. The inspectors general who were greatly disturbed by the deplorable conditions resulting from over-crowding, took

---

[1] 3 & 4 Vict., c. 44.

[2] *Fifteenth report of the inspectors general on . . . the prisons of Ireland*, p. 8, H.C. 1837 (123) xxxi and *Eighteenth report*, p. 7, H.C. 1840 (240), xxvi.

[3] *Prisons of Ireland, sixteenth report of the inspectors general*, p. 6, H.C. 1837–8 (186), xxix, *Seventeenth report*, pp. 16–7, H.C. 1839 (91), xx.

one important step. On discovering that the superiority of the prison to the workhouse dietary was inducing paupers to try to be sent to gaol, they reduced the scale of the prison dietary. And in their next report they were able to congratulate themselves that this decision had led to a reduction in expenditure while not apparently adversely affecting the prisoners' health.[1]

After 1850 the prison population began to fall—a trend which continued to the close of the century. But besides the immediate difficulties created by the famine the end of the forties saw the emergence of a permanent problem in Irish prison administration. The growing reluctance of the colonies to accept convicts (the last ship-load left Ireland in 1856) compelled the authorities to confine and punish them at home. In 1853 it was made possible to substitute a sentence of penal servitude for transportation, and in 1857 it was enacted that a sentence of penal servitude could be abridged by good behaviour.[2] In Ireland the government, as the overseas outlets narrowed, found itself with a mass of convicts, numbering in 1855 about 4,000, on its hands. Drastic measures had to be taken to house and control them, Mountjoy (completed in 1850), a depot at Smithfield and the barracks at Spike Island being used.[3] In 1849 Hitchins, a clerk in the chief secretary's office, was appointed superintendent of Mountjoy and inspector of government prisons. He seems to have found his duties almost overwhelming and in 1854 a commission which included Crofton and Knight of the English prison service reported that the Irish government prisons were over-crowded and the prisoners' labour ill-organized.[4]

In 1854 legal authority for the management of the government prisons (i.e. the convict prisons) was secured by legislation. The lord lieutenant was empowered to appoint a board of directors of convict prisons composed of not more than three persons.[5] The first chairman of this board was Sir Walter

[1] *Prisons of Ireland, twenty-eighth report of the inspectors general,* p. ix, H.C. 1850 [1229], xxix, *twenty-ninth report,* p. xii, H.C. 1851 [1364], xxviii.

[2] 20 & 21 Vict., c. 3.

[3] *Annual report of the inspector of government prisons in Ireland for the year ended 31 Dec. 1851,* H.C. 1852-3 [1634], liii.

[4] *Convict prisons etc. (Ireland); copies of correspondence,* H.C. 1854 (344), lviii.

[5] 17 & 18 Vict., c. 76; *First report of the select committee on transportation,* p. 139, H.C. 1856 (244), xvii.

Crofton, who had served in the Royal Engineers and the English prison service. With tremendous zeal for his work he held strong views on prison administration, as can be seen from his pamphlets and the evidence he gave before parliamentary committees. The criminal class, he thought, constituted a serious and expensive social menace, but the convict, he believed could often be turned into a useful member of society. Therefore Crofton was especially concerned both to prepare the convict for freedom and to keep a watch over him for some time after his release.[1] Crofton's two colleagues were Captain Knight, who had been governor of Portsmouth prison, and Lentaigne, an Irish medical man who played an important part in the creation of the Irish reformatory and industrial school system and who was an early and enthusiastic advocate of photography as a method of criminal identification.

Crofton and his colleagues quickly took steps to improve the Irish convict system. Additional accommodation was provided by a prison of iron huts set up at Philipstown, discipline in the prison service was tightened up, it being made clear that any officer found drunk would be dismissed, prisoners were classified and graded and their records carefully compiled, and it was arranged that a convict at the beginning of his sentence should have a period of separate confinement. After release convicts were subject to a period of police supervision, and before release they might spend some time in an intermediate prison. Of these there were two, Smithfield (closed in 1869) and Lusk, to which a farm was attached (closed in 1886). In these establishments, of which Crofton was exceedingly proud, convicts were employed in trades or in farming, and allowed a wide measure of freedom. They were also given a series of educative and morally improving lectures on subjects such as the pursuit of knowledge under difficulties, remarkable inventions, temperance and the cost of drunkenness, the wonders of science, and what a man with brains may do. The 'individualism' which was a feature of the intermediate prison enabled the conduct of the

---

[1] W. Crofton, *A few remarks on the 'convict question'* (1857) and *The immunity of 'habitual criminals' with a few propositions for reducing their number* (1861); *Royal commission on prisons in Ireland*, vol. I . . ., pp. 151–6, H.C. 1884–5 [C. 4233], xxxviii and *Reformatories and industrial schools commission . . . report . . . together with minutes of evidence*, p. 508, H.C. 1884 [C. 3876–1], xlv.

convict to be observed and prepared him for the outside world.[1]

The Irish and English convict systems were in general similar. But two striking features of the former which have been mentioned, attracted considerable attention, police supervision and the intermediate prison. Jebb, the energetic surveyor general of British convict prisons, stung by suggestions that he had overlooked ideas of value to the English system, strongly criticized the intermediate prison in a report he published in 1858.[2] Crofton was 'very sore' on reading this report and the Irish directors in their next report launched into a long justification of the intermediate prison.[3] Thus two government departments clashed publicly over an issue of policy. Jebb and Crofton expounded their views at the 1862 meeting of the Social Science Association and a number of fiercely partisan pamphlets and articles on penal methods appeared.[4] Jebb had a fiery Irish supporter in Gibson, the presbyterian chaplain of Spike Island, who was a prolific miscellaneous author.[5] Gibson strongly disapproved of 'police espionage' and had little faith in intermediate prisons. 'The prisoners', he remarked, 'of course liked them and make "prison character" to get where they say they will be comfortable'.[6] Gibson when preparing a book on Irish prison life in which he denounced the distinctive features of the Irish system, got in touch with Jebb. And Jebb, though he advised him to eschew personalities, supplied him with information and corrected his proofs.[7] Characteristically, in contemporary Ireland, Gibson disapproved of Crofton for theological reasons. He believed that Crofton was acting under the

---

[1] *Report of the commissioners appointed to inquire into the working of the penal servitude acts . . . minutes of evidence*, p. 1032, H.C. 1878–9 [2368–11], xxxviii; *First report from the select committee on transportation*, p. 143, H.C. 1856 (244), xvii.

[2] Jebb to Waddington, draft, 16 Apr. 1861 (Jebb papers), *Report on the discipline of convict prisons for 1856 and 1857*, pp. 90–106, H.C. 1857–8, 2414, xxix.

[3] Whitty to Jebb, 17 Oct. 1861 (Jebb papers).

[4] *Transactions of the national association for the promotion of social science, 1861*, pp. 493–5, *1862*, pp. 358–95.

[5] C. B. Gibson, *Life among convicts*, 2 vols.

[6] Gibson to Jebb, 15 Sept. 1862 (Jebb papers).

[7] Jebb to Gibson, 5 Dec. 1862 (Jebb papers).

influence of the ultramontane party and was a danger to freedom and the constitution.[1]

Whitty, Crofton's second-in-command, was in an awkward position. He had served under Jebb and wanted to get back to England, but loyalty to his superior debarred him from supplying Jebb with information which could be used in an attack on the Irish system.[2] He did not in fact think there was anything distinctive in the treatment of convicts in Ireland except the intermediate prison, the success of which he argued was largely the result of Irish conditions. Irish prisoners, he explained, were usually 'biddable fellows' and did not suffer so badly from association as English ones. 'There are', he wrote, 'fierce and accomplished scoundrels among them, and when a fellow is bad it comes out so decidedly and openly that there is less of the under-current of evil than prevails among the English convicts who are such adepts at dodges'.[3] Whitty indeed regretted that the two convict systems were regarded as being completely separate. Otherwise, he explained, Jebb could send catholic convicts to Ireland and dispense with catholic chaplains on his side of the channel, 'a happy arrangement for you'.[4]

In 1862 Crofton retired and Lentaigne became an inspector general of prisons. The result was that, for a short time there was only a single director of convict prisons, Whitty; and though in 1863 Murray, the inspector of reformatories, was appointed a director (continuing, however, to hold his inspectorship), again from 1873 to 1877 Barlow was the sole director of convict prisons. Both Crofton and Whitty deplored the reduction in the number of directors, arguing that the efficiency of the system depended on close attention to detail.[5] On the other hand by 1870 the convict population had fallen to about 1,200.

In the same year the number of prisoners detained in local prisons amounted to only a little over 2,000. The central government's control over local prison administration had been

[1] Gibson to Jebb, undated, (Jebb papers).
[2] Whitty to Jebb, 27 Apr., 18 Aug. 1858, 1 Sept. 1862 (Jebb papers).
[3] Whitty to Jebb, 1 Jan. 1858 (Jebb papers).
[4] Whitty to Jebb, 29 May 1858 (Jebb papers).
[5] *Penal servitude acts commission, report . . .*, pp. 996–7, H.C. 1878–9, [C. 2368–11], xxxviii.

strengthened by the prisons act of 1856. Plans for new prison buildings had to receive the lord lieutenant's sanction, and he was empowered to alter rules made by local boards of superintendence and to dismiss prison officers. It was also laid down that prisons were to be lit by gas, that prisoners serving a sentence of longer than a year should wear prison dress, and that all prisoners were to be provided with two bed sheets.[1]

By the 'sixties however the inspectors general were pressing for sweeping changes. They favoured the abolition of imprisonment for debt and a repeal of the act authorizing the confinement of dangerous lunatics in gaol. They also strongly advocated a reduction in the number of local prisons, since, as they frequently pointed out, many of the prisons were not designed to provide for an adequate degree of separation.[2] In 1866 and 1867 a prisons bill was introduced in the commons. The first bill fixed higher standards for local prisons and strengthened the powers of the inspectors general. The second bill, introduced by Lord Mayo, who took a keen interest in prison reform both in Ireland and India, went further. It provided for the creation of district prisons serving several counties. Both these bills failed to reach the statute book as did two other Irish prison bills, introduced in 1872 and 1876. Finally, in 1877, the general prisons (Ireland) act was passed. It abolished the directors of convict prisons, the inspectors general of prisons, the boards of superintendence, and the registrar of criminals, vesting their powers in the newly created general prisons board, composed of a chairman and not more than three other members. All prisons were placed under the control of this board and all prison expenditure was to be met from the imperial exchequer. A visiting committee of justices of the peace was to be appointed by the grand jury of each county which was to visit prisons in the county, hear complaints and report abuses.[3]

The general prisons board took over four convict prisons, thirty-eight local prisons and ninety-five bridewells. Ten years

[1] 19 & 20, Vict., c. 68.
[2] *Forty-fifth report of the inspectors general on . . . the prisons of Ireland*, pp. xl–lviii, H.C. 1867 [3915], xxxv; *Forty-seventh report*, pp. xliv–v, H.C. 1868–9 [4205], xxix.
[3] 40 & 41, Vict., c. 49.

before, the inspectors general in a published memorandum had condemned the Irish bridewells as being damp, insanitary and insecure, adding that the bridewell keepers were often eking out their scanty salaries by engaging in a second occupation or occasionally by 'trenching upon the prisoners' allowance, or by the falsification of the diet accounts'.[1] The general prisons board immediately shut 52 bridewells. This was in accordance with the board's general policy. Believing that larger units made for better administration, it adopted from the first a policy of prison consolidation. And by 1914 the 137 prisons placed under the board in 1877 had been reduced to 23, this latter figure comprising a convict prison (Maryborough), a convict and local prison (Mountjoy), 14 local prisons (including one solely female and three solely male), 5 bridewells, an inebriates' reformatory and a borstal.

From the start the board was eager to emphasize the reformatory as well as the punitive aspect of prison treatment. The board's rules, which granted privileges for good behaviour, encouraged prisoners to conduct themselves properly.[2] By the 'nineties all non-productive labour (such as the treadmill) had been abolished in Irish gaols. A considerable amount of work was done for government departments (such as the manufacture of mail bags) and prisoners were also employed on prison construction work and sometime in agriculture. And the board was so eager to encourage agricultural work that it purchased a farm of 34 acres adjoining Maryborough.[3] The plank bed was abolished in gaols (except as a punishment), prisoners were allowed to associate at work, prison libraries were provided and efforts were made to improve the educational facilities in prison. The 1902 rules permitted lectures to be arranged in Irish prisons and in 1904 the first of these was given, in Dundalk gaol, on temperance.[4] Indeed in its report

---

[1] *Forty-fifth report of the inspectors general on . . . the prisons of Ireland*, pp. xlv–lii, H.C. 1867 [3915], xxxv.

[2] For the board's rules see *Prisons (Ireland) . . . general rules . . .*, H.C. 1882 (31–4) liv; *Rules and regulations in force in prisons in Ireland*, H.C. 1888 (329) lxxxii; *Dublin Gazette*, 12 Aug. 1902, 9 Apr. 1915.

[3] *Seventeenth report of the general prisons board, Ireland*, p. 10, H.C. 1895 [C. 7806], lvi; *Eighteenth report*, pp. 11–2, H.C. 1896 [C. 8252], xliv.

[4] *Twenty-seventh report of the general prisons board, Ireland*, p. xii, H.C. 1905 [Cd. 2659], xxxvii; *Twenty-eighth report*, pp. x–xii, H.C. 1906 [Cd. 3103], li.

for 1908 the board went so far as to assert that for many Irish prisoners 'the shelter of a prison with its wholesome food, equable temperature (the cells and passages during the winter months are heated day and night) and healthy occupation, is not merely a beneficial but stimulating change—a real though not luxurious sanatorium'.[1] If the board was somewhat complacent, it seems to have been trying hard to manage its prisons efficiently and by a mixture of firmness and leniency to reform their inmates, who were largely, in the board's eyes, 'human derelicts, drink-sodden and mentally or physically deficient'.[2]

The board was concerned at the high proportion of prisoners who were committed for offences arising from drunkenness, and in 1895 it pointed out that habitual drunkards when committed to prison had to be treated as patients not prisoners.[3] In 1899 it opened an inebriates' reformatory at Ennis. In this reformatory an attempt was made to cure habitual drunkards who had been given a prison sentence, by subjecting them to steady, healthy work and religious and educational influences in cheerful surroundings.[4] The board also strongly disapproved of juveniles being sent to prison. In 1892 it suggested that magistrates should make more use of the first offenders act.[5] And about this time the chairman of the board when he discovered that a boy of ten had been sentenced to 14 days in Clonmel gaol and two years in a reformatory for throwing missiles at the electric telegraph, reported the case to the lords justices who cancelled the reformatory sentence.[6] In 1896 the board issued rules providing that juveniles should be separated from other prisoners and taught a trade.[7] In 1904 it drew magistrates'

[1] *Thirtieth report of the general prisons board, Ireland*, p. xii, H.C. 1908 [Cd. 4253], lii.

[2] *Thirty-sixth report of the general prisons board, Ireland*, p. x, H.C. 1914 [Cd. 7469], xlv. For a general summary of the improvements in prison conditions which occurred between 1895 and 1905 see *Twenty-eighth report of the general prisons board, Ireland*, pp. x–xiv, H.C. 1906 [Cd. 3103], li.

[3] *Seventeenth report of the general prisons board, Ireland*, p. 4, H.C. 1895 [C. 7806], lvi.

[4] *Twenty-third report of the general prisons board, Ireland*, pp. 16–20, H.C. 1901 [Cd. 707], xxxii.   [5] 50 & 51 Vict., c. 25.

[6] *Fourteenth report of the general prisons board, Ireland*, p. 12, H.C. 1892 [C. 6789], xlii.

[7] *Nineteenth report of the general prisons board, Ireland*, p. 7, H.C. 1897 [C. 8589], xl.

attention to the youthful offenders act, and it was very pleased with the children's act of 1908 which practically put a stop to sending children (i.e., those under 16) to prison.[1] For offenders between 16 and 21 the board took steps in 1906 to provide borstal training, a system which combined education, technical instruction and physical training under skilled super-vision. And in 1910 Clonmel prison became a borstal.[2]

Other special institutions for young delinquents had been established during the nineteenth century. In the early 'fifties a house of commons select committee investigated juvenile delinquency. A number of witnesses, several of them from Ireland, stressed the need for reformatories to which juvenile offenders could be committed. Berwick, the assistant barrister for County Cork, an intelligent and sensitive man, told the committee that children could be sent to gaol for 'mere begging' and that he had tried children 'who were so small that the turnkey in the dock was obliged to hold them up that I could see them'. He also pointed out that 'once a child passes the threshold of a gaol a change certainly takes place in its own feelings and in the feelings of the public towards him'. In prison, Berwick added, the bad prisoners were generally the cleverest and so able to 'produce an effect on the mind of a young and clever boy'.[3]

The committee recommended that penal reformatories for young persons should be established and in 1856 Crofton took steps to acquire land at Lusk for a reformatory which would be managed by the directors of convict prisons. But another solu-tion was adopted. In 1858 an act was passed authorizing the chief secretary to certify institutions established by voluntary effort as reformatories. The treasury and local bodies could make grants to certified reformatories and the lord lieutenant was empowered to appoint an inspector of reformatories. A person under 16 convicted of any offence (except vagrancy)

[1] *Twenty-sixth report of the general prisons board, Ireland*, p. xii, H.C. 1904 [Cd. 2194], xxxv; *Thirty-first report of the general prisons board, Ireland*, p. xii, H.C. 1909 [Cd. 4792], xlv.

[2] *Twenty-ninth report of the general prisons board, Ireland*, pp. x–xi, H.C. 1907 [Cd. 3698], xxxi; *Thirty-third report*, pp. xv–xvii, H.C. 1911 [Cd. 5785], xxxix.

[3] *Report from the select committee on criminal and destitute children together with the . . . minutes of evidence*, pp. 342–51, H.C. 1852–3 (674,) xxiii.

could be sent to a reformatory.[1] The reformatory was obviously meant to be an alternative to prison, but when the bill was passing through the house of commons an important amendment was carried to the effect that no offender could be sent to a reformatory unless also given a prison sentence of at least 14 days. The object of this amendment was 'to prevent children being made chargeable without sufficient cause on these reformatories'.[2] The result of the amendment was of course to bring children into contact with prison life before reaching the reformatory. In 1868 the exception of vagrancy from the offences which might lead to committal to a reformatory was abolished.[3] And in 1893 the obligation to impose a prison sentence on an offender committed to a reformatory was done away with.[4]

In 1868 the treasury was empowered to make grants to industrial schools established by voluntary efforts. Children under 14 who were destitute and children under 12 convicted at petty sessions could be sent to these schools. The inspector of reformatories was thenceforth in addition inspector of industrial schools.[5] He also was usually one of the prison commissioners, an arrangement which promoted the co-operation of two systems with similar problems. In 1914 there were 5 reformatories and 66 industrial schools.

[1] 21 & 22 Vict., c. 103. [2] *Hansard*, 3 series, cli. 1067–9.
[3] 31 & 32 Vict., c. 59. [4] 56 & 57 Vict., c. 48.
[5] 31 & 32 Vict., c. 25.

VI

LOCAL GOVERNMENT, POOR LAW AND PUBLIC HEALTH

~~~~~~

LOCAL GOVERNMENT, poor relief and public health were so closely related in nineteenth-century Ireland that it is convenient to group together the departments which handled them. At the beginning of the century the central government had not much contact with the local authorities, the grand juries in the counties and the corporations in the cities and boroughs. There was no government department specially responsible for local affairs. Admittedly a very substantial proportion of the legislation passed by the Irish parliament could be classified under 'local government'. But the great bulk of this legislation simply consisted of acts authorizing a local body to carry out a specific project—very often the improvement of a stretch of road or the construction of a bridge. Again the crown annually appointed the high sheriffs (who selected the grand juries) and the assize judges approved the grand jury presentments.[1] But it must be quickly added that the judge's fiant (assent) seemed to have been usually a formality, and the crown in the appointment of a high sheriff and the high sheriff when selecting grand jurors were limited in their choice by contemporary convention. On the whole, then, at the beginning of the

---

[1] *Report of the method of raising and appropriating money by presentments*, pp. 20, 24, 36, 46, H.C. 1814–5 (283), vi.

nineteenth century the state interfered very little with local administration. One exception, however, to this generalization should be mentioned immediately. From the middle of the eighteenth century the government intervened vigorously in the municipal affairs of the capital, and for this reason Dublin will be dealt with in a short section at the end of this chapter.

As the nineteenth century progressed, the government both began to supervise in some detail the activities of local bodies and even took over some of their more important functions. The lord lieutenant was empowered to make arrangements for the audit of county (in 1836) and borough (in 1840) accounts. The government supervised local lunatic asylums (from 1817) and took over from the county authorities the control of the police (in 1836) and of prisons (in 1877). During the nineteenth century the state co-operated with local authorities in attempting to tackle some of the problems created by poverty and sickness. And the government department created to supervise the working of the poor law system became in time responsible for public health and finally was transformed into the local government board.

The achievements of the state in the related fields of poor relief and public health during the eighteenth and early nineteenth centuries can be easily summarized. It attempted little and its efforts were almost entirely confined to encouraging the action of local authorities and charitable institutions. The Elizabethan poor law had not been extended to Ireland, so the destitute and impotent poor had no right to relief and the English poor law machinery based on the parish did not exist. In 1772 the Irish parliament had enacted that in every county and county of a city or town a corporation should be constituted, composed of clergymen, M.P.s, magistrates and those who subscribed substantially, to erect and maintain 'workhouses or houses of industry'. The helpless poor were to be badged and licensed to beg or supported in these houses. Vagrants were to be swept into the houses and kept for terms of hard labour. This act remained inoperative over most of Ireland. Only half-a-dozen corporations seem to have been constituted, and if to their houses of industry there are added a few others founded under local acts there were half a score of such institutions functioning in Ireland at the beginning of the nineteenth century.[1]

Little then was done by the state, even indirectly, for the destitute and impotent. There was, however, a section of the poor whose condition especially appealed to eighteenth-century benevolence—the sick. During the century a number of hospitals were founded in Ireland. And in 1765 parliament made a statutory annual grant to three Dublin hospitals (the Charitable Infirmary, Mercer's and the Hospital for Incurables) and took steps to encourage the foundation of county infirmaries.[2] The subscribers to an infirmary were to form a corporation responsible for its erection and management, the grand jury could make grants for its maintenance, and the surgeon of each infirmary was to be paid a salary of £100 per annum 'out of the public money' (i.e. by the government). These infirmaries were obviously of little value to the sick poor outside a narrow radius round each house, so they were supplemented by dispensaries where advice and medicine could be obtained. In 1815 it was enacted that, whenever the governors of an infirmary certified that a dispensary had been established, the grand jury could subsidize it up to the amount subscribed. By 1845 there were scattered through Ireland about 660 dispensaries. The system had obvious defects. There was a lack of supervision. The distribution of the dispensaries depended on local generosity, and as setting up a dispensary was a way of helping a medical man or attracting a new doctor to the neighbourhood, needless to say there were competing charities in some areas.[3] Still the main aim of the subscribers was to help the sick poor, and the voluntary dispensary system proved an important forerunner of the public system which was to be founded in 1851.

The great fever epidemic of 1817–18 shocked the state into taking steps for the preservation of public health. In the autumn of 1817 a small committee, known as 'the fever committee', was

---

[1] 11 & 12 Geo. III, c. 30, *Commissioners for auditing public accounts of Ireland, sixteenth report*, H.C. 1824, (330), xii and *Select committee on the state of the poor in Ireland*, pp. 30–2, H.C. 1830 (667), vii.

[2] *Comm. Journ. Ire.*, xiii. cxcv, 5 Geo. III, c. 20.

[3] *Poor relief and medical charities, appendix . . .*, p. 473, H.C. 1846 (694), xi.

set up to advise the government on applications for financial aid from districts which were suffering severely, and a year later a central committee was formed by the government 'to promote communication and concert' among the Dublin hospitals. The government also appointed four inspectors, one for each province.[1] Their reports were referred to a select committee of the house of commons, and its recommendations formed the basis of an act passed in 1819 which empowered parishes to appoint officers of health who were to direct the cleansing of the streets. In the previous year (1818) as 'fevers of an infectious nature had for some time prevailed among the poor in several parts of Ireland, whereby the health and property of the whole country had been considerably endangered', steps were taken to set up fever hospitals. In each county and county of a city or town a corporation was created consisting of *ex-officio* members and subscribers with the object of building and maintaining fever hospitals. The grand jury could pay for the erection of a fever hospital and make grants for its support up to double the amount subscribed. If fever appeared in any area the lord lieutenant, at the request of a public meeting, could appoint a board of health for the district which could take steps to cleanse the streets and fumigate houses.[2]

When the cholera threatened Ireland in 1832 the government again appointed an *ad hoc* body, the general board of health. It consisted of four commissioners who employed a secretary and six medical inspectors. For over a year from its appointment in March 1832 the board worked hard, collecting and publishing statistics relating to the disease, giving advice, and issuing directives. Early it emphasized the importance of providing small local hospitals and of removing the sick immediately to hospital, and it implored the clergy to give prompt information of cases they met. It defined the spheres of duty of the Dublin board of health and the parish officers of health, and it explained the principles on which advances from the consolidated fund for public health purposes were made. Realizing one reason which made the poor reluctant to enter a

[1] S. Cheyne & F. Barker, *An account of the . . . fever lately epidemic in Ireland*, (1821), i. 111–2, 128, ii. 374–7.
[2] 59 Geo. III, c. 41; 58 Geo. III, c. 47.

hospital, it suggested that the Dublin schools of medicine should temporarily suspend dissections.[1]

In 1846, during the great emergency created by the famine, temporary legislation which was extended until 1850 empowered the lord lieutenant to appoint a central board of health of five unpaid commissioners. This board could require the guardians of any union to provide a fever hospital, dispensaries and medicines 'including nutriment'. The board could also appoint in any union a medical officer of health 'for the relief of the destitute poor'.[2] The board was at first composed of Edward Twistleton, the poor law commissioner, Sir Robert Kane, Philip Crampton, the celebrated surgeon, and Dominic Corrigan, a vigorous, public spirited physician who seems to have proved the most active member of the board (Crampton was seventy, Kane was engaged in setting up Queen's College, Cork). The board was severely criticized by the medical profession for the rates of remuneration it fixed for medical men attending fever hospitals. But the under-secretary pointed out that these rates had been approved by the treasury which considered them as high as it was justified in granting.[3] And the *Dublin Evening Post*, defending the board, explained that it was 'acting as a broker for the rate-payers of Ireland in purchasing medical attendance for Irish fever hospitals'.[4]

The fever committee, the general board of health and the central board of health were all temporary bodies set up to deal with an emergency. In addition to these boards the Government also constituted in 1820 'a general permanent board of health' composed of a dozen unpaid members from which it could obtain information and advice on matters relating to public health. This body made numerous reports to the government and submitted to the lord lieutenant a monthly return on the number of fever cases in Dublin. It advised the lord lieutenant as to the necessity of constituting a local board of health, and it advised local boards of health

[1] *Saunders newsletter*, 27, 30 Mar., 7, 12, 25, 30, Apr. 1832 and *A return of the receipts and expenditure of the central board of health for Ireland*, H.C. 1834 (447), li.

[2] 9 Vict., c. 6.

[3] 'A letter . . .' by R. J. Graves in *Dublin quarterly journ. of medical science*, iv. 513–43.

[4] *Dublin Evening Post*, 4 Nov. 1847.

and checked their expenditure. It also reported on the claims for remuneration of medical men occasionally employed by government departments.[1]

Besides creating a permanent board of health and making small grants to the county infirmaries there were only two other ways in which the state at the beginning of the nineteenth century attempted to provide for the sick poor. It helped some medical charities in Dublin, where there was a mass of poverty on the government's door-step, and it tried to provide accommodation for the lunatic poor. Since lunacy administration and the government's relations with a group of Dublin hospitals each led to the creation of a separate department, and since both subjects stand somewhat apart from the general story of state intervention in the field of public health, they will be disposed of at this point.

During the eighteenth century the Irish parliament in an unsystematic, sporadic way had assisted medical charities in Dublin, and in its last session it voted substantial grants to the Dublin House of Industry and the Westmoreland Lock Hospital, the former receiving nearly £12,000, the latter nearly £5,000. The Dublin House of Industry, one of the few houses founded under the act of 1772, had 'with the implied sanction of the parliament and government of Ireland assumed the character of a national establishment', and from 1777 it received an annual parliamentary grant. In 1816, as the house was seriously overcrowded, Sir Robert Peel in a businesslike letter suggested to the governors that they should exclude pensioners and refractory beggars and impose on the able-bodied unemployed 'as much labour as is consistent with their health'. These measures practically reserved the institution for the aged and infirm, lunatics and orphans. Moreover during the early years of the nineteenth century there were founded in connection with the House of Industry three hospitals, the Hardwicke Fever Hospital (1803), the Richmond Surgical

---

[1] *Estimates, miscellaneous services for the year ending 31 Mar. 1848*, pp. 39–40, H.C. 1847 (229), xxxv. 415–6. Maunsel, a vigorous medical controversialist, contended that by 'taxing' medical men's bills the board was exercising an illegally assumed power 'in an arbitrary and improper manner' (*Report from the select committee on medical charities, Ireland, . . .*, p. 371, H.C. 1843 (412), x.)

Hospital (1811) and the Whitworth Chronic Hospital (1818). Taken together they had about 300 beds and were regarded as 'forming one great institution'. As patients were admitted 'solely because the individual is considered so ill as to stand in need of hospital accommodation', beds were seldom vacant, the three hospitals in the early 'forties having about 4,000 admissions a year. Clinical instruction was given and as early as 1819 the managers of the House of Industry pointed out that their hospitals had been of essential service in training surgeons for the army and navy. With the introduction of an Irish poor law system in 1838 the main House of Industry building became the North Dublin Union Workhouse, but the three hospitals were detached, placed under a board partly nominated by the lord lieutenant and given an annual grant.[1]

The Westmoreland Lock Hospital for the treatment of patients suffering from venereal disease was founded in 1792 by the direction of the lord lieutenant acting on the advice of several leading medical men. It was governed by a board nominated by the government and maintained almost entirely by a government grant. Subscriptions for the hospital, it was explained by a medical man, were hard to obtain, 'It is a hospital', he pointed out, 'you can never bring well before the public through the newspapers, and ladies could not be asked "to go and beg" for the Lock Hospital.' During the early years of the nineteenth century the hospital was overcrowded and disorderly, and after two commissions appointed by the government had reported in 1820, a new board of governors was appointed. In 1854 the hospital was found to be economically and efficiently administered and its value in a garrison city was emphasized.[2]

Shortly after the union the government was partly at least responsible for the foundation of another medical institution in Dublin. In 1804 the Cow-pox Institute was founded with the

[1] *Report of the commissioners appointed by the lord lieutenant to inspect the House of Industry*, pp. 15, 19–21, H.C. 1830 (84), viii; *Report from the select committee on Dublin hospitals*, p. v, H.C. 1854 (338), xii. 5; *Charitable institutions (Dublin) copies of the reports of George Nicholls, Esq.* . . ., p. 14, H.C. 1842 (389), xxxviii.

[2] *Report from the select committee on the Dublin hospitals*, p. 9, H.C. 1854 (338), xii; *Select committee . . . on the laws relating to the destitute poor in Ireland . . ., appendix*, pp. 240–58, H.C. 1846 (694), xi; T. P. C. Kirkpatrick, *History of Dr Steevens hospital* (1924), pp. 189–90.

object of 'disseminating genuine cow-pox infection by inoculating gratuitously the children of the poor'. From the outset it was under the patronage of the lord lieutenant and received a small annual government grant. It was managed by a group of Dublin medical men, the directors, and gave valuable service to the public at a comparatively small cost. In 1877, the Cow-pox Institute was taken over by the local government board, the collection and distribution of lymph being henceforth controlled by the board's vaccine department which supplied workhouses and dispensaries gratuitously.[1]

In the years following the union, annual grants were secured by five other Dublin hospitals—the Rotunda (from 1803), Steevens (from 1805), the Cork Street Fever Hospital (from 1808), the Meath (from 1828) and the Hospital for Incurables (from 1817).[2] The select committee of the house of commons on the Irish miscellaneous estimates of 1829, when considering the grants to the seven Dublin hospitals, defined 'the principles on which alone any fair claim to public assistance on the part of these establishments can be advanced' as follows: 'the proved utility of the charity, the improbability of its maintenance by private aid only, the contribution of funds locally raised by subscription or taxation, and the strictest economy in salaries and all other expenses'. These principles pointed to a discontinuation or reduction of the grants, and twenty years later another select committee on the estimates, having pointed out that no state support was given to similar institutions in other parts of the empire, bluntly recommended that the grants to the Dublin hospitals should be progressively diminished until they ceased. This aroused the Irish members to action, and with striking unanimity, led by Grogan and Reynolds, the members for Dublin, the former a conservative, the latter a liberal, they set to work to protect the interests of the Dublin hospitals. After three set-backs they secured the appointment of a select committee in 1854.[3] Grogan seems to have taken

[1] *Charitable institutions (Dublin) return* . . ., pp. 146–51, H.C. 1842 (337), xxxviii; *Local government board for Ireland, fifth report*, pp. 25–6, 57–9, H.C. 1877, [C. 1761], xxxviii.

[2] *Report from the select committee on the Dublin hospitals*, pp. vi–viii, *evidence*, p. 45, H.C. 1854 (338), xii.

[3] *Hansard*, 3 series, cxi. 721–3, 649–56, cxxx. 1143–51, and P. Kirkpatrick, *The book of the Rotunda hospital* (1913), p. 162.

good care that the hospitals' case should be effectively presented, and the committee reported in favour of continuing the grants. The hospitals were important teaching hospitals and provided an extensive system of medical relief for the poor of Dublin, a city which was 'a metropolis for the poor but not for the rich'. The committee was averse to putting the hospitals under the poor law authorities but recommended that a supervisory commission should be appointed.[1] This recommendation was implemented by the Dublin hospitals regulation act, which empowered the lord lieutenant to appoint an unpaid board to supervise those Dublin hospitals which received an annual parliamentary grant. The board, which employed a secretary, could make general rules for the grant-aided hospitals and annually published a report on their condition.[2] In 1914 it had nine hospitals under its supervision.

There was one section of the Irish sick poor for which little was done during the eighteenth century—the insane. Swift, as is well known, left a munificent legacy to found a hospital for idiots and lunatics, and parliament made a couple of grants to his foundation. Parliament also empowered the grand juries to provide wards for insane persons, but at the beginning of the nineteenth century the only public provision for the lunatic poor was a large asylum in Cork, erected in 1788, and cells, attached to infirmaries and houses of industry, which were frankly described as being 'for mere custody sufficient' but 'very different from what they ought to be with a view to accomplishing the cure of the patient'.[3] In 1804 and 1811 select committees of the house of commons considered what provision should be made in Ireland for the insane poor. Both committees recommended that the government should set up lunatic asylums, the first committee suggesting four provincial institutions, the second a number of district asylums.[4] In 1810 steps were taken to erect in Dublin a government controlled asylum, the Richmond, which was opened in 1815 for 'the

[1] *Report from the select committee on the Dublin hospitals*, H.C. 1854 (338), xii.
[2] 19 & 20 Vict., c. 110.
[3] *Report from the select committee on the lunatic poor in Ireland*, p. 7, H.C. 1817 (430), viii.
[4] *Report from the committee respecting the poor of Ireland*, H.C. 1803-4, (109), v; *Report from the select committee on the lunatic poor in Ireland*, H.C. 1817 (430), viii.

reception and management of lunatic patients'.[1] In 1817 the lord lieutenant in council was empowered to establish district asylums. Each of these was to be managed by a board of governors appointed by the lord lieutenant and to be built and maintained at the expense of the area served, the grand juries voting the necessary sums. The lord lieutenant by the same act was also empowered to appoint an unpaid board for 'the general control of district asylums' and general rules for the management of district asylums were to be made by the lord lieutenant in council. A board of eight (including four medical men) was appointed in September 1817. The power to issue rules was not, however, exercised until 1843, when the first of a series of codified regulations was issued.[2] By 1835 there were ten district asylums (including the Richmond, which in 1830 was converted into the district asylum for the Dublin area). In that year the members of the board of control 'having completed the erection of the number of asylums then considered requisite for the whole of Ireland', resigned. They were replaced by the commissioners of public works who henceforth formed *ex officio* the board of control. The new board, as might be expected, did not attempt to supervise the management of asylums but restricted itself to dealing with building questions.[3]

In 1826 the inspectors of prisons had been directed to inspect mad-houses, and in 1842, when private asylums were required to be licensed, the inspectors were empowered to make a recommendation to the lord chancellor when they considered that a licence should be withdrawn. Three years later the powers and duties of the inspectors of prisons in respect of asylums were transferred to two inspectors of lunatics appointed by the lord lieutenant. In the same year, 1845, an act was passed establishing a criminal lunatic asylum at Dundrum (opened 1850) under the direct control of the government, the lord lieutenant appointing the staff and making regulations for its management.[4]

---

[1] 55 Geo. III, c. 107.

[2] 57 Geo. III, c. 106. For these general rules, issued in 1843, 1862, 1865, 1872, 1874 and 1875, see Council order books (S.P.O.I.).

[3] *Report of the commissioners of inquiry into the state of the lunatic asylums . . . in Ireland . . .*, p. 5, H.C. 1857–8, (2436), xvii.

[4] 7 Geo. IV, c. 74; 8 & 9 Vict., c. 107; 5 & 6 Vict., c. 123.

The legislation of the 'forties settled the pattern of Irish lunacy administration for the next eighty years. Naturally there were some changes. Between 1852 and 1869 twelve more district asylums were erected. In 1867 the lord lieutenant was empowered to appoint the superintendents of district asylums. In 1898 the management of the district asylums was transferred to the newly-constituted county councils which henceforth were responsible for providing accommodation for the lunatic poor. Each asylum was to be managed by a committee appointed by the county councils of the area it served, and if its district comprised more than a single county the committee was to be composed of representatives of the several counties concerned. The district asylums continued to be inspected by the inspectors of lunatics and the lord lieutenant's approval was required for plans and contracts relating to a district asylum, its rules and the appointment and removal of its medical officers.[1]

During the nineteenth century much was accomplished in the sphere of Irish lunacy administration. But even so, at the beginning of the twentieth century there was serious over-crowding in the district asylums and a number of pauper lunatics who should have been receiving asylum treatment were still to be found in workhouses. Moreover as great advances were being made from the beginning of the nineteenth century in the study of mental deficiency, the standards of care and treatment demanded by informed opinion were steadily rising. It was suggested more than once that a drastic reconstruction of the administrative machinery was needed. In 1878 a viceregal commission of inquiry recommended that the whole lunacy administration of Ireland should be placed under the supervision of the local government board. A decade or so later another viceregal commission put forward a different plan. Considering that the local government board had quite enough to do, it recommended the creation of a general board of commissioners in lunacy for Ireland. It was to be composed of five unpaid and two paid members and was to deal with all lunacy questions and supervise all establishments for the care of the insane.[2] But the system remained unchanged until 1922.

---

[1] 61 & 62 Vict., c. 37.

[2] *Poor law union and lunacy inquiry commission (Ireland), report and evidence* . . . , p. ciii, H.C. 1878–9 [Cd. 2239], xxxi; *First and second reports of the committee*

During the early 'thirties the question of an Irish poor law was continuously being discussed. Fundamental issues of social policy were involved. Contemporary opinion, especially in England, was deeply concerned about both the need to relieve destitution and the importance of checking extravagance and encouraging self-reliance. In 1833 the government appointed a strong commission of inquiry into the relief of the Irish poor. This commission, which reported early in 1836, recommended the creation of a board to plan and supervise wide schemes of national improvement which would be financed by state loans and local rates. It also recommended the creation of a poor law commission to supervise local boards which would be responsible for the care of the infirm, aged, sick and lunatic poor.[1] The commission's approach to the great problem of Irish poverty was bold and constructive, but its recommendations did not accord with contemporary economic thinking. If the government had accepted the report it would have been obliged to bring in a very contentious measure with a minute parliamentary majority. It is scarcely surprising then, that a few months after the publication of the report, the prime minister, Lord John Russell, should have directed Nicholls, an English poor law commissioner and a man of immense energy, with strong views on the poor law question, to visit Ireland and report. Nicholls, after making a quick tour of the country, produced a long, lucid and decided report. He was strongly in favour of simply providing a severely limited system of poor relief. The destitute were not to have a legal right to relief (Nicholls seems to have regretted the existence of such a right in England), but a number of workhouses were to be built and maintained by a local rate and within their walls relief was to be provided. There was, Nicholls emphasized, to be no outdoor relief. Nicholls admitted that the poor law he recommended would not work miracles, and he added that it could not cope with the situation which would be created by a general famine. But

[1] *Third report of the commissioners for inquiring into the condition of the poorer classes in Ireland*, H.C. 1836 (43), xxx.

. . . *on lunacy administration (Ireland)*, H.C. 1890–1 [Cd. 6434], xxxvi; *Royal commission on the care and control of the feeble minded: minutes of evidence relating to Scotland and Ireland . . .*, vol. III, pp. 75, 95, H.C. 1908 [Cd. 4217], xxxvii; *Report of the royal commission on the care and control of the feeble minded*, p. 417, H.C. 1908 [Cd. 4202], xxxix.

he believed that the system would improve social conditions, and improved social conditions promoting peace and quiet would encourage capital investment in Ireland.[1]

The government accepted Nicholls's recommendations and in 1837 introduced an Irish poor law bill, which passed in the following session. The administration of relief in Ireland was placed under the control of the poor law commission which had been established in England in 1834. The country was to be divided into unions in each of which there was to be a work-house and a board of guardians composed of members elected by the ratepayers and of justices of the peace resident in the union. The commission was given wide powers, being authorized to audit the unions' accounts, and to make orders for the management of workhouses and for 'the direction and control, appointment and removal' of guardians and poor law officers.[2]

A month after the bill received the royal assent the commission decided that Nicholls should go to Ireland and exercise the powers of the commission there. Thus, as the commissioners themselves admitted, the board was divided in two. But to insure 'a perfect unity of action' Nicholls was instructed to send to London all orders and regulations which required the seal of the commission. Nicholls stayed in Ireland for four years, and when he returned to England permanently the commission delegated power to supervise the poor law system in Ireland to two of the assistant commissioners working there. Later, at the close of 1845, when the membership of the poor law board was raised to four, Twistleton, the new commissioner, was made resident commissioner in Ireland.[3]

The commission set to work with tremenduous vigour to get its system functioning in Ireland, which as Nicholls pointed out, was 'entirely a blank' so far as poor law administration was concerned.[4] At the outset eight assistant commissioners—four experienced Englishmen and four newly appointed Irishmen— were assigned to work in Ireland. The country was quickly divided into 130 unions; arrangements were made for the

---

[1] R. B. McDowell, *Public opinion and government policy in Ireland*, pp. 186–95.
[2] 1 & 2 Vict., c. 56.
[3] *Poor law commissioners, fifth annual report*, p. 24, H.C. 1839 (239), xx; *Ninth annual report*, p. 41, H.C. 1843 (468), xxi; *Twelfth annual report*, p. 26, H.C. 1846 (704), xix.   [4] *Poor law commissioners, fifth annual report*, p. 24.

election of guardians, the levying of rates and the construction of workhouses. Detailed regulations were issued relating to the keeping of accounts, the conduct of elections, the duties of poor law officers and the management of workhouses. Nicholls himself had pointed out that the 'governing principle' of the workhouse system had been that relief given in the workhouse should 'on the whole be less desirable than the support to be obtained by independent means'. He realized that 'it would be vain even if it were desirable to make the lodging, the clothing, the diet of the inmates of the Irish poorhouses inferior to those of the Irish peasant', but he thought that the discipline of the house would be 'irksome' enough to the Irishman to make it a satisfactory test.[1] The workhouse regulations were certainly strict. On entry paupers were classified by age and sex. This meant the separation of husbands and wives. When it was said that the separation of an aged couple was over-harsh the commissioners replied that a workhouse should not be managed so as to 'invite the aged and infirm of the labouring classes to take refuge in it'.[2] In the workhouse paupers were to be put to work. They were not to be allowed tobacco or alcohol. Their day was to begin by the ringing of a bell. Their diet if healthy was monotonous, the commission prescribing oatmeal, buttermilk and potatoes, though it did not object to 'animal food being introduced sparingly into the dietary'—that is to say, a pint of soup might be given to every adult twice a week. And workhouse masters and boards of guardians were empowered to punish disorderly and refractory paupers.[3]

The commission itself had to deal with refractory ratepayers and guardians. During 1843 and 1844, the payment of poor rate was violently resisted in some unions, and police and even in places military had to be employed in support of the collectors. Boards of guardians also gave trouble. The Cork guardians disregarded the commission's rule that newspaper reporters should not be admitted to their meetings, and implied that in issuing the rule the commission had acted *ultra vires*.

[1] *Report of George Nicholls . . . on poor law, Ireland . . .*, H.C. 1837 (69), li.
[2] *Report of the poor law commissioners on the amendment of the poor law*, pp. 30–31, H.C. 1840 (226), xvii.
[3] *Poor law commissioners, eighth annual report, appendix*, pp. 151–4, H.C. 1842, 389, xix; *Tenth annual report, appendix*, pp. 194–203, H.C. 1844 (589), xi.

The commission secured an opinion from the law officers, which the Cork guardians did not receive 'with the deference which ought to have been paid to an opinion proceeding from such high legal authority'. And as other boards followed the example of Cork, the commission with an ill grace yielded.[1] It was more successful in other disputes. When the Limerick and Rathkeale boards on being refused permission to suspend their clerks resigned, the commission secured a mandamus against them and the guardians resumed their duties. When the Tuam and Castlerea boards failed to open their workhouses or take satisfactory steps to collect their rates, the commission first proceeded against them by mandamus and then dissolved the boards.[2]

The most important dispute between the commission and the local poor law authorities arose over the construction of workhouses. The commission had hoped that this would be carried out by the board of works, but difficulties arose and in the event the commission employed its own architect, Wilkinson, who with a small staff planned and supervised the building of workhouses on standard patterns all over Ireland. Nicholls himself admitted later that the architect had too small a staff, owing to 'our endeavour to economize in every way, striving to make up by individual exertion for deficiency in numbers'. Soon over twenty boards were complaining that in the construction of their workhouses estimates had been exceeded and work carelessly done. The home secretary sent over James Pennethorne, the well-known English architect and town planner, to investigate. He reported that mistakes had been made and that the unions affected had been 'improperly put to an expense of not less than £50,000'. Nicholls replied to his criticisms of the commission in a couple of indignant letters, and a select committee of the house of commons decided that a further inquiry was necessary. The treasury then appointed Colonel Barney, of the Royal Engineers, to inquire into the expenditure on Irish workhouses. Barney reported that from his calculations it seemed as if about £46,000 excess expenditure had been incurred as a result of

[1] *Poor law commissioners, seventh annual report*, pp. 56-8, H.C. 1841 (327), xi.
[2] *Poor law commissioners, eleventh report*, pp. 22-4, H.C. 1845 (624), xxvii, *Twelfth report*, pp. 20-1, H.C. 1846 (704), xix.

faulty work. And the treasury relieved the unions of this liability.[1]

But it would be unfair to conclude this sketch of the commission's preliminary work in Ireland by dwelling on its mistakes. In a remarkably short space of time it had brought into being an elaborate relief system covering the whole country, and had unceasingly striven by precept and example to instill into everybody who came in contact with the system, whether as administrators or as paupers, the new ideals of efficiency and economy.

But the poor law commissioners when dealing with Ireland were unfortunate. Just when they had completed the task of setting up the new system in Ireland they were called upon to take a major share in coping with an overwhelming catastrophe, and a system designed to relieve about 100,000 paupers had to function in a country where millions were clamouring for help. From the summer of 1845 to the autumn of 1848 the potato crops were blighted. That meant that the bulk of the Irish peasantry who normally relied on their potato plots for their main food-supply found their main means of subsistance gone. At first the poor law commissioners maintained a firm or doctrinaire attitude, taking their stand on the principles of the poor law. But they did not ignore the worsening situation. As early as December 1845 they urged guardians to provide fever hospitals, offering them a plan for a temporary building—though characteristically the commissioners emphasized that a board of guardians must not think that the erection of a temporary fever ward absolved it from the duty of providing a proper hospital.[2] Ten months later, in December 1846, alarmed by the despondent reports about the prospects for the new potato crop which were pouring in from the clerks of the Irish unions, the commissioners strongly warned guardians to review their stocks of clothing and provisions and to budget for a period when the whole of their accommodation would be

---

[1] *Report of the commissioner for inquiring into the execution of the contracts for certain union workhouses in Ireland* . . ., H.C. 1844 (562), xxx; *Report of the commission appointed to inquire into the execution of the contracts for certain union workhouses in Ireland* . . ., H.C. 1845 (170), xxvi.

[2] *Poor law commissioners, twelfth report, appendix,* pp. 92–3, H.C. 1846 (745), xix.

required. The commissioners also supplied the guardians with plans for enlarging a workhouse, for improving its ventilation and drainage, and for manufacturing a cheap bedstead. But about the same time, in October 1846, they firmly restrained the guardians of a number of unions in Cork and Tipperary from giving outdoor relief. Justifying this decision, the commissioners argued in their thirteenth report that when parliament passed the Irish poor law act it implicitly decided against outdoor relief. If outdoor relief was to be introduced without fresh legislation, it would lead to 'great abuse and confusion'. Moreover, few Irish unions could afford to grant it.[1] The importance of preventing unions slipping into slack financial habits was emphasized by Twistleton, the commissioner resident in Ireland. Scarcely any circumstances, he declared, would make it expedient for the government to advance a loan to a union for the payment of current expenses. But he agreed that in an emergency the government might for a severely limited time pay interest on a loan raised by a union. About the same time as Twistleton made this suggestion, the poor law commissioners thought of a method by which they might 'be able to prevent formal applications for loans from boards of guardians to the government'. They suggested that a poor law union might be allowed to borrow from its treasurer, since 'as all the union funds pass through his hands he will undoubtedly be able to repay himself'.[2]

The poor law commissioners were able to adhere closely to their principles for over a year, because the government was struggling to meet the emergency through other agencies. Indeed the commissioners themselves grudgingly acknowledged this. In their report for 1846–7 they pointed out that since poor law relief was limited by the workhouse accommodation available, the main means of coping with the calamity would have to be the public works organized by the government. But during the session of 1847 the government carried legislation which modified the Irish poor law and created a new board with enlarged powers and responsibilities. A temporary relief

---

[1] *Poor law commissioners, thirteenth annual report*, p. 24, 132–8, H.C. 1847 (816), xxviii.

[2] *Copies or extracts relating to the state of the union workhouses in Ireland*, pp. 2, 17, H.C. 1847 (766), lv.

act, which ran for six months, supplemented the existing poor law machinery by the creation of a relief commission. The lord lieutenant could direct the formation of a relief committee in one or more electoral divisions of any union. The committee was to be composed of the poor law guardians elected for the area, resident justices of the peace, such other persons as the lord lieutenant might nominate, and an inspector of the relief commission. Along with the relief committee the lord lieutenant could also nominate a finance committee composed of the inspector and not more than four other persons. The relief committees were to draw up lists of destitute persons in their areas and estimates of the costs of providing them with the necessities of life according to rules laid down by the relief commission. The finance committee was to revise these lists and estimates. When the finance committee had decided on the amount required, the lord lieutenant or the chief secretary could issue a warrant directing the board of guardians responsible for the area to raise the money by a rate. And the treasury might advance a loan to the committee on the security of the rate. If a board of guardians refused to act on the warrant it could be dissolved.[1]

Two other acts passed in 1847 made important permanent changes in Irish poor law administration. boards of guardians were empowered to grant outdoor relief to the aged, infirm and sick poor and to poor widows with two or more dependent children. And the poor law commissioners were empowered to permit boards to give out door relief in the form of food to the able-bodied poor for limited periods (but occupiers of more than quarter an acre were not to be eligible for such relief). Finally, a major administrative change was made. A separate poor law commission for Ireland was created consisting of the chief secretary, the under-secretary and the chief commissioner. To this commission were transferred the powers and duties relating to Ireland of the poor law commission. The Irish commission's general rules were to be approved by the lord lieutenant in council and it was to have a staff of inspectors and clerks whose numbers and salaries were to be fixed by the treasury.[2] In fact the commission took over the poor law commission's Irish staff, the first chief commissioner being

---

[1] 10 Vict., c. 7. [2] 10 Vict., cc. 31 & 90.

Twistleton, who since 1845 had been the commissioner resident in Ireland. Twistleton held his new post for less than two years, resigning early in 1849 because he disapproved of the government's rate-in-aid bill, which provided that the more distressed unions should be assisted by a special rate struck in the others. Twistleton, who thought that it was 'of much more importance that we should attach the Irish people to Great Britain than that we should make conquests in India or even establish colonies', considered that the distressed unions should have been helped by a grant from the imperial exchequer.[1]

It must be said at once that the poor law commissioners (whether appointed under the 1836 or the 1847 act) displayed throughout the famine era an unceasing devotion to their own exacting standards of duty. The immense mass of their correspondence, a selection from which for the years 1846 to 1848 almost fills four large printed volumes, evinces this, as does the department's casualty list—for during the years 1847–9, nineteen inspectors and vice-guardians and 164 workhouse officers died from fever.[2] From the correspondence it is clear that the commissioners were inspired by a disciplined, hard-driving, determination to make the system work, despite all obstacles—including especially human frailty. The correspondence also at times reflects the commissioners' inevitable isolation from the brutal realities of poor law administration amongst a starving and desperate population. Their position in fact was analogous to that of the staff in the eyes of the fighting soldier. In their Dublin office, at a decent distance from the struggle for survival, they were able to enunciate general principles with cold lucidity. Theirs was the unpopular but necessary task of forcing the others into the fight. This meant continuously reminding officials of the board's rules and wishes, urging boards of guardians to perform their functions efficiently, and above all to try to collect the rates which supplied them with the necessary resources for their work. But in the most acutely distressed areas, where the small ratepayers were almost desti-

---

[1] *Select committee on poor laws (Ireland), fifth report*, pp. 1–2, H.C. 1849 (148), xv.

[2] *First annual report of the commissioners for administering the laws for the relief of the poor in Ireland*, p. 16, H.C. 1847–8 (963), xxxiii; *Second report*, pp. 15–6, H.C. 1849 [1118], xxv.

tute and the large landowners were hard hit, it seemed to many of the guardians simply impossible to collect the rates required. At least two boards of guardians, Kanturk and Athlone, were so depressed by their difficulties that they tried to surrender their powers to the poor law commissioners. In both instances the commissioners accepted the surrender—clearly with disgust. They pointed out that they were empowered to dissolve a board 'quite irrespective of a desire on the part of the guardians to be released from their duties'. And they emphasized that they were exercising their right because the guardians had failed to discharge their duties efficiently.[1] Over a year before these two boards collapsed a number of other boards had shown themselves in the opinion of the commissioners incapable of performing their duties. The first three to collapse were Ballinrobe, Castlebar and Westport. As early as December 1846 the Ballinrobe guardians warned the commissioners that they could no longer feed the paupers in their house because their poor rate was proving unproductive. The commissioners recommended the guardians to use their powers 'which are as great as are possessed by any body in the state for the imposition or collection of a rate or tax'. Six months later the commissioners dissolved the board, pointing out that it was not meeting regularly, had failed to collect sufficient money to meet its expenses and had allowed its workhouse to become disorganized. Castlebar was the next board to be dissolved. In October 1846 the Castlebar guardians, considering that 'the collection of the outstanding rate was wholly impractical', decided to refuse admission to their house unless the government would advance them some money. Otway, an assistant commissioner, told the guardians that they were guilty of 'a cruel neglect of their highest duties', and urged them to strive to collect arrears and strike a new rate. In the end the commissioners dissolved the board. The Westport board of guardians was dissolved because, though they knew they had no funds, they 'failed to meet and face the difficulties of their position'.[2]

[1] *Copies or extracts of correspondence relating to . . . union workhouses in Ireland, fourth series*, pp. 190–1, H.C. 1847–8, (896), liv; *Fifth series*, pp. 404–5, H.C. 1847–8 (919), lv.

[2] *Copies or extracts of correspondence relating to . . . union workhouses in Ireland, first series*, pp. 26–7, 36–40, 58–9, H.C. 1847 (863), lv; *Fourth series*, pp. 37–40, H.C. 1847–8 (896), liv.

During the emergency thirty-nine boards of guardians in all were dissolved, the administration of their unions being temporarily transferred to vice-guardians. Both vice-guardians and inspectors, surrounded as they were by destitution, sickness and hunger, toiled exceedingly hard. Two extracts from their reports tersely illustrate how they worked. The vice-guardians in charge of the Lowtherstown union reported that 'it has required nothing less than our repeated daily and almost hourly inspection, remonstrances, and personal directions to enforce, and that but indifferently, attention to meal hours and cleanliness and to maintain a semblance of order and arrest the unruliness of all classes of the paupers'. And Kennedy, a temporary poor law inspector, summarized the conditions under which he was working by saying 'that though Saturday is set apart for the transaction of routine and financial business, every day in the week is alike—one of labour'.[1]

During the summer of 1850 a sharp fall in the number of those receiving outdoor relief showed that the crisis was passing. A year later the pressure on the workhouses was decreasing and by May 1853 the poor law commissioners felt that 'the state of administration of relief to the destitute poor in Ireland may now be looked upon as nearly identical with its normal state as originally contemplated on the passing of 1 & 2 Vic., c. 58'.

After the famine, generally speaking, the poor law was administered in a more lenient spirit. The commissioners expressed their anxiety that workhouse inmates should be given vegetables and good milk, that the aged should be permitted bread and tea instead of stirabout, that fireguards should be supplied in workhouse schoolrooms, and that workhouse schoolmasters and mistresses should not only be teachers but act as parents to the friendless or orphaned child. And the poor law commissioners vigorously and publicly defended workhouse educated children when the prison commissioners in one of their reports spoke of them in a derogatory fashion. Near the end of the

[1] *Papers relating to . . . the relief of distress . . . in Ireland, fifth series*, p. 112, H.C. 1847–8, (919), lv; *Papers relating to . . . the distressed unions in the west of Ireland*, p. 54, H.C. 1849 [1010], xlviii. Kennedy, an army officer, had been educated at T.C.D. After serving as a poor law official he had a distinguished career as a colonial governor.

century, boards of guardians were authorized to allow tobacco and snuff to aged and infirm paupers and to permit an aged husband and wife to share a small compartment in the workhouse instead of being separated.[1]

The legislature too showed itself ready to mitigate the severity of the poor law. The poor relief act of 1862 abolished the quarter-acre clause, provided for the relief of children outside the workhouse, and permitted guardians to admit to their infirmaries poor persons who could afford to contribute towards their own maintenance, thus, as the poor law commissioners put it, supplying the last link 'in the connection between the poor law and the system of medical charities in Ireland'. As time went on, the number of the able-bodied in the workhouse fell and by the beginning of the century able-bodied paupers formed only ten per cent of the workhouse population, the bulk of the inmates being children, sick, infirm, aged or insane. Moreover, while the workhouses held about 45,000 poor persons, about 57,000 were receiving outdoor relief.[2]

Shortly after the great emergency created by the famine ended, the poor law commission was entrusted with new functions, being made the department responsible for public health. As has been pointed out, at the beginning of the nineteenth century the state in a very limited way tried to assist the sick and preserve the health of the community. When in the 'thirties the need for a system of poor relief was being discussed, the question of providing medical relief was also considered. As early as 1830 a committee of the house of commons suggested that every grand jury should appoint a committee to supervise medical charities in its county. And between then and 1846 not only did another house of commons committee, a house of lords committee and the poor law commission issue reports dealing with medical relief, but no fewer than five attempts were made to put things on a

---

[1] *Commissioners for administrating the laws for the relief of the poor, seventh annual report, appendix*, p. 17, H.C. 1854 [1785], p. 555; *Twelfth report, appendix*, pp. 24, 26, H.C. 1859, second session, 2546, xi. 340, 342; *Local government board for Ireland, twenty-second report*, p. 5, H.C. 1894 [7454], xli. 13.

[2] *Poor law reform commission (Ireland)*, vol. i, p. 65, H.C. 1906 [Cd. 3202], li.

satisfactory footing by legislation—one by a conservative government, another by a liberal government and three by private members.[1]

There was general agreement on two points. The cost of medical relief should be met out of local taxation and there should be a central board empowered to inspect and issue rules for rate-aided hospitals and dispensaries. But how the board should be formed was after 1840 a subject of controversy. The poor law commission (in fact Nicholls 'acting in Ireland as a board of poor law commissioners') recommended that fever hospitals and dispensaries should be maintained out of the poor rate and managed by the poor law guardians.[2] This of course would have put them under the ultimate control of the poor law commission, and Nicholls, though he did not emphasize this implication, carefully explained that the central medical board, which he recommended should be appointed, should have only 'advisory' functions. Nicholls's report provided the basis for a bill introduced by Eliot, the chief secretary, in 1842. It provided that hospitals and the dispensaries should be supported by the poor rate. There was to be a medical charities board which was to employ inspectors and make regulations governing the 'medical economy' of institutions in the system, while the poor law commission was to supervise their finances. There was considerable opposition, both medical and lay, to increasing the powers of the poor law commission, and this opposition led to the chief secretary dropping his bill. A year later a committee of the house of commons decided by the casting vote of the chairman in favour of placing medical relief under a medical charities board, and three years later in 1846, a committee of the house of lords recommended a similar scheme. The board of health set up as an emergency measure during the famine might have become a new permanent department supervising public health. But the poor law board, if unpopular, was composed of experienced administrators, possessed a trained staff and controlled a nation-wide system. So it is not surprising that when the government, shortly after the famine,

[1] Bills were introduced in the following sessions—1836, 1837–8, 1840 and 1843.

[2] *Report of the poor law commission on medical charities, Ireland*, H.C. 1841 (324), xi.

decided to tackle the question of Irish medical relief, it adopted the simple course of using the poor law machinery.

The famine had brought home in the most forcible possible form the need for an adequate system of medical relief. So the dispensaries act of 1851 reached the statute book remarkably easily. It provided that guardians should divide their unions into dispensary districts, in each of which there would be a dispensary committee consisting of guardians, justices of the peace and the larger ratepayers. It would maintain a dispensary and appoint and pay a medical man. 'A poor person' granted a ticket by a member of the committee was entitled to medical relief. The expenses of the system were to be met out of the poor rates. The poor law commission was to be reinforced by two additional commissioners one of whom was to be a medical man, and medical inspectors were to be appointed. Large powers were vested in the commission, which could revise the boundaries of dispensary districts, fix the qualifications and salaries of dispensary doctors and remove them from office, and issue rules for the management of dispensaries.[1] The bill as first introduced included the county infirmaries, but this part of the scheme was dropped in deference to the opposition of Irish M.P.s. The poor law commission found the guardians anxious to implement 'the benevolent intentions of the legislature', and the act was soon put into force all over Ireland, the country being rapidly divided into over seven hundred dispensary districts. At first medical men complained about the quantity of records they were expected to keep but the commission firmly insisted that full record-keeping was indispensible.[2] By 1861, the chief poor law commissioner could see only one serious defect in the dispensary system, the failure of dispensary committees to meet regularly, since their duties were neither interesting nor exciting.[3] And six years later an English poor law inspector, who was much impressed by the system, criticized 'the extreme facility' with which tickets for medical relief could be obtained.[4] But at this very time the Irish poor law commission was em-

[1] 14 & 15 Vict., c. 68.

[2] *Medical charities, Ireland; first annual report of the commissioners . . .*, pp. 6–7, [1609], l.

[3] *Report from the select committee on poor relief (Ireland) . . . minutes of evidence*, pp. 70–1, H.C. 1861 (408), x.

[4] *Medical relief dispensaries (Ireland)*, p. 4, H.C. 1867 (17), lx.

phasizing with pride that in Great Britain, on the recent appearance of cholera, an immense amount of time, trouble and expense had been absorbed in creating a system which in Ireland was already in existence.[1] And in 1870 the commission was able to record that smallpox was no longer indigenous to Ireland. Four years earlier the duties of the poor law commission had been further extended by the public health act of 1866, which provided that all persons employed or appointed under the dispensaries act were to aid local authorities in its execution, and that the poor law commission should, when required to do so by the lord lieutenant, inquire into public health and be the authority for issuing regulations under the prevention of diseases act (1850).[2]

In 1872, the new emphasis in the commission's functions was recognized by its transformation into the Local government board. Theoretically a new board was created, composed of the chief secretary, the under-secretary, a vice-president and two commissioners, one of whom was to be a medical man. And in this board were vested the government's powers in matters relating to public health. In fact the new board was the poor law commission under a new name, and as might be expected the first vice-president and commissioners were the Poor law commissioners.[3]

As time went on the local government board became entrusted with a wide variety of duties. Of course it continued to administer the poor law and dispensary systems. In the 'eighties and early 'nineties it played an important part in organizing relief in the areas which suffered especially from distress. In unions where there was exceptional distress the guardians were permitted to grant relief in the form of food and fuel and the government made interest free loans for the purchase of seed potatoes, made loans at a low rate of interest for improvements and in 1890–1 started the construction of light railways. The local government board through its inspectors had the task of 'diagnosing the distress and discriminating between the real and simulated destitution'. And it was on its recommendation that unions were scheduled as distressed.

[1] *Poor relief (Ireland), annual report of the commissioners*, p. 32, H.C. 1867 (3877), xxiv.
[2] 29 & 30 Vict., c. 90.   [3] 33 & 36 Vict., c. 69.

Acting under the local government of Ireland act of 1872 the local government board issued provisional orders changing local government boundaries, transferring powers from one local authority to another, and authorizing loans and new forms of rate. It also audited the accounts of local bodies. Naturally the great local government act of 1898 thrust an immense amount of work on the board, since it was responsible for constituting electoral divisions, for framing rules to govern the election of aldermen and councillors, and for preparing the financial basis upon which the local bodies established by the act were to rest. The board could close burial grounds. It was expected to examine local and personal bills. It was 'the confirming authority' under a series of statutes beginning in 1875 providing for the housing of the working classes by local authorities, and it supervised the administration by boards of guardians of the seed potato supply acts. By the locomotive highways act of 1896, it was empowered to make rules relating to the design and speed of motor cars (in later years it had to resist the demands of local authorities for too severe speed limits). It supervised the hospitals set up under the tuberculosis prevention act (Ireland) and the distress committees established by local authorities under the unemployed workmen's act of 1905. The old age pensions act of 1908 made the board the central pensions authority for Ireland. In conjunction with the treasury it issued regulations for carrying out the act and it heard appeals from local authorities. Between 1908 and March 1914 there were 70,000 of these appeals, for the administration of the act in Ireland proved exceptionally difficult, since statutory registration of births had begun only in 1864 and in addition the determination of the 'means' of many of the occupiers of small-holdings in the south and west presented numerous knotty problems[1].

The increase in the department's duties from the late 'nineties is reflected in the growth of its staff. In the middle 'fifties, when the famine emergency was completely over, the poor law commission had a staff of just under seventy. In the 'nineties the local government board was managing with a staff of about seventy-seven. Then after the passing of the local

---

[1] *Local government board for Ireland, twentieth report*, appendix, pp. 96–103, H.C. 1892 [Cd. 6801], xxxix.

government act of 1898, the department's staff in one bound had increased by fifty per cent (the work also increased so rapidly that several of the staff broke down under the pressure).[1] In the next five years the staff mounted by thirty per cent, and by 1914 it was three times as large as it had been in the middle 'nineties.

As has been said earlier the state had special relations with Dublin, the seat of government and, until well into the nineteenth century, by far the largest urban centre in Ireland. From 1786 (with an interval between 1795 and 1808) the government controlled the metropolitan police, and at the time of the union a body largely composed of government nominees, the wide streets commissioners, was playing an important part in Dublin development. This commission had been constituted by statute in 1757 'to make a wide and convenient way, street and passage' between Essex Bridge and 'the royal palace or castle of Dublin.'[2] Later the commmission was entrusted with the execution of a series of schemes for widening, and forming new, streets. It was composed originally of twenty-one members, the lord mayor and twenty members named in the act of 1757. Vacancies were to be filled by the lord lieutenant, and it was enacted that if a member failed to attend for six months he lost his seat. In 1767 the members for the city and county were added.[3] The commission had wide powers, including that of compulsory purchase, and funds derived from a variety of sources—parliamentary grants, a coal tax, a tax on cards and, after 1807, a rate assessed on the metropolitan area. The commission had a very small staff, a secretary, a clerk and a surveyor and engineer. And when necessary it employed a solicitor. By 1847, Sherrard, who had been secretary for forty years (in succession to his father) was also acting as surveyor and seems to have been the only whole-time employee of the commission.[4] The commission was largely responsible for the shaping of central Dublin and could pride itself on the bold planning which gave the city some of its finest streets. But in

[1] H. Robinson, *Memories: wise and otherwise*, p. 128.
[2] 31 Geo. II, c. 19.   [3] 7 Geo. III, c. 7.
[4] *Dublin Wide Streets bill: minutes of evidence* . . ., p. 3, H.C. 1846 (519), xii.

the 'forties it was severely criticized by an influential and vocal section of the Dublin public as being an unrepresentative body imposing taxation,[1] and in 1851 it was abolished, the commissioners' power and duties being transferred to the Dublin corporation.[2]

Shortly after the union a government department, the paving board, was constituted to supervise important municipal services in Dublin.[3] During the eighteenth century several unsuccessful attempts had been made to create a satisfactory municipal authority which would be responsible for the Dublin streets. In 1806 a commission of inquiry found that the streets were in a dangerous and neglected condition, and in 1807 the drastic step was taken of entrusting their paving, cleansing and lighting to a government-nominated commission. The new paving board, which was empowered to levy a rate, was composed of three paid commissioners nominated by the lord lieutanant, who also appointed their four principal subordinates, a secretary, treasurer and two supervisors.[4] The first chief commissioner was Major Alexander Taylor, of the Royal Irish Engineers; his two colleagues were both aldermen.

The paving board greatly improved the condition of the streets but early in 1824 it became involved in a serious dispute with the corporation over the cost of laying water-pipes. About the same time there was a violent public clash between the paving board and the lord mayor. The lord mayor, Richard Smyth, at the head of a market jury, insisted on having an interview with the commissioners, who ordered him and his companions out of their board room.[5] Two years later, Smyth was nominated a commissioner. He promptly began to detect abuses and he detailed them at length to a commission of inquiry appointed by the government in 1826. This commission (composed of two barristers) reported that Major Taylor had been borrowing large sums of public money from the board's treasurer, that the board's accounts were badly

---

[1] *Ibid.*, p. 24. [2] 12 & 13 Vict., c. 97.

[3] *Report of the commissioners appointed to inquire into the conduct of . . . of the corporation for paving, cleansing and lighting the streets of Dublin,* H.C. 1806 (17), viii.

[4] 47 Geo. III, c. cix.

[5] *Saunders News Letter,* 18 Feb. 1824, *Cal. anc. rec. Dublin,* xviii. 69–73.

kept, and that its general business was being conducted with the greatest irregularity, 'one commissioner often acting as the board'. The commissioners of inquiry also listed some grave instances of negligence and extravagence.[1] As a result of this inquiry Taylor was removed from office, being replaced as chairman by Smyth. And thenceforth the board functioned efficiently (if somewhat expensively)[2] but in 1851, it was abolished along with the wide street commission, its duties and powers being vested in the Dublin corporation.[3]

It is understandable that the new Dublin corporation constituted under the municipal reform act should quickly absorb nominated bodies such as the wide streets commission and the paving board. But strange to say, in 1849, shortly before these departments disappeared, another government office responsible for an important branch of Dublin municipal administration was established. By the middle of the nineteenth century there were no fewer than seven distinct rates being levied in Dublin by different public bodies, and in 1849 it was enacted that a collector general should be appointed who would collect all these rates and allocate the revenue raised to the bodies entitled to strike a rate. The collector general, whose salary was fixed at £800 per annum, and his staff, were to be appointed by the lord lieutenant who was also empowered to make rules for the management of the collector general's office.[4] The department was a small one—in the 'seventies its staff consisted of seven clerks and eleven collectors—and its management was 'practically left to the discretion of the collector general'.

The department was an easy-going official backwater, and in 1878 a viceregal commission of inquiry into its working produced a grim report. The collector general, though very polite (and apparently an adept at turning away the wrath of irritated citizens by soft answers), was elderly and incapable. Duties were not systematically distributed amongst the staff, and the department's books were for the purposes of accountancy

---

[1] *Report of the commissioners for inquiring into the management . . . of the paving board, Dublin*, H.C. 1826-7 (329), xi.

[2] *Dublin improvement: report of the commissioners . . .*, H.C. 1847 (124-77), xxvi.

[3] 12 & 13 Vict., c. 97.   [4] 12 & 13 Vict., c. 91.

'utterly useless'.[1] The receiver-master in chancery was supposed to audit the collector general's accounts, and Gerald Fitz-Gibbon, who was appointed receiver-master in 1860 attempted to investigate the causes of arrears. The collector general contended that the master was exceeding his powers, and the privy council in 1865 decided that the collector general's decision on arrears was final. Thenceforth the master certified the accounts as correct in a carefully qualified form of certification.[2] The commission of inquiry suggested that the methods of collection should be improved and the viceroy's control over the department strengthened. The government introduced a bill implementing these recommendations but failed to carry it. Some years later a group of nationalist M.P.s tried to place the collector general's office under the control of the corporation. Conservatives were averse to this and in the discussions over the Dublin corporation act of 1890 a clumsy compromise was evolved. A separate department, 'the municipal department', was established in the collector general's office, for the applotting and levying of the municipal rates. The officials in this department were to be appointed by the corporation, except that one-third of the rate collectors were to be nominated by the lord lieutenant. This eccentric arrangement was terminated by the local government act of 1898, which transferred the collection of rates in Dublin to the corporation and abolished the collector general's office.[3]

[1] *Report . . . of commissioners of inquiry into the collection of rates in the city of Dublin with minutes of evidence*, H.C. 1878 [Cd. 2062], xxiii.

[2] *Ibid.*, p. 16.

[3] 53 & 54 Vict., c. cccxlvi, *Hansard*, 3 series, cccxlviii. 617–65. James Joyce's father worked in the office for some years (R. Ellman, *James Joyce* (1959), pp. 16–9, 121.

VII

DEPARTMENTS CONCERNED
WITH ECONOMIC
DEVELOPMENT

~~~~~~~~~~~~~~~~~~~~~~~~~~~~~~~~~~~~

THE BEGINNING of the nineteenth century coincided with the opening of the epoch of *laissez-faire* domination over British political and economic thought. During the eighteenth century the state had been expected to promote by active intervention what were regarded as healthy developments in economic life. During the first half of the nineteenth century there was a growing belief that the less it meddled in economic matters the better. But it was difficult for even the most resolute doctrinaire to insist on a rigid application of *laissez-faire* principles to Ireland. For while English industry was advancing by stupendous strides and English agriculture was steadily improving, over most of Ireland industry was stagnant or declining and agriculture (on which the bulk of the population depended) backward. Distress was endemic and whenever it became acute over large areas there were urgent demands for public assistance. The orthodox official attitude was expounded in 1824, with considerable lucidity and force by the then chancellor of the exchequer, Frederick Robinson. If, he explained, Irishmen secured lavish loans for economic development from the state instead of trusting 'to their own resources and the energies of their country' they would tend to rely for support on the government, and in the end discover they were incapable of exerting themselves.[1] But Adam Smith had listed amongst the duties of the state the promotion and maintenance of public works (such as roads, bridges, canals and harbours), which, though they might be of the highest degree advantageous to a great society, are 'of such a nature that the profit could never repay the expense to any individual or small number of individuals, and which it therefore could never be expected that any individual or small number of individuals should erect or maintain'. Some of the building and engineering operations undertaken or financed by the Irish government during the first half of the nineteenth century would clearly have been permissible by Smith's canons. But in a poor country there was naturally a tendency to press the government to extend its activities, in the hope that they would stimulate normal economic development. It was argued that if the government would pave the way by improving communications and encouraging drainage then private enterprise would exert itself vigorously in many directions. And of course public works were sometimes called for simply as an immediate form of relief.

At the close of the eighteenth century there were two government departments in Ireland specifically responsible for encouraging economic development, the linen board and the directors of inland navigation. The trustees of the linen manufacture were constituted in October 1711 in accordance with an act passed a year earlier.[2] Set up to improve and regulate the linen manufacture, the board both punished and rewarded, striving to enforce the legislation for maintaining standards in the cultivation of flax and the manufacture of linen and encouraging the development of the industry by granting bounties, paying premiums, giving prizes, and—especially during the early nineteenth century—promoting the introduction of improved machinery. The board tried to maintain standards by arranging for the inspection and sealing of cloth, and managed a linen hall in Dublin. This was a large building containing 550 rooms, and the distribution of these

[1] *Hansard*, new series, xi. 72.
[2] For the work of the linen board see *Proceedings of the trustees of the linen and hempen manufacture of Ireland*, published annually from 1784 and C. Gill, *The rise of the Irish linen industry* (1925).

between the Dublin linen merchants and the general management of the building gave the board a considerable amount of trouble. The trustees met regularly. But as they were usually peers or M.P.s, it is scarcely surprising that during the early part of the nineteenth century meetings were badly attended, and it was said that sometimes the secretary collected separately the signatures of the necessary quorum. On one occasion, indeed, in 1822 over twenty trustees met in London, and admitting that the law 'did not justify' a meeting of the linen Board except in Dublin they nevertheless directed that the inspector general of Munster should visit Holland and report on Dutch methods of treating flax.[1] Shortly afterwards a board meeting in Dublin, attended by three trustees, ratified this decision. It must, however, be said that the trustees who did attend board meetings dealt competently enough with a large quantity of detailed business and they displayed robust self-confidence by publishing annually the minutes of their meetings.

The staff of the board in 1822 consisted of a secretary (with emoluments of £800 per annum), who was assisted by three clerks, three provincial inspectors (one for Ulster, the other two for the remainder of Ireland), thirty-five county inspectors, five port inspectors, and five seed inspectors. The county inspectors received salaries of £40 per annum, and an additional sum averaging £50, made up of travelling expenses, fees for branding utensils, fines and seizures.

In the first few years of the nineteenth century the officials of the board were involved in three administrative scandals, the first of which at least had elements of pathos. In 1795 James Corry succeeded his father as secretary to the board. He had intended to be called to the bar, and during the later years of his father's life, 'passing through the graduations of a classical education' (he was a Trinity graduate), he was not interested in the working of the linen office. Shortly after he was placed at its head he began to improve the system on which its accounts were kept, with the result that it emerged that his father had appropriated £16,000. For this, filial feeling found an excuse. The elder Corry's predecessor after his resignation had become involved in an expensive law suit over an estate in Cavan.

[1] *Proceedings of the trustees . . . for the year ending 5 January 1823*, pp. 183–4.

Corry, out of gratitude supported him enthusiastically, and having exhausted his own resources he imperceptibly (as his son explained) began to use public money. This he found was easily done by the simple method of not making up a year's accounts until he had received on account of issues in the succeeding year a sufficient amount to replace what he had appropriated. And by procuring undated vouchers he was able to present satisfactory accounts. As a result of his son's candour the commissioners of imprest accounts in 1805 detected the deficiency and reported to the trustees, who promptly suspended Corry, appointing the inspector general, Charles Duffin, to act in his place.[1] Six months later Corry, who had transferred his interest in his father's property to trustees acting for the board, was restored to office and by 1812 all the elder Corry's arrears were fully discharged.[2] James Corry, it may be added, was not only an honest man, but during the thirty years he held office he was a most zealous official, the mainstay indeed of the department which he twice warmly defended before parliamentary committees of inquiry in 1822 and 1825.

Ironically enough Charles Duffin who took over Corry's duties when he was in disgrace was himself in serious trouble five years later. In February 1810 the commissioners of accounts requested detailed information concerning sums of money which had passed through the hands of the inspector general. And soon Duffin was accused of issuing two sets of receipts for the same looms. Further, it was discovered that he had tried to prevent two county inspectors giving evidence against him, telling one of them that 'the duplicates must be denied or I am ruined' and suggesting that to avoid giving evidence on oath the inspector could claim to be a Quaker. Duffin was dismissed from office and prosecuted for fraud, and his office was discontinued.[3]

The third scandal concerned subordinate officials. In 1816 it was discovered that the chief clerk had accepted for himself and his two subordinates gratuities from Edmund Shanahan, a Cork linen manufacturer whom the linen board was prosecu-

---

[1] *Proceedings of the trustees . . . from 5 Jan. 1807 to 5 Jan. 1808*, pp. 69–77.

[2] *Proceedings of the trustees . . . for the year 1812*, pp. 72–3.

[3] *Proceedings of the trustees . . . from 5 July 1810 to 7 Jan. 1811, Appendix*, I.

ting for fraudulently claiming bounties. The chief clerk in his defence explained that 'Mr Shanahan possessed the character and manners of a gentleman and hence succeeded in ingratiating himself as well with the other gentlemen in the office as with me. His invitations to dinner were accepted and followed by the ordinary result, an interchange of the compliment on all sides, and these perfectly reciprocal civilities gave a familiar feature to the intimacy he had already cultivated with me'. This intimacy paved the way for Shanahan's gifts of money, which the chief clerk insisted had not influenced him or his subordinates in the discharge of their duties. But only four years previously the clerks had emphasized that they strictly observed the rule of the office forbidding the acceptance of fees. Then they had been petitioning for an increase in their salaries to meet the rising cost of living. The board had acted generously on that occasion so it is scarcely surprising that it punished the breach of the rule severely, dismissing the chief clerk and fining each of his subordinates a quarter's salary.[1]

The value of the board's work is not easily assessed. At the beginning of the nineteenth century the linen industry, especially in Ulster, was certainly in a flourishing condition. It clearly owed something to the board, but it is also clear that it was not an industry greatly in need of state assistance. And though two parliamentary committees in the early 'twenties recommended that the board be maintained, it was urged in the house of commons that a great industry should not be shackled at a cost to the public of £20,000 per annum. In 1827 the grant to the linen board was sharply cut, and in the following year the board itself was abolished.[2]

The directors of inland navigation were the successors of an eighteenth-century body, the corporation for promoting inland navigation, founded in 1752 and dissolved exactly a quarter of a century later after distributing in a negligent fashion an enormous amount of public money. In 1800 a committee of the Irish house of commons, in a long report, recommended that parliamentary grants for the construction of canals should be made under regulations approved by parliament, and by an act passed in the last session of the

[1] *Proceedings of the trustees . . . for the year 1816*, pp. 105–21.
[2] *Hansard*, new series, xvii. 245; 9 Geo. IV, c. 62.

Irish parliament £500,000 was assigned for the purpose of promoting canals. The lord lieutenant was empowered to appoint five directors. All canals constructed at the public expense were to be vested in these directors, and they were to examine all requests for grants for canals and if a grant was made, were to supervise the progress of the work. Each director was to receive a salary of £500 per annum—a parliamentary critic was quick to point out this would be an inducement to them to prolong their duties—and it was enacted that a proportion of their salaries could be deducted for non-attendance at directors' meetings.[1] In 1825 the directors were also appointed commissioners for maintaining those roads and bridges towards the construction of which the state had contributed at least half the cost. The commissioners were authorized to expend on this work at least £10,000, the expenditure to be repaid by the grand juries of the counties concerned.[2]

Besides supervising and inspecting projects the directors were soon responsible for working two existing waterways (the Tyrone Navigation and the Upper Shannon) and (indirectly) for managing the Newry Canal.[3] In 1813 they were entrusted with the completion of the Royal Canal, the Royal Canal Company being 'hopelessly insolvent'. Three years previously the directors had approved of the canal being extended to reach the Shannon at Termonbarry. The Grand Canal Company, fearing competition, appealed against this decision to the Irish privy council, which decided against the proposed extension. But a committee of the house of commons agreed with the directors, who were empowered to extend the Royal Canal on the line they favoured. In 1818 the completed canal was vested in the New Royal Canal Company, a body composed of the holders of loan debentures in the old company.[4] The directors were less fortunate in dealing with a minor project. In 1803 they took over from a local company a section of the Lower Shannon for repair and improvement. When the work was complete the company, unwilling to be burdened

---

[1] 40 Geo. III, c. 51; *Hansard*, 2 series, xxiii. 739.

[2] 6 Geo. IV, c. 101.

[3] The directors appointed nine of the principal inhabitants of Newry to act as 'local conductors' of the Newry canal.

[4] 39 Geo. III, c. 101; 58 Geo. III, c. 35.

with the maintenance costs, refused to take their property back and the board was unable to get it off their hands until 1830.[1]

To the two departments concerned with economic development which have been mentioned as in existence at the union, the linen board and directors of navigation, a third was temporarily added in 1809, the commissioners for inquiring into the nature and extent of the Irish bogs. Wellesley, when chief secretary, was concerned about 'the probable want of flax seed in Ireland' and he suggested that a commission should be appointed to inquire into the possibility of large-scale drainage operations.[2] In the summer of 1809 such a commission was constituted by a measure introduced by John Foster. An increase in Irish productivity, the preamble of the act explained, 'would not only increase the agriculture of Ireland and contribute much to its resources for the sustenance of the British Empire and its profitable export of corn, but is highly expedient towards promoting a secure supply of flax and hemp within the United Kingdom for the use of the navy and the support of the linen manufacture independent of foreign nations and of the interruptions of political events upon foreign trade'. The lord lieutenant was empowered to appoint five unpaid commissioners to conduct an inquiry into the extent of the bogs and the feasibility of draining them.[3] A warrant for the commissioners appointment was issued in September 1809 and they set to work immediately. They obtained permission to use the Royal Dublin Society's house as their headquarters and 'with a view to economy' they appointed as their secretary the society's assistant secretary with another of the society's employees as his clerk. The commissioners also employed nine engineers (at two guineas a day each) together with forty surveyors and a number of staffmen, chainmen and labourers.[4] Two of the engineers, Griffith and Nimmo, had later outstand-

---

[1] *Commission of inquiry into fees . . . thirteenth report*, pp. 37–8, H.C. 1813 (70), vi and 11 Geo. IV and I Will. IV, c. cxvvi.

[2] C. G. Andrews, 'Some precursors of Bord na Mona' in *Journal of the statistical and social inquiry society of Ireland*, xx, 146 ff.

[3] 49 Geo. III, c. 102.

[4] *Commissioners on the nature, extent and practicability of draining and cultivating the bogs of Ireland: reports*. The staff of the commission is given in its fourth report, pp. 19–22.

ing professional careers. Another, Richard Lovell Edgeworth, was already well-known as an educationalist, inventor and agriculturalist. When he was asked to serve on the commission Edgeworth was in poor health, but declaring that 'he would rather die doing something than doing nothing' he threw himself into the exhausting work of surveying difficult country with the greatest enthusiasm. Characteristically he began by 'remonstrating in vain against instructions which he thought would lead to great and needless expense'.[1]

The commission functioned for four and a half years, and its engineers produced detailed reports, which the commission published, relating to areas covering over a million acres. Undoubtedly the commission organized its survey competently and achieved a great deal at a relatively small cost in a short time. But the commission was against State intervention in economic life. It firmly pronounced that the future development of the Irish bogs should be left to private enterprise, hoping that, with the coming of peace, the value of Ireland 'as a field for the employment of British capital' would be appreciated. There was only one function which the commission suggested the state should perform. Through 'a commission of perambulation' it should try to establish precisely the boundaries of estates, since where they were uncertain, the fear of litigation stopped proprietors engaging in drainage schemes.

In 1819 another commission, the fishery board, was set up to supervise and encourage economic activity in a special sphere. The Irish parliament had attempted to encourage the fisheries, 'that rich but uncultivated waste surrounding our shores',[2] by a system of bounties, administered towards the close of the eighteenth century by a few inspectors working under the revenue commissioners.[3] In 1819, since the Irish fisheries were of 'the most essential importance to the wealth and commercial prosperity as well as to the naval strength of the United Kingdom', the Irish fisheries board was set up. The lord lieutenant was empowered to appoint between seven and twenty unpaid commissioners who were to pay

[1] *Memoirs of Richard Lovell Edgeworth* (1820), ii. 313–9.
[2] *Royal commissioners on Irish oyster fisheries: report on the coast and deep sea fisheries of Ireland*, p. 15, H.C. 1870 [Cd. 224], xiv.
[3] 25 Geo. III, c. 35; *Comm. Journ. Ireland*, xi. ccclxxxvi.

bounties for boats and on catches. The commission quickly recruited a small staff—a secretary, a clerk, four inspectors general and twenty local inspectors—and employed Alexander Nimmo, the engineer, to make a survey of the Irish coast. They also made loans for boats and equipment and built small piers. The commission was convinced that the fishing industry, paralysed by poverty, needed the fostering protection of the legislature, and in 1829 it pointed with pride to the fact that the number of Irish fishermen had almost doubled since it began operations. But bounties were going out of fashion and a critic of the commission suggested that it had been responsible for 'an excess of stimulation', the bounty system attracting more men to the industry than it could support.[1] So, understandably, in 1830 the bounties and the commission were abolished, the latter's functions in so far as they survived being vested in the board of works.[2]

In 1817, disturbed by post-war unemployment, parliament made lavish grants for public works, a quarter million being earmarked for Ireland. The lord lieutenant was empowered to nominate fifteen unpaid commissioners (the commissioners for advancing money from the consolidated fund) on whose advice loans were to be made. Seven commissioners were to be nominated to advise on loans urgently required.[3] In 1820 the lord lieutenant was empowered to appoint another unpaid commission to advance loans to merchants and manufacturers who were temporarily distressed. This commission operated until the middle 'fifties. The commissioners for advancing money from the consolidated fund advanced money for a wide variety of objects, making loans to grand juries to build roads, bridges and court-houses, to the churchwardens of a parish to build a steeple, to Lord Bantry to start a local linen manufacture, to Lord Clancarty to build a market house, and to the wide street commissioners in Dublin and Cork. Though only a handful of commissioners usually acted, projects seem to have been closely scrutinized and loans were on the whole repaid. The commission employed a secretary, a solicitor, and several inspecting engineers.[4]

[1] *Tenth report of the commissioners of Irish fisheries*, p. 5, H.C. 1829 (329), xiii.
[2] I Will. IV, c. 54.   [3] 57 Geo. III, c. 34.
[4] 57 Geo. III, c. 34, 123; *P.R.O.I., guide*, p. 272; P.W.I/I.4 (P.R.O.I.)

In 1831, the government decided to consolidate the agencies advancing public money by reorganizing the board of works. It may be said at once that the connection between the old and the new boards of works was slight. Still, as there was a continuity of title and to some extent of duties, this is an appropriate place to mention the department which at the end of the eighteenth century was usually known as the barrack board and board of works. It was formed of seven commissioners, of whom one was in sole charge of the barrack department. The work of the barrack department has already been discussed. The civil branch of the board was responsible for the upkeep of the Castle, the law courts, the residences in Phoenix Park, the park itself, and a few government and ecclesiastical buildings scattered through Dublin. The staff of this branch was composed of a secretary, an architect, four other officials, a couple of foremen (overseers), an unspecified number of labourers, a group of about a dozen, who performed humble but useful service in the board's own office, and the buildings under its care, the Castle fire-engine keeper, the keeper of the Castle stable yard, and the overseer of the lord lieutenant's garden.[1]

In December 1801, the lord lieutenant, Hardwicke, had issued instructions for the commissioners. These laid down that the commissioners were to meet once a week at a fixed time, that at least three commissioners must be present to form a board, and that an attendance list was to be furnished to the lord lieutenant. All items of expenditure exceeding £5 were to be submitted by the architect to the board and those exceeding £100 were to be laid before the lord lieutenant. Careful accounts were to be kept, estimates laid before parliament, and no fees received by any subordinate officer. The architect was to supervise the works carried out by the board and to survey annually the buildings under the care of the commissioners. He was to be paid half his salary in advance so as to be able to meet small incidental expenses. The overseer of buildings was to supervise the conduct of all workmen employed by the board, 'taking care that they attended regularly and performed their several duties with diligence and in a workmanlike manner'.[2] The commissioners replied promptly, promising to comply

[1] *Commissioner of inquiry into fees . . . twelfth report*, p. 42, H.C. 1812 (33), v.
[2] *Papers respecting instructions to the commissioners of works, Ireland*, 1805 (26), vi.

with these instructions, but ten years later a commission of inquiry discovered that frequently a board meeting was attended by only two commissioners, documents being sent to a third commissioner for his signature and his name being then inserted in the minutes. Money was being spent without previous authorization by the board, and the board's architect, Francis Johnston, celebrated for his bold, orginal and graceful handling of architectural problems, had on several occasions gravely underestimated the cost of his schemes. When asked for an explanation, he referred to the rising prices of materials, 'unforeseen casualties' and 'in some instance want of sufficient accuracy' in framing the estimates. The main reason why the board could be accused of over-spending during the first decade of the nineteenth century is, however, clear. Half its expenditure was on the official residences of the leading members of the Irish administration, and a commissioner admitted that 'orders from the lord lieutenant and the chief secretary are considered as peremptory, the board conceiving it had no control over them'. The commission of inquiry recommended that the board be dissolved and the buildings under its control placed under an architect responsible to the lord lieutenant or chief secretary.[1] This step was not taken and sixteen years later the committee on the Irish miscellaneous estimates seems to have been satisfied that the board's expenditure was on the whole being carefully controlled.

In 1831, as has been said, the board of works was reconstituted. The new board was composed of three commissioners appointed by the treasury. The treasury also was empowered to approve the board's establishment and sanction its expenditure. The board was empowered to make loans for public works and improvements to public bodies and individuals. The powers and duties of the commissioners for issuing money out of the consolidated fund (constituted in 1817) and the directors of inland navigation were vested in the board, and it was entrusted with the maintenance of public buildings in Dublin and of Kingstown and Dunmore harbours. The first three commissioners were Burgoyne, as chairman, Radcliff and Otterly. Burgoyne, a military engineer who had distinguished himself in the Peninsula, had an informed and sympathetic

[1] *Commission of inquiry into fees . . . twelfth report*, pp. 24, 30.

interest in the condition of the Irish peasantry, Radcliff who had been for some time a director of Inland Navigation had also been trained as a military engineer, Otterly was a Cambridge graduate.[1]

As time went on the board acquired new functions. The number of buildings for which it was responsible steadily grew. By 1857 it had taken over the constabulary buildings and all buildings connected with the customs, the inland revenue, the post office and the national education system.[2] In 1842, the board of works with an additional commissioner was constituted a commission for administering the drainage act passed in that year. In the same year the board was made responsible for the supervision of fisheries and in 1846, the powers of the Shannon commissioners were vested in the board.[3]

Drainage, fisheries and the Shannon were thus all entrusted to the board of works in the 'forties, and the board's handling of each subject was to be severely criticized. In 1835, since it was believed that the improvement of the Shannon would 'contribute to the general prosperity, commerce, agriculture and revenue of Ireland', the treasury had been empowered to appoint commissioners to survey the river, plan works which would render it navigable, and settle the compensation which ought to be paid to landowners whose properties were adversely affected. Five commissioners were appointed, the chairman being Burgoyne, chairman of the board of works. And the treasury warned the commission that 'while nothing is [to be] omitted that is requisite for the substantial and permanent character of the works, the whole should be executed in the most plain and economical manner, all extra expense for decoration and ornament being rejected, as the magnitude and importance of the work will be in fact its own most appropriate ornament'.[4] The commissioners carefully inspected the river,

---

[1] Burgoyne, *Letters on the state of Ireland*, 1831. For Radcliff's career see *Report from the select committee on miscellaneous expenditure, minutes of evidence*, p. 370, H.C. 1847–8 (543), xvii. 434.

[2] The Board was incorporated for the performance of its duties under the Queen's Colleges Act of 1845 (8 & 9 Vict., c. 66).

[3] 5 & 6 Vict., c. 89 and c. 106; 9 & 10 Vict., c. 86.

[4] 5 & 6 Will. IV, c. 67; *River Shannon: copy of the instructions given to the commissioners . . .*, p. 2, H.C. 1836 (61), xlvii.

and their fourth and last report, published in 1839, was accompanied by 120 maps and plans.[1] In the same year an act was passed 'for the improvement of the navigation of the river Shannon'. The treasury was empowered to appoint three commissioners for the purpose, who were permitted to draw up to £586,000 from the treasury to spend on the works, the money to be repaid by the counties and individuals benefiting. When the necessary works were completed the whole undertaking was to be handed over to the board of works.[2] Between 1839, and 1850 when the work was considered to be finished, the commissioners built piers, bridges and weirs, and deepened and cleared the channel.[3]

When these works were undertaken it was held that the improvement of the Shannon navigation should take precedence over the prevention of flooding. This, a later inquiry agreed, was a reasonable policy in the pre-railway age.[4] But after the middle of the century the Shannon was superseded as a means of communication and on the other hand severe flooding in 1861 led to complaints from riparian landowners. A house of lords select committee severely censured the Shannon commissioners for making unsanctioned departures from the plans approved by parliament, and the treasury appointed Bateman, the well-known hydraulic engineer, to survey the river. He suggested measures to prevent flooding which included the insertion of sluices in the solid weirs constructed by the Shannon commissioners. The government decided that parliament should be asked to meet only half the cost of Bateman's scheme. But as the proprietors who would benefit proved reluctant to come forward and shoulder the other half of the burden, nothing was done, until in 1880–2 parliament voted the necessary sums to enable the board of works to carry out part of Bateman's scheme.[5]

[1] *Reports of the commissioners for the improvement of the River Shannon,* 1836–9.

[2] 2 & 3 Vict., c. 61.

[3] *Reports of the commissioners for improving the navigation of the Shannon,* 1840–50.

[4] *Board of Works (Ireland) inquiry, committee's report,* pp. xxxvi–xxxviii, H.C. 1878 [Cd. 2060], xxiii.

[5] *Report from the select committee of the house of lords on the River Shannon . . . together with the . . . minutes of evidence,* p. iii, H.C. 1863 (292) 1; *First report of the royal commission on Irish public works,* pp. 22–7, H.C. 1887 [Cd. 5038], xxv.

The drainage act of 1842 seems to have been inspired by the Shannon scheme. It was enacted that if a scheme was suggested to the commissioners, they were to make a preliminary survey, give notice of what was intended so that objections might be lodged at quarter sessions, undertake a more detailed survey and if the proprietors of two-thirds of the lands affected agreed, execute the scheme, raising the necessary funds by a loan from government or private sources, charged on the lands improved. Very few works were begun under this act but with the famine 'there arose a cry for reproductive works' and the act was modified, detailed surveys and estimates being dispensed with and the consent of the proprietors of half the lands improved being taken as sufficient.

The board was severely criticized for its use during the famine of the powers it presumed that it possessed under the drainage acts. Relying on a clause in the act of 1842, which permitted it to make necessary 'deviations' when executing a drainage scheme, it considerably extended some schemes, saddling the proprietors of the lands improved with heavy additional expenses. Trevelyan, usually a firm upholder of *laissez-faire* ideals, defended this bold behaviour by arguing that 'the words of the act must be interpreted by the subject matter of the act', it being notorious that 'of all engineering works river drainage works are least capable of an exact estimate'. Moreover, he explained, Irish conditions were exceptional. 'In England', he said, 'for the business of private society to be done by private society is the rule and for the government to do that business is the exception. . . . In Ireland for the government to do this class of work is the rule; for individuals to do it is the exception'. But, Trevelyan emphasized, when the government accepted responsibility for executing a drainage scheme, it acted not only as the agent of the proprietors concerned but as trustee for the whole community.[1]

As a result of loud complaints from landowners, the house of lords in 1852 appointed a select committee to inquire into the drainage of land in Ireland. This committee declared that 'the reasoning which would transform the commissioners of public works into trustees invested with almost irresponsible authority' was inconclusive. And shortly afterwards a measure

[1] 5 & 6 Vict., c. 89; 9 Vict., c. 24.

was enacted under which the treasury remitted much of the debt involuntarily incurred by Irish proprietors whose lands were included in drainage schemes amended by the board of works.[1]

In 1863, a new drainage act was passed. It relieved the board of works of the responsibility of executing drainage works. But if in any area a group of landed proprietors took the initiative and prepared a scheme, the board of works could, after inquiry, approve it and confirm it by a provisional order which would constitute the area a drainage district with a drainage board. The board of works could then make loans to the drainage board to enable it to carry out the scheme. One hundred and twenty districts were constituted under the drainage code of 1842, and sixty-three more were formed under the code of 1863, but nevertheless flooding continued to be a serious Irish problem and the board of works was sometimes blamed for not being more active. But at the beginning of the twentieth century a vice-regal committee on drainage reported that the legislation under which the board was functioning had been rendered obsolete by the land acts.[2]

By the fisheries act of 1842 (the first of a series of fishery acts) the board of works was empowered to appoint two inspectors to enforce the regulations on river and deep sea fishing imposed by the act. Three years later the treasury was empowered to appoint a fishery commissioner, and Mulvany, already a member of the board, was made commissioner for fisheries. In 1848 it was enacted that the two existing fishery inspectors should become fishery commissioners and members of the board when it was considering fishery questions. The

[1] *Report of the select committee of the house of lords appointed to inquire into the operation of the acts relating to the drainage of land in Ireland*, pp. 10–11, H.C. 1852–3 (10), xxvi. After the publication of this report Mulvany, the commissioner especially responsible for drainage, resigned on pension. He then went to Germany where as an engineer and financier he played a great part in the industrial development of the Ruhr. (See J. Ryan, 'William Thomas Mulvany' in *Studies*, xii. 378–90 and J. O'Loan, 'Origin and development of arterial drainage in Ireland and the pioneers' in *Department of agriculture, journ.*, lix.

[2] *Viceregal committee on arterial drainage: report* . . ., H.C. 1907 [Cd. 3374], xxxii; *Hansard*, 4 series, clxxii. 1113–37, 5 series, iii. 1681–1759; *Eighty-second annual report of the commissioners of public works in Ireland*, p. 8, H.C. 1914 [Cd. 7563], xlvii.

board's management of its fishery duties was from time to time sharply criticized. Redmond Barry, one of the first fishery commissioners and an experienced official, in the early 'forties wanted the board to make loans to fishermen. The board turned his suggestion down, and later Sir Richard Griffith, when chairman of the board, enunciated that it 'was the special duty' of the fishery commissioners 'never to recommend any course calculated to produce any expenditure'. The board sometimes deleted from Barry's reports, before publication, passages which suggested expenditure, and when in 1861 Ffennell, the other fishery commissioner, was appointed a commissioner in England, Barry, then over seventy, was left to carry on alone with the occasional help of a clerk.[1]

In 1849 and again in 1867 a select committee of the house of commons expressed the opinion that, considering the number of duties devolved on the board of works, the administration of the fishery acts should be entrusted to a separate department. And though leading officials of the board were quite confident that the board was capable of handling fishery business, it was in the 'sixties removed from its hands. In 1863, by the salmon fishery act, three commissioners were appointed to decide issues which might arise over the management of the salmon fisheries—especially in respect to the weirs. And in 1869 the powers of these commissioners and of the board of works under the fishery acts were transferred to three fishery commissioners appointed by the lord lieutenant. These commissioners with a staff of less than a dozen formed a small independent department, which was absorbed after thirty years existence by the department of agriculture and technical instruction in 1899.[2]

An immense amount of work was thrust on the board of works as a result of the famine. Between the close of 1845 and the beginning of 1847 an attempt was made to provide employment by a series of acts encouraging an extensive programme of

---

[1] 5 & 6 Vict., c. 106; 11 & 12 Vict., c. 92.

[2] Griffith declared that what he had said was that no expenditure should be suggested in a report until it had been considered by the treasury. *Report from the select committee on fisheries (Ireland)*, p. ix, H.C. 1849 (536), xiii; *Report from the select committee on sea coast fisheries (Ireland) Bill*, pp. vii, 128, 134, 242, H.C. 1867 (443), xiv; 32 & 33 Vict., cc. 9, 92

public works. These were initiated by local bodies, acting through the machinery of presentment sessions. It was the duty of the board of works to inspect the plans, decide whether a grant towards the cost should be made, and supervise the execution of the approved works.[1] Secondly, in 1846 the board was entrusted with the expenditure of £50,000 for the improvement of Irish fisheries. Thirdly, land improvement schemes and arterial drainage schemes had to be pushed forward as fast as possible.[2] Throughout, as has been mentioned earlier, the treasury firmly supervised the board's activities. At the beginning of operations, in 1846, Trevelyan, writing to Colonel Jones, emphasized that 'care ought to be taken that the funds granted by parliament for the relief of the people during the scarcity are not to be misappropriated to serve the interested views of private individuals and that the permanent interests of the community do not suffer by an advantage being taken of this temporary emergency to get rid of rules which have been found by experience to be of much practical utility'. Trevelyan also insisted that, when a grant was made for public works, a local contribution should be obtained, either from landowners in the area or from the country. But, he added, 'this and every other rule must however be modified or suspended in cases when it is evident that the consequence of our insisting on the strict execution of our rule would be that the people would starve'.[3] Some months later, to prevent labourers leaving their proper employment to congregate on relief works, the treasury, when issuing detailed instructions for local committees, insisted that wages on relief works should be 'at least' 2d. a day below the average in the district and that persons employed on relief works should if possible be paid in proportion to the work done by them. Also Trevelyan instructed the board of works to make it quite clear that the advances made for relief works were being sanctioned 'not for the sake of the works themselves, but for the sake of the relief afforded by them', and that the works would be discontinued when no longer necessary for relief.[4]

[1] 26 & 27 Vict. c. 114, 32 Vict. cc. 9, 92, 62 & 63 Vict. c. 50.

[2] 9 Vict., c. 1; 9 & 10 Vict., cc. 85, 86, 101, 108; 10 & 11 Vict., c. 106.

[3] *Correspondence explanatory of the measures adopted . . . for the relief of distress . . .*, pp. 270, 279, H.C. 1846 (735), xxxvii.

[4] *Relief of distress in Ireland correspondence . . . (Board of works series)*, pp. 67–71, 97, H.C. 1847 (764), l.

To carry out its emergency duties the board rapidly enlarged its staff, so that by February 1847 there was engaged in supervising relief schemes a staff of over 14,000, including 76 inspecting officers, over 500 engineers, 8,000 overseers, 4,000 check clerks, and 550 pay clerks. Moreover at the central office in Dublin, 'the heart of a colossal organization', into which there poured on an average eight hundred letters a day, over a hundred extra clerks were employed.[1] It was naturally difficult to recruit quickly staff on such a scale. Assistant engineers were difficult to find, many pay clerks, overworked, were unable to keep their accounts up-to-date, many others resigned. As for the overseers, these, Jones declared, were 'generally persons recommended by gentlemen in the county. When we get one good and trustworthy, ten will be found to be the reverse'. However, the board had the utmost confidence in their inspecting officers, all military men. These officers, the board reported, 'under great and constantly varying difficulties had been guided by one simple principle—duty'. And the sappers and miners who had been appointed overseers had also done 'good service, well conducted and very useful'.[2]

Down in the country this staff had to prepare schemes quickly, largely for road-making and drainage, to provide work for the immense masses who were starving. As might be expected, many of the schemes were, the board admitted, of doubtful utility. Also the board was often exasperated by the behaviour of the local bodies with which it had to co-operate. The presentment sessions, Jones complained, very often sanctioned a scheme without proper investigation, and the relief committees, whose duty it was to scrutinize applications for employment, exercised 'little or no discretion'. 'Each body', Jones wrote, 'is ready to excuse itself with the people by throwing its duty upon our shoulders and then they appeal clamorously to

[1] *Correspondence . . . relating to the measures adopted for the relief of distress . . . (Board of Works series), Second part,* p. 190, H.C. 1847 (797), lii; *Correspondence . . . relating to the measures adopted for the relief of distress (Board of Works series),* p. 349, H.C. 1847 (764), l.

[2] *Correspondence . . . relating to the measures adopted for the relief of distress (Board of Works series),* p. 263, H.C. 1847 (764) l; *Correspondence . . . to the measures adopted for the relief of distress (Board of Works series), Second part,* p. 191, H.C. 1847 (797), lii.

the government against the result of the non-performance of their own duty'.[1]

The head office in Dublin was painfully aware of the crisis with which its machinery was struggling to cope. Stickney, who was appointed accountant to the board towards the close of 1846, wrote to Trevelyan shortly after arriving in Dublin, 'I assure you I am without hope of ever reaping either satisfaction or credit from this appointment beyond that negative satisfaction of having toiled daily from a few minutes before ten in the morning (this *dark* season) until after *seven* in the evening. A dinner after that makes it 8½ p.m. before one can have a moment for quiet or reflection. . . . It is of little avail to talk about system and theory, etc. We have people to deal with who are regardless of rules and regulations, and *their places cannot be supplied if you dismiss them* (engineers, assistant engineers, etc.)'.[2] And Jones himself declared that 'a stranger can form no idea of our office work; the passages and corridors are blocked up with deputations and expectants for office, and this we cannot prevent unless our doors were kept constantly locked. Instead of the quiet of a well-regulated London office, ours resembles a great bazaar'.[3]

By the early 'fifties the audit of the relief accounts was completed and the board's work was back to normal. But the diversity and range of its activities continued to grow. As was pointed out in 1870, the Irish commissioners of public works conducted all the business entrusted in England to two separate departments (the commissioners of works and the public works loan commissioners). And during the next twenty years the board's duties were largely increased 'both by automatic development and as the result of legislation'.[4] One of its most important duties was the issue of loans under a series of land improvement acts, beginning in 1847, for drainage, sub-soiling, farm buildings, and labourers' cottages. The board also made loans for sanitary improvements (from 1874), and for building

---

[1] *Correspondence . . . relating to the measures adopted for the relief of distress* (*Board of Works series*), p. 196, H.C. 1847 (764), i.

[2] *Ibid.*, p. 477.   [3] *Ibid.*, p. 263.

[4] *Board of Works* (*Ireland*) *inquiry committee report* . . . p. x, H.C. 1878 [Cd. 2060], xxiii; *Sixty-sixth report of the commissioners of public works, Ireland*, p. 5, H.C. 1898 [Cd. 9029], xx.

working-class dwellings (from 1866), glebe houses for clergy-men of any denomination (from 1870), national school teachers' residences (from 1875) and dispensaries (from 1879). From 1851 it arbitrated between railway companies and landowners over the acquisition of land by the former, from 1871 it made loans for the construction of railways and conducted inquiries into the merits of tramway and railway schemes. Under the Irish church act of 1869 it was entrusted with the care of disused churches deemed to be national monuments, and in 1882 it was constituted the authority for the preservation of national monuments. From 1883 it administered the funds provided under the sea fisheries act for the construction of piers and harbours.

It was unfortunate that a department which was being en-trusted with such a variety of duties should have been severely crippled about the middle of the century by a successful effort to achieve a small and ill-advised economy. It has been pointed out that the board as originally constituted consisted of three members. In 1846 two more were added, and by a treasury minute certain duties were assigned to each member. However, when Jones and Larcom left the board in 1850 and 1853 respectively, the treasury did not fill the consequent vacancies, and when Griffith resigned in 1864, 'his services were retained for any special occasion . . . but generally as a non-effective member of the board'. Thus, though the board in practice consisted of only two members, its statutory size was theoretically maintained. Naturally enough, formal meetings were aban-doned—'a board of two', it was remarked, 'is scarcely a board' —though the two commissioners and the assistant commissioner who was appointed in 1873 frequently consulted one another. The chairman was dissatisfied and pressed for the appointment of a third commissioner, pointing out that office routine and the reception of callers absorbed the two commissioners' time, making it impossible for one of them to make an inspection of work in progress. A departmental commission appointed by the treasury in 1878 reinforced his plea by listing instances where the board had shown vacillation and hesitancy. A few years later a third commissioner was appointed and board meetings seem to have been resumed. In fairness it must be added that the commission of 1878 considered that, generally speaking, the board had displayed great energy and achieved a considerable degree of success in its 'multifarious and extensive dealings'.[1]

The board of works was for nearly half a century the principal agency through which the government influenced Irish economic development. There were a few other departments with economic functions, but they merely supervised relatively narrow spheres. The cattle diseases act of 1866 empowered the lord lieutenant to make regulations for checking infection amongst animals. And in 1873 the officials appointed by the lord lieutenant to administer these regulations were constituted by statute the veterinary department of the privy council.[2] This department which comprised a director, a couple of assistants and a few clerks, was absorbed in 1899 by the newly created department of agriculture and technical instruction. Under the home office there were inspectors of factories (from 1833) and mines (from 1872). And in 1855 a registrar of friendly societies for Ireland was appointed to whom these societies had to submit their accounts.[3]

Under the merchant shipping acts the board of trade appointed surveyors in Irish ports and from 1872 it controlled the government emigration officers in Ireland. From their first appointment in 1833 until 1840 these officers were under the colonial office. In 1840, they were placed under the superivision of the colonial land and emigration commission and thirty-two years later they were transferred to the board of trade.[4] In 1862, the board of trade, acting under the powers conferred by the companies act, appointed a registrar of companies in Dublin. In 1909, the board was empowered to open labour exchanges throughout the United Kingdom. And by 1914, it was operating twenty-one of these exchanges in Ireland.[5] The board of trade also from 1854 strictly controlled

[1] *Board of works (Ireland) inquiry committee report* . . ., pp. x–lxii, 3, 17, H.C. 1878 [Cd. 2060], xxiii.

[2] 29 & 30 Vict., c. 4; 35 & 36 Vict., c. 16.   [3] 18 & 19 Vict., c. 63.

[4] F. H. Hitchins, *The colonial land and emigration commission*, chapters III & IV; O. MacDonagh, *A pattern of government growth, 1800–60*.

[5] 9 Edw. VII, c. 7; *Industrial directory of the United Kingdom*, H.C. 1914 [Cd. 7483], lxxx.

the expenditure of the Irish lighthouse authority. In 1810, the management of the Irish lighthouses (apparently about a dozen in number) had been transferred from the revenue commissioners to the commissioners for preserving and managing the port of Dublin (the ballast board). In 1867 the duties of the port commissioners were divided between two bodies, the Dublin port and dock board and the commissioners of Irish lights, the latter body, working under the supervision of the board of trade, being responsible for Irish lighthouses.[1]

In 1836, the loan fund board, whose members were appointed by the lord lieutenant and unpaid, was set up to supervise charitable loan societies, formed 'for the benefit and advantage of the industrious classes of His Majesty's subjects'. Such societies had to submit their rules and accounts to the board, which could inquire into their management. The board was empowered to appoint a staff, but, presumably by an oversight, was not empowered to pay it. However, in 1843, the board was provided with a source of revenue from the sale of official forms to the societies it supervised, and then it appointed a secretary and an inspector. In 1850 Richard Robert Madden, the historian, was appointed secretary to the board, a position which he was to hold for thirty years. Madden, who had had an adventurous career as a physician and magistrate in the Levant, the West Indies and on the west coast of Africa, was an energetic secretary. Soon after his appointment he secured the dismissal in rapid succession of two inspectors, one for negligence, the other for incompetency, and he drew up new rules defining the inspector's duties. He also strongly recommended to a parliamentary committee of inquiry that the board's powers should be increased and that a paid commissioner should be

---

[1] The commissioners of Irish lights were not a government department, since the commissioners consisted of *ex officio* members belonging to the Dublin corporation and co-opted members. But the co-opted members had to be approved of by the lord lieutenant, the commission's clerks sat an examination conducted by the civil service commission and the board of trade exercised close financial control. For Irish lighthouse administration see 36 Geo. III, c. 18; 50 Geo. III, c. 95; 17 & 18 Vict., c. 104; 30 & 31 Vict., c. lxxxi; *Report of the select committee appointed to inquire into the state and management of the lighthouses*, pp. lxx—lxxvii. H.C. 1834 (590), xii; *Royal commission on lighthouse administration, vol. I: report*, pp. 3–10, H.C. 1908 [Cd. 3923], lxix.

appointed, explaining that he often found it difficult to assemble a board, 'having to send pressing notes to the members to secure their attendance'.[1] The committee agreed with him, but no legislative action followed, and a committee of inquiry authorized by the loan fund board in 1896, found that most of the Irish loan societies were being badly mismanaged. The committee recommended that the board should not only have power to dissolve a society which failed to comply with the rules on which it held its certificate but should also be empowered to recall a certificate and to impose on societies rules which it thought necessary to their proper management. Some years later the loan fund board found itself in a most undignified situation for a government department. Its revenue was insufficient to meet its modest expenditure and it was approaching bankruptcy. It suggested it should be given an annual grant from the exchequer. Instead, however, after two committees had reported, in December 1915, by an order in council, its powers and duties were transferred to the department of agriculture and technical instruction.[2]

In the late 'sixties a comparatively large, if temporary, department with important economic functions was established, the church temporalities commission.[3] Its creation was a result of the decision in 1869 to sever the connection between church and state, and it had two distinct sets of duties to perform. It had both to arrange for the payment of compensation to interests adversely affected by disestablishment and manage a mass of ecclesiastical property taken over by the state. The

[1] *Report from the select committee on loan fund societies (Ireland) . . . and minutes of evidence*, pp. 9, 22, 337, H.C. 1854-5 (259), vii.

[2] *Report of the committee appointed to inquire into . . . charitable loan societies in Ireland*, pp. 383-415, H.C. 1897 [Cd. 8381] xxiii; *Report of the departmental committee on agricultural credit in Ireland*, pp. 81-118, H.C. 1914 [Cd. 7375], xiii.

[3] *Irish church temporalities commission report . . . from the commencement of the commission to 31 Dec. 1874*, H.C. 1875 [Cd. 1148], xx; *Irish church temporalities commission, report for the period 1869-80*, H.C. 1881 [Cd. 2773], xxviii; *Return of the officers and persons in the employment of the commissioners of the Irish church temporalities*, H.C. 1877 (122) lxvi; *Reminiscences of Lord Kilbracken* 1931), p. 17.

commission was composed at first of three commissioners, Lord Monck, a moderate liberal who had been governor general of Canada, James Lawson, a justice of the common pleas with a keen interest in economics, and Hamilton, who having been for years a leading Irish conservative M.P. had been appointed by Lord Derby, permanent secretary to the treasury. On Hamilton's death in 1871, his colleagues intimated that in their opinion two commissioners would henceforth be sufficient, and his place was therefore not filled. The commission took over the ecclesiastical commission's headquarters (Mornington House, Upper Merrion Street), and quickly with treasury assistance recruited and organized a staff which by the middle 'seventies numbered about sixty.[1] At its head was Godley, a soldier 'with great social gifts' who had been Monck's secretary in Canada. Directly under the secretary was the chief clerk's department, with about twenty clerks. It not only handled the general correspondence of the commission, but also was made responsible for the sale of rent charges and land. The collection department which was responsible for the receipt of revenue was even larger, having a staff of about thirty. The commission also employed a registrar, an accountant and a solicitor, each with a few clerks to assist him.

Within a few years of setting to work the commission had almost accomplished one of its two main duties. It had assessed and met (usually by the payment of a lump sum) the claims of the Church of Ireland clergy, of laymen who had held office in the established church, of the owners of advowsons, and of the presbyterian clergy. It had also handed over to the Church of Ireland the buildings and attached lands to which it was entitled under the church act, it had paid to the trustees of Maynooth and to the presbyterian church compensation for the annual grants paid to their respective theological colleges, and it had decided which ruinous buildings should be handed over to the board of works to be maintained as ancient monuments.

The commission's other important function was the administration of the property, consisting of the rent charges and land belonging to the established church, vested in it by the church act. The commission strove to sell these assets as quickly as

[1] The church temporalities commission took over members of the staff of the ecclesiastical commission. For the ecclesiastical commission see p. 14.

possible, and in accordance with the intention of the 'Bright clauses' in the church act it tried, by accepting only a quarter of the price in cash, the remainder being treated as a mortgage, to induce the tenant to purchase his holding. In this operation the commission displayed considerable ingenuity in devising methods to remove as far as possible 'every difficulty of a technical or mechanical nature which stood in the way of an uneducated man undertaking and bringing to conclusion what is usually an embarrassing and complicated legal proceeding'.

Gladstone's second land act (1881), set up a new department, the land commission, which was responsible both for fixing 'fair' rents and for making loans to tenants who wished to purchase their holdings. The commission was also entrusted with the administration of the property controlled by the church temporalities commission which was dissolved. The powers of the land commission were at first vested in three commissioners, the judicial commissioner, who had to be a barrister of at least ten years standing and who had the status and tenure of a high court judge, and two other commissioners appointed for seven years.[1] The first judicial commissioner was John O'Hagan, an able lawyer who had been a contributor to the *Nation*. His two colleagues were Litton and Vernon. Litton, a Q.C., had distinguished himself at the general election of 1868 by defeating a Hamilton in Tyrone, and 'this service to the liberal party gave him a claim' which contemporary opinion believed was met by his appointment as a land commissioner.[2] But it was generally agreed that he was fair and able and if his decisions were generally in favour of the tenant he was firmly opposed to straining the act in favour of either side. He was balanced by Vernon, a conservative who had been agent for the Pembroke and other estates and was noted for his intelligent broad-minded approach to the land problem. In 1882 Lord Monck was added to the commission for two years. In 1885, when the Ashbourne act provided for the advance by the commission of the entire purchase money to a tenant who agreed with his landlord to purchase his holding, two new commissioners, both court officials with considerable knowledge of land matters, were added to the commission, it being enacted that they were 'especially to attend to' land purchase. In 1891,

[1] 44 & 45 Vict., c. 49.   [2] For Litton see *The Times*, 29 Nov. 1890.

the commission was made permanent, and twelve years later Wyndham's great land purchase act of 1903 which provided facilities for the purchase of estates *en bloc* either by the tenants or the land commission, also remodelled the commission. One of the commissioners, Fitzgerald, was created a judicial commissioner, and three estates commissioners were appointed to supervise purchase operations under the act. One of the estates commissioners was to be a land commissioner and the next two vacancies in the land commission were not to be filled, so that ultimately the commission was to be composed of two judicial and three estates commissioners.[1] A non-judicial commissioner was removable between 1891 and 1903 only by an order of the lord chancellor and after 1903 only by an order in council and the order of removal had to be laid before parliament. Under the act of 1881, the lord lieutenant had power to appoint assistant commissioners, and a sub-commission composed of two or more assistant commissioners acted as a local court of first instance in 'fair rent' cases. Some of the assistant commissioners had legal qualifications, while the others were expected to have a 'practical' knowledge of farming and agriculture. A sub-committee was composed of a legal and one or more lay assistant commissioners. The assistant commissioners who were comparatively well paid were at first temporary officials. In 1891, some were given permanent appointments, but as the work fluctuated a number were retained on a temporary basis. As might be expected, their qualifications were closely scrutinized by the public and their decisions frequently disappointed either the landlord or the tenant. Even the commissioners, it was sometimes suggested, had an ineluctable bias when dealing with rents. Still it is probably true that the commission and its staff strove hard to find a series of principles on which agricultural profits might be fairly divided between landlord and tenant. And their work at least helped to simplify the problem of land purchase.

The land commission had from the outset a large staff, numbering by 1882 about 120, including 36 sub-commissioners, five valuers and about 60 clerks. By 1914, the commission's staff numbered about 550, including 30 sub-commissioners, 39 inspectors, 49 surveyors and about 360 clerks. This staff was

[1] 54 & 55 Vict., c. 48; 3 Edw. VII, c. 37.

divided amongst seventeen 'branches'. Of these, twelve were occupied solely with land purchase and three with duties on the fair rent side, the rest performed duties common to both sides.[1]

The liberals devised machinery for coping with a specific Irish problem, land tenure, the conservatives devised machinery for dealing with a special area—the congested districts. Over much of the west of Ireland, the rural population, 'wretchedly housed and insufficiently fed', lacking knowledge and capital, was struggling to extract a mere subsistence from the soil. Balfour who toured the west in the summer of 1890 believed that what the region required was a department that would give 'paternal assistance' to districts which were too poor to help themselves, 'acting as a very wealthy and benevolent landlord might act towards an estate . . . in which he found people sunk in great difficulties from which they were quite incapable of extricating themselves'. And in the land purchase act of 1891, Balfour embodied provisions establishing a department of this nature—the congested districts board. The term 'congested' was somewhat misleading. It simply meant a zone where acute poverty prevailed. A statutory definition of congested district was decided on, which enabled the government to de-limit the zone in which it wanted the board to function. It was an electoral division of which the rateable value was less than thirty shillings per head, situated in a county, twenty per cent of whose inhabitants lived in divisions of such a rateable value. In 1891 the congested districts, stretching from Donegal through Connaught to West Cork, included about a sixth of the area and a ninth of the population of Ireland. The board consisted of ten members all unpaid, two *ex officio*, (the chief secretary, or in his absence the under-secretary, and a land commissioner), and eight members nominated by the crown. Its functions were defined in wide terms. Within the congested districts it could purchase tenants' interests with the object of enlarging holdings, and take steps to encourage agriculture, industry and fishing. Balfour was anxious to avoid trammelling the new department 'by I won't say red tape, for that is rather an offensive word, but by rules and precedents which are very

[1] *Royal commission on civil service, fourth report, evidence*, pp. 304, 607–8, H.C. 1914 [Cd. 7340], xvi.

proper limitations to the action of a great government department'.[1] So the board was granted almost unlimited control over the fixed income placed at its disposal. In January 1892, Balfour, by then first lord of the treasury, stated his views on the position of the board in a short memorandum which Micks, the board's secretary and historian, described as its 'charter of freedom'. The board, Balfour laid down, was not 'in the ordinary sense a government department, nor is it subordinate either to the chief secretary's office or the ministry of the day'.[2] While Sir Antony McDonnell was under-secretary (1902–8) Micks saw symptoms of a design to subordinate the board to the chief secretary's office—and undoubtedly McDonnell, who was an unflagging administrator, gathered an important share of the board's business into his own hands. But on the whole the board both preserved its autonomy and had amicable relations with departments with which it came in frequent contract—the land commission, and the department of agriculture and technical instruction.

The board, which had a very varied membership, including civil servants, catholic ecclesiastics, landlords and members of parliament, threw itself with alacrity and enterprise into a variety of useful activities. At the outset Balfour suggested that a survey of the area under its care should be made, which would provide precise knowledge of the problems facing it and a 'base-line' by which to calculate the progress made. Six temporary inspectors were appointed and an immense amount of information collected. The board then initiated a series of schemes. It distributed seeds, planted trees, took steps to encourage the breed of horses, cattle, donkeys and poultry, sent out agricultural instructors, and encouraged the spraying of potatoes, bee-keeping and fruit growing. It made loans to a few weaving factories, and promoted cottage industries, crochet work, lace work and cloth weaving. It improved communications, building roads and causeways, constructed piers, planned the marketing of fish, set up curing stations, and made loans

---

[1] *Royal commission on congestion in Ireland, fifth report, appendix,* p. 1, H.C. 1907 [Cd. 3630], xxxvi.

[2] *Royal commission on congestion in Ireland, first report, appendices,* pp. 4, 7, H.C. 1906 [Cd. 3267], xxxii. 633; A. L. Micks, *An account of the . . . congested districts board* (1925), p. 17.

for the purchase of fishing boats. But soon, owing to a curious, and it might be added unexpected, shift in the balance of the board's work all these activities became overshadowed by its land programme. It very soon was clear that tenants in the west were most reluctant to relinquish their interest in the soil but on the other hand there were landlords who were prepared to sell their estates. Now 'it is', as Micks wrote, 'a fascinating occupation to Irishmen to buy, sell and deal with land', and soon the board was busy taking over estates for re-sale to the tenants.[1] At first the board had to use the land commission, but in 1893 by a bill backed by Balfour and Morley it was empowered to appoint trustees to hold land on its behalf and later legislation granted the board increased facilities for land purchase, including power to obtain from the land commission stock (in 1896) and cash (in 1903).

By the land act of 1909, the board's powers were extended, its resources increased and its composition altered. The area under its supervision was about doubled. It was given exclusive control of land purchase in the congested districts, its powers in relation to estates which it handled were strengthened, and it was empowered to take steps to acquire land compulsorily. From January 1910, the board was composed of the chief secretary, the under-secretary, the vice-president of the department of agriculture and technical instruction, nine unpaid members and two paid members. A paid member could only be removed by an order in council which was to be laid before both houses of parliament, and if either house demanded its annulment the king in council could revoke it.[2] The first two paid members were Micks and Doran, both of whom remained in office until the dissolution of the board in 1923.

In 1914 the congested districts board had a staff of about 200, divided into two almost equal sections, the staff of the office in Dublin, and the 'outdoor' staff of the estates branch, concerned with the purchase, preparations for re-sale, and improvement of estates. This latter section was composed of men

---

[1] A. L. Micks, *op cit.*, p. 101. Micks later regretted the tendency of the Board to concentrate on land purchase since he was anxious to obtain state encouragement for industrial development. But he admits that as secretary to the Board he was keenly interested in land purchase.

[2] 9 Edw. VII, c. 42.

with engineering and surveying qualifications, who as a body, according to Doran, were not only full of enthusiasm but displayed great tact and patience in reorganizing the boundaries of 'little holdings' in remote districts.[1]

Just before the century ended, a third major department with important duties in the agricultural sphere, the department of agriculture and technical instruction, was created. There was a widespread belief that the state should make a sustained effort to improve Irish agriculture. This belief was expressed forcibly by Horace Plunkett, paradoxically an idealist who urged his fellow countrymen to think less about politics and more about economic matters. Irishmen, divided and embittered by politics, might become united in a high-minded endeavour to make their country more productive and prosperous. Plunkett combined crusading zeal with experience and great persuasiveness, in his writings gracefully blending epigrams and earnestness. In 1895 he collected a powerful committee, 'the recess committee', composed of men drawn from differing political camps. This committee published a report which emphasized that the administration of state assistance to agriculture and industry in Ireland should be entrusted to a single department which would also be responsible for technical education.[2]

The government—Lord Salisbury had become prime minister for the third time in 1895—had even before the report appeared been considering the creation of a department of agriculture, and in 1899 the department of agriculture and technical instruction was set up. In addition to being responsible for the organization of agricultural and technical education, the new department took over from other departments a number of duties relating to agriculture and fisheries, including the collection of agricultural statistics, the prevention of animal and plant disease and the inspection and encouragement of the Irish fisheries. It was also entrusted with the supervision of the National Museum, the National Library and the Botanical Gardens at Glasnevin. And the lord lieutenant was empowered, with the consent of the treasury, to transfer to the new

[1] *Royal commission on the civil service, second appendix to the fourth report*, pp. 319–29, 609–10, H.C. 1914 [Cd. 7340], xvi.
[2] *Report of the Recess committee . . .* (1896).

department any duties performed by any other Irish government department which were analogous to the duties transferred to it on its foundation.[1] In 1905 the geological survey of Ireland, which was being administered by the English board of education, was transferred to the department.

Gerald Balfour, the chief secretary, who introduced the bill constituting the department, was exceedingly anxious that it should be in touch with the groups it was designed to benefit. Therefore he took the unusual step of establishing a group of semi-representative advisory bodies, the council of agriculture, the agricultural board and the board of technical instruction, which were to assist the department. The council was composed of persons nominated by the county councils and by the department in the ratio of two to one, the department being obliged to nominate a number of persons resident in each province equal to the number of counties in the province. The agricultural board was composed of two representatives from each province, elected by the members of the council of agriculture from the province, together with the president, the vice-president and four persons nominated by the department. The board of technical instruction was composed of persons appointed by the county boroughs, the urban district councils, the county council representatives on the council of agriculture, the board of national education, the intermediate education board and the department itself. The two boards were to advise the department on all matters it submitted to them, and had a veto over the expenditure of a portion of the department's revenue. The council of agriculture was to meet at least once a year to discuss matters connected with the act.

At the head of the department was the vice-president (the president, who was expected to be a figurehead, being the chief secretary) who could sit in parliament and who ranked as a junior minister. This arrangement was administratively and politically convenient. It spared the already over-burdened chief secretary by not imposing on him the management of a complex department, and it was a conciliatory gesture towards those nationalists, who, though critical of the whole system of government in Ireland, welcomed the foundation of the new department. Constitutionally the department could not be an

[1] 62 & 63 Vict., c. 50.

independent enclave in the Irish administration. A minister had to be responsible for its working. But by refraining from putting it directly under the minister responsible for law and order, something was done to keep the department out of the political line of fire.

The department had a wide and varied range of duties and touched Irish life at many points. As its title implied it was founded to promote education on practical lines. But it was also entrusted with a number of functions relating to agriculture hitherto performed by other departments, and it was in fact a ministry of agriculture. In its educational work the department co-operated with the county councils and the councils of urban districts which appointed committees to deal with agricultural and technical education. It drew up schemes, maintained standards, gave grants-in-aid, assisted institutions which provided technical instruction and tried to supply teachers. By 1914 it managed ten institutions in which approved courses in agriculture were given, including the Royal College of Science, the Albert College, the forestry centre at Avondale and stations where short courses were given to farmers' sons and daughters. And it was in process of taking over the Royal Veterinary College. In co-operation with the national board it established classes for national teachers in experimental science, drawing, domestic economy and rural science. It tried to ensure a supply of teachers in commercial subjects by granting scholarships to the London School of Economics. In agreement with the intermediate board it published programmes in science and art for the secondary schools. Immediately after it was constituted the department sent out 'pioneer lecturers' on agricultural subjects. By 1914 there were 138 lecturers, appointed by the county committees and paid by the department, giving 'itinerant instruction' in agriculture, horticulture, poultry and butter making.

In co-operation with the county committees the department devised schemes to improve livestock, poultry and flax. It arranged for seed testing, it conducted experiments in plant breeding, made loans for agricultural purposes, and purchased land for afforestation. It investigated complaints against transport companies, encouraged local authorities to enforce the food and drugs acts and took proceedings against British firms 'for falsely describing articles purporting to be of Irish origin'. The veterinary branch was active in checking animal disease. The fisheries branch made loans to fishermen, improved harbours, restocked oyster beds and scientifically investigated fishery problems. The statistics and intelligence branch not only published a vast mass of material relating to Irish economic life, but also produced for the department a quarterly journal and a number of reports and leaflets.

The department was organized in nine branches—the secretariat, the accounts, agriculture, technical instruction, fisheries, veterinary, transit and markets, statistics and intelligence, and science and art institutions. Among these branches there was distributed in 1914 a staff of 370 (including over 100 inspectors). And the growing importance of the department's work is illustrated by the fact that between 1906 and 1914 this staff had increased by fifty per cent. Moreover, half a dozen institutions controlled by the department had staffs which in 1914 totalled over 200. If instructors employed by the county committees are also taken into account, the department with a staff of about 700 was easily the largest of the Irish government departments.[1]

The first vice-president was Plunkett, who was fortunately in parliament, having won South County Dublin for the unionists in 1892. Plunkett was determined that the secretary and permanent head of the new department should be T. P. Gill, a catholic, who had been secretary to the recess committee. But Gill had been a nationalist M.P. and there was considerable Unionist opposition to his appointment. In January 1900 Plunkett had what he described as 'a very disagreeable interview' with the lord lieutenant, who 'poured out his grievances on the Gill extravagance'. And Gerald Balfour also expressed distrust of Gill. But Plunkett was in a strong position. It was clear that he would resign if he could not choose the senior members of his staff. So Gill became secretary and Plunkett

---

[1] For the work and organization of the department see *department of agriculture and technical instruction (Ireland): report of the department committee of inquiry*, H.C. 1907, [Cd. 3572], xvii; *Minutes of evidence and appendix*, H.C. 1907 [Cd. 3574], 3573, xviii; *Department of agriculture and technical instruction for Ireland: fourteenth annual report . . .*, 1913-14, H.C. 1914-16 [Cd. 7839], vi.

also made two other important appointments from outside the civil service, an under-secretary and a statistician.

Shortly after his meeting with Gerald Balfour, the chief secretary, Plunkett met 'the bosses' of his constituency and explained to them that he would not take politics or other irrelevant considerations into account when making appointment in his department. And though there was 'some blowing off of steam' they unanimously asked him to stand again. But at the general election which occurred at the close of the year, a section of Plunkett's constituents, feeling that he was displaying a dangerous degree of political latitudinarianism, put up another unionist candidate, with the result that the nationalists secured the seat.[1]

The government, however, appreciating the value of Plunkett's work, encouraged him to remain in office and when the liberals came into power in 1905, the new chief secretary, Bryce, requested Plunkett to regard his appointment as 'outside the considerations of party', and to continue as vice-president. Bryce explained that he was willing to consider Plunkett as a temporary official but the nationalists were not prepared to forget that Plunkett had been a unionist minister and remembered his epigrammatic comments on Irish politics. In April 1907 Redmond demanded that the 'anomalous, illogical and untenable position' should be terminated and Plunkett was compelled to resign his vice-presidency.[2] He was succeeded by T. W. Russell, a versatile and pugnacious Ulster M.P., who by 1906 was a liberal (the only liberal representing an Irish constituency). In January 1910 he lost his seat and the unionists naturally tried to embarrass the government by suggesting that he ought to resign his post. But Russell hung on and in October 1911 was returned by another Ulster constituency. In January 1919 he was succeeded by H. T. Barrie, an Ulster unionist M.P., the last vice-president.

The most unusual feature in the constitution of the new department was the advisory bodies connected with it. Of these the most impressive was the council of agriculture, described by Plunkett as almost 'a parliament representative of Irish

[1] Plunkett, diaries, 4, 14, 25 Jan. 1900.
[2] *Hansard*, 4 series, clii. 352-6, clxvii. 366-7, clxx. 876-84, clxxiii. 136-71; 5 series, xiv. 1620, xviii. 196, 837.

agricultural and industrial interests'. The relations between these bodies and the department were remarkably harmonious. According to Gill a 'principle of common and friendly action among different sections of Irishmen made a living and inspiring element in every branch of our organization'.[1] Anderson, a member of the council of agriculture, put it rather differently when he spoke of the council as being so disciplined a body that 'an orderly formality' characterized its meetings.[2] Plunkett's prestige and the ability of his staff seem to have enabled him to keep the advisory bodies firmly under control. Referring to an early meeting of the agricultural board he remarked, 'I am getting quite a lion tamer'. And later he noted in his diary that the agricultural board was really 'an excellent body, we practically nominate the elected members'.[3]

Ironically enough Plunkett after he left office was to see one of his cherished schemes rejected by the council of agriculture on the advice of his successor. After his resignation of the office of vice-president Plunkett was elected president of the Irish Agricultural Organization Society, the body which co-ordinated the activities of the Irish co-operative societies. He believed that this body and the department should work together—the department standing for better farming, the I.A.O.S. for better business—and he had arranged for the department to pay an annual subsidy to the society. But co-operation was unpopular with many Irish businessmen and Plunkett was regarded with suspicion by many nationalist politicians. Therefore it is not altogether surprising that his successor discontinued the subsidy in 1908. In January 1911 the I.A.O.S. applied for a grant to the newly constituted development commission. The commission referred the request to the treasury which passed it on to the department. Russell recommended that a grant should not be made. Some months later he justified his attitude at the council of agriculture in a vigorous speech in which he claimed to have done more for the Irish farmer than the whole of the I.A.O.S. put together. To make a grant to the I.A.O.S. would be to set up a state-endowed authority hostile

[1] *Department of agriculture and technical instruction for Ireland, Journ.*, xx. 316.

[2] R. A. Anderson, *With Horace Plunkett in Ireland*, pp. 118–9.

[3] Plunkett, diaries, 12 Sept. 1900, 6 Mar. 1901.

to the department.[1] The council of agriculture endorsed this decision on a vote by 47 to 33. But Plunkett and his ardent supporter George Russell, refused to accept defeat. They vehemently urged the case of the I.A.O.S., Plunkett declaring that the real issue was between bureaucracy and democracy, and in the end the I.A.O.S. secured a substantial grant on acceptable conditions.[2]

[1] *Department of agriculture and technical instruction for Ireland, Journ.*, xii. 217–31.

[2] *Report of the I.A.O.S. for 1911*, p. 37.

VIII

DEPARTMENTS CONCERNED
WITH EDUCATION

∿∿∿∿∿∿∿∿∿∿∿∿∿∿

DURING THE nineteenth century the state encouraged education in Ireland at three levels—primary, post-primary and university. In addition it took steps to provide facilities for technical, artistic and scientific education. Needless to say, the interventions of the state in the educational sphere were productive of controversy—political and theological as well as educational. And the administrative machinery through which the state strove to assist and supervise educational effort, being formed of different sections, created at different times, with different but occasionally over-lapping purposes, was highly complex. Fortunately one important aspect of the subject need be dealt with only very briefly in this work. The Irish university question in the nineteenth century was involved and bristled with controversy. But from the administrative point of view the relationships between the government and the Irish universities were simple and no special department was formed to deal with university matters.

At the beginning of the nineteenth century there was only one university in Ireland, the University of Dublin (Trinity College). There was also the great national seminary of Maynooth founded in 1795. Though Trinity College had been well endowed by crown and parliament, and Maynooth was largely maintained by the state, the government had little official contact with either institution. The provost of Trinity College was appointed by the crown and changes in the college statutes required until 1911 a 'king's letter' (letters patent). Between 1800 and 1845 the lord chancellor and the heads of the three common law courts were *ex officio* visitors of Maynooth, and from 1845 until 1871, when the connection between the college and the state came to an end, the board of works maintained the college buildings.

Between the union and 1914, four universities were founded by State action in Ireland, the Queen's University (1850), the Royal University (1880), the National University (1908) and the Queen's University of Belfast (1908). Moreover, in 1845, the three Queen's Colleges of Belfast, Cork and Galway were founded. These colleges composed the Queen's University and after its dissolution in 1882 their students took their degrees in the Royal University. In 1908, Queen's College, Belfast became Queen's University, the other two colleges became colleges of the National University. The crown appointed the presidents and professors of the Queen's Colleges, the chancellor and the greater part of the senate of the Queen's University, and the chancellor and thirty of the thirty-six members of the senate of Royal University. In practice these appointments were made by the lord lieutenant and the chief secretary. The treasury of course also exercised some influence on the development of these institutions, carefully scrutinizing suggestions for expenditure on new lines.[1]

The state's effort to assist and plan educational activities in other spheres led to important and at times confusing administrative developments which will now be dealt with. From about the middle of the sixteenth century education was regarded as an instrument of state policy in Ireland, and crown and parliament took steps to encourage education at different levels. Towards the close of the century the University of Dublin was founded. Sixty years earlier, in 1537, when the strength of the crown in Ireland was beginning to revive, it was enacted that every parish clergyman should endeavour to learn, instruct and teach the English tongue to 'all and every' under his rule and with that object maintain a school in his parish.[2] Thirty-three

---

[1] For the university question in Ireland in the nineteenth century see T. W. Moody and J. C. Beckett, *Queen's Belfast, 1845–1949: the history of a university.*   [2] 28 Henry VIII, c. 15.

years later the state thrust on the clergy another educational burden, it being enacted in 1570 that as the greatest number of Irish people had lived in rude and barbarous states, ignorant of the divinely-ordained duty of obedience to their sovereign, the bishop and clergy of each diocese were to be taxed to maintain a free school which was apparently intended to be a grammar school. In five dioceses the headmaster was to be appointed by the bishop, in the others by the lord lieutenant.[1] This legislation was to a remarkable degree ineffective. At the close of the eighteenth century it was discovered that the majority of parishes did not possess a parish school and many dioceses were without a diocesan school.[2]

At the beginning of the seventeenth century the parish and diocesan schools were supplemented by the 'Royal Schools', founded and endowed with landed estates as part of the plantation policy. Seven royal schools existed at the beginning of the nineteenth century, five in Ulster and two in Leinster. The Ulster schools and one of the Leinster schools were grammar schools; the school at Carysfort in Wicklow had become a primary school. The headmasters of two of the schools (Armagh and Dungannon) were appointed by the archbishop of Armagh, the headmasters of the other five by the lord lieutenant.[3]

In the early eighteenth century the state began to assist primary education. In 1733 the Incorporated Society was founded with the aim of instructing children in English, writing and arithmetic, manual trades and Church of Ireland doctrine. The society, which was inefficiently managed by a large board of *ex officio* governors, was given parliamentary grants from 1746. And in 1792 the Association for Discountenancing Vice and Promoting Religion, which was active in promoting parish schools, secured a small annual grant. During the eighteenth century four other educational institutions managed to secure annual parliamentary grants—the Female Orphan Society, the Marine School, the Hibernian School founded in 1769 for soldiers' orphans and children, and the Foundling Hospital.

---

[1] 12 Eliz., c. 1.

[2] *Endowed schools, Ireland, commission . . . evidence*, vol. II, pp. 366–8, H.C. 1857–8 [2336], xxii.

[3] *Endowed schools, Ireland, commission, report*, pp. 47, 64, 121, H.C. 1857–8 [2336], xxii.

The Foundling Hospital produced one of the greatest administrative scandals of the century. At the beginning of the century a general workhouse was erected to the south-west of Dublin near James's Gate. By 1776 it had ceased to take in adults and had become simply a foundling hospital. A few years later it was highly commended by a house of commons committee for having saved the lives of a great number of children who would otherwise have perished, and from henceforth it received a substantial parliamentary grant. In 1791 and 1792, however, committees of the house of commons investigated the hospital and discovered that it was not only in debt but very badly managed—the mortality rate amongst the children being exceedingly high. Public opinion was shocked but no action was taken until after a third committee had reported in 1797.[1] Several acts were then passed which vested the control of the institution in a committee composed of the Irish chancellor of the exchequer and nine named persons, who could fill vacancies in their number by co-optation. As a result conditions greatly improved. Several 'ladies of distinction' set to work to reform the infant department. The arrangements for conveying children to the institution were greatly improved. There was more careful nursing, many of the children being sent to wet-nurses in the country, and efforts were made to give the older children a good primary and technical education. In 1822 it was enacted that no child should be admitted unless a payment of £5 was made by the parish from which it was sent. Numbers of admissions dropped and in 1827 a commission of inquiry when reporting on the Foundling Hospital was exceedingly critical of institutional upbringing for children (they were careful to point out that boarding schools for the upper ranks were exempt from their criticisms. These schools were chosen by the parent and the child was in them for only a stated period of the year). A few years later, in accordance with a recommendation of a select committee of the house of commons it was decided there should be no further admissions to the Foundling Hospital after 1 January 1830. In 1839 the institution was vested in the poor law commission. The commission decided that the hospital building should be used

[1] *Commons Journ., Ire.*, xiv. *appendix*, p. ccxcix; xv. *appendix*, p. cciii; xvii. p. ccxl.

as the workhouse for the south Dublin union, the foundlings being transferred to a house in Cork Street. In 1848 the Cork Street house was closed, the remaining foundlings being boarded out in the country. And in the financial year 1907–8 the last annual grants to 'invalid foundlings' were paid.[1]

At the time of the union £28,000 was being voted for educational purposes, and already parliament was clearly uncertain whether this sum was being wisely applied. In 1787 the house of commons approved of a striking plan proposed by Orde, the chief secretary, for expanding educational facilities in Ireland. There were to be numerous parish schools. Existing secondary schools were to be improved and new ones founded. Some of the secondary schools were to be 'classical' schools, in others the curriculum was to emphasize 'practical' subjects. And there was also to be a second university. The cost of the scheme was to be met out of the grants to the charter schools, a tax on clerical incomes, and local taxation. In the following year a statutory commission to inquire into educational problems was appointed. The commission in 1791 suggested a new plan much on the lines of Orde's scheme but with one important addition—the creation of a government. department with duties in the educational sphere. A 'board of control' composed of unpaid commissioners was to be constituted, which was to supervise the application of educational endowments. But Orde's scheme was never implemented nor was the board of control created.[2]

In 1806 as a result apparently of the joint efforts of Newport, who was chancellor of the exchequer for Ireland in the ministry of all the talents, and of the archbishop of Armagh, a statutory commission to inquire into Irish education was set up. The primate who was, according to Maria Edgeworth, 'a man of the warmest feelings with the coldest exterior'[3] was one of the most active members of the commission, and its

[1] 38 Geo. III, c. 35; 40 Geo. III, c. 33; 50 Geo. III, c. 192; *House of industry and foundling hospital Dublin: accounts . . .*, H.C. 1828 (176), xxii; *Charitable institutions (Dublin) . . . copies of the reports of George Nicholls . . . on . . . the foundling hospital, Dublin, and the house of industry, Dublin,* H.C. 1842 (389), xxxviii.

[2] *Endowed schools, Ireland, commission, report,* vol. II, pp. 362–5, H.C. 1857–8 [2336], xxii.

[3] A. Hare, *Life and letters of Maria Edgeworth* (1894), ii. 107.

membership included another dignitary of the established church, Verschoyle, dean of St Patrick's and later bishop of Killala, Hall, provost of Trinity College, his successor Elrington, Disney, a benevolent barrister, Foster, later a judge, Isaac Corry, who had been Irish chancellor of the exchequer, and Richard Lovell Edgeworth, a keen experimentalist who had attempted to provide his own son with an education on the principles of Rousseau. The commission assembled in Dublin from time to time, accumulated a large amount of information, and issued fourteen reports. As these reports show, the state had until the beginning of the nineteenth century confined itself in the educational sphere to legislation, investigation and granting subsidies to voluntary educational agencies. It had not attempted to supervise or direct. In their fourteen reports the commissioners recommended that there should be sustained state intervention in the educational field. A permanent commission should be set up, empowered to operate a national system of primary education. 'The difficulty of changing long-settled establishments and the waste of time to the commissioners who would be much more profitably employed in forming new seminaries than in altering old ones' induced the commission to recommend that the permanent commission should not be expected to interfere with existing schools.[1]

Strangely enough, though it accepted the suggestion that there should be a permanent commission, the government entrusted to it the supervision of existing establishments not on a primary but on a secondary level. In 1813 an education bill created a permanent commission for 'the regulation of the several endowed schools of private foundation'. It was ultimately composed of eleven *ex officio* members (the archbishops, the chief secretary, the provost of Trinity, the member for the University of Dublin, the lord chancellor, the lord chief justices, the chief baron) and four bishops and six other persons appointed by the lord lieutenant. Three members, of whom one had to be an *ex officio* member, formed a quorum. The commission was empowered to visit the schools under its control, the property of the Royal Schools was vested in it, and it could appoint a secretary and subordinate officials and apply

[1] *Fourteenth report from the commissioners of the board of education in Ireland*, H.C. 1813–4 (47), vi.

to the lord lieutenant for a subsidy to defray its expenses.[1] The commission (usually known as the commissioners of education) had a long and undistinguished history. To begin with a number of schools were expressly exempted from its jurisdiction —the Incorporated Society's schools, the Erasmus Smith schools, schools with visitors created by statute and schools for persons of religious opinions other than those of the established church. Secondly, the commissioners (with weighty backing) held that the power to visit did not imply a right to inspect, visitatorial powers being of a judicial not of a supervisory nature. Hampered by these restrictions, the commission functioned cautiously within narrow limits. It supervised the finances of the Royal Schools, managing their estates, recovering some endowments and improving the school buildings. From 1830 it offered exhibitions tenable at Trinity College, to 'young gentlemen of merit' educated at the Royal Schools, it secured reports from headmasters and infrequently arranged for the visitation of a school. The commissioners themselves seem to have felt it necessary to apologize for the monotony of their short, stereotyped reports, pointing out that their duties were of a routine nature which did 'not supply materials for much variety' in their reports. And from 1870 the commissioners were pressing for increased powers. They wanted to be able to remove masters, to employ inspectors, to plan courses and to transfer a portion of the income of one school to another. And as early as 1831 they wanted the rule that an *ex officio* commissioner must be included in a quorum to be abolished. This last request touched on a great weakness of the board which explains its inertia. Its members, busy men, attended very badly. In the 'thirties it was stated that sometimes, owing to the absence of all the *ex officio* members, other members were kept waiting impatiently, unable to form a board. And as time went on, the number of *ex officio* members fell. When Dublin University was given a second M.P. in 1832, the commissioners on taking legal opinion were informed that neither M.P. could attend their board as member for the university. As a result of the church temporalities act, the number of archbishops was halved and the number of bishops appointed by the lord lieutenant reduced to two. And after the passing of the Irish

[1] 53 Geo. III, c. 107.

church act of 1869 it was held that prelates of the Church of Ireland could not be appointed to the ecclesiastical seats on the board. For long periods the only *ex officio* commissioner who attended regularly was the provost, and the secretary had often considerable difficulty in getting business done. For instance, on one occasion, 'owing to the provost and Mr Jellett being obliged to meet His Excellency the lord lieutenant in Trinity . . . and Mr Kirkpatrick having been bitten by a dog', a board could not be held. Sometimes in practice two commissioners dealt with business and the secretary 'made out a quorum' later by securing the acquiescence of a third commissioner.[1]

The members of the educational endowments commission of 1878 having examined the board's secretary and its books, were so impressed by 'the difficulties, defects and irregularities in the performance of the functions of the board' which emerged that they transmitted the evidence to the board and asked if any commissioner would like to appear as a witness. The secretary of the board replied in a long letter. In the first sentence he intimated that no commissioner intended to give evidence. The rest of the letter expounded the board's theory that their powers were too limited to be effective. A few years later in 1885 when asked by the government what were their opinions on educational reform, the commissioners, unabashed by the comments which had been made on their behaviour, restricted themselves to declaring that any commissioners appointed to supervise secondary education should be unpaid.[2] In 1889 the educational endowments commissioners surveyed the schools under the commissioners of education. As nearly all the diocesan schools had vanished with disestablishment, there were only the Royal Schools and a few small endowed schools to be considered. The educational endowment commissioners decided that two of the Royal Schools should be closed, and that in five Ulster counties where there was a Royal School its endowment should be split in two, and in each

[1] *Endowed schools, Ireland, commission, report*, ii. 7–13, 31, 613–4, H.C. 1881 [2831], xxxv; *Report from the select committee on foundation schools and education in Ireland together with the minutes of evidence*, pp. 158–60, H.C. 1835–6 (630), xiii.

[2] *Annual report of the commissioners of education in Ireland for the year 1884–5*, p. 1, H.C. 1884–5 [Cd. 4509], xxiv.

county each half should be administered for purposes connected with secondary education by a catholic and protestant committee respectively. The work of these ten committees was supervised by a board of educational commissioners, regarded as the commissioners of education in a reconstituted form. It was composed of ten persons nominated by the government and ten elected by the local committees. This board had a very small staff, a secretary and a clerk, which the treasury agreed should be remunerated by a parliamentary vote.[1]

Sixty-five years after the commissioners of education were constituted the state made another attempt to encourage secondary education in Ireland. This time it intervened on a far wider front. By the intermediate education act (Ireland) of 1878 an unpaid board of seven members appointed by the lord lieutenant was constituted. Its function was to promote intermediate education by holding examinations, granting prizes and certificates to successful candidates, and paying fees depending on the results of the examinations to managers of schools which complied with certain conditions. The funds of the board were at first drawn from the interest on one million pounds handed over by the commissioners of church temporalities, and this was supplemented in 1890 by an annual grant from the customs and excise and in 1914 by an annual grant under the intermediate education act of that year. The board's rules had to be laid before parliament and its staff consisted of two assistant commissioners who acted as secretaries and such other officers and examiners as the board, with the approval of the lord lieutenant and the treasury, might appoint.[2]

The board quickly built up the necessary machinery for conducting its annual examinations at a number of local centres and awarded grants to the schools based on the results—the grant for each pupil being carefully calculated in accordance with the standard he attained. In January 1898 the board took the unusual course of unanimously representing to the lord lieutenant that there were defects in the system they were administering and requesting to be constituted a commission

---

[1] *Educational endowments (Ireland) commission . . . annual report for the year 1890–1*, p. iv; *appendix*, pp. 211–53, H.C. 1890–1 [Cd. 6544], xxviii.

[2] 41 & 42 Vict., c. 66; 53 & 54 Vict., c. 60; 4 & 5 Geo. V, c. 41.

of inquiry. This was done and the commissioners having heard a number of witnesses, reported in the summer of 1899. It emphasized that the grant to a school should not be related merely to the number of its pupils who passed an examination and the number of subjects they were successful in. Other factors which reflected the school's efficiency should be taken into account when fixing its annual grant. And the report emphasized the part inspection could play in raising standards. As a result a new intermediate education act was passed in 1900, raising the board's membership to twelve and allowing it to substitute grants on a capitation basis for the prevailing results system, and, subject to the approval of the lord lieutenant and the treasury, to appoint inspectors. The board at once modified its rules respecting the basis for grants, but it soon discovered that it would have to fight hard to secure a permanent inspectorate. The government procrastinated, the board's communications being left for six months unanswered. In July 1905 the government suggested that the whole matter might be reconsidered in the light of suggestions for co-ordinating Irish intermediate and primary education, and a committee of inquiry was set up composed of representatives of the intermediate and national boards and of the department of agricultural and technical instruction. Though this committee reported in favour of a permanent inspectorate under the intermediate board, nothing was done. Admittedly for three years, 1901–3, the board was allowed to appoint temporary inspectors, but in 1904 it refused to accept this makeshift solution and turned a section of its published report for 1906 into a manifesto in favour of inspection. The report argued that the inspectors could both advise and stimulate the teaching profession and their visits would help to dispel 'the pernicious idea that the highest end of school life is to pass an examination and to win so many pounds sterling'. And the government were warned that if the decision to appoint inspectors 'be longer deferred, it will have to be made, not as a result of deliberate statesmanship but in obedience to angry clamour'. In 1909 sanction was at last obtained for the appointment of six permanent inspectors (afterwards increased to eight).

While discussions over the inspectorate were proceeding, relations between the board and the government were still further aggravated by a minute constitutional crisis. In May 1906 the house of commons, on the motion of a nationalist member, refused to sanction the rules of the board for 1906–7 unless amendments were made improving the status of Irish and 'domestic economy and hygiene'. The board, as a temporary expedient, laid before parliament the rules which had been adopted for 1905–6 but declined in the interests of intermediate education to accept the amendments suggested by the house of commons. In the correspondence which it conducted with the under-secretary, the board complained that as the lord lieutenant had sanctioned the rules for 1906–7 the government accepted responsibility for them, and should have defended them in the house where the board was not represented. The under-secretary replied that all the information the board had supplied to the government was given to the house but that the 'information was, as regards two of the points raised, extremely scanty and gave the government no material for arguing the question'. If the lord lieutenant had been informed that the teaching of Irish 'had become a subject of warm discussion', he would have communicated with the board before sanctioning the rules. In July the board took a firm, some might say aggressive, line, with both the government and parliament. It declined, on the ground that they were confidential, to comply with the government's desire that the minutes of its discussions on the rules should be laid before parliament. And the board contended that the veto possessed by each house over its rules did not give either house the power to dictate how they should be framed. In preparing their rules the board would always recognize the lord lieutenant's 'constitutional responsibility' and 'respectfully consider his views and wishes'. But the board emphasized that its members had to exercise 'that independent judgement which the act [of 1878] requires them to use and which they consider it inconsistent with their duty to abandon'. If a serious disagreement arose between the board and the government there was 'a constitutional method of determining it'—the dismissal by the lord lieutenant of those members of the board whose 'opinions were not in harmony with his own'. The government retorted that 'the power of veto necessarily implies that effect is to be given to the veto', and this interpretation was supported by both the English and Irish law officers. The board promptly secured an opinion in favour of their interpretation of the act of 1878 from Stephen Ronan, and at the same time declared that the peremptory tone adopted by the Irish executive made it difficult 'to see how men of any standing and self-respect can continue to hold a position which will be rendered not only irksome but humiliating'. In the event the board, though it stoutly refrained from making any concessions on the legal issue, incorporated the changes demanded by the house of commons in its rules for 1908, having, as they put it, 'regard not only to the interests of secondary education in Ireland, but also to the express wishes of His Excellency in reference to the resolutions of the house of commons'.[1]

An immense amount of legal and financial tidying up in the Irish educational sphere was accomplished by a short-lived body, the Irish educational endowments commissioners. The educational endowments act of 1885 set up a temporary commission of five composed of two judicial and three assistant commissioners. The judicial commissioners, the first two of whom were named in the act, were supreme court judges, were unpaid and held office during good behaviour.[2] The assistant commissioners were appointed by the lord lieutenant and were removable and remunerated. The first two judicial commissioners were both protestants, FitzGibbon, a conservative, and Naish, a liberal. On Naish's death he was replaced by O'Brien, a catholic conservative. The first three assistant commissioners were the Rev. Gerald Molloy, the rector of the Catholic University, Anthony Traill, a pugnacious episcopalian and future provost of Trinity, and Rev. J. B. Dougherty, a presbyterian professor of philosophy. And when Dougherty retired in 1892 he was succeeded by another presbyterian minister, Rev. Hamilton Wilson. The commissioners were empowered to draft schemes for the future government and management of educational endowments in Ireland (with cer-

[1] *Intermediate education board for Ireland, report for the year 1901*, pp. xiii–xv, H.C. 1902 [1092], xxix; *Report for the year 1906*, pp. xi, xvi, H.C. 1907 [Cd. 3544], xxii; *Intermediate education (Ireland) . . . copy of correspondence between the Irish government and the commissioners of intermediate education for Ireland . . .*, H.C. 1906 [Cd. 3213], xci; *Viceregal committee on intermediate education (Ireland), report*, p. 8, H.C. 1919 [Cd. 66], xxi; *Hansard*, 4 series, clxxiii. 886–7, cxciii. 886–7, cxciii. 1710–11.   [2] 48 & 49 Vict., c. 78.

tain exceptions). Before drafting a scheme they could if necessary hold a public inquiry, and after the scheme was prepared and published they could hear the objections of interested parties. Finally the judicial commissioners could frame a scheme and submit it to the lord lieutenant in council, and he, having heard any objections which might be made, could confirm it or refer it back to the commissioners. Furthermore, the governing body concerned or a group of ratepayers in the area affected by the scheme could insist that it whould be laid before parliament, but if neither house disapproved of the scheme the lord lieutenant in council could approve it.

The commission, which worked with a small staff of a secretary and a few clerks, sat frequently both in public, where interested parties often stated their case with vigour, and in private. It usually met in Dublin, but it held sittings in other places. Just over 200 schemes affecting about 1,350 primary schools, more than 80 intermediate schools and 22 'collegiate or other especially important institutions' were submitted to the lord lieutenant. Only 22 were remitted to the commission for amendment, only five had to be laid before parliament, and on only one of these did either house take action.[1] ·

The educational commissioners appointed in 1807 had in their fourteenth report visualized a state-aided system of elementary education. In fact, as has been shown, what was created was an ineffective body supervising schools on a higher level. During the first three decades of the nineteenth century state intervention in elementary education was limited to making grants to voluntary bodies. By 1825 three societies were being subsidized, and between 1819 and 1825 an annual parliamentary grant to assist education in Ireland was placed at the disposal of the lord lieutenant. The administration of this grant was entrusted to three unpaid commissioners, Rev. Dr James Dunn, a viceregal chaplain, Digges La Touche, a benevolent business man, and Major Benjamin Woodward, an inspector of prisons, who made grants towards the building of primary schools. Before a grant was made, substantial financial

[1] *Educational endowments (Ireland), final report of the commissioners*, H.C. 1894 [Cd. 7517], xxx.

support for the school from local sources had to be guaranteed: so most of the money went to the clergy of the established church since catholic applicants found it difficult to produce a satisfactory local subscription list.[1]

The government's policy of subsidizing private enterprise, while sparing in administrative effort, soon involved the state in religious controversy. The grant-aided societies were in practice under protestant control and catholics naturally suspected that they would try to influence the religious views of the children attending their schools. Catholic opinion was a growing power in Ireland, and from 1827 the government began to reduce the parliamentary grants to the societies.[2] This, while tending to protect the state against accusations of religious partiality, left Irish elementary education in a parlous condition.

In 1829 a house of commons select committee recommended that a salaried board should be appointed to exercise general control over a system for the education of the poorer classes in Ireland. The board would receive a parliamentary grant and make grants to individuals or charitable societies towards building school-houses and paying teachers. In the schools supported by the board there was to be 'combined literary and separate religious education'. In 1831 Stanley, then chief secretary, boldly adumbrated a scheme similar to that of the select committee's in his famous letter (or rather letters) which laid the foundations of the Irish system of primary education.[3] A board—which soon became known as the national board—carefully balanced denominationally, was set up to administer an annual parliamentary grant for Irish primary education. A local committee or an individual were expected to provide at least part of the cost of building the school, to maintain it, and to pay part of the teacher's salary. The board might assist the building of the school, would provide cheap textbooks, and a fixed grant towards the teacher's salary. To enable members of all denominations to co-operate in managing a school

[1] *First report of the commissioners of education in Ireland*, pp. 58–9, H.C. 1825 (400) xii; *Report from the select committee on the Irish miscellaneous estimates*, pp. 5–8, H.C. 1829 (432), iv.

[2] *Hansard*, new series, xvii. 245; 3 series, vi. 1258.

[3] *Royal commission of inquiry into primary education (Ireland)*, vol. I, report, pp. 22–6, H.C. 1870 [Cd. 6], xxviii.

and children of all denominations to attend any school assisted by the board, it was laid down that there was to be combined literary and separate religious education. The formula was a neat one. Its application proved difficult. To begin with, there were those in the three major denominations who argued that the separation of secular and religious instruction, if possible, was wrong. And even those who accepted or acquiesced in the system—and in time it was almost universally accepted—were quick to criticize any interpretation of its principles which might put them at a disadvantage, and were afraid that the board in its anxiety not to give offence to any section might dangerously minimize the importance of religion in education. As can be seen from its first four great reports the national board was subjected to continuous pressure on religious matters and was constantly struggling both to preserve the basic principle of the system and to conciliate the major denominations. From the outset the most active of the commissioners fervently believed that united education should be encouraged as promoting political and social goodwill. But influential leaders in each of the three major denominations emphasized the importance of preserving and strengthening their children's faith. The episcopalians and presbyterians were at first reluctant to surrender the right to read and explain the scriptures to all children attending schools under their management. And the presbyterians in 1840 secured an important concession. A school, it was agreed, might receive support from the board (though not a building grant) although a clergyman who belonged to a different denomination to the management committee was not permitted to give religious instruction to children of his own persuasion on the school premises.[1] Amongst the catholics, Archbishop MacHale of Tuam denounced the board's latitudinarianism, and the Christian Brothers, whose aim was to give a thoroughly catholic education, after a short experiment broke off all connection with the board. Concessions were made and in the event the system could be described as denominational in practice with a conscience clause.[2] By 1900 nearly all the

[1] T. O'Raifeartaigh, 'Mixed education and the synod of Ulster, 1831–40' in *I.H.S.*, ix. 281–99.

[2] *Royal commission on the civil service, fourth report, second appendix*, 425, H.C. 1914 [Cd. 7430], xvi.

schools were under denominational control, nearly sixty-five per cent of the children were in schools attended by adherents of a single denomination, and the bulk of the teachers were trained in denominational training colleges.

It would be a mistake—if an understandable one—to imply that the commissioners were concerned only with denominational diplomacy. They were engaged in a triple task—maintaining the principles of the system; emphasizing sound educational ideals; and building up and working an administrative machine. In their reports, especially the earlier ones which reveal an enthusiasm rare in official documents, and in their directives to inspectors and teachers, the commissioners displayed their concern to provide a sensible, thorough and comprehensive training for the children in their schools. The virtues of precision, orderliness, tidiness, obedience, restraint and tolerance were continually hammered home. Discipline, inspired by good intentions and intelligently enforced, was intended to be an outstanding feature of the system. The teachers were expected to be 'of Christian sentiment, of calm temper and discretion', loyal and law-abiding, possessing not only 'the art of communicating knowledge' but the capacity to mould the mind. And the extracts in the reading books provided by the board conveyed a remarkable amount of miscellaneous information.[1]

Political rather than administrative considerations determined the form of the controlling authority. It was obvious that a board of unpaid members, chosen to represent the different sections of the community, would command a greater degree of public confidence than a department directly controlled by the government. At first the board had seven members; as time went on other members were added, and in 1844, when it was incorporated by charter, the number of commissioners was fixed at fifteen, all nominated by the lord lieutenant. During the first thirty years of its existence there was always a substantial majority of protestants on the board, but in 1860 a new charter raised the number of commissioners to twenty and provided that ten of them should be catholic and ten protestant. The commissioners included eminent lawyers and divines,

[1] *Ninth report of the commissioners of national education in Ireland*, appendix, p. 21, H.C. 1843 (471), xxviii.

university dons and public-spirited peers and country gentlemen. Towards the end of the century a few retired senior officials of the board were appointed commissioners, and finally, in 1910, Ward, an able national school teacher from Belfast, was appointed a commissioner. The board met weekly until about 1866, when it tended to meet fortnightly, and attendance was, as might be expected, somewhat erratic, but, as was pointed out, it always rose whenever there was business of real importance—this being defined as anything 'that touches religious feeling or any appointments of importance'.[1] On the whole the board worked harmoniously, because there was plenty of genuine goodwill, and partly because, as will be shown, it delegated some of its functions to an important permanent official who scrutinized much of its business in advance. Only twice during the nineteenth century was there a serious rift amongst the commissioners, each occasion being marked by an archi-episcopal resignation. In 1853 when a majority of the board decided to omit *Lessons on the truth of Christianity* from its list of books for combined secular instruction, three members, all belonging to the established church, left the board, including Whately, the archbishop of Dublin, one of whose books had supplied the basis for the work which had been dropped from the list. Nearly half a century later another dispute, which will be described in due course, led to the resignation from the board of the catholic archbishop of Dublin. In neither case did the majority of the board reverse its decision.[2]

The board's relations with the Irish government were anomalous. The commissioners themselves (with one important exception) were unpaid, and the great majority of the persons working under their direction, the teachers, were certainly not civil servants, for they were appointed and removed by the managers of the schools. But the commissioners were of course appointed by the lord lieutenant and could be removed by

---

[1] *Royal commission of inquiry into primary education (Ireland)*, pt. III, pp. 458-60, H.C. 1870 [Cd. 6-11]; *Viceregal commission of inquiry into primary education (Ireland)*, second report, appendix, p. 314, H.C. 1914 [Cd. 7229], xxviii. 322.

[2] *Report from the select committee of the house of lords appointed to inquire into the practical working of the system of national education in Ireland with the minutes of evidence*, H.C. 1854 (352), xvi.

him (though this power was never exercised); the funds at their disposal were voted by parliament, and their expenditure was closely scrutinized by the treasury; the staff at the central office and the inspectors were civil servants; and the teachers were almost entirely remunerated out of the annual parliamentary grant. In 1855 what seems to have been an accepted practice was legalized when, in the code of rules drafted by the board and approved by the lord lieutenant, it was laid down that the commissioners should not change any fundamental rule without the express permission of the lord lieutenant. This consent was secured in 1883 when it was arranged that the denominational training colleges for teachers could receive financial assistance from the board, but later an attempt to change the rules involved the board and the Irish administration in an awkward collision. In 1895 the chief secretary, John Morley, requested the board to amend its rules so that it could afford assistance to some existing denominational schools in certain localities whose exclusion was rendering the school attendance act inoperative, the local authorities refusing to enforce it. A minority of the board was reluctant to make any concessions to denominationalism, but the majority responded to the chief secretary's suggestion by making numerous amendments which would have allowed denominational schools in general to enter the system. Morley, who was anxious merely to deal with a limited problem, 'not to enter on these large issues', asked the board to reconsider its scheme. But the majority firmly adhered to its plan, pointing out that 'it is the function of the commissioners of national education in Ireland to prepare such rules as they may think expedient to the good working of the system entrusted to their management'. Finally, when Rosebery's government was compelled to resign in June 1895, the minority of the board prevailed, for the new conservative administration refused to sanction the majority's scheme.[1]

A board of busy men distracted by other duties would have accomplished little if the sheer pressure of business had not at an early stage created a post—that of resident commissioner

---

[1] *Correspondence . . . between the Irish government and the commissioners of national education in Ireland . . .*, H.C. 1895 (324), lxxvii; *Further correspondence between the Irish government and the commissioners of National Education in Ireland*, H.C. 1896 (89), lxvi.

—which provided a mainspring for the system. Shortly after the board was set up, one of the commissioners, Rev. James Carlile, a presbyterian minister who was resident 'not merely in Dublin but in the house' in Marlborough Street, where the board had its headquarters, was appointed to handle matters arising between board meetings, and by a treasury warrant was granted £300 per annum and apartments in the house.[1] When he resigned in 1839 he was succeeded by Alexander Macdonnell, then chief clerk in the chief secretary's office.

The resident commissioner's position was analogous to that of the permanent head of a department, and he exercised considerable power through a transparent fiction. The board's duties were largely performed by three committees, the sub-committee, the finance committee, and the agricultural committee. And these committees were in fact the resident commissioner working with several of the board's senior officials, the secretaries, the accountant, the chiefs of inspection. But there was no doubt that these officials were only present in a consultative capacity. The committees were the resident commissioner. As a resident commissioner explained, the phrase that he was on these committees 'attended by' the senior officials was misleading, as it might convey the idea that these officials were members of the committees 'and not officials who consulted the resident commissioner'. According to one of the board's secretaries, giving evidence in 1870, ordinary routine business was dealt with by the office staff, 'serious routine business' came before the resident commissioner, and the decisions taken by him in committee were laid 'in globo' on the table of the board whose members barely glanced at them. Needless to say, the secretary implied that the system worked well enough. For instance the dismissal of a teacher would be considered by the resident commissioner, and 'if there was any doubt . . . in regard to the propriety of dismissing him, the case is brought fully before the board'. In 1902 William Starkie, then resident commissioner, simplified the system. He secured a resolution from the board abolishing the sub-committee, on the ground that it was simply the resident commissioner sitting permanently in his office, and providing that important administrative acts

[1] *Report from the select committee on plan of education, Ireland*, pp. 1–3, H.C. 1837 (485), ix.

should be embodied in provisional orders which would come before the board for confirmation.[1]

The board in its early days had a very small staff, its first secretary, Thomas Frederick Kelly, a barrister of about ten years standing, who later became a judge of the admiralty court, for some years managing both the correspondence and the financial business of the board. But in 1835 an accountant was appointed to manage financial business, and about the middle of the century a book-keeper and a pay clerk were appointed to assist him. In 1838, on Kelly's retirement, two secretaries were appointed, Maurice Cross, who had been a bank manager and secretary to a Lancastrian school in Belfast, and Hamilton Dowdall. The secretaries, who were equal, conducted the correspondence of the board. In practice they divided the business between them, one dealing with office organization and finance, sanctioning items of expenditure, the other dealing with the inspectors. But either was prepared to handle the other's work in his absence. By the middle of the nineteenth century the staff at the central office, senior officials and clerks, numbered about 45. By 1914, it had grown to 140, including the resident commissioner, the two secretaries, the accountant, the examiners (who considered the reports of the inspectors), and about 100 clerks as well as boy clerks and typists.

The board kept in continuous touch with the schools through its inspectorate. At the outset eight inspectors were appointed, 'gentlemen of respectable character', of whom several were reading for the bar and one had kept a reputable school in Dublin. 'Almost accidentally' four of them were catholics. By 1854 the inspectorate was composed of six head inspectors, 39 district and seven sub-inspectors, a total of 52, an insufficient force if the board's aim, a quarterly inspection of every school, was to be attained. By 1870 it had increased to 66, including six head and 60 district inspectors—the sub-inspectors being

[1] *Royal commission of inquiry into primary education (Ireland)*, pp. 31, 106–8, 168, 176–9, H.C. 1870 [Cd. 6–11], xxviii; *Viceregal commission of inquiry into primary education (Ireland), second report, appendix*, pp. 97, 259–60, 315, H.C. 1914 [Cd. 7229], xxviii. 267, 323 *Select committee of the house of lords appointed to inquire into the progress . . . of the new plan of education in Ireland, minutes of evidence*, pt. II, p. 1152, H.C. 1837 (543–11), viii.

by then termed third-class inspectors as 'it was more gratifying to them and there was no objection to giving them the name'. In 1900, the system was reorganized, the country being divided into twenty-two districts, in each of which there were placed a senior and two junior inspectors, and it was arranged that every school should be inspected at least three times a year. In 1914, the inspectorate comprised two chief inspectors and 72 inspectors, two women inspectors, and 18 organizers for Irish and for scientific and technical instruction. At first inspectors were appointed by the board on testimonials, with sometimes an interview, but from 1860 the civil service commissioners conducted a competitive examination for inspectorships from a select list of candidates provided by the board. Later, the board adopted a different system. Vacancies were advertised and from the applications the resident commissioner and a group of the board's senior officials prepared a select list of candidates, who were then subjected to a qualifying examination and interviewed by the board. By 1914 the majority of the inspectors were graduates and twenty-two had been national school teachers.[1]

There were also from the middle 'fifties two chiefs of inspection whose duty was to read the inspectors' weekly journals and reports. They had to deal with about six hundred reports weekly. These were first scrutinized by clerks, who passed them on to the chiefs of inspection with notes as to any relevant information or previous decision. The post of chief of inspection had emerged as the result of a temporary congestion of business in the office. The examination of reports having fallen badly into arrears about 1855, the commissioners called in six head-inspectors to assist the office staff for a few months. One of them 'did not care to go about the country again and he continued to stay on in the office and the people in power at the time applied to the treasury for his payment as chief of inspection'. A second chief of inspection was appointed shortly afterwards. The other five chief inspectors who had to go back to their districts 'did not like it, and they sent a round robin to the

---

[1] *Report of the select committee on the plan of education, Ireland*, p. 57, H.C. 1837 (485), ix. 63; *Viceregal commission of inquiry into primary education (Ireland), first report, appendix*, p. 1, H.C. 1913 [Cd. 6829], xxii; *Estimates for civil services for the year ending March 1915*, pp. 460–4, H.C. 1914 (132), lv.

commissioners which was considered insubordinate, indiscreet and indecorous'.[1]

The number of schools controlled by the board in 1850 was 4,547, attended by 511,000 children. By 1913 it had almost doubled, the schools numbering 8,255, attended by 699,000 children. And these increases occurred over a period when the population fell by about fifty per cent. The schools were in 1850 staffed by 5,136 teachers (male and female), and by 1913, the board's 'teaching power' had risen to 15,600 teachers. The appointment and dismissal of teachers was in the hands of the managers, though the board of course practically possessed the power of dismissing a teacher by withholding his salary. Up to 1874 the manager could summarily dismiss a teacher. But in 1874 the board introduced a rule obliging a manager who dismissed a teacher to be prepared to show sufficient cause to the board or to the courts or to give three months notice or three months salary. A vigorous resident commissioner admitted that the board might be involved in grave difficulties if it decided in favour of a teacher against a clerical manager on any but the very strongest grounds.[2] Fortunately, however, appeals from catholic teachers did not come before the board since, by a resolution of the hierarchy, a catholic manager had to secure his bishop's sanction before dismissing a teacher. Up to 1908, a teacher could appeal to the board against a decision of either his manager or an inspector only through the other. In that year he was given the right of direct appeal.[3]

From 1840 the teachers were divided into three classes each with its own salary scale. Teachers could present themselves for the purpose of classification at examinations conducted by inspectors. In 1872 a strenuous effort was made to raise Irish educational standards by the adoption of a simple, almost automatic, device, the results system. In addition to his class

[1] *Viceregal commission of inquiry into primary education (Ireland), second report, appendix*, pp. 259–60, H.C. 1914 [Cd. 7229], xxviii.

[2] *Royal commission of inquiry into primary education (Ireland)*, iii. 3, H.C. 1870 [Cd. 6–11], xxviii; *Royal commission on the civil service, fourth report, second appendix*, p. 425, H.C. 1914 [Cd. 7340], xvi.

[3] *Viceregal commission of inquiry into primary education (Ireland), first report, appendix*, p. 133, H.C. 1913 "Cd. 6829], xxiii; *Royal commission on the civil service, fourth report, evidence*, p. 425; *Irish ecclesiastical record*, 3 series, xvii. 174.

salary a teacher was to be annually paid a sum calculated on the answers of individual pupils in an examination by an inspector. In less than thirty years this system was being widely condemned as encouraging a narrow approach to education and mechanical methods of instruction, and on its abolition in 1900 the teachers were regrouped in three grades, of which the highest was divided into two sections. To be eligible for the higher grades and the higher section of the highest, a teacher had to have minimum numbers of pupils and both salary increments and promotion from grade to grade was made to depend on inspectors' reports, an inspector being required to classify schools and teachers as 'excellent', 'very good', 'good', 'fair', 'middling' or 'bad'. As the treasury fixed the maximum numbers which could be recognized in each grade, the practice of 'paper promotion' came into being, the teacher being promoted but not receiving the salary of his new grade until a vacancy arose.[1]

The board also managed directly several institutions, the Marlborough Street teachers' training college, about thirty model schools, and for a long period a number of agricultural training centres. In the 'thirties the commissioners were very eager to promote a better knowledge of agriculture, hoping that their schools would 'tend as far as practicable to bring forward an intelligent class of farm labourers and servants'. Between 1836 and 1838 the board established at Glasnevin an agricultural college with about fifty (later increased to one hundred and twenty) acres attached, where young men were given both scientific and practical training in agriculture. In addition, the board by 1870, supervised nineteen model agricultural schools, many with substantial farms attached, and recognized eighteen which were under local management. Moreover, eighty-three national schools had gardens. The board's farms were severely criticized as being equipped on too expensive a scale and as being frequently worked at a loss. In a report prepared for the Powis commission on primary education it was pointed out that 'there clearly could be no more useless expenditure of the public funds than to teach Irish farmers to

[1] *Viceregal committee of inquiry into primary education (Ireland)*, pp. 35–9, H.C. 1919 [Cd. 60], xxi. 779–83.

lose money'.[1] After the Powis commission reported, the board started to dispose of its agricultural schools, and after 1881 it managed only two, the Glasnevin College (known from 1853 as the Albert College) and the Munster Institute in Cork, which developed into a centre for dairy instruction. In April 1900, these two institutions were handed over to the department of agriculture and technical instruction.

At the beginning of the twentieth century a sustained effort to improve the educational system supervised by the board produced a series of administrative crises. Strained relations developed between members of the board, between the resident commissioner and members of his staff, and between the department and many of the teachers. The results system, which was introduced in 1872, undoubtedly 'raised the average attendance of children and made their progress more regular and rapid'. But at the same time it tended to encourage 'monotonous and mechanical cramming'. During the 'nineties several leading members of the board, Archbishop Walsh, the chief baron and Professor George Fitzgerald became convinced that drastic changes were required, and in 1896 two deputations from the board waited on the lord lieutenant and pressed for the introduction into the Irish primary schools of an organized and comprehensive scheme of manual instruction to supplement a programme regarded as too 'bookish'. A viceregal commission with Lord Belmore as chairman was appointed in 1897 to see how far manual and practical instruction could be incorporated into the curriculum. It heard 186 witnesses, held some sittings in England, sent a quorum to take evidence in Sweden and Denmark and finally produced an unanimous report recommending that the curriculum should include subjects in which manual and practical instruction could be given and that the results system should be abolished.[2]

The board appointed a committee to consider the report of Lord Belmore's commission and several senior officials were requested to draw up schemes giving effect to the commission's recommendations. But little or nothing was done

[1] *Royal commission of inquiry into primary education (Ireland)*, vol. I, pt. II, p. 833, H.C. 1870 [Cd. 6–A], xxviii.

[2] *Commission of manual and practical instruction in primary schools in Ireland . . . final report*, H.C. 1898, c. 8923, xliv; *Sixty-seventh report of the commissioners of national education*, p. 8, H.C. 1901 [Cd. 704], xxi.

until William Joseph Myles Starkie was appointed resident commissioner in February 1899. Starkie, a distinguished scholar who had been a fellow of Trinity and president of Queen's College, Galway, was an educational enthusiast—but with few illusions. He came to his new post, in the opinion of his private secretary, 'as a new man with the best intentions' towards his senior officials.[1] But these good intentions were laced with reforming zeal, for Starkie had been warned by the government on his appointment that the education office was 'an Augean stable'. Reddington, his immediate predecessor, 'one of the most charming of men', had at the time of his appointment little official experience and at the end of his short term of office had been in poor health. Reddington's predecessor, Keenan, at the close of his career, had also been a sick man.[2] As a result the office had become disorganized. The chiefs of inspection were failing to bring important decisions, such as those relating to the dismissal or punishment of teachers, before the resident commissioner. Moreover, the chiefs of inspection themselves left too much to their subordinates. In the early 'nineties Keenan's attention was drawn to the fact that 'the reports were being dealt with almost entirely by the clerical staff of the office, the notings were made on the back of them suggesting action, and the chiefs of inspection were merely attaching their initials in a perfunctory manner'. Keenan summed up the position as follows: 'the chiefs of inspection are destroying their position. I must insist they deal with the reports themselves and put notings on the back of the reports themselves. Let the clerks in the office supply them with the material for their action but the clerks must not deal with the reports in their entirety, because if they do there will be no necessity for the chiefs of inspection'. The result was that the chiefs of inspection told the clerks not to make any more notings for action on the backs of the reports, but instead to put such notes on a slip and insert it in the reports. These notes were then copied out on the backs of the reports by the chiefs of inspection. Finally, a serious episode involving several senior officials occurred a few years before Starkie's appointment. In

[1] *Viceregal commission of primary education* (*Ireland*), *second report, appendix,* pp. 266–8, H.C. 1914 [Cd. 7229], xxviii.
[2] *Ibid.*, p. 281.

1895, a number of teachers complained that their promotion examination had been too severe, and that a number of the questions set had been wrong. The board referred this to the chiefs of inspection and the head inspector responsible who showed the greatest reluctance to revise their work. In the end some members of the board had themselves to re-mark the papers—much to the disgust of the original examiners, one of whom expressed himself with considerable force in a correspondence he conducted with the board.[1]

Starkie set to work with terrific drive to put the new programme into operation. Shortly after his appointment the curriculum was revised and broadened, while the 'results' system was abolished and replaced by a grading scheme. In carrying out these changes Starkie, as might be expected, found the senior officials unsympathetic. On one occasion, when Starkie and Professor George Fitzgerald were conferring with one of the chiefs of inspection, and Fitzgerald was 'giving his views with regard to what the commissioners would like to have done' and the chief of inspection 'was controverting them', Fitzgerald was so exasperated that he declared: 'Remember that we are the commissioners and wish this to be done. You are not a commissioner, you are one of our officers, and it is our views that must obtain with regard to this new programme'. After this the chief of inspection left the room and abstained from giving any further assistance in drafting the new programme. Some time later, at the beginning of 1900, when the resident commissioner produced a memorandum setting out the changes he intended to make, the chiefs of inspection reacted violently. The point which they fastened on was a personal one —their duties, title and (in their own eyes at least) status. They were to become chief inspectors, supervising the whole inspection, which meant they should spend a considerable amount of time away from the office. Inspectors' reports were to be dealt with by 'examiners of reports', of which two were appointed in 1900 and another later. The examiners' duty was to read the reports and when necessary suggest action. Both chiefs of inspection wrote indignant letters as soon as they heard of the proposed changes. They argued that the examination of reports could only be carried out by experienced educational-

[1] *Ibid.*, pp. 260–1, 266.

ists, and contended that they were not inspectors, but heads of a department in the office, the senior emphasizing that if the resident commissioner's behaviour was justifiable 'my vested interests as a civil servant are a myth, and my position one of slavery'. Starkie immediately suspended one of the chiefs of inspection; and the board confirmed his decision and suspended the other for insubordination. The chiefs of inspection had to apologize before being restored to office. In fairness it should be added that Starkie, when changing the functions of the chiefs of inspection, generously arranged that their salaries should be increased. The aggrieved officials completely ignored this in their letters.[1]

The basis of the teacher's remuneration having been altered, the salary of every primary teacher had to be recalculated according to the new rules, and though a great effort was made to handle the vast array of varying cases on equitable lines, the decisions of the board produced an avalanche of appeals. In order to check futile correspondence the resident commissioner instructed the financial assistant secretary 'to cease from the fruitless task of trying to explain to individual applicants why their claims could not be entertained', and to classify and hold over for the consideration of the board the cases that were accumulating. The assistant secretary did not strictly obey. Instead, by firmly giving adverse decisions in many instances he tried to put an end 'to an unduly prolonged correspondence'. Archbishop Walsh, to whom a number of managers and teachers indignantly wrote, soon found himself overwhelmed with grievances, many of which he felt were well founded. He took the drastic step of writing a couple of letters to the *Freeman's Journal*, complaining that decisions were being given without the board being consulted. A few weeks later, dissatisfied with the very moderate censure administered by the board to the erring secretary, he resigned, and immediately afterwards gave a couple of interviews to the press in which he stated that confusion prevailed in the national board's office. His fellow commissioners accepted a memorandum, composed with his accustomed verve by the resident commissioner, demonstrating to

[1] *Viceregal commission of inquiry into primary education* (*Ireland*), *first report, appendix*, pp. 5–6, 75, 118, H.C. 1913 [Cd. 6828], xxii; *Second report, appendix*, pp. 266, 270–6, 280–4.

their satisfaction that the archbishop had exaggerated the importance of some mistakes made in the office. On the same day the board by four votes to two agreed to a harsh repudiation of the archbishop's charges prepared by Judge Shaw.[1]

From about 1900 strained relations developed between many of the teachers and the board. The working of the merit system gave the inspectorate considerable power over the teacher's economic prospects. Failure to obtain a satisfactory sequence of 'marks' might delay the award of an increment, and it was believed by many teachers that the 'marks' were often awarded in an arbitrary and unfair fashion. There was much grumbling and agitation amongst the teachers, and finally a viceregal committee of inquiry, appointed in 1913, having heard numerous witnesses (and much acrimonious evidence), strongly recommended the abolition of the merit mark system. This recommendation was implemented when a new salary scale was introduced in 1917.

As has been shown the state played a vigorous part in general education at each of the three levels, university, secondary and primary, on which it is usually assumed to be conducted. And there was another educational sphere in which the state was exceedingly active, technical instruction. The division between general and technical education is no doubt in some respects an arbitrary one. Nevertheless it was assumed that technical education was both in content and intention a distinct subject. In Ireland from the middle of the nineteenth century the state encouraged technical instruction and indeed was largely responsible for the growing importance of the subject in Irish education.

The government promoted technical education in Ireland from the middle of the eighteenth century indirectly by subsidizing the Royal Dublin Society, and from the middle of the nineteenth century directly through the Museum of Irish Indus-

[1] *Extracts from minutes of the proceedings of the commissioners of national education (Ireland) . . . in relation to recent action taken by the Most Rev. W. J. Walsh, D.D., archbishop of Dublin . . .*, H.C. 1901 (261), lvii; *Second memorandum considered at the board of national education, Ireland . . . in connection with the recent resignation of the Most Rev. Dr. Walsh . . .*, H.C. 1901 (366), lvii; *Viceregal committee of inquiry into primary education (Ireland), second report, appendix*, pp. 239–91.

try. The Royal Dublin Society, that famous Irish institution, founded in 1731 and chartered in 1749, had as its object the 'promoting of husbandry and the useful arts'. Early in the nineteenth century its aims were summarized as being 'the diffusion of knowledge of natural history and physical science and the advance of the useful and ornamental arts'.[1] It maintained a natural history museum, a botanical garden, a library, drawing schools and a group of scientific professors who gave courses of public lectures. Having a membership embracing peers, M.P.s and many public-spirited country gentlemen, it had managed from 1761 to secure a regular parliamentary grant. By the middle of the nineteenth century this grant which constituted the bulk of the society's revenue, stood at over £5,000. Naturally the government considered at times that it had the right to supervise and even interfere in the activities of a society which was largely supported by public money. The society, on the other hand, was proud of its autonomy and traditions. Twice in the 'thirties and again in the early 'sixties there was serious tension between the Irish administration and the society. The crisis in the 'thirties ended in the society having to modify its rules. The 1861 crisis arose because the society refused to open the botanic garden to the public on Sundays, arguing that to do so would violate the sanctity of the Sabbath and expose the plants to danger from disorderly crowds. Lord Granville, the lord president of the council, disposed of the first argument by pointing out that fellows of the society were admitted on Sunday; and Lowe, the vice-president of the committee of the council for education, announced that he would withhold the society's annual grant if it refused to change its policy. In the event the society yielded.[2]

In 1845, the government began to provide directly facilities for technical and scientific education. The committee of inquiry into the Irish ordnance survey memoir, when it reported in 1843, recommended that an Irish geological museum should be set up in Dublin.[3] The government accepted this recommenda-

[1] *Report of the select committee on the Royal Dublin Society*, p. 111, H.C. 1836 (445), xii.

[2] *Proc. Royal Dublin Society*, 1860–1, p. 73, 1861–2, pp. 1–7; *Hansard*, 3 series, cliv. 16–28, 344–63, 759–61.

[3] *Report of the commissioners . . . to inquire into . . . the ordnance memoir for Ireland*, p. xiv, 78–9, H.C. 1844 (527), xxx. 272, 345–5.

tion, and the museum, for which a large house in Stephen's Green was secured, was placed under the control of the commissioners of woods and forests, who appointed as its first director Robert Kane, a distinguished Irish chemist. The appointment was a significant one. Kane was not only an able scientist with a gift for systematic exposition but was an ardent and eloquent believer in the importance of applying scientific knowledge in every possible way to increasing Irish productivity. In a memorandum submitted to the committee on the ordnance survey memoir, he had made it clear that he hoped the Irish geological museum he recommended would become 'an Irish technical museum'. As soon as he was appointed director he started to widen the new museum's scope. To the geological collections he added technological collections, labelled with great thoroughness, illustrating the use of raw materials in Irish industry. And he even panelled the museum's entrance hall with various specimens of Irish marble, setting, he declared, an example, which was followed by other Irish institutions including Trinity College in its new museum building. In 1847, Kane persuaded Carlisle, the first commissioner of works, to sanction a change in his museum's name which would indicate its range. He suggested it should be called the Irish Industrial Museum. But Carlisle thought that 'the word "industrial' was not strictly speaking known in this country; that it was rather a foreign word'. So the name finally chosen was the Museum of Irish Industry.[1]

In 1853 the control of the museum was transferred to the newly established science and art department. This department was itself under the board of trade, having been created because it was feared that Great Britain would be outstripped by industrial rivals with more science and better taste. Shortly after the new department was set up, one of its secretaries, Henry Cole, who had played an important part in organizing the exhibition of 1851, made a survey of Irish technical education. He believed that technical education could to a very great extent be provided by the Queen's Colleges and the primary schools. Still he thought that there should be 'a culminating

[1] *Report from the select committee appointed to inquire into the condition of the scientific institutions of Dublin . . .*, pp. 66, 69, 363–5, H.C. 1864 (495), xiii.

point for industrial education', and that this should be the Museum of Irish Industry. Since it would obviously be unsatisfactory to have 'two centres in Dublin both supported by public funds ostensibly promoting the same objects', he emphasized that all responsibility for direct instruction should be vested in the museum, the Royal Dublin Society being left with its other functions. Cole submitted his views to the science and art department in January 1854, and three months later the department informed the Royal Dublin Society that 'it would be entirely relieved from the superintendence of its educational staff'. In future the professors of chemistry, physics, geology and botany who had been maintained by the society, were to be appointed by the board of trade and attached to the Museum of Irish Industry. The society remonstrated strenuously against this decision, arguing that it was unfortunate the government should have set up in close proximity to the society another institution to perform duties which the society, 'a great instrument for the diffusion of practical and scientific teaching on Ireland' was perfectly competent to discharge.[1] A deputation from the society met the president of the board of trade, Cardwell, and a compromise was arrived at. The government insisted on the transfer of the professors but agreed that they should deliver some lectures in the society's theatre. And a committee of eight (four appointed by the science and art department and four by the Royal Dublin Society) was set up to make arrangements for the lectures to be given in the museum, the society's theatre and at provincial centres. Besides these lectures, which were 'popular', from the close of 1854 systematic courses were given by the professors at the museum. So as 'to make the class a real student class and not a class of mere loungers', fees were charged for the courses, examinations were held, and prizes awarded.[2]

The arrangements made in 1854 did not last long. In 1861

---

[1] *Royal Dublin Society . . . return to an order of the honourable the house of commons dated 8 May 1854*, H.C. 1854 (330), lviii. 537–57; *Report from the select committee on scientific institutions (Dublin) . . ., appendix*, pp. 363–5.

[2] *Second report of the department of science and Art, appendices*, pp. 188, 240, H.C. 1854–5, 1962, xvii. 460, 512; *Report from the select committee on scientific institutions together with . . . minutes of evidence*, p. 153, H.C. 1867–8 (432), xv.

the Royal Dublin Society started a fresh discussion on Irish technical education by informing the government that it would need £10,000 to complete plans for improving its buildings and grounds. The science and art department, which was responsible for the society's vote, was irritated to discover that the society had managed to secure a little extra money by getting a vote in the board of works estimates. Nevertheless the department, after an inquiry conducted by one of its inspectors, Captain Donnelly, agreed to increase the society's grant from £6,000 to £7,000 in the 1862 estimates. This increase aroused some interest in the house of commons. Adderley, a conservative keenly interested in education, suggested that the Museum of Irish Industry could be 'incorporated with the Royal Dublin Society', and he dwelt on the awkward fact that Kane, who was deservedly closely identified with the museum in the public mind, was also president of Queen's College, Cork. Another conservative member, Whiteside, had already drawn attention to this, pointing out that, unless 'he possessed something of the quality of Sir Boyle Roche's bird of being in two places at once', Kane could scarcely perform his duties properly. Several other Irish M.P.s rallied to the defence of the museum which, it was said, was fulfilling its mission of developing the industrial resources of Ireland with remarkable success. From what was said both in the debate and later it was clear that many catholics and nationalists, guided as much by instinct as anything, regarded the Royal Dublin Society, which was dominated by protestants and landowners, as sectarian and snobbish.[1]

The government appointed a treasury committee of inquiry composed of Trevelyan (spending a short spell at home between Indian appointments), Donnelly of the science and art department, Blackburne, an ex-lord chancellor, and Griffith, chairman of the board of works. This committee recommended that the Museum of Irish Industry should be abolished, its functions being transferred to the Royal Dublin Society. The committee was convinced that it was inadvisable to have two bodies in Dublin with similar objects both supported by public money. This report was in accordance with the general policy of the science and art department. After an 'experimental' period in

---

[1] *Royal Dublin Society . . . return dated 1 Apr. 1862 . . .*, H.C. 1862 (264), xxx. 631–48; *Hansard*, 3 series, clxvi. 1450, 1526.

the 'fifties the department had in 1859 decided that the best way to promote technical and scientific education was not by giving fixed salaries to teachers but by giving prizes to pupils and payments to teachers based on examination results. And the head of the department for practical purposes in 1864 was Robert Lowe, an outspoken doctrinaire liberal, who was ready to apply as far as possible *laissez faire* principles to educational administration. Lowe welcomed the report, pointing out that general elementary scientific instruction was fully provided for by the system adopted by his department. If an advanced industrial college was to be founded it obviously should not be in Dublin, but at 'a place where manufactures were largely carried on'. The treasury agreed with him, emphasizing that if an industrial college was set up in Dublin it might reasonably be expected that claims would be made by Manchester and the other great seats of manufacture in Great Britain, and if these claims were granted it would add largely to the education estimates. The views of the Irish government, which of course could not ignore Irish liberal opinion, were forcibly expressed by Larcom, the under-secretary, in a communication addressed to the treasury. He argued that there should be an industrial college in Dublin and that it would be a retrograde step to remove 'a branch of national instruction' from public control and entrust it to a private, or, as he termed it, proprietary body, aided by public money.[1]

In so far as the weight of departmental opinion counted, the Museum of Irish Industry seemed doomed. But in April 1864 Gregory, an Irish liberal-conservative M.P., secured the appointment of a select committee on the Dublin scientific institutions, arguing that the treasury committee was 'packed', Trevelyan having a treasury bias, Donnelly being on the staff of the science and art department and Blackburne and Griffith being members of the Royal Dublin Society. The select committee, which was largely composed of Irish M.P.s, recommended generous financial support for several Irish cultural institutions, including the Royal Dublin Society. It was also strongly in favour of the Museum of Irish Industry being trans-

[1] *Scientific institutions of Dublin, copy of any correspondence between the lord lieutenant . . . and the treasury or the department of science and art*, pp. 2–8, H.C. 1863 (401), xlvi. 604–10.

formed into a college giving systematic instruction on the same lines as the Royal School of Mines in London.[1]

The government proved surprisingly acquiescent (Lowe had resigned in 1864 and had been replaced by a gentler minister, Henry Bruce). It agreed that the Royal Dublin Society's museum, library and botanic garden should be wholly supported out of public funds, the society acting as trustee, and that the Museum of Irish Industry should become 'a college affording a complete and thorough course of instruction in those branches of science which are more immediately connected with and applied to all branches of industry'. The department of science and art appointed a commission which included Huxley, Tyndall, Kane and Lord Rosse, who acted as chairman, to make recommendations on the curriculum and organization of the new college. And in the autumn of 1867 the Royal college of science for Ireland, under the control of the department, with Kane as dean and a staff of ten professors, began to function.[2]

At the beginning of 1876 Lord Sandon, vice-president of the committee of the council for education, placed before the Royal Dublin Society a scheme 'for augmenting and extending the facilities for science and art instruction in Ireland'. The society was to surrender its library, natural history museum, botanic garden, and art schools to the government, which was to provide in Dublin a national library, a science and art museum, and a metropolitan school of art. There were prolonged negotiations, but finally in 1877 the terms of transfer were settled by a deputation from the society, Sandon and the chief secretary, the society securing a substantial grant and other privileges.[3]

The collections of the Royal Dublin Society were vested in the science and art department and the buildings which contained them in the board of works. And between 1885 and 1890

---

[1] *Hansard*, 3 series, clxxiv. 663 ff.; *Report from select committee on scientific institutions (Dublin): together with the . . . minutes of evidence*, H.C. 1864 (495), xiii; Science and art department of the committee of the council on education, minute, 21 Sept. 1865 (Naas papers, MS 11143).

[2] *Report of the commissioners on the College of Science, Dublin . . .*, H.C. 1867 (219), lv.

[3] *Proc. Royal Dublin Society, 1876-7*, pp. 66-70.

Sir Thomas Deane, the celebrated Irish architect, flanked Leinster House with two buildings in a sixteenth-century Italian style, one of which housed the National Museum and the other the National Library.[1]

The management of the National Museum was entrusted to a board of trustees which reported to the department. The department controlled directly the museum and the botanic gardens but to assist it in their management a board of visitors was constituted, composed of members nominated by the lord lieutenant, the Royal Dublin Society, and Royal Irish Academy. Relations between this advisory body and the department and its successor, the department of agriculture and technical instruction, were not altogether happy. The visitors felt that insufficient attention was paid to their opinions and complained both to the lord lieutenant and to a departmental commission of inquiry.[2]

At this point something might be said about the institution analogous and in close proximity to the National Library and the Museum, the National Gallery, which, strange to say, retained complete administrative independence. Founded in 1854, it was governed by a board of governors of which four were nominated by the lord lieutenant. It was maintained by the state and received an annual grant, for which its director (who with the registrar comprised its administrative staff) was the accounting officer. In the 'seventies Doyle, the director, whose judicious purchases greatly enhanced the gallery's reputation, had to plead 'official inexperience upon a matter of form' to excuse a discrepancy in his accounts. At the close of the century his successor Armstrong, a distinguished art critic, annoyed the treasury by failing to present his accounts in time and not answering letters. In 1903 his conduct was discussed in the house of commons, the financial secretary to the treasury describing him as 'a gentleman of great artistic temperament with no love for accurate accounting'. In the following year Armstrong was warned that if he failed to produce his accounts in proper form he would have to appear before the committee on public accounts. Twelve months later the treasury reported

---

[1] *The Builder*, lix. 194.

[2] *Department of agriculture and technical instruction (Ireland), inquiry committee, minutes of evidence*, pp. 767–76, H.C. 1907 [3574], xviii.

that his accounts were being produced punctually and in proper form.[1]

For nearly half a century the science and art department played an important part in Irish educational life. At the close of the 'sixties it was urged that a separate science and art department for Ireland should be constituted. The need for such a department—adequately housed in Dublin—was strongly argued by an influential group which was trying to induce the government to purchase the premises in Earlsfort Terrace owned by the unsuccessful Dublin Exhibition Palace and Winter Garden Company. The advocates of a separate Irish department mobilized educational arguments and national sentiment in support of their case, and though Larcom was scornful (writing to the chief secretary he asked how many more bankrupt companies would the government be expected to redeem) the government yielded. In 1868 the treasury appointed a committee with Lord Kildare as chairman, to report on how an Irish science and art department should be organized. But the committee, which was a strong one, decided to consider also the question whether such a department should be constituted at all, and in the event reported that it would be better for Ireland 'to retain the imperial system by which students throughout the kingdom are examined together'.[2]

In 1899, the functions of the science and art department in Ireland were entrusted to the newly created department of agriculture and technical instruction. The new department's activities in some spheres touched or overlapped those of the national education and intermediate boards. It gave instruction in subjects which were also taught in the national schools, and it gave grants for science and art to secondary schools. The act constituting the department set up a consultative committee composed of the vice-president of the department and

[1] *Hansard*, 4 series, cxix. 1003–6; *First, second and third reports from the committee of public accounts, with . . . minutes*, p. 14, H.C. 1904 (152, 207, 228), v. 225; *First, second, third and fourth from the committee of public accounts with . . . minutes*, p. 195, H.C. 1905 (176, 240, 248, 260), vi. 549; and *First report from the committee of public accounts, minutes*, p. 14, H.C. 1876 (133), viii. 28; *Third report*, p. 23, H.C. 1876 (324), viii. 147.

[2] *Report of the committee on the science and art department in Ireland . . .*, H.C. 1868–9 [4103 4103–1], xxiv and documents in Naas papers (N.L.I., MS 11200).

one member appointed by each of following: the National education board, the intermediate education board, the agricultural board and the board of technical instruction. This committee tried to co-ordinate the educational work of the different bodies represented on it, but in 1906, Starkie, one of its most energetic members, declared that what was needed was a single education department for Ireland. A year earlier a report on intermediate education had recommended the creation of such a department, and twelve years later in 1919 a viceregal committee on intermediate education recommended emphatically that there should be a central authority responsible for primary, secondary and technical education.[1]

[1] *Department of agriculture and technical instruction (Ireland), minutes of evidence taken before the departmental committee of inquiry,* pp. 232–3, H.C. 1907 [Cd. 3574], xvii; *Intermediate education, Ireland, report of Messrs F. H. Dale and T. A. Stephens,* pp. 84–5, H.C. 1905 [Cd. 2546], xxviii; *Viceregal committee on intermediate education (Ireland),* p. 21, H.C. 1919 [Cd. 66], xxi.

IX

ARCHIVES AND
INFORMATION

~~~~~~

BY THE BEGINNING of the nineteenth century many Government offices in Ireland possessed large accumulations of documentary material.[1] The courts of justice and some of the financial departments, notably the auditor general's office, had substantial archives, the chief secretary's office had attached to it the state paper office, and other departments had collections of varying importance. In addition there were four offices, the registry of deeds, the Bermingham Tower, the office of arms and the parliamentary record office which had as their *raison d'etre* the preservation of records. Nothing will be said at this point about the registry of deeds, which functioned and developed historically, in so far as it altered at all, in almost complete isolation from other Irish offices. In the Bermingham Tower, which had been used as a repository for centuries, there was stored an immense mass of material including patent, pleas and close rolls, sheriffs' accounts and the contents of 'three large closets full of papers' which it was impossible to open 'without being enveloped in dust and dirt'.[2] In 1775, when the tower was being reconstructed, the records had been

---

[1] For the condition of the records in Ireland at the beginning of the nineteenth century see *Record commission, Ireland*, fifteen reports published between 1810 and 1825.

[2] *Record commission, Ireland, reports, 1810–15*, pp. 51, 398.

shoved into sacks and left in the Battle Axe Hall. Later, when they were put back in the tower they were squeezed into inadequate space. And though these records had in the past suffered from fire, at the beginning of the nineteenth century the bottom floor of the Bermingham Tower was being used as a kitchen. The office of keeper of the records in the Bermingham Tower, to which at the beginning of the eighteenth century a substantial salary had been attached, was held from 1805 by the earl of Stanhope. An absentee, he was represented by two deputies, William Warburton and William Betham. Warburton is remembered as a joint author of a bulky work on Dublin. Betham, an Englishman, was a genealogist by descent, being the son of William Betham, the author of *Genealogical tables of the world*. A fluent writer on historical, heraldic, antiquarian and philological subjects, industrious, self-assured and at times quarrelsome, Betham was for years a prominent figure in the social and scholarly life in Dublin. After his appointment as deputy keeper he toiled assiduously to build up a great private collection of references to the Irish records, the foundation of his well-advertised practice as a pedigree expert. In accomplishing this task he admitted that he had one advantage in addition to his unremitting industry: he was given 'ready access' to the records and exempted from paying the customary fees, though, as he was careful to explain, the custodians ultimately gained from their records being more easily and therefore more frequently consulted.[1]

Betham was also, from about 1800, deputy Ulster King of Arms and in 1820, on the death of his principal, Admiral Sir Chichester Fortescue, he succeeded him as Ulster. The office of Ulster King of Arms, along with that of Athlone Pursuivant, had been created in 1552. Its holder was responsible for granting and confirming arms and recording pedigrees. He was also a member of the viceregal court and the principal officer of arms of the order of Saint Patrick. At the beginning of the nineteenth century, the records of the office were kept in Betham's private house in Cope Street, where there was always a clerk in attendance. In 1830 they were removed to the Record Tower. On Betham's death in 1853, he was succeeded

[1] W. Betham, *Observations . . . on the record commission*, Dublin 1837, pp. 20–1.

by another hereditary genealogist, Sir Bernard Burke, a son of the founder of the *Peerage*, who held office for nearly forty years, also acting as keeper of the state paper office.[1]

The parliamentary record office was established after the union as a repository for the records of the Irish parliament. The architect who adapted the Parliament House to the purposes of the Bank of Ireland sent off the records in cart-loads to the new office, which was in a house in Anglesea Street, described as 'insecure, but not much more insecure than most private houses'. The keeper of the collection was Edward Cooke, who, after the union, left Ireland to pursue a very distinguished civil service career in England. He was represented by two deputies, both in other posts, who were paid for whatever work they did in the parliamentary record office by fees, which annually amounted to an infinitesimal sum.[2]

It had long been recognized that the Irish archives contained material of great historical value. About the middle of the eighteenth century, Walter Harris, the editor of works which he hoped would 'fill up a few void spaces in Irish history' had remarked that 'it was obvious to mankind that the records of nations must be the main basis and foundation upon which the history of these nations ought to be built'. And he suggested that some experienced clerks should be set to work under expert direction to 'transcribe and methodize in a chronological series all records relating to Ireland'. A few years later Lodge in the preface to his *Peerage of Ireland* referred to 'those inexhaustable funds of history the rolls office and the Bermingham Tower'. Finally, just after the union, Duhigg, a barrister and the author of a history of the King's Inns—in which much antiquarian knowledge is almost inextricably entwined with his views on a multiplicity of contemporary questions—in a couple of pamphlets pressed Abbot, then chief secretary and Manners, then

---

[1] Rymer, *Foedera*, xv. 314–5; *Record commission, Ireland, second report*, pp. 64–5; *Report from the select committee on miscellaneous expenditure, minutes of evidence*, p. 296. *Burke's landed gentry*, 1952, xcvii.

[2] *Record commission, Ire., and reports*, 1810–15, pp. 58–9; *Record commission, proceedings, report of searches, 1806*, pp. x–xi. Cooke's deputies were Thomas Tayler, a clerk in the chief secretary's office, and T. R. O'Flaherty, registrar of the office of arms and an attorney.

chancellor, to institute an inquiry into the state of the Irish records.[1]

In the year in which Duhigg's second pamphlet was published the Irish record offices were caught in a wave of reform arising in England. In 1800, a select committee of which Abbot was chairman was set up to inquire into the condition of the British public records. As a result of its report a record commission was appointed to examine and organize the archives. In 1806 two of its sub-commissioners engaged in searching for original statutes and charters visited Ireland and reported briefly on the condition of some of the Irish repositories.[2] Their comments reinforced Redesdale's[3] plea that steps should be taken to reorganize the public records, and in 1810 an Irish record commission was appointed. It was composed of six ex-officio members, the lord chancellor, the master of the rolls, the heads of the three common law courts, and the chief secretary, the bishop of Kildare,[4] three Irish peers, the provost of Trinity and Dr Duigenan. The commission was empowered to take steps for the better arrangement and preservation of the records and for the composition of calendars and indexes, and to supervise the publication of 'original records'.

At its first meeting the commission appointed as its secretary William Shaw Mason and recruited a staff of sub-commissioners, most of whom were lawyers or officials in offices with valuable archives. In 1822, there were thirteen sub-commissioners. Five (including Mason) who were salaried were preparing 'works of literary character'. The rest 'remunerated by hourly rates' were abstracting and transcribing. In addition there were eight or nine assistants.[5] Among the sub-commissioners were Betham and Duhigg, who have already been mentioned, Hardiman and John Erck, who were to do solid work based on manuscript sources, Henry Joseph Monck Mason who according to

[1] W. Harris, *Hibernia*, Dublin 1747, pp. 18–9; Lodge, *Peerage of Ireland*; B. T. Duhigg, *A letter to Charles Abbot . . .* (1801) and *A letter to Lord Manners . . .* (1810).

[2] *Record commission, proceedings, 1806–7*, pp. 3–5, *appendix*, pp. 96–7.

[3] Redesdale was lord chancellor of Ireland 1802–6.

[4] Charles Lindsay.

[5] For the work of this commission see *Record commissioners, Ireland*, fifteen reports, 1810–25 and M. Griffith, 'The Irish record commission, 1810–30' in *I.H.S.*, vii. 17–28.

the *D.N.B.* 'possessed much general knowledge and an extremely good opinion of himself', and Rowley Lascelles, an enthusiastic student of history and an opinionated, prolix and turgid author, who was to be the villain—or in his own eyes the victim—of a major administrative scandal. An Englishman and a barrister who became a bencher of his Inn, Lascelles was employed from 1815 as a sub-commissioner to prepare for publication Lodge's manuscript lists of the patentee officers. In 1820 he quarrelled with the commissioners, because he claimed he was denied the credit he deserved and the salary he had been promised, and also because he gave honest expert evidence against the crown. He returned to England and arranged with the chief secretary that he was to continue his work at a salary of £500 per annum. It seems to have been expected that Sir Thomas Tomlins, who was parliamentary counsel to the chief secretary, would supervise him. But Lascelles himself declared that Sir Thomas exercised supervision 'not in the vulgar sense of the word' but 'with a more than ordinary deference, honour and delicacy'. He considered 'with his usual good sense that an architect if honest might be trusted with his own work'. An arrangement 'so satisfactory to the employee, so improvident on the part of the public' having been made, it is scarcely surprising that Lascelles found his work 'enlarged as discoveries opened upon my view', and by 1829 he was unable to say when it would be finished.[1]

Besides starting an extensive programme of arranging and indexing, the commission also planned a radical reorganization of the records. By 1815 the contents of the Bermingham Tower, of the state paper office of the parliamentary record office and of the office of arms (which had been stored in a private house) were concentrated in the tower, henceforth known as the Record Tower, the massive medieval building which sturdily commands the lower castle yard. The commission also had an ambitious scheme for moving the registry of deeds, the auditor general's records and some ecclesiastical records to a new repository beside the King's Inns on the north side of the city. And their schemes were facilitated by an act of 1817 which provided that the offices of surveyor general of crown lands,

[1] *Report from the select committee on the Irish miscellaneous estimates*, pp. 36–40, H.C. 1829 (342), iv; *Gentleman's magazine*, new series, xvi. 333.

keeper of the records in the Bermingham Tower and keeper of the state paper office were each to be abolished on the next vacancy and their records removed to any record office the lord lieutenant might designate.[1] But owing to the reluctance of the government to meet the expense involved, the scheme for a great consolidated record office fell through.

After it had been functioning for about twelve years the commission was attacked by two well-informed critics, Betham and Lascelles. Betham in 1811 had bitterly compared the amount of space in the Record Tower allotted to his Bermingham Tower records with that appropriated by Shaw Mason and his clerks, and he appears to have tried to prevent the commission's staff having access to his records.[2] In 1822 he prepared for the chief secretary a long, carefully drafted memorandum on the commission's activities. While admitting it was doing useful work, Betham alleged that it had committed grave blunders. Some of its work had been marred by inaccuracies, material had been indexed before it was arranged, abstracts had been made on too great a scale, and proof correcting had cost 'as much if not more than the whole printing would if the copy had been properly prepared for the press'. The commission, in Betham's opinion, had even shown a lack of political awareness by choosing to print inquisitions whose appearance would excite discontent amongst the descendants of attainted proprietors. One of the commission's worst mistakes was its failure to make sufficient use of officers well acquainted with the records. Instead it had employed a number of young men who learned their business as they worked on (and in Betham's opinion sometimes disorganized) the collections. Betham also understood that the sub-commissioners 'were prohibited from working too hard for fear of doing the work too fast', and he had heard that some of them were performing their duties while detained in a debtor' prison.[3]

In the same year (1822) as Betham produced his memorandum, Lascelles presented a petition to the house of commons

---

[1] *Record commission, Ireland, reports, 1810–15*, pp. 409, 472, 551.

[2] Betham to lord chancellor, 6 Nov. 1813, Mason to Betham, 6 July 1814 (Shaw Mason papers).

[3] Betham to chief secretary, 1822 (Unregistered papers, C.S.O./1833/50).

accusing the record commission of mismanaging its affairs.[1] Significantly enough the house called for a return of the expenses of the commission, which showed that it had cost up to date nearly £70,000, but no further step was taken.

A few years later a friendly official from an English department had a startling experience of the commission's methods. Weale, a principal clerk in the department of woods and forests wanted to have a reliable list of the crown rentals in Ireland drawn up. This, he thought, could be done comparatively cheaply by the record commission, whose staff was already dealing with the records which would have to be consulted. Mason was very helpful, but suddenly Weale, who had returned to England, was alarmed to hear on what scale the work was being planned. If, he wrote, making a perfect abstract of the patent rolls was going to occupy three sub-commissioners for twelve months, 'I have been most egregiously mistaken in my estimate of the cost of the entire work'. He emphasized that all that had to be done was 'straightforward work and chiefly mechanical', and that it did not demand the 'painful accuracy' Mason suggested, after all, they were not editing classical texts. Weale was not prepared, he emphasized, 'to plunge headlong *in medias res* trusting to the chapter of accidents, or placing the treasury ultimately in the situation of being compelled to authorize the expenditure of more money than they could now sanction or to abandon the work after useless expenditure'. In the end Weale's views prevailed, and the work was accomplished at a reasonable cost.[2]

It is hard to say what weight should be attached to the charges made against the record commission and it is not easy to assess the value of its work. After all it was pioneering amongst the accumulations of centuries, and it would probably have been better if it had not attempted to do so much at once. In any event, by the end of the 'twenties it was threatened by a powerful economy drive, a select committee on the Irish miscellaneous estimates being appointed by the house of commons in 1829. It was a sign of impending danger that Lascelles began corresponding with Mason in the most friendly

[1] *Commons' jn.*, lxxvii. 369.

[2] James Weale to Mason, 18 Oct. 1826, 1, 28 Feb. 1827 (Shaw Mason papers).

fashion, writing in March 1829 that he contemplated 'with pleasure re-entering the embrace or bosom of that Holy Roman Catholic Church the Irish records, drowning in oblivion all past discords between it and me'. He was very anxious that the commission should sanction the work he had been engaged on, and he warned Mason that the situation was serious, since the government, with deplorable weakness, had decided to sacrifice the Irish estimates in the hope of saving the English estimates.

The select committee examined only one witness on the workings of the Irish record commission—Lascelles. He had a strenuous examination, the committee taking great interest in the terms of his employment, but when he started describing his work in grandiloquent language, he was cut short with the direction to submit a written statement. The committee also examined him on his petition of 1822. This Lascelles thought was unfair, for it compelled him either to attack the commission or to abandon his petition. He explained at some length that the commission was at last behaving better and that his feelings had changed, with the result that, according to himself, 'the committee cheered me as they do in the house itself when they hear a member express himself handsomely and with candour'. But he proved a true prophet when he declared the committee was meeting 'not to inquire but to execute', since in its report it doubted if the record commission had given good value for the £100,000 it had cost, and unhesitatingly recommended that Lascelles' employment should be terminated.[1] In 1830 the treasury ceased to pay Lascelles and in 1832 it asked the English record commission to report on his work, much of which was already in print. The commission had no hesitation in recommending the cancellation of the section in which 'Mr Lascelles has embodied his opinions on Roman Catholic emancipation, the state of the church, Adam Smith and the Scoto-Gallic economists'. And they pronounced the work in general to be 'a miscellaneous mass of extracts'.[2] As a result of this report the treasury decided not to publish the work. But it was

[1] Lascelles to Mason, 11 Mar., 23 May, 22 June 1829 (Shaw Mason papers); *Report from the select committee on the Irish miscellaneous estimates*, pp. 35–43, H.C. 1829 (342), iv.
[2] T. 1/3051.

found to be of use by those who were able to consult it and finally in 1852 publication was sanctioned.

Lascelles' compilation, the *Liber munerum publicorum Hiberniae*, is one of the most fantastic of record publications, masses of padding, including a long excursus on Irish history and summaries of the statutes being added to the lists of patentee officers. Lascelles himself described the work as 'a storehouse of facts and documents for the use of the statesman, the lawyer, the churchman, the peer and the commoner, the antiquary, as well as the ordinary man of business. Nor will it be found, I trust, unworthy the regard of the philosophical scholar and historian'.[1] And in 1836 Lascelles appeared before another select committee volubly claiming compensation for the termination of his employment, which, he argued, he had a right to under his interpretation of the terms of the gentleman's agreement on which he had been engaged. The committee, however, refused to pronounce an opinion on the matter.[2]

The Irish record commission ceased to function in 1830, Mason being instructed to hand over its papers to Betham. There were henceforth two offices specifically concerned with the preservation of records, the Record Tower under Betham's control, and the registry of deeds. In addition there were two sub-offices or sections of departments which were responsible for the care of large and important manuscript collections, the rolls office, attached to the court of chancery and what was ultimately (from 1861) known as the landed estates record office. The nucleus of the collection in the landed estates record office was the auditor general's records. In 1830 a portion of these records was in the vice-treasurer's office in the castle. Another portion was stored in the dome of the Four Courts, an arrangement, which, it was pointed out, was 'most unfavourable to their preservation and reference' and which moreover created 'some apprehensions with regard to the safety of the building'.[3]

In 1831 the vice-treasurer suggested to Weale, the principal

---

[1] *Liber Mun. Hib.*, introduction, p. 3. For variations in the editions of the *Liber Mun. Hib.* see *I.H.S.*, iv. 23.

[2] *Report from the select committee on the record commission together with . . . evidence*, pp. 511–6, H.C. 1836 (429, 565), xvi.

[3] *Record commissioners, Ireland, fifteenth report*, p. 25.

clerk in the department of woods and forests, that all the records relating to 'the crown's territorial rights and revenues' should be placed in 'one general repository'.[1] Weale strongly favoured the suggestion and in 1832 the auditor general's records were removed to the west wing of the Custom House. Other financial records were later added to the collection. The commissioners of woods and forests recommended that the officials in the record department of the vice-treasurer's office should not be employed in the new office. Its staff, they suggested, should be the sort of persons 'in the service of a public library', and its head, they thought, should be selected by the head of the English commission on the public records.[2] However, Hardinge, who was the senior clerk in the record department of the vice-treasurer's office, successfully asserted his claim to be put in charge of the custom house collection. The control of the Custom House collection was first vested in the vice-treasurer, later, in 1837, it was transferred to the paymaster of civil services. In 1861, by a treasury minute, the record branch of the paymaster's office was converted into the landed estates record office.[3]

In 1838 a great general repository, the public record office, was established in England, and it was soon being suggested that a similar office should be established in Ireland. Betham clearly considered himself to be the doyen of Irish archivists, but two other keepers of large collections of departmental records, Hardinge, who was in charge of the Custom House collection, and Hatchell, clerk of the enrolments, who was in charge of the records of the court of chancery, prepared printed statements emphasizing the claims of their offices to be the central repository. Hardinge dwelt both on the size of his collection and his own experience. He was an hereditary archivist, having entered the civil service in 1815 under his father, clerk of the records in the auditor general's office, whom he had succeeded in 1831. Nobody, Hardinge declared, who did not know the former 'filthy, unarranged, inaccessible condition' of the records under his care could appreciate 'the labour of

---

[1] James Weale to commissioners of woods and forests, Dec. 1831 (T. 1/4152).

[2] Commissioners of Woods and Forests, 24 July 1833 (T. 1/4152).

[3] *P.R.I. rep. D.K.I., appendix*, p. 107.

mind and body' involved in reorganizing them. And he compared himself in general with 'men of less experience . . . and more limited record intelligence [who] have by ephemeral press productions caught the attention of those in power', and particularly with Betham, whose extensive practice as a pedigree agent disqualified him from being head of a great public office.[1] Hatchell both enumerated the important categories of documents in his office and explained how, by rearranging the office accommodation in the Four Courts, a space could be secured for a large record office. It would both hold the legal records and any other documents the government might order to be deposited, and would be 'the most perfect, extensive and convenient receptacle for records in the empire'.[2]

A few years before Hatchell put forward his plan, William Shaw Mason, living in embittered retirement, drafted a bill for the establishment of a public record office. The registrar of deeds was to be keeper of the records, and there was to be a deputy keeper who was to be responsible for the management of the new office. Mason himself was prepared to accept the office of deputy keeper without salary and devote the rest of his life to carrying out 'this truly national and important measure', on the understanding that the treasury paid him the compensation for loss of office to which he considered himself entitled. But Peel, while referring the question to the Irish government, made it clear to one of Mason's supporters that he 'was not inclined to view with much favour any legislative measure which suggests an office to be conferred on the author of it'.[3]

In 1856, witnesses appearing before a committee on the court of chancery recommended strongly that better provision be made for the keeping of its records.[4] Two years later, by the Four Courts extension act the board of works was empowered to acquire ground on which to build a repository, and in 1862 the building of a new record office was begun.[5] Just about this time, public and parliamentary attention was drawn to the

[1] Statement of claim of W. H. Hardinge (1849) (P.R.O.I. M. 4971.).

[2] Printed paper by George Hatchell, P.R.O.I. M. 4970.

[3] W. S. Mason to Bishop of Kildare, 24 June 1842, Peel to Bishop of Kildare, 6 Aug. 1842 (Add. MS 40511).

[4] *Report from the select committee on the Court of Chancery (Ireland) Bill, together with . . . minutes of evidence*, pp. 18–9, 165–6, H.C. 1856 (311), x.

[5] 21 & 22 Vict., c. 84.

management of the Irish records by fierce scholarly dispute. An edition of the patent rolls was published by James Morrin, the clerk of the enrolments, under the direction of the master of the rolls. Gilbert, the energetic editor of Irish historical manuscripts, denounced Morrin's work as being disfigured by plagiarisms, inaccuracies, omissions, and blatant mistranslations.[1] The master of the rolls appointed a commission of inquiry, composed of Thomas Duffus Hardy, the deputy-keeper of the public records, and Brewer, the well-known editor. Their report, while admitting defects in Morrin's work, exonerated him from some of Gilbert's charges.[2] Gilbert returned to the attack, demonstrating that the commissioners themselves had made mistakes in their report.[3] Gilbert had a strong if over-stated, case, but, what was perhaps more important, the whole episode showed the importance of entrusting the care of the records to a special department. In 1864 Hardy and Brewer in a second report insisted on the importance of having an Irish record office, recommending that it be placed in the New Record Building beside the Four Courts.[4] Three years later, the building being completed, the Irish public records act of 1867, modelled on the English act of nearly thirty years earlier, was passed.[5] The new Dublin record office and the Record Tower were both placed under the supervision of the master of the rolls, the former being managed by the deputy keeper of the records, the latter by the keeper of the state paper office. The latter office was revived for Sir Bernard Burke, Betham's successor as Ulster King at Arms, and was to be assumed by the deputy keeper on Sir Bernard's retirement (which occurred in 1892). In the record office were to be deposited legal records over twenty years old, the contents of the landed estates record office, wills, papers from the Record Tower over fifty years old, and any other government records the lord lieutenant might direct to be so deposited. The staff at first consisted of a deputy-keeper, an assistant-deputy keeper, a secretary

---

[1] An Irish Archivist, *Record revelations* . . . (1863).

[2] *Report of Messrs Brewer and Hardy . . . in reference to the publication of the calendar of the patent and close rolls of Ireland*, H.C. 1865 (35), ilv.

[3] An Irish Archivist, *Record revelations resumed* (1864).

[4] Report by Hardinge and Brewer to G. A. Hamilton, 7 Oct. 1864 (copy in P.R.O.I.).   [5] 30 & 31 Vict., c. 70.

and eight clerks.[1] In knowledge and productivity Gilbert had an unrivalled claim to the deputy-keepership. But his controversial vigour must have been a handicap and he was fobbed off with the secretaryship—an office which the treasury managed to abolish in 1876.[2] The first deputy-keeper was Samuel Ferguson, a poet and an antiquary, an amiable man, well-liked by a large and influential circle. But Ferguson was also a competent lawyer who prided himself on his practicability, and from the time he was appointed at the close of 1867 he displayed tremendous energy and organizing power in managing the transfer to the new office of immense masses of documents.[3] From the Custom House alone 169 tons were moved by 'floats' and covered wagons, to be stored in the great granite-faced record treasury, where during the next fifty years one of the greatest collections of official documents in Europe was to be steadily and systematically built up.[4]

The staff of the new office was at first composed of about half a dozen officials (with archival experience) transferred from other offices, and four clerks appointed by competitive examination. Amongst the first group was Digges La Touche, the first assistant deputy-keeper, who succeeded Ferguson in 1886, and William Hennessy, the well-known Irish scholar. La Touche after a distinguished career at Trinity had in 1857 been appointed to a clerkship in the rolls office, the assistant keeper of the rolls being anxious to have on his staff 'a young man who had received a collegiate education for the purpose of having him study the black letter and learn to decipher and read the old records of the office'.[5] Hennessy, who had already edited a volume in the rolls series, was transferred to the Public Record Office from what must have been the less congenial post of clerk to the inspectors of lunatics.[6]

The registry of deeds, which, as has been mentioned, was isolated in its work and development from the other record

---

[1] P.R.O.I. rep. D.K., I, pp. 8–9.

[2] R. M. Gilbert, *Life of Sir John T. Gilbert*, pp. 87–93, 205.

[3] Lady Ferguson, *Sir Samuel Ferguson in the Ireland of his day*, ii. pp. 327–45.

[4] See reports of the deputy keeper of the records.

[5] *Chancery office, Ireland, commission, report*, p. 132, H.C. 1859 [2473], xii. 492.   [6] P.R.O.I. rep. D.K., I, p. 9.

offices, was the most active of these offices at the beginning of the nineteenth century. In 1707 it had been enacted that a deed or conveyance registered in accordance with a stated procedure would be effectual against an unregistered instrument. The primary object of this measure was to check evasions of the penal land laws by catholics, but before the close of the century it was considered to be of 'great and general utility'. At the head of the office, which shortly after the union was moved from the Castle to the Four Courts, was the registrar. In 1800, the registrar was George Ogle, a genial and popular M.P. and the composer of some celebrated airs. He rarely visited the office and in 1814 he was succeeded by Lord Kilwarden, who never attended. Kilwarden's deputy was George Moore, a practising barrister, who according to himself visited the office daily for the greater part of the year—though he admitted that he did not attend 'for any specific time'. Routine business seems to have been managed by the two senior clerks who were also assistant registrars, and under whom worked a dozen 'common clerks', registering, indexing and searching. The two assistant registrars also practised as solicitors, doing the greater part of their business in the office. Though Moore was convinced that 'the business of the office is the first object of each and that they only attended to their own concerns when at occasional leisure from their public duty', an investigating commission considered 'this arrangement which seems to suppose the possibility of a concurrent attention to public and private business' very objectionable. The commission also discovered that, as in other legal offices, the fees demanded were far in excess of those sanctioned by statute, with the result that the registrar's income (including his salary) amounted to about £3,600 a year. His deputy enjoyed about £700 a year, and as for the 'common clerks' their incomes ranged from £50 to £150 per annum.[1]

The commission of inquiry into the courts of law reported on the registry of deeds in 1820, and in 1828 and 1832 acts were passed reorganizing the office which at the beginning of the 'thirties was moved to a wing of the King's Inns, Henrietta Street. The treasury was given power to appoint its senior officials and to fix duties and salaries.[2] The first registrar under

[1] *Courts inquiry: eighth report*, pp. 6–12, 24–5, 68, H.C. 1820 (94) viii.
[2] 9 Geo. IV, c. 57; 2 & 3 Will. IV, c. 87.

the new regime was George Moore, who had been Kilwarden's deputy for thirty years. He was lucky in one respect. After some deliberation the treasury decided that his salary should be £1,200 per annum. But owing to a departmental blunder, a treasury clerk assuming that what was merely a draft minute was a board decision, he was appointed at £1,500 a year. And a select committee of the house of commons which investigated the matter decided that his salary should remain at this figure. But when his successor was appointed the treasury fixed his salary at £1,200.[1]

From the early 'thirties the office had an uneventful history. In 1876 it was made a lower division office, and some years later a commission of inquiry commended the 'zeal and intelligent interest' displayed by the clerks in spite of 'the monotonous nature' of much of their work. On half a dozen occasions extensive modifications of the systems of registration and indexing were proposed.[2] But any major change required legislation, and measures embodying important changes which were introduced in the early 'sixties and early 'nineties failed to pass. In the early 'sixties the work of the office was badly in arrears owing to the elaborate procedure which had to be employed. In 1862 and 1863 the government introduced a bill which would have simplified procedure and placed the office under the control of the judges of the landed estates court, who would have appointment of its temporary staff—while the permanent staff was to be appointed by the Irish government. The bill was strongly attacked by Cairns and Whiteside. The latter denounced it 'a crochet', declared that the office was well managed, and quoted Sir James Graham to the effect that if an Irish bill of a complicated nature was ever introduced by the government 'look for the patronage clause and in that clause you will find the key of the measure'. In the face of this resistance the government withdrew the bill, the attorney general sardonically explaining that, with the threat of

---

[1] *Report from the select committee on registry of deeds (Ireland) Bill,* H.C. 1831–2 (592), xviii.

[2] *Suggestions for improving the mode of registering deeds, Ireland.* p. 466, H.C. 1862 (190), xliv; *Report of the committee appointed to inquire into the registry of deeds . . .,* p. 33, H.C. 1887 (37), lxvii. 463; *Report upon the office of registry of deeds,* H.C. 1861 (2867), ii.

reorganization, the staff of the registry had suddenly 'summoned up such an extraordinary amount of energy' that the arrears had disappeared. When in the 'nineties Madden, the Irish attorney general, failed to carry a registration bill, he complained bitterly that 'it would not be expected that a measure of purely legal reform unconnected with patronage or politics should excite any particular enthusiasm'.[1]

A group of departments must now be dealt with which had functions analogous to those of the record offices, the departments concerned with the collection and publication of information about the country and its inhabitants. These were the ordnance survey, the geological survey, the valuation office and the registrar general's office. At the beginning of the nineteenth century the state in Ireland paid little attention to the collection of statistical and geographical information, except in respect of trade and public finance. By the close of the century there was available an immense amount of scientifically organized information about Ireland collected by government agencies.

In 1812, just after the second British census was taken, a measure was passed providing for the taking of an Irish census, and under this measure and later legislation attempts to enumerate the population were made in 1813, 1821 and 1831.[2] Local authorities, in 1813 the grand juries, after that date the justices of the peace in quarter session, appointed enumerators for their areas and transmitted and made returns to the chief secretary's office. In 1813, the lord lieutenant was empowered to appoint an officer to arrange and digest the returns, and in 1831 that officer was entrusted with the task of drawing up the question paper. In 1813 and 1821 William Shaw Mason, the remembrancer of first fruits, was appointed to receive the returns; the census of 1831 was supervised by George Hatchell.[3]

---

[1] *Hansard*, 3 series, clxx. 448–59, 1211 and D. H. Madden, *A practical treatise on the registration of deeds, Dublin 1901.*

[2] For the Irish census up to and including 1841 see K. H. Connell, *The population of Ireland, 1750–1845*, chapter I.

[3] See P.R.O.I., Official papers, second series, 543/394/38, 556/413/24, 3380/713/2.

The census of 1813 was very defective, the county officials being remiss over making their returns. The censuses of 1821 and 1831 were more thorough. But the increase of population shown by the census of 1831 may have been exaggerated, since the enumerators were paid in accordance with the numbers they returned.

The census of 1841 compared with its predecessors was not only much better organized but much wider in scope. It was supervised by a commission of three, appointed by the lord lieutenant, consisting of William Tighe Hamilton, of the chief secretary's office, Brownrigg, the inspector general of the constabulary, and Larcom, of the ordnance survey, who seems to have been mainly responsible for the planning of the commission's work. It was decided that the census 'should be a social survey, not a bare enumeration', and the constabulary, a disciplined force distributed throughout the country, were employed to collect the information required. The result of the commission's labours was a bulky volume containing an immense amount of detailed and precise information on population, distribution, the housing and occupations of the people, agricultural production, education and vital statistics.[1] From 1851 to 1911 a regular decennial census was taken. Each census was organized by a commission of three appointed by the lord lieutenant. The senior commissioner was always the registrar general, and usually one of the other commissioners was a member of his staff. On each occasion the information required was collected by the constabulary, and was tabulated and prepared for publication in the registrar general's office.

The post of registrar general was created in 1844, when, with the object of removing the presbyterians' disabilities, the Irish marriage law was amended. The registrar general was entrusted with the duty of keeping records of Irish marriages from April 1845, with the exception of those celebrated by the catholic clergy. From 1864 he kept records of all marriages celebrated in Ireland, and he also kept records of all births and deaths.[2] In addition he was responsible for compiling agricultural statistics. By the 'forties the value of such statistics was being realized. Attempts were made in various parts of Great

[1] See Larcom papers, *N.L.I.*, MSS 7525-7.
[2] 7 & 8 Vict., c. 81, and R. E. Matheson, *Digest of the Irish marriage law.*

Britain to obtain accurate information about the quantities of agricultural produce, and in 1847 a bill was introduced empowering the board of trade to collect agricultural statistics for England and Wales. It failed to obtain a second reading, but in the same year Clarendon, the lord lieutenant, realizing the urgent necessity of securing precise information about Irish productivity, directed the board of works to organize a census of agricultural production in Ireland. Larcom took charge of the operation and used the constabulary to obtain the required information. For a few years the board of works continued to compile agricultural statistics, but in 1853 this duty was transferred to the registrar general. Nearly half-a-century later, in 1898, this duty was transferred from the registrar general to the new department of agriculture and technical instruction.[1]

The first registrar general was William Donnelly, a barrister and a cousin of Young, the influential conservative M.P. for Cavan. Donnelly began with a small office, his staff consisting of one permanent and two temporary clerks. Soon he was complaining that they were overworked. Sometimes, he explained, he had to keep all three working until six, occasionally he had even to keep one in the office until ten. His complaints bore fruit since by 1848 he had a staff of five clerks, and later he built up a separate section for dealing with agricultural statistics. In 1874, when the work of the office was greatly increased, its permanent staff was about doubled, and when to this permanent staff were added the unestablished staff, fourteen temporary clerks and nearly fifty 'task-workers', the office had a total staff of over eighty.[2]

In 1824 a committee of the house of commons recommended that a complete survey of Ireland should be made as a basis for a fair valuation which could be used for local taxation. The ordnance survey of Great Britain had been begun in 1784 and the committee suggested that the corps of Royal Engineers

[1] *Report from the select committee of the house of lords appointed to inquire into the best mode of obtaining accurate agricultural statistics . . ., pp. iv, 84–9, H.C. 1854–5 (501), viii.*

[2] *Freeman's Journal,* 11 September 1844; S.P.O.I., 1876/10576; *Estimates, civil services for the year ending 31 May 1865,* ii. 34–5, H.C. 1864 (103–11, 108–9).*

should also undertake the Irish survey.[1] The recommendations of this committee had far-reaching results since they led directly to the boundary survey, the ordnance survey, the geological survey, and the townland, tenement and 'Griffith's' valuations. Each of these will now be dealt with.

As a prelude to the ordnance survey it was decided to ascertain and mark all townland and parish boundaries. The lord lieutenant, who was empowered to appoint a chief boundary surveyor, selected for the post Richard Griffith, an outstanding nineteenth century engineer and civil servant.[2] Starting in the Royal Irish Artillery, shortly after the union, he resigned his commission and qualified as a civil engineer, studying mineralogy and geology in Cornwall and at Edinburgh and practising as a valuator in the Scottish lowlands. About 1809 he began working in Ireland for the commission of inquiry into the Irish bogs. Later he worked hard constructing subsidized roads in the west. Griffith thought that he could carry out the survey with a staff of three assistant surveyors but 'on trial it was soon found the first establishment was far too small' and the boundary survey was unable to keep sufficiently ahead of the ordnance survey. So the establishment was increased until it numbered five assistant boundary surveyors, each of whom had several assistants, and a staff of clerks and draughtsmen in the Dublin office.[3] By 1830 the boundary survey was completed and Griffith was able to begin work on the valuation.

The ordnance survey, having been given legislative sanction in 1825,[4] was begun in the following year on a scale of six inches to the mile. It was under the direction of Major (later Major General) Colby of the Royal Engineers. Short and bustling, Colby possessed 'a singular nervous and elastic frame which no fatigue could overcome'. He was also a first-class organizer, and as he was convinced that 'any attempt to obtain ready trained surveyors in large numbers by means of high

---

[1] For a brief history of the ordnance survey see *Report of the progress of the ordnance survey*, pp. 3–4, H.C 1890 [Cd. 5959], lviii.

[2] 6 Geo. IV, c. 99.

[3] *Second report from the select committee on the public income and expenditure of the United Kingdom, appendix*, pp. 374–5, H.C. 1828 (110), v.

[4] 6 Geo. IV, c. 99.

prices would be costly and ineffectual in the result', he employed on the survey a number of officers from his own corps, including two future under-secretaries, Drummond and Larcom, Robert Dawson, who did outstanding work on the English survey, Reid, later governor of Malta, and Portlock, a soldier with wide scientific interests.[1] At first some of Colby's subordinates did not realize 'the importance of the fastidious progress of accuracy' which he demanded. But his persistence and military discipline prevailed, and soon a high standard of accuracy was attained. Under the engineer officers were civilian assistants, three companies of sappers carefully instructed at Chatham in practical geometry, and hundreds of civilian labourers. A central office was set up in Phoenix Park where information was amassed, calculations made, and maps engraved and printed. And by 1840 the total staff of the survey numbered about 1,600, including 21 officers, nearly 200 sappers and about 600 labourers.[2]

Soon after it started the survey widened in scope. Some of the officers employed in surveying were assiduous in collecting geological specimens, and in 1832 a geological department was established under Portlock. He formed a geological museum in Belfast, the contents of which were in 1840 moved to Dublin, and in the early 'forties he published a thorough work on the geology of County Londonderry. Furthermore, an attempt to establish the precise orthography of Irish place-names expanded into a great scheme of antiquarian and historical research, conducted by several outstanding pioneers in modern Gaelic studies, including Petrie, O'Donovan and O'Curry.[3]

These developments were welcomed and encouraged by Larcom whom Colby had put in charge of the Phoenix Park office. Larcom had arrived in Ireland in 1826 as a young lieutenant strongly influenced by the scientific tradition of his corps, eager to use the machinery of the survey 'to draw together a work embracing every kind of local information'.[4]

---

[1] J. E. Portlock, *Memoir of the life of Major General Colby*, pp. 1–2, 6, 226.

[2] *Report from the select committee on the ordnance survey, (Ireland) together with the minutes of evidence, appendix*, p. 47, H.C. 1846 (664), xv.

[3] *Report of the commissioners to inquire into the facts relating to the ordnance memoir of Ireland*, pp. vi–viii, H.C. 1844 (527), xxx.

[4] *Ordnance survey of the county of Londonderry.*

He persuaded Colby to issue a memorandum to officers engaged on the survey suggesting they should collect information on a very wide range of topics. Larcom projected a series of county memoirs, and his conception of the form it should assume is illustrated by the one fragment which was completed and published, the volume devoted to the parish of Templemore in County Londonderry. A work of over three hundred pages, it presents an enormous quantity of systematically arranged information, since, beginning with the natural history of the county it goes on to show how man has modified nature, and then, treating of the inhabitants, their history and activities, it demonstrates how man has been influenced by his environment.

The publication of this volume precipitated a crisis in the affairs of the survey. In 1838 Drummond had warned Colby that the treasury would expect full details of the cost of producing the Templemore volume, and as soon as it appeared Spring-Rice, the chancellor of the exchequer, wrote vigorously about it to Morpeth, the chief secretary. Having 'run through' the volume, Spring-Rice strongly doubted the expediency of continuing publication on such a scale. It would, he wrote, divert the officers engaged in the survey from their topographical duties, and he did not think the government should 'run a race with public money against private enterprise and literary industry'. Finally, he pointed out, in sanctioning such a work the government was accepting responsibility for the opinions expressed in it on historical questions and issues of social policy. A couple of months later the master general of the ordnance directed that the survey should 'revert immediately to its original object under the valuation act'. The specimens and memoranda collected by Portlock and Larcom were to be preserved and arranged, but not with a view to publication. Colby ruefully told Larcom that 'the inspector general is going to make a record against me for authorizing the geological and statistical expenditure', and he warned Larcom that he should make it quite clear that the historical and archaelogical material which had been collected all related to orthography.[1]

[1] Drummond to Colby, 15 Mar. 1838, Spring-Rice to Morpeth, 1845 (Larcom papers 7553), Colby to Larcom, 27 Mar., 1 Apr. 1840 (Larcom papers 7535), Master general of the ordnance to Morpeth, 25 Apr. 1840 and E. Fanshawe to Colby, 1 July 1840 (WO/47/1866).

There was a considerable amount of indignation at the abandonment of the county memoirs, and a group of Irish peers and gentlemen and the Royal Irish Academy asked that the question be reconsidered. Peel in 1843 appointed a commission of inquiry composed of three M.P.s. Probably influenced by one of their number, Adair, a keen archaeologist who was in close touch with Larcom, this commission recommended that the publication of the descriptive memoirs be resumed.[1] The government ignored the recommendation but it accepted another—that the geological survey of Ireland be removed from the control of the ordnance and entrusted to an office which, under the supervision of the commissioners of woods and forests, would undertake a geological survey of the whole United Kingdom. This office in 1853 was placed under the control of the science and art department, but in 1905 the geological survey of Ireland was transferred to an Irish department, the department of agricultural and technical instruction.[2]

By the early 'forties the ordnance survey as envisaged in 1824 being nearly completed, the bulk of its permanent staff was transferred to England, a branch with a small staff being left in Ireland. This branch not only revised the maps of Ireland but also carried out work for the landed estates court and the land commission, surveying 5,400 estates for these two bodies during the latter half of the nineteenth century.[3]

The historical labours of the ordnance survey in Ireland during the 'thirties were indirectly responsible for an important state-aided contribution to Celtic scholarship. In 1851 Charles Graves, a fellow of Trinity College, who although primarily a mathematician was ardently interested in Irish antiquities, published a short pamphlet in which he urged that an effort should be made to publish the manuscript material relating to the Brehon laws. These laws, he explained, were of the greatest interest to the jurist and the historian and he added (presumably with government assistance in mind) their publication

[1] *Report of the commissions to inquire into the facts relating to the ordnance memoir of Ireland*, H.C. 1844 (527), xxx.

[2] 9 & 10 Vict., c. 63; *First report of the department of science and art, appendix*, pp. 1–2, H.C. 1854 (1783), xxviii.

[3] *Report of the progress of the ordnance survey to 31 Mar.*, p. 8, H.C. 1900 [Cd. 327], lxviii.

would show that 'false or exaggerated notions' had 'been entertained of the well-being of society and the advance of civilization in early times'. A most powerful argument for immediate action, Graves emphasized, was the availability of men who had become 'instructed and disciplined scholars' while employed on historical work for the ordnance survey.[1]

Clarendon, the lord lieutenant, requested Graves and Todd, another fellow of Trinity, to report on the problem of publishing the ancient law of Ireland. At the beginning of 1852 they presented a report which was a repetition of the arguments in Graves's pamphlet buttressed by a collection of letters from a number of well-known historians (including Hallam, Guizot and Ranke) supporting the proposal to publish the laws.[2] And before the close of 1852 an unpaid commission was appointed to supervise the publication of the laws. The commission employed several distinguished scholars (O'Donovan, O'Curry, Handcock and Richey) in the cataloguing, transcribing and editing of the manuscripts. There was a vast amount of difficult material to be handled and numerous technical problems arose but by 1879 four volumes had been published. In 1886, the commission was reconstructed and by 1901 its work was completed in two volumes, edited by Atkinson, the professor of Sanscrit in Trinity College, the second of these being a glossary to the preceding five volumes.[3] Atkinson was a bold and prolific scholar and his work for the commission provided a target for a scarifying attack by Whitley Stokes, an able philologist with the most austere standards. He listed Atkinson's errors under nine heads and referred contemptuously to the commission's volumes with their inaccurate texts, guesswork translations and pathetically feeble footnotes.[4] But Stokes admitted that Celtic philology had advanced rapidly in the closing decade or so of the nineteenth century and it is only fair to the commission to remember it was doing pioneering work in a field in which rapid advances were being made.

[1] C. Graves, *Suggestions with a view to the transcription and publication of the manuscripts of the Brehon laws . . .*

[2] *Laws and institutes of Ireland: return . . .*, H.C. 1852 (356), xviii.

[3] See *the reports of the commission for the publication of the ancient laws and institutes of Ireland.*

[4] W. Stokes, *A criticism of Dr Atkinson's glossary to vols. I–V of the Ancient Laws of Ireland.*

In 1830, the ordnance survey being well under way, Griffith began the valuation of Ireland, townland by townland. While this townland valuation was in progress, it was enacted in 1838 that there should be a poor rate based on a tenement valuation made by the poor law guardians in each union.[1] It was obviously unsatisfactory to have a county and a poor rate each based on a different valuation, so in 1846 it was enacted that the commissioner for valuation should arrange for a tenement valuation to be made in ten counties and counties of cities.[2] Later in 1852, it was enacted that the commissioner for valuation should make a tenement valuation for the whole of Ireland.[3] This valuation, known as 'Griffith's valuation', was completed by 1865 and thenceforth it was being continually revised in detail by the valuation office. The valuation office at the beginning of the twentieth century was entrusted with the duty of making a new valuation on different principles, with the object of ascertaining capital values for the purposes of the finance act of 1909–10.

The valuation office was largely Griffith's creation. When in 1830 he began the townland survey in County Londonderry, he started by collecting the names of a number of professional surveyors and valuators employed in the north-east of Ireland. He selected nine and for a month trained them in his methods of valuation. After this 'it was perfectly extraordinary', he declared, 'how near they came together' in their estimates. Later he published a couple of works explaining in some detail his principles of valuation. An autocratic head of the valuation department—for some years he even housed a section of it in his own house in Fitzwilliam Square—Griffith was also from 1846 a member of the board of works of which, in 1850 he became chairman. When it was suggested that he must have found it difficult to direct simultaneously two important departments, he explained that his subordinates in the valuation office were so well selected, and each office so systematically organized, that he could run them both. He added that he always travelled by night so as to have the whole day for official work.[4]

[1] 1 & 2 Vict., c. 56.   [2] 9 & 10 Vict., c. 110.   [3] 15 & 16 Vict., c. 63.
[4] *Report from the select committee on the general valuation etc. (Ireland), together with . . . minutes of evidence and appendices*, pp. 43–8, H.C. 1868–9 (362), ix.

Up to 1860 the staff of the valuation office was selected and appointed by Griffith. In that year the office was placed under the supervision of the treasury which was empowered on Griffith's retirement to appoint the commissioner of valuation and to fix the establishment of the office.[1]

[1] 23 Vict., c. 4.

EPILOGUE

~~~~~~~~~~~~~~~~~~~~~~~~~~~~~~~~~~~~

FROM THE BEGINNING of 1912 a drastic reconstruction of the Irish administration in the near future seemed inevitable. The third home rule bill, despite the house of lords, was bound to reach the statute book about the middle of 1914. This bill provided that 'the public services in connection with the administration of the civil government of Ireland' (save those which were 'reserved') were to be managed by departments constituted by the Irish parliament. And as early as 1912 Lord MacDonnell published a scheme for grouping the Irish offices, 'the disjecta membra of Irish government', under nine ministries, the heads of which would be responsible to the Irish parliament.[1] But though the home rule bill received the royal assent in September 1914, its operation was suspended for the duration of the war and administrative reconstruction postponed.

The war influenced the Irish administration pattern only slightly. Two new United Kingdom ministries, formed to cope with wartime problems, the ministry of munitions and the ministry of food, both functioned in Ireland. The ministry of munitions appointed two joint directors of munitions for Ireland in October 1915, and an Irish food control committee to administer the rationing and distribution of food was set up in August 1917.[2] But neither ministry played much part in Irish life. Ireland, outside a small corner in the north-east, had little industrial potential which could be used for the manufacture

---

[1] Morgan, J. H. *The new Irish constitution* (1912), pp. 53–80.

[2] W. H. Beveridge, *British food control* (1928), p. 415, *History of ministry of munitions* (1921), vol. I, pt. II.

of munitions, and only a very small degree of food control was attempted. In 1917, a new Irish department was established, the department of national service. It was headed by a director who had a small staff and who was expected to work in co-operation with the director general of national service in Great Britain. But the department was under the control of the Irish government, the chief secretary answering for it in parliament. Since conscription was never applied in Ireland, the department's functions were very limited. It was responsible for making the best use of any Irish labour available for war work in England while ensuring a sufficient supply of labour for agriculture in Ireland.[1] The Irish department which probably contributed most to the war effort was the department of agriculture and technical Instruction. It was empowered under the defence of the realm act and the corn production act of 1917 to enforce compulsory tillage schemes. Under the latter Act it was empowered to set up an agricultural wages board to regulate the wages of agricultural labourers, and such a board was constituted in February 1918.

From 1919, the hostility of the more extreme nationalists to the government created conditions which greatly impeded the working of the administration. Indeed by 1920 the maintenance of law and order in some areas had become a military operation. The government's first post-war attempt to find a solution for the Irish question was embodied in the government of Ireland Act, 1920. This act provided for an extensive reorganization of the Irish administrative system. Some services were to be retained under imperial control. The others were to be entrusted within their respective areas to the government and parliaments of Southern and Northern Ireland. In June 1921 the lord lieutenant, acting under the government of Ireland act, authorized the creation of seven government departments in Northern Ireland, defined their functions and listed the United Kingdom and Irish departments whose duties were to be transferred to them. Some months later the king in council fixed the dates on which the responsibility for the different services was to be transferred to these departments (the date fixed for the last transfer being 1 February 1922). And at the beginning of 1922 a civil service commission established under the govern-

[1] *Hansard*, 5 series, xci. 45, 843–4, 872, xcii. 30, cvii. 22, 1538.

ment of Ireland act, was busy allocating staff from the Irish departments to the Northern Ireland offices.[1]

Early in 1922, the southern section of the now divided administration was summarily reshaped. On 16 January 1922, the members of the provisional government, approved by the Dáil, and members elected to the parliament of Southern Ireland, were received by the lord lieutenant who informed them they were duly installed in office. And on 1 April by an order of the king in council, and an order of the provisional government, issued simultaneously, the duties performed by government departments functioning in Southern Ireland were assigned to departments of the provisional government.[2]

The lord lieutenant, 'a transient and embarrassed phantom', remained in office until almost the close of the year. Theoretically he was at the head of the executive in both Southern and Northern Ireland. The provisional government regarded him as a form of 'liaison officer'. The Northern government, when he paid a short visit to Northern Ireland in October 1922, gave him 'a hearty and loyal welcome' as the king's representative.[3] Upon the appointment of a governor general of the Irish Free State on 6 December 1922, the lord lieutenant's powers ceased to be operative in that area. Two days later they lapsed in Northern Ireland.

[1] *Dublin Gazette*, 7 June 1921; 15 Nov. 1921; *Irish Times*, 17 Jan. 1922.
[2] *London Gazette*, 1 Apr. 1922; *Iris Ofigiuil*, 4 Apr. 1922; *Irish Times*, 5 Jan. 1922.
[3] *Iris Dáil Eireann, official report: debate on the treaty between Great Britain and Ireland*, p. 398. *The parliamentary debates . . . of Northern Ireland, 1 series*, ii. 939, 1137.

APPENDIX I

Irish Government Departments, 1800

For details relating to the establishments of these departments
see:

*a Accounts and papers . . . relating to the increase and diminution of
salaries in the public offices of Ireland . . .*, H.C. 1821 (287), xiii.
*b Increase and diminution of salaries: returns . . . for an account of
all offices in Great Britain and Ireland*, H.C. 1821 (712), x.
*c Return of the establishments of the public departments and offices in
1821 and 1829 respectively . . .*, H.C. 1830 (386), xvii.
*d Return of the persons employed . . . in all public offices or departments
in the year 1797 and in the years 1805, 1810, 1815 and 1819 . . .*,
H.C. 1830–1 (92), vii.
e Reports of the commissioners respecting the courts of justice.
*f Reports of the commission of inquiry into fees and emoluments in
public offices in Ireland, 1806–14.*
*g Reports from the commissioners respecting the public records of
Ireland, 1810–25.*

Accounts, Commissioners of, *a, b, c, d*.[1]
Arms, Office of, *g*.
Army accounts, Examinator and Comptroller of, *a, b, c, d*.[2]
Barrack Board and Board of Works, *a, b, c, d, f12*, W.O. 44/111.
Bermingham Tower, Record repository in, *g*.
Chief Secretary's Office, *a, b, c, d*.
Commissariat, *a, b, c, d*.

---

[1] From 1812 known as the commissioners for auditing the public accounts.
[2] From 1812 the powers of the examinator and comptroller of army
accounts were vested in the commissioners of military accounts.

Deeds, Registry of, *a*, *b*, *e20*.
Exchequer, Revenue side of, *e12*.
First Fruits, Board of, *a*, *b*, *c*, *d*.
Inland Navigation, Directors General of, *a*, *b*, *c*, *d*, *f13*.
Linen Manufacture, Trustees of, *a*, *b*.
Lottery Office.
Muster-Master General's Office, *a*, *b*.
National Debt, Commissioners for the reduction of, *a*, *b*.
Ordnance, Board of, *a*, *b*.
Post Office, *a*, *b*, *f9*.
Privy Council Office, *a*, *b*, *c*, *d*.
Stamps, Commissioners of, *a*, *b*.
Treasury, Commissioners of, *f14*.
Revenue, Commissioners of, *a*, *b*, *f6*.
Wide Streets, Commissioners of, *a*, *b*.

APPENDIX II

IRISH GOVERNMENT DEPARTMENTS, 1914

For details relating to the establishments of these departments see:

a *Estimates of civil services for the year ending 31 March 1915*, H.C. 1914 (132), lv.
b *Royal commission on the civil service, fourth report, second appendix*, H.C. 1914 [Cd. 7340], xvi.
c *Royal commission on the civil service: memorandum as to the organization and staff of the chief secretary's office* . . . [1913].

Agriculture and Technical Instruction, Department of, *a.*
Arms, Office of, *a.*[1]
Charitable Donations and Bequests, Commissioners of, *a.*
Chief Crown Solicitor and Treasury Solicitor, *a.*[1]
Chief Secretary's Office, *a.*
Congested Districts Board, *a*, p. 362 and *b*, pp. 609–10.
Criminal Lunatic Asylum, Dundrum, *a.*
Dublin Hospitals, Board of Superintendence, *a.*
Dublin Metropolitan Police, *a.*[1]
Education, Commissioners of, *a.*
General Prisons Board (and Reformatory and Industrial Schools), *a.*[1]
Intermediate Education, Commissioners of, *a.*
Land Commission, *a*, and *b*, pp. 607–8.
Loan Fund Board, *c*, p. 12.[1]
Local Government Board, *a.*
Lunatic Asylums, Inspectors of, *a.*

[1] A department under the immediate control of the chief secretary's office.

National Gallery of Ireland, *a.*
National Education, Commissioners of, *a.*
National Health Insurance, Commissioners of, *a.*
Petty Sessions Clerks, Registrar of, *c*, p. 11.[1]
Public Record Office, *a.*
Public Works Office, *a.*
Quit Rent Office, *a.*
Registrar General's Office, *a.*[1]
Registry of Deeds, *a.*
Royal Irish Constabulary, *a.*[2]
Teachers' Pensions Office, *a.*
Treasury Remembrancer's Office, *a.*
Valuation and Boundary Survey, *a.*

[1] A department under the immediate control of the chief secretary's office.
[2] The Dublin metropolitan police and the Royal Irish Constabulary each had an administrative office with a civil service staff.

APPENDIX III

~~~~~~~~~~~~~~~~~~~~~~~~~~~~~~~~~~

United Kingdom Departments Functioning in Ireland, 1914

For the number of officials in these departments employed on solely Irish business see *Public departments (Scotland and Ireland) return showing . . . the number of established and unestablished officials . . .*, H.C. 1912–13 (104), lvi. In this return the quit rent office is included but as it was a pre-union Irish office it is not included in the following list.

> Admiralty.
> Customs and Excise.
> Exchequer and Audit.
> Friendly Societies Register.
> Home Office.
> Inland Revenue.
> Ordnance Survey.
> Post Office.
> Stationary Office.
> Trade, Board of.
> War Office.

APPENDIX IV

~~~~~~

OFFICIALS DISCUSSED, pp. 46–51.

Under-Secretary (Sir James Dougherty).
Assistant Under-Secretary (Edward O'Farrell).
Principal Clerks, Chief Secretary's Office (W. P. J. Connolly, J. J. Taylor).
Chief Crown Solicitor (Sir Malachy Kelly).
Treasurer Remembrance (M. F. Headlam).
Resident Commissioner of National Education (W. J. M. Starkie).
Secretaries, Board of National Education (P. E. Lemass, W. J. Dilworth).
Assistant Commissioners, Intermediate Education Board (W. F. Butler, W. A. Houston).
Chairman, Board of Works (Sir G. Stevenson).
Members of the Board of Works (P. Hanson, T. P. Le Fanu).
Vice-President, Local Government Board (Sir H. Robinson).
Members of Local Government Board (Sir T. Stafford, E. Bourke).
Secretary Department of Agriculture and Technical Instruction (T. P. Gill).
Assistant Secretaries, Department of Agriculture and Technical Instruction (J. R. Campbell, G. Fletcher).
Land and Estates Commissioners (W. F. Bailey, S. L. Lynch, W. H. Stuart, F. S. Wrench).
Congested Districts Board, Permanent Members (H. Doran, W. L. Micks).
Registrar of Deeds (R. Manders).

300

Secretaries, Board of Charitable Donations and Bequests (A. F. Graves, R. M. Sweetman).

Commissioner of Valuation (J. G. Barton).

Deputy Keeper of the Records (J. Mills).

Registrar General (Sir William Thompson).

Inspector General, R.I.C. (Sir Neville Chamberlain).

Chief Commissioner, D.M.P. (Sir John Ross-of-Bladensburg).

Chairman, General Prisons Board (M. Green).

Members, General Prisons Board (The MacDermot, D. E. Flinn).

Registrar of Petty Sessions Clerks (H. Caddell).

Inspectors of Lunatic Asylums (T. I. Considine, W. R. Dawson).

Secretary, General Post Office (A. H. Norway).

Chairman, National Health Insurance Commission (J. A. Glynn).

National Health Insurance Commissioners (W. S. Kinnear, W. J. Maguire, Mrs M. L. Dickie).

Secretary, National Health Insurance Commission (J. Houlihan).

Solicitor, Inland Revenue (R. Martin).

Assistant Secretary, Inland Revenue, Stamp and Tax Department. (J. Simpson).

BIBLIOGRAPHY

I. SOURCES

    (A) Manuscript material

LONDON

    British Museum
        Aberdeen papers
        Balfour papers
        Campbell-Bannerman papers
        Gladstone papers
        Hardwicke papers
        Peel papers

    Public Record Office
    There is a large amount of material relating to Ireland in three departmental collections, those of the Home Office, the War Office and the Treasury. T.14 (Treasury outletters, Ireland) is an especially useful series.

Surrey County Record Office
    Goulburn papers
    This collection contains a large number of letters from
    Sir William Gregory when Under-Secretary.

The Plunkett Foundation
    Sir Horace Plunkett's papers (correspondence and
    diaries)

The London School of Economics
    The Jebb papers

OXFORD

    Bodleian Library
    Lord MacDonnell's papers

DUBLIN

    Public Record Office
    H. Wood in *A guide to . . . the Public Record Office of
    Ireland* (Dublin 1919) describes the collections in the
    office before almost all its contents were destroyed in
    1922. He also gives in this work some useful information
    about the development of some of the legal and
    administrative offices. 'A short guide to the Public
    Record Office of Ireland', by M. Griffith in *I.H.S.*,
    viii. 45–58, lists the material in the office in 1952.
    Board of Works records

    State Paper Office
    Official papers, 2nd series
    Registered papers
    This enormous collection comprises the correspondence
    of the Chief Secretary's Office.

    National Library of Ireland
    Bryce papers
    The Kilmainham papers
    Larcom papers
    Naas papers

BELFAST

    Public Record Office
    Hill papers

(B) Printed material

    Where London is the place of publication, location is not
mentioned.

(1) *Parliamentary records*

Commons Journals, Ireland, 21 vols., Dublin, 1796–1802.

The parliamentary history of England from the Norman conquest to the year 1803, 36 vols., 1806–20.

The parliamentary debates from the year 1803 to the present time (1820), 41 vols., 1804–20.

The parliamentary debates published under the superintendence of T. C. Hansard . . . new series (1820–30), 25 vols., 1820–30.

Hansard's parliamentary debates . . . 3rd series (1830–91), 356 vols., 1831–91.

Hansard's parliamentary debates . . . 4th series (1892–1908), 199 vols., 1892–1908.

Hansard's parliamentary debates . . . 5th series (1909–), 1909– .

(2) *Directories*

For an account of the Dublin directories see 'The first hundred years of the Dublin directory' in Proc. Irish Bibliog. Soc., vii

Wilson's Dublin directory, 1751–1837.

Pettigrew and Oulton's directory, 1834–50.

Post office directory, 1832– .

Thom's official directory, 1844– .

(3) *Biographical guides*

F. Boase, *Modern English biography*, 6 vols., 1892–1921.

Burke's landed gentry of Ireland (1912), 1958.

Dictionary of national biography.

Who was who (1897–1960), 5 vols.

(4) *Departmental reports*

The following Irish departments published regular (usually annual) reports which, with the exception of those of the Linen Board, appeared as parliamentary papers.

Accounts, Commissioners of, –1833.

Agriculture and technical instruction, Department of, 1902– .

Ancient laws and institutions of Ireland, Commission for publication of, 1859–64, 1886–98.

Charitable donations and requests, Commissioners of, 1846– .

Church temporalities, Commissioners of, 1875–81.

Congested districts board, 1893– .

Dublin hospitals, Board of superintendence of, 1858– .

Ecclesiastical commission, 1845–69.

Education, Commissioners of, 1834– .

Education, Board of intermediate, 1880– .

Fisheries, Commissioners of, 1814–1830.

Land commission, 1882– and Estates commissioners, 1905– .

Linen manufactures, Trustees of, 1784–1828.

Local government board, 1873– .

Lunatic asylums, Inspectors of, 1845– .

National education, Commissioners of, 1834– .

Poor, Commissioners for administrating the laws for the relief of, 1848–1872.

Prisons, Inspectors general of, 1823–1878.

Prisons, Convict, Board of directors of, 1854–1878.

Prisons, General prisons board, 1879– .

Public loan fund board, 1839–1916.

Public record office, 1869– .

Records, Commissioners of, 1813–25.

Works, Board of, 1832– .

(5) *Parliamentary papers*

Arranged chronologically. Papers which are especially valuable since they deal with a large section of the Irish administration are asterisked.

An account of the particulars of compensation awarded in consequence of the union with Ireland, H.C. 1803–4 (158), viii.

Report from the committee respecting the poor of Ireland, H.C. 1803–4 (109), v.

Papers . . . respecting instructions from the lord lieutenant to the commissioners of the board of works in Ireland, H.C. 1805 (26), vi.

Commissioners appointed to inquire into fees, gratuities, perquisites and emoluments which are or have lately been received in certain public offices in Ireland . . . and into the present mode of receiving . . . and accounting for public money in Ireland, first report, on customs, H.C. 1806 (6), viii; Second report, stamps, H.C. 1806 (270), viii; Third report, on assessed taxes, H.C. 1806–7 (1), vi; Fourth report, on the land revenue of the crown, H.C. 1806–7 (2), vi; Fifth report, on excise: distillation, H.C. 1806–7 (124), vi; Sixth report, on excise: malt, H.C. 1808 (4), iii; Seventh report, on excise: auctions, cards and dice, glass bottles, hides and skins, paper . . . wrought place, H.C. 1809 (15), vii; Eighth report, on the mode of accounting for excise duties, H.C. 1809 (52), vii; Ninth report, on general post office, H.C. 1810 (5), x; Tenth report, on arrears and balances, H.C. 1810 (234), x; Eleventh report, 1810–11 (55), vi, 1812–13 (123), vi; Twelfth report, on the board of works, H.C. 1812 (33), v; Thirteenth report, on inland navigation, H.C. 1812–13 (61), vi; Fourteenth report, on the treasury, H.C. 1813–14 (102), vii.

A copy of the report of the commissioners of paving, etc. in Dublin to the lord lieutenant of Ireland . . ., H.C. 1809 (148), vii.

Report from the commissioners appointed to inquire into . . . the state prisons and other gaols in Ireland . . ., H.C. 1809 (265), vii.

Copies of any official letters . . . to the first commissioner or commissioners of the Customs department . . . relating to the suppression of fees, H.C. 1810 (97), xii.

Report from the select committee on grand jury presentments of Ireland, H.C. 1814–15 (283), vi.

Commissioners appointed to inquire into the duties, salaries and emoluments of the officers, clerks and ministers of justice in all temporal and ecclesiastical courts in Ireland, First report of the court of chancery, H.C. 1817 (9), x; *Second report, on the court of exchequer*, H.C. 1817 (10), xi; *Third report, on the court of error*, H.C. 1817 (287), xi; *Fourth report, on offices in disposal of the crown*, H.C. 1818 (140), x; *Fifth report, on the court of common pleas*, H.C. 1819 (5), xii; *Sixth report, on the court of King's bench*, H.C. 1819 (6), xii; *Seventh report, on the clerks of nisi prius*, H.C. 1819–20 (33), iii; *Eighth report, on registry . . . of deeds*, H.C. 1820 (94), viii; *Ninth report, on the court of exchequer*, H.C. 1822 (322), xiv; *Tenth report, on the equity side of the court of exchequer*, H.C. 1822 (31); *Eleventh report, on the court of exchequer*, H.C. 1822 (322), xiv; *Twelfth report, on the revenue side of the court of exchequer*, H.C. 1824 (467), xii; *Thirteenth report, on the sheriff's office*, H.C. 1825 (373), xv; *Fourteenth report, on the judge and commissary of the prerogative and faculties*, H.C. 1826 (68), xvii; *Fifteenth report, on the office of sheriff*, H.C. 1826 (310), xvii; *Sixteenth report, on the crown office*, 1826–7 (341), xi; *Seventeenth report, on the courts of quarter sessions*, H.C. 1828 (144), xii; *Eighteenth report, on the high court of admiralty*, H.C. 1829 (5), xiii; *Nineteenth report, on the courts of prerogative and faculties*, H.C. 1830 (311), xx, and H.C. 1830 (518), xv; *Twentieth report, on the office of registry of deeds*, H.C. 1830–31 (365), vi; *Twenty-first report, on the metropolitan and consistorial courts*, H.C. 1831 (146), x.

Report from the select committee on the lunatic poor in Ireland with minutes of evidence, H.C. 1817 (430), viii.

Report from the select committee on the state of gaols, H.C. 1819 (575), vii.

Report of the commissioners appointed . . . to inspect the house of industry . . ., H.C. 1820 (84), viii.

Accounts and papers . . . relating to the increase and diminution of salaries etc. in the public offices of Ireland in the year ending 1st January, 1821, H.C. 1821 (287), xiii.

Report of the commissioners of inquiry into the collection and management of the revenue, First report, on the collection and management of the revenue *in Ireland*, H.C. 1822 (53), xii; *Second report, on the incorporation of the revenue boards*, H.C. 1822 (563), xii, xiii; *Third report, on counter-vailing duties*, H.C. 1822 (606), xiii; *Fourth report, on the union duties* . . ., H.C. 1822 (634), xiii; *Fifth report and supplemental report, on distillation*, H.C. 1823 (405) (498), vii; *on customs and excise estab-lishments in Dublin*, H.C. 1824 (100), xi; *Eighth report, on excise*, H.C. 1824 (331), xi; *Tenth report, on the ports in Ireland*, H.C. 1824 (446), xi; *Sixteenth and seventeenth reports, on stamps, Ireland*, H.C. 1828 (7), xiv, xv; *Nineteenth report, on the post office, Ireland*, H.C. 1829 (353), xii.

*Accounts and papers . . . relating to the increase and diminution of salaries in the public offices of Ireland, H.C. 1823 (198), xii.

*Papers and accounts relating to the exchequer offices in Ireland . . . and to the office of vice-treasurer of Ireland, H.C. 1823 (81), xii.

Prisons of Ireland: report of inspectors general, H.C. 1823 (342), x.

Grand jury presentments: abstracts of accounts of presentments, H.C. 1824 (258), xxii.

Public works . . . an account of all sums of money advanced by the com-missioners for the issue of money out of the consolidated fund for public works in Ireland . . ., H.C. 1824 (278), xxi.

A statement of the average annual salaries and emoluments of the several individuals composing the late establishment of the office muster-master general in Ireland . . ., H.C. 1824 (28), xii.

Report of the commissioners for inquiring into the management and system of conducting the affairs of the paving board, Dublin, H.C. 1826–7 (329), xi.

House of industry and foundling hospital, Dublin, accounts . . ., H.C. 1828 (176), xxii.

Report from the select committee on the admiralty court in Ireland . . ., H.C. 1829 (293), iv.

Report from the select committee on the Irish miscellaneous estimates, H.C. 1829 (342), iv.

*Appointments in public departments . . ., H.C. 1830 (449), xvii.

*Return of the establishments of the public departments and offices in *1821* and *1829* . . ., H.C. 1830 (386), xvii.

*Returns of the names and offices of all persons now employed in the respective civil departments of the United Kingdom, whose salary and emoluments exceed £250 per annum . . ., H.C. 1830 (480), xvii.

Accounts and papers relating to first fruits in Ireland, H.C. 1830–31 (12) (328), vii.

Report from the select committee on King's printers' patents with the minutes of evidence, H.C. 1831–32 (713), xviii.

Report from the select committee on the registry of deeds (Ireland) bill, H.C. 1830–31 (512), xvii.

*Return of persons employed, and of the pay or salaries granted to such persons in all public offices or departments in the year 1797 and in the years 1805, 1810, 1815 and 1819 . . ., H.C. 1830–31 (92), vii.

Vice-treasurer of Ireland: copy of treasury minute regulating the office, H.C. 1830–31 (50), xvii.

Vice-treasurer of Ireland: copies of treasury minute . . . relating to the office . . ., H.C. 1830–31 (100), xvii.

*Report from the select committee on civil government charges together with the minutes of evidence, H.C. 1831 (337), iv.

Report from the select committee on the King's printers' patents with the minutes of evidence, H.C. 1831–32 (713), xviii.

Copy of treasury minute . . . on . . . regulations for ascertaining the fitness of persons appointed to situations in the public service, H.C. 1833 (680), xxiii.

A return of the receipts and expenditure of the central board of health for Ireland . . . [and] a similar return for the general board of health for the city of Dublin, H.C. 1834 (447), li.

Third report of His Majesty's commissioners on ecclesiastical revenue and patronage in Ireland, H.C. 1836 (246), xxv.

Report from the select committee on county cess (Ireland) with the minutes of evidence, H.C. 1836 (527), xii.

Report from the select committee on record commission, H.C. 1836 (429), xvi.

Report from the select committee on Royal Dublin Society together with the minutes of evidence . . ., H.C. 1836 (445), xii.

Report from the select committee of the house of lords appointed to inquire into the state of Ireland in respect of crime, H.C. 1839 (486), xi and xii.

Charitable institutions (Dublin): copies of the reports of George Nicholls . . . on . . . Foundling hospital, Dublin, house of industry, Dublin, H.C. 1842 (389), xxxviii.

Report from the select committee on medical charities, Ireland, together with the minutes of evidence . . ., H.C. 1843 (412), x.

Report of the commissioners appointed to inquire into . . . the ordnance memoir of Ireland . . ., H.C. 1844 (527), xxx.

Correspondence explanatory of the measures adopted by H.M. government for the relief of distress . . . in Ireland, H.C. 1846 [735], xxxvii.

Report from the select committee on ordnance survey (Ireland), together with the minutes of evidence . . ., H.C. 1846 (664), xv.

Report from the select committee of the house of lords on the laws relating to the relief of the destitute and into the . . . medical charities in Ireland with the minutes of evidence . . ., H.C. 1846 (694), xi.

Correspondence and accounts relating to the different occasions on which measures were taken for the relief of the people suffering scarcity in Ireland between the years 1822 and 1839, H.C. 1847 [734], xxxvii.

Correspondence from July 1846 to January 1847 relating to the measures adopted for the relief of distress in Ireland and Scotland: commissariat series, H.C. 1847 [761], [56], li.

Correspondence . . . relating to the measures adopted for the relief of distress in Ireland: commissariat series, second part, H.C. 1847 [796], lii.

Correspondence . . . relating to the measures adopted for the relief of distress in Ireland: board of works series, first part, H.C. 1847 [764], l, *second part*, H.C. 1847 [797], lii.

Copies or extracts of correspondence relating to the state of the union work-houses in Ireland, first, second and third series, H.C. 1847 [766], [790], [863], lv; *Fourth series*, H.C. 1847–8 [896], liv; *Fifth series*, H.C. 1847–8 [919], lv; *Sixth series*, H.C. 1847–8 [955], lvi; *Seventh series*, H.C. 1847–8 [999], liv; *Eighth series*, H.C. 1849 [1042], xlviii.

Distress (Ireland), reports of relief commissioners, H.C. 1847 [799], [819], [836], [859].

*Report from the select committee on miscellaneous expenditure, together with minutes of evidence and appendix, H.C. 1847–8 (543), xviii.

Poor law unions (Ireland): returns of each union in Ireland for which guardians and temporary inspectors have been appointed . . ., H.C. 1848 (240), liii.

Dublin wide streets bill . . . minutes of evidence taken before the committee . . ., H.C. 1846 (519), xii.

Papers relating to the aid afforded to the distressed unions in the west of Ireland, H.C. 1849 [1010], [1019], [1023], [1060], [1077], xlviii.

Report from the select committee on fisheries (Ireland): together with . . . minutes of evidence, H.C. 1849 (563), xiii.

Report from the select committee of the house of lords appointed to inquire into the operation of acts relating to the drainage of lands, Ireland, H.C. 1852–3 (10), xxvi.

*Reports of committee of inquiry into public offices, H.C. 1854 [1715], xxvii.

Report from the select committee on Dublin hospitals, H.C. 1854 (338), xii.

Report from the select committee of the house of lords appointed to inquire into the practical working of the system of national education in Ireland, H.C. 1854 (525), xv.

Report from the select committee of the house of lords appointed to consider the consequences of extending the functions of the constabulary in Ireland . . ., H.C. 1854 (53), x.

Report from the select committee of the house of lords appointed to inquire into the best mode of obtaining accurate agricultural statistics . . ., H.C. 1854–5 (501), viii.

Report of the commissioners appointed to inquire into the hospitals of Dublin, H.C. 1856 [2063], xix.

Report from the select committee on court of chancery (Ireland) bill, together with the . . . minutes of evidence, H.C. 1856 (311), x.

Select committee on transportation: first, second and third reports, H.C. 1856 (244), (296), (355), xvii.

Endowed schools, Ireland, commission: report: minutes of evidence, documents and tables . . ., H.C. 1857–8 [2336], xxii.

Lunatic asylums, Ireland, commission, report . . . with minutes of evidence . . ., H.C. 1857–8 [2436], xxvii.

Chancery office, Ireland, commission, report, H.C. 1859 [2473], xii.

Report from the select committee on civil service appointments . . . together with the . . . minutes of evidence . . ., H.C. 1860 (440), ix.

Report from the select committee on miscellaneous expenditure . . ., H.C. 1860 (483), ix.

Report from the select committee on poor relief (Ireland), H.C. 1861 (408), x.

Report upon . . . the registry of deeds . . ., H.C. 1861 [2867], li.

Copy of a report made by Mr Bateman . . . with reference to the means of preventing injury by flooding to the lands adjoining the river Shannon . . ., H.C. 1863 (292), l.

Scientific institutions (Dublin); copy of any correspondence between the lord lieutenant of Ireland, or any other member of the Irish executive and the treasury or the department of science and art on the proposed amalgamation of the museum of Irish industry with the Royal Dublin society, H.C. 1863 (401), xlvi.

Report from the select committee on scientific institutions (Dublin): together with the . . . minutes of evidence, H.C. 1864 (495), xiii.

Report from the select committee on the Shannon river, together with . . . minutes of evidence, H.C. 1865 (400), xi.

Constabulary, Ireland, report of commissioners, H.C. 1866 [3658], xxxiv.

Second report of H.M.'s commissioners appointed to inquire into the superior courts . . . of England and Ireland, H.C. 1866 [3674], xvii.

College of science (Dublin) . . . copies of the commission on the college of science, Dublin . . . of the minute of the committee of the privy council for education, directing the abolition of the office of director of the museum of Irish industry and of all correspondence which had taken place with different departments of the government with reference to the abolition of that office . . ., H.C. 1867 (219), lv.

Report of the commissioners on the college of science, Dublin . . ., H.C. 1867 (219), lv.

Report from the select committee on the sea coast fisheries (Ireland) bill, together with . . . minutes of evidence, H.C. 1867 (443), xiv.

Report from the select committee on the grand jury presentments (Ireland) together with the . . . minutes of evidence, H.C. 1867–8 (392), x.

Report of H.M.'s commissioners on the revenues and constitution of the established church (Ireland), H.C. 1867–8 [4082], [4082–1], xxiv.

Report from the select committee on scientific instruction together with the . . . minutes of evidence, H.C. 1867–8 (432), xv.

Report from the select committee on general valuation (Ireland), together with . . . minutes of evidence, H.C. 1868–9 (362), xxii.

Report from the commission on the science and art department in Ireland . . ., H.C. 1868–9 [4103–1], xxiv.

Royal commission of inquiry into primary education (Ireland) report, appendix, reports of assistant commissioners, minutes of evidence, educational census returns, miscellaneous papers and returns, H.C. 1870, [C. 6], [C. 6A], [C. 6–I–C.–6–VII], xxvii.

*Report of the commissioners . . . to inquire into the condition of the civil service in Ireland on the local government board, general register office and general report together with minutes of evidence and appendix, H.C. 1873 [C. 789], xxii.

Report of the commissioners appointed . . . to inquire into the condition of the civil service in Ireland (Royal Irish constabulary), H.C. 1873 [C. 831], xxii.

Report of the commissioners appointed . . . to inquire into the condition of the civil service in Ireland (Dublin metropolitan police), H.C. 1873 [C. 788], xxii.

Report of the commissioners appointed . . . to inquire into the condition of the civil service in Ireland (resident magistrates), H.C. 1873 [C. 923], xvi.

Select committee on civil service expenditure, three reports, H.C. 1873 (131), (248), (352), vii.

Civil service inquiry: reports I–III with the proceedings of the committee, H.C. 1873, [C. 1113], [C. 1226], [C. 1317], xxiii.

*Local government and taxation (Ireland) inquiry, special report from W. P. O'Brien Esq. . . ., H.C. 1878 [C. 1965], xxiii.

Report . . . of the commissioners of inquiry into the collection of rates in the city of Dublin with the minutes of evidence, H.C. 1878 [C. 2062], xxiii.

Report of the committee appointed to inquire into the board of works, Ireland, together with minutes of evidence . . ., H.C. 1878 [C. 2060], xxiii.

First report of H.M.'s commissioners appointed to inquire into the law relating to the registration of deeds and assurances in Ireland, H.C. 1878–9 [C. 2443], xxxi.

Poor law union and lunacy inquiry commission (Ireland), report and evidence . . ., H.C. 1878–9 [C. 2239], xxxi.

Endowed schools, Ireland, commission, H.C. 1881 [C. 2831], xxxv.

Dublin metropolitan police, report of the commission of inquiry, H.C. 1883 [C. 3576], xxxii.

Training schools (Ireland), H.C. 1883 (144), liii.

Prisons in Ireland: preliminary report of the royal commission appointed to inquire into the administration, discipline and condition of the prisons in Ireland, H.C. 1883 [C. 3496], xxxii, first report with digest of evidence . . ., H.C. 1884–5 [C. 4233], xxxviii, second report [C. 4145], xlii.

Royal Irish constabulary: report of the committee of inquiry, H.C. 1883 [C. 3576], evidence, H.C. 1883 [C. 3576–I], xxxii.

Civil service expenditure returns . . ., H.C. 1884 (327), xlvii.

Reformatories and industrial schools commission: report . . . together with minutes of evidence . . ., H.C. 1884 [C. 3876–I], xlv.

Correspondence between the treasury and the Irish government as to the remunerations of the attorney general and solicitor general for Ireland, H.C. 1887, (261), (336), lxvii

Royal commission on Irish public works, first report, H.C. 1887 [C. 5038], appendix [C. 5038–I], xxv, second report, H.C. 1888 [C. 5264], appendix [C. 5264–I], xlviii.

First and second reports of the committee . . . on lunacy administration (Ireland), H.C. 1890–1 [C. 6434], xxxvi.

Educational endowments (Ireland), 48 & 49 Vict. c. 78; Final report of the commissioners, H.C. 1894 [C. 7517], xxx.

National education (Ireland) (conscience clause) . . . copies of correspondence in the year 1895 between the Irish government and the commissioners of national education for Ireland, with extracts from the minutes of the proceedings of the commissioners . . ., H.C. 1895 (324), lxxvii.

National education (Ireland) (conscience clause) . . . copy of further correspondence between the Irish government and the commissioners of national education for Ireland, with extracts from the minutes of the proceedings of the commissioners . . ., H.C. 1896 (89), lxvi.

Report of the committee appointed to inquire into . . . the proceedings of charitable loans societies in Ireland, H.C. 1897 [3381], xxiii.

Calendar, history and general summary of the regulations of the department of science and art, H.C. 1898 [C. 8937], xxxi.

Royal commission on local taxation: report on valuation in Ireland, H.C. 1902 [Cd. 973], xxxix.

Intermediate education (Ireland), copy of correspondence between the Irish government and the commissioners of intermediate education for Ireland, H.C. 1906 [Cd. 3213], xci.

Royal commission on congestion in Ireland, first report and appendices, H.C. 1906 [Cd. 3266, Cd. 3267], xxxii.

Vice-regal commission on arterial drainage (Ireland), report . . ., H.C. 1907 [Cd. 3374], xxxii.

Department of agriculture and technical instruction (Ireland): report of the departmental committee of inquiry, H.C. 1907 [Cd. 3572], xvii, minutes of evidence and appendix, H.C. 1907 [Cd. 3574, Cd. 3573], xviii.

*Government departments (Ireland), return setting forth the . . . official position of all salaried officials . . . who have been appointed by (a) nomination with examination, (b) by nomination with limited competition, (c) by nomination with a qualifying examination, H.C. 1907 (8), lxviii.

Royal commission on the care and control of the feeble minded: minutes of evidence relating to Scotland and Ireland . . ., vol. III, H.C. 1908 [Cd. 4217], xxxvii.

Report of the Royal commission on the care and control of the feeble minded, vol. viii, H.C. 1908 [Cd. 4202], xxxix.

Royal commission on the poor laws and the relief of distress: report on Ireland, H.C. 1909 [Cd. 4630], xxxviii.

*Public departments (Scotland and Ireland) return showing . . . the number of established and unestablished officials employed . . ., H.C. 1912–3 (104), lvi.

Viceregal committee of inquiry into primary education (Ireland), 1913, First report, H.C. 1913 [Cd. 6828], evidence and appendices, H.C. 1913 [Cd. 6829], xxii; Second report, H.C. 1914 [Cd. 7228], evidences and appendices [Cd. 7229]; Third report, H.C. 1914 [Cd. 7479], evidences and appendices, [Cd. 7480]; Final report [Cd. 7235], xxviii.

*Royal commission on the civil service, fourth report with appendices, H.C. 1914 [Cd. 7338, Cd. 7339, Cd. 7340], xvi.

Royal Irish constabulary and Dublin metropolitan police: appendix to the report of the committee of inquiry, H.C. 1914–6 [Cd. 7637], xxxii.

Royal commission on the rebellion in Ireland: report, H.C. 1916 [Cd. 8279], xi.

Viceregal committee of inquiry into primary education (Ireland), 1918, report, summaries of evidence . . ., H.C. 1919 [Cd. 60], [Cd. 178], xxi.

(6) OTHER PRINTED SOURCES

Abraham, G. W., The law and practice of lunacy in Ireland, Dublin, 1886.

Anderson, R. A., With Horace Plunkett in Ireland, 1935.

Barker, F. & Cheyne, J., An account of the fever lately epidemical in Ireland, 2 vols., 1921.

Betham, W., Observations on the evidence taken before the committee of the house of commons on the record commission, Dublin, 1837.

Colchester, Lord, ed., The diary and correspondence of Charles Abbot, Lord Colchester, 3 vols., 1861.

Crofton, W., A few words on the 'convict question', Dublin, 1857.

Crofton, W., The immunity of 'habitual criminals' with a few propositions for reducing their number, Dublin, 1861.

Duhigg, B., A letter to . . . Lord Manners . . . on the expediency of an immediate and separate record commission, Dublin, 1810.

Gibson, C. B., Life among convicts, 2 vols., 1863.

Gilbert, T. J., *Record revelations: a letter . . . on the public records of Ireland and on the 'Calendar of patent and close rolls of chancery in Ireland' recently published . . .*, by An Irish Archivist, 1863.

Gilbert, T. J., *Record revelations resumed: a letter*, by An Irish Archivist, 1864.

Godley, A., *Reminiscences of Lord Kilbracken*, 1931.

Gordon, John Campbell, 1st marquess of Aberdeen and Temair, *We twa: reminiscences of Lord and Lady Aberdeen*, 2 vols., 1925.

Headlam, M., *Irish reminiscences*, 1947.

Howard, G. E., *A treatise of the exchequer and revenue of Ireland*, Dublin, 1776.

Mackail, J. W. & Wyndham, G., *The life and letters of George Wyndham*, 2 vols., 1925.

Morley, John, *Recollections*, 2 vols., 1917.

Nun, R. & Walsh, J. E., *The powers and duties of justices of the peace in Ireland*, 2nd ed., Dublin, 1844.

O'Connor, J., *The Irish justice of the peace*, Dublin, 1911

Robinson, H. A., *Memories wise and otherwise*, 1923.

Robinson, H. A., *Further memories connected with local government administration in Ireland*, 1924.

II. LATER WORKS

Andrews, C. S., 'Some precursors of Bord na mona', in *Journ. of statistical and social inquiry society of Ireland*, xx. 132–55.

Ball, F. Elrington, *The judges in Ireland, 1221–1921*, 2 vols., New York, 1927.

Berry, H. F., *A history of the Royal Dublin Society*, 1915.

Blackwood, S. A., *Some records of the life of Stevenson Arthur Blackwood*, by his widow, 1896.

Butler, B. B., 'John and Edward Lees', in *Dublin Hist. Rec.*, xii. 138–50.

Digby, M., *Horace Plunkett: an Anglo-American Irishman*, Oxford, 1949.

Ferguson, M. C., *Sir Samuel Ferguson in the Ireland of his day*, 2 vols., Edinburgh, 1896.

Gilbert, R. M., *Life of Sir John T. Gilbert*, 1905.

Gill, C., *The rise of the Irish linen industry*, Oxford, 1925.

Griffith, M., 'The Irish record commission, 1810–25', in *I.H.S.*, vii. 17–28.

Hammond, J. W., 'The King's printers in Ireland', in *Dublin Hist. Rec.*, xi. 29–31, 58–64, 88–96.

Hitchins, E. H., *The colonial land and emigration commission*, Philadelphia, 1931.

Hughes, J. L. J., 'The chief secretaries in Ireland', in *I.H.S.*, viii. 59–72.

Kiernan, T. J., *History of the financial administration of Ireland until 1817*, 1930.

King-Harman, R. D., *The earls of Kingston*, Cambridge, 1959.

Kirkpatrick, T. P. S., *The book of the Rotunda Hospital*, Dublin, 1913.

Lascelles, R., *Liber munerum publicorum Hiberniae*, 1852.

MacDonagh, O., *A pattern of government growth, 1800–60*, 1961.

Micks, W. L., *An account of the congested districts board for Ireland, 1891–1923*, Dublin, 1925.

Moody, T. W. and Beckett, J. C., *Queen's Belfast, 1845–1949: the history of a university*, 2 vols., 1959.

Morgan, J. H., ed., *The new Irish constitution*, 1912.

O'Brien, R. B., *Dublin castle and the Irish people*, 1909.

O Raifeartaigh, T., 'Mixed education and the synod of Ulster 1831–40', in *I.H.S.*, ix. 281–99.

Petrie, C., *Walter Long and his times*, 1936.

Spender, J. A., *The life of the Rt. Honourable Sir Henry Campbell-Bannerman*, 2 vols., 1923.

Todd, A., *On parliamentary government in England*, 2nd ed., 2 vols., 1887.

Webb, B., *Our partnership*, 1948.

White, T. de V., *The story of the Royal Dublin society*, Tralee, 1955.

Wilkinson, N. R., *To all and singular*, 1925.

Wrottesley, G., *Life and correspondence of Sir John Burgoyne*, 2 vols., 1873.

INDEX